Gleanings

Gleanings

Essays 1982–2006

Christine Downing

iUniverse, Inc.
New York Lincoln Shanghai

Gleanings
Essays 1982–2006

iUniverse books may be ordered through booksellers or by contacting:

iUniverse
2021 Pine Lake Road, Suite 100
Lincoln, NE 68512
www.iuniverse.com
1-800-Authors (1-800-288-4677)

ISBN-13: 978-0-595-40036-2
ISBN-10: 0-595-40036-1

Printed in the United States of America

In celebration of

my 75th birthday

and Sigmund Freud's 150th

and 25 years of knowing and loving River

Contents

For Chris Downing

So many candles, so large a luminous light,
so daring a voice ahead of all our thoughts.

Beckoning us to take up in our own hands
Our Freud
Our Persephone
Our Buber
Our-selves
and knot it into the bundle of our own Birth-
Days and Nights.

We stand here now and salute you from the
shadows—made so deep and dark by the
Lumen of so many sweet and sturdy cycles
of time—a fragrant lap
a diadem of good cheer
a Downy, down-turning, a deep-delving
Chris—gazing at us all
within a circle of fire.

> Dennis Patrick Slattery

Foreword

Last year after putting together *Preludes: Essays on the Ludic Imagination,* a collection of essays from the time I was in graduate school at Drew University up to the publication in 1981 of my book, *The Goddess: Mythological Images of the Feminine,* I realized I would also like to gather together essays from the most recent twenty-five years, the period since the publication of *Goddess.* I knew that in a sense the pickings would be more slim, since not surprisingly many of my articles and talks from these years made their way into the six books I published in a burst of creativity between 1987 and 1994 (my *Journey through Menopause, Psyche's Sisters, Myths and Mysteries of Same-Sex Love, Mirrors of the Self, Women's Mysteries, Gods in Our Midst,* and *The Long Journey Home*) or into *The Luxury of Afterwards,* which presented written-out versions of talks I had given at San Diego State University between 1995 and 2004 (though in many instances more elaborated versions of these papers also appeared elsewhere).

So the title was immediately obvious: these are *GLEANINGS* from the most recent quarter century. The timing (as the dedication makes clear) is important to me: this book represents a seventy-fifth birthday present to myself (I remember now that *Women's Mysteries* came out as part of my sixtieth birthday celebration) and a celebration of twenty-five years of sharing my life with River Malcolm. It is also an honoring of the 150th birthday of Sigmund Freud.

The ever-increasing importance of Freud as a prompter of my own thinking, my own working-through, is I believe inescapably evident in these pages—as is also an ever deeper concern with the relations between polis and psyche, city and soul, history and archetype. The move toward personal voice so clearly underway in *Goddess* (and I think achieved in the other books that appeared before our move to Orcas Island in 1994) seems now more muted, still present, but as an undertone. So I like the somewhat paradoxical way this book ends: with an essay on Narcissus that includes no explicit self-reference.

Although the choice of title was obvious, I did not at first realize how many associations it would evoke. To be honest, I hadn't come to it quite directly. When the idea for this volume first appeared I remembered that toward the end of his life Martin Buber had brought together some of his uncollected pieces under the title *Nachlese.* I thought this meant "gleanings"—as it does. But it also means "re-readings," what one finds when one looks something up or when one returns to something read earlier and discovers in it more than one had initially. Discovering that reminded me of another "*nach*" word: *Nachtraglichkeit:* Freud's word, clumsily translated as "deferred action" or "belatedness," which refers to the way historically earlier moments become endowed with originally unsuspected significance and power when evoked, usually unconsciously, by later ones. (This served to confirm my initial hunch that the best way to order these "leftovers" would be chronologically.)

The German word set off bookish associations and connections to my most important fatherly mentors—whereas the English word, gleanings, has (or certainly had initially) a more tangible implication and immediately reminds me of my mother and her stories about gleaning in the sugar beet fields to the south of Zeitz, the Thuringen town in which she grew up, during the last years of the First World War. Of course, it also reminds me of the biblical Ruth and the powerful identification with her I explored in my essay, "How Little It Resembles Memory" (included in *Luxury of Afterwards*).

"Gleanings" for me (as I imagine for many others) also immediately brought to mind Jean-François Millet's 1857 painting *The Gleaners*. Somehow Elaine Rother found a way for us to get permission to use it on the cover. For that, and for everything else she did to help this book make its way into the world, I thank her. I also want to thank Dennis Patrick Slattery, my colleague at Pacifica Graduate Institute, for letting me use some lines from his poem.

Christine Downing
Orcas Island, Washington
Spring 2006

1

The Eros of Teaching

When I was in high school my best friend was Anne Martin. Anne was the only other scholarship student in our small class at one of northern New Jersey's fancy private schools for girls. I'd been there since fifth grade, she came in ninth. I was almost surely the first even remotely Jewish student ever to attend the school, she probably the first Catholic. But what really set us apart from our classmates and drew us to one another was how much we both loved books, reading them and talking about them. I remember how that first year we read all of Jane Austen together, book by book, and how the next year it was George Eliot. But I also remember how disappointed I was when I told her of my ongoing love for Jo March and she let me know that Louisa May Alcott was not a good writer, not worth spending one's time on. She said this with great authority; her father was an English Literature professor.

Now that I have begun remembering Anne, I need to go on. We spent so much time together all through high school, especially on weekends. Of course, we had differing interests, too. In one of our art classes, she discovered that she loved working with clay. I still remember the amazingly perfect copy she made of the famous Nefertiti head and the months she spent working on it. I loved playing hockey, basketball, lacrosse, pursuits that bored her. Perhaps another telling clue: for our senior theses she wrote on Emily Dickinson, I on Dostoevski. When it came time to go to college, she went to Vassar where all the best students from our school had always gone; I chose a coeducational school, Swarthmore. She majored in sculpture, I in literature. I got married at the end of my junior year, she became more and more devoted to her art. We drifted apart but never quite lost touch. She won a Prix de Rome and went to Italy and a year or two later killed herself—I think because she had discovered that though she was, indeed, gifted, indeed, *good,* she was never going to be great.

What led me to think of Anne was trying to explain my appreciation of May Sarton's *A Small Room.*[1] It is so clearly *not* a great book—the characters are not

1

fully realized, the plot is a bit contrived, the language never sings, the metaphors are too obvious, the resolution too pat. I am even prepared to call it a small book—and yet I am moved by it, moved by it to reflect on my own experience as a teacher in a way that no other academic novel has called me to do. Perhaps because it is about *teaching* and *about love*—not about adultery (as fiction set in the academy so often turns out to be) but about the love of teaching.

I find myself wondering what it would have been like to have read this novel about Lucy Winter's initiation into the world of teaching when it first came out twenty years ago, just before I began my own academic career. I am conscious even now of reading with a double perspective. Of course, I read it from my own present standpoint, that of a fairly seasoned professor just over 50, that is of someone just about Sarton's age when she wrote the book. But I also find myself identifying with 27-year-old Lucy Winter and her fascination with Carryl Cope, the 50-ish professor who serves as her initiator and "makes her fall in love with a profession." Strange sometimes how a book falls into our hands just when we are ready for it—just before beginning this one I had found myself engaged in a powerful inner dialogue between just these two "selves," my 27-year-old self and the me of now.[2]

My hunch is that when we academics read novels set in a college or university we will amplify what is actually given in the text with our own experience and that a novel about initiation will recall us to our own beginnings—to our perhaps almost romantic sense of vocation, to the inevitably naïve and innocent dreams and hopes that we brought to our first jobs—and to the vital fears, self-doubts, conflicts, confusions, and failures that were also present (and that we have gradually learned we never fully leave behind). A novel like this gives us an opportunity to step outside for a moment and to see this world freshly. At her first faculty party, Lucy is told that she and the other newly hired faculty are in the position of anthropologists confronting a strange tribe. And throughout the novel Lucy remains a little outside—and thus is trusted with confidences from all the major players in the story that unfolds. She seems able to see more wholly than she will ever be again once she becomes an insider with a clearly defined role of her own.

The language of initiation pervades the novel. It opens with a train ride that marks Lucy's separation from her earlier world. She has recently lost a loved but emotionally distant father and has just broken an engagement to a male lover; she is on her way to her first teaching assignment at a small prestigious women's college. It feels to her that she might be entering upon a "novitiate"; she wonders if she is on her way to finding her true vocation. The entire novel takes place during her first fall semester; it begins and ends with a faculty party in a "small room" of the home of one of the established professors. At the first such gathering there is much talk of the school being a world set apart, like a mystery cult or secret society. Lucy feels that everyone seems to be wearing masks and talking a different language. She is pointedly asked, "Is this just an interlude for you?"

Lucy herself isn't clear; she knows that she has just stumbled into this world. As she confides that she had only gone to graduate school at Harvard so as to be near her fiancé while he was in medical school, that she had never really thought beyond that, I remember how I, too, really made my way into teaching only by accident. I had so loved being in graduate school in the midst of others who enjoyed thinking seriously and talking passionately about the things that interested me most; it was only as I had completed my course work that I realized that the only way to stay in such a world was to move from being a student to becoming a teacher. For me as for Lucy (and I suspect for many of us) it is teaching itself that teaches us to love it.

Though the fictional "Appleton" is a women's college, it is not quite an all women's world. There are a few male faculty and they have wives. But the focus really falls on the interactions among the women faculty—none of whom are married or have children—and between them and their female students. My own first twelve years of teaching were spent at a women's college—larger than this one and more closely connected to a male counterpart—but I recognize the scene. At my institution also there were very few married female professors and I remember well what an anomaly I with my five children represented. In the novel there are two middle-aged women who've been together for 20 years and whom everyone recognizes as a couple—as was true at just about every women's college of that era. I also recognized the intensity of the connections between female faculty and students that never becomes explicitly erotic (as in my experience it did by the end of the decade). Because students enter this novel only as the faculty come to know them, there is no hint of the quasi-lesbian intensities of their involvements with one another, that I remember so clearly. However, even during her interview for the job, Lucy is emphatically told, "We are not interested in producing marriageable young ladies," but rather in nurturing our students' intellects and fostering excellence.

In the book about the Greek goddesses I published a year ago I wrote about the powerful role that what Athene represents has played in my life—a role she plays in this novel as well. (I think I am right in remembering that she is the only goddess invoked.) We are shown how much Athene can *give* women: a blessing of their intellectual gifts, their creativity, their courage, but also of the costs of devotion to her. Like Athene, all the major figures in the novel are father's daughters; all seem to carry a deep father wound (whereas there are almost no references to mothers).

There are several wonderful classroom scenes, including one account of an experienced teacher's subtle guidance of a seminar that evokes awe in Lucy—and, I must admit, in me. The report of Lucy's own very first upper-division class serves to introduce the central theme of the novel—the place of *eros* in the relation between faculty and student. Lucy spends that first hour talking very personally about herself, about her relation to her father and to the important teachers (all male) who inspired her own love of literature—and is then dismayed when after class a student tries to share with her how devastated she remains by the recent death of her father. "You're confusing me with an imaginary someone, a father confessor or friend," she tells her, "I won't be that." Yet she is appalled by the cruelty of her rejection and hastens to consult Hallie Summerson, the older teacher whom she already views as a mentor. "I don't believe in personal relationships between teachers and students, do you?" she asks. "Theoretically, no," Hallie somewhat ambiguously replies. The novel explores this topic in a rich, complex way that serves to underline my own sense of how hard—impossible, perhaps—it is to find the right balance. Later Carryl Cope will tell Lucy, "The relation between student and teacher must be about the most complex and ill-defined there is." Lucy comes to sense how difficult it will always be to know when to withdraw, when to yield or approach; she comes to appreciate that such relationships are "as various, as unpredictable, as a love affair." Hallie affirms that "what we give our students, whether we are personal with them or not, is the marrow, the essence of ourselves, what true lovers ask of love."

Later Carryl helps her see that one cannot just evade or eliminate the transferences that are inevitably invoked, not only the transferences that students project on their teachers but also those projected by teachers on students. Carryl recognizes that her own favorite student, Jane Seaman, has transferred longings for recognition from her father onto her—but also that she had seen herself in Jane, sought to give the student what she had once hoped for for herself. Carryl also tries to help Lucy understand, "We couldn't do this without all of who we are—without our personal lives, our passions, our conflicts."

Throughout the novel Lucy wonders what it is that she is really trying to teach—content, knowledge, or how to live. She does so in a way that leads me to wonder about this for myself. My (tentative) answer is that I want to communicate my love—not exactly of my students, though not exactly *not* of my students—but more explicitly my love of the books, the authors, the way of looking at the world, that has moved and inspired me, and my love of the process of inquiry that has brought me to those books, those writers; I want to encourage my students to find what might move them in the same way—and to come to love looking for it. In the novel Carryl is clear she wants to teach her students to *think*—but I guess I want to encourage them to *love*—and yet I sense that we are not as far apart as this formulation might suggest, for I would wish they might come to love thinking and to discover that one can think with one's whole being!

The plot of the novel revolves around an exceptionally brilliant student, Jane Seaman, who had been mentioned at that initial party as a protégé of Carryl Cope. Almost by accident Lucy shortly later discovers that Jane has plagiarized an at that time little-known essay on the *Iliad* by Simone Weil; Jane's only slightly paraphrased version is being published as the lead article in a publication of Appleton student essays. Lucy—and later everyone else—is puzzled by why such an unquestionably gifted student would have done something so incredibly risky and stupid. As the story unfolds we learn that Jane herself believes that she has done it in order to be found out, in order to free herself from what has become an unbearable pressure to excel. Initially she had responded with great joy to the encouragement Carryl Cope had given her but then felt that the bar kept being raised higher and higher; the pressure had become too great. Jane essentially ends up having a nervous breakdown, which forces Carryl to come to terms with the limitations of her blindness to anything about Jane other than her intellectual gifts. Carryl comes to accept responsibility both for expecting too much from Jane and for not having given her the more personal attention she really longed for. "I wasn't there," she says (though the novel encourages us to trust Carryl's lesbian partner's insistence that Carryl had really loved Jane).

At the December party that completes Lucy's initiation almost everyone present tries to make sense of the crisis into which this episode had plunged the whole college. One of her male colleagues stammeringly protests, "C-C-Carryl, it's very noble of you, and all that, to feel responsible for Jane, but I doubt actually if it would have been such a very great help if you had given whatever it was you think you withheld." Lucy recognizes that perhaps there is no generalizable lesson to be drawn.

What I take away from the novel is a reminder that (like Carryl—but in our own ways) we *will* fail, will get it wrong, will do damage sometimes (and I've been reminded of damage I've done)—but also that the opportunity being a teacher offers us to share what we love and to encourage others to find what they can love is an incomparable gift.

Notes

1.   May Sarton, *The Small Room* (New York: Norton, 1961).

2.   See my "Dear Chris...Love, Christine," *Preludes* (New York: iUniverse, 2005).

2

Whitmont's Return to the Goddess

There are two quite different functions a reviewer may take upon him or herself: descriptive or critical. One may choose to focus on trying to persuade one's readers that a book they might otherwise ignore is worth their attention by presenting its arguments in the author's own terms but more compactly, or one may opt to discuss with what are assumed to be fellow readers (and implicitly with the author himself) the questions the book has raised for the reviewer. I have deliberately made the second choice in agreeing to write about Edward C. Whitmont's new book, *The Return Of The Goddess: Femininity, Aggression, and the Modern Grail Quest* (Crossroad, 1983), for the author has explicitly asked for "readers willing to enter a dialogue with me and personally work through their reaction to the material." Thus I write not as a disinterested observer but as a woman who is herself deeply concerned with the relevance of goddess imagery to contemporary experience and who wholeheartedly supports Whitmont's "right [as] a man to be speaking of the Goddess and of feminine dynamics"—although (as I will explain at greater length in what follows) I wish he would more often remember that he is speaking as a man.

The book is, indeed, as Whitmont warns in his introduction, a complex one. I sometimes found it needlessly so: repetitive and grandiose. Whitmont sometimes appears unclear about his presumed readership, unsure where he might presuppose familiarity and sympathy with Jung, where he should speak as though to the completely uninitiated. He seems to restate his central theses again and again as though we would be too slow, too resistant, to let him penetrate otherwise. He seems to want to encompass as his subject matter the whole past and future of human history and to address all humankind. There is a beauty in this urgency. I sense the book to be a consciously late work like Freud's *Civilization and its Discontents*, one which grows out of profound social concern about the future of civilization, which is written in painful awareness of the threat of ultimate destruction we face and of the inadequacy of external political measures to avert that threat. Whitmont communicates the imperative need for a radical overcoming of the repression of aggression that is likely to undo us all. It is a grand theme—and a petty feminist response is beside the point.

Nevertheless, I often found myself maddened by the impersonality of the book as a whole, by the magisterial "we" that seems either to lecture me or to include me, willy-nilly, without my assent. The more confessional introduction, the occasional compassionate portrayal of a patient's struggle, help—but the style still strikes me as that of one who resists full participation in the fellowship I would see "The Goddess" inviting him to join. Whitmont stands so alone in his quest. With the exception of Sylvia Perera's work on Inanna, he seems singularly unaware of recent efforts by Jungians to work on the same issues that concern him. His discussion of Dionysos completely ignores James Hillman's reflections at the end of *The Myth of Analysis*; his attempt to rethink "anima" and "animus" proceeds as though Hiliman had never written his two essays in *Spring*. Likewise, his insularity from recent feminist scholarship is remarkable. That leads one to wonder how genuinely open he is to having his ideas brought into a community of concern. Yet, again, I remember Freud's deliberate disassociation from Nietzsche, Freud's sense that truly to develop his own thinking required such solitary incubation.

Let me begin my more focused discussion of the content rather than the style of Whitmont's book by looking at Whitmont's own announced purpose: to pick up where Erich Neumann's *Origins and History of Consciousness* left off.

> Neumann was the first to describe the evolution of consciousness from the matriarchal to the patriarchal level, collectively and individually. Written more than thirty years ago, his work concludes with the achievement of patriarchal consciousness. Neumann does not deal with the return of the archetypal Feminine. He did not go on to forecast the reappearance of the Goddess and her Dionysian companion who embody desire, neediness, and aggression in both their destructive and their consciousness-expanding possibilities (p. 49).

The least necessary part of the book to my mind is Whitmont's own rehearsal of the move from matriarchal to patriarchal consciousness (which adopts uncritically once again Levy-Bruhl's fantasy of primitive mentality as being fully describable in terms of *participation mystique*). Whitmont's review is consistently Hegelian in its recognition of the necessity of the now out-moded earlier phases:

The next development, falling due in our own epoch, is towards freedom of ethical and moral choice. This step has been prepared for by those religious and social disciplines which have made restraint of purely animal desires a matter of personal responsibility (p. 99).

We must first learn to operate and live as conforming members of state and community before we can move toward guidance by a self as a center that directly addresses the individual psyche (p. 101).

A person who would be self-motivated needs a prior initiation (p. 106).

The new pattern of maleness requires a prior adequate development of ego-firmness and discipline (p. 204).

I wince when this recognition seems to include an easy acceptance of the necessity of the devaluation of the feminine—and of the oppression of women—for the sake of ego-development:

It caused both sexes to devalue, not so much women per se, but the feminine...since women are by and large more feminine than men, they were declared inferior by mutual consent (p.136).

Whitmont argues that the confusion between sexual and archetypal gender leads us to overlook the psychological factor in favor of the sociological, to "see discrimination against *women*, primarily, where we must deal with a repression of femininity in women *and* men" (p. 140, his emphases). But, surely, his own interpretation fails equally in favoring the opposite factor.

In any case, the point as he sees it is that it is now time to move beyond the patriarchal ego, for to stay with it "threatens to starve our soul and to destroy our world" (p. 113). In a sense there is nothing new here, yet this does need to be resaid for our time: both because our situation is more urgent and because Jung's (as well as Freud's) way of posing the issue assumes, as Whitmont recognizes, too simple an understanding of "masculinity" and "femininity."

For Whitmont the transition beyond patriarchal consciousness entails the return of "The Goddess." Here he clearly participates in Jung's great move beyond Freud, already heralded in the disputes that issued in the break between them about the psychological meaning of incest fantasies. Jung saw that return is not always only regression, something Freud was still not able to recognize in that powerful first chapter of *Civilization* in which he reduces "oceanic feeling" to primary narcissism. Whitmont knows that by "The Return of the Goddess" he means the emergence of a new consciousness, one that "will have to be endowed with greater clarity, freedom, self-awareness, and a new and different capacity to love" (p. 50).

He struggles to get past what he takes to be Jung's and Neumann's limitations. He clearly believes that he has something new to say. Yet I see him as still tied to their presuppositions in a way that insures that the reunion with the feminine as he experiences and imagines it will indeed be the return of "The Goddess." Much as Whitmont may wrestle with the absurdities of Neumann's identification of consciousness and ego with masculinity, of the unconscious with femininity, much as he may question Jung's confusion of anima and animus with contrasexuality, he remains caught in a psychology which sees the feminine only as the Great Mother, in a psychology of the son. In the final pages of *The Myth of Analysis*, Hillman speaks to the inadequacy of this perspective: "But what of the God*desses*?: Athene, Demeter, Aphrodite, Artemis and Psyche. Are these not modes of consciousness reflected in the existence of women? (my emphasis). That for women the archetypal feminine is not simply The Great Mother is, of course, the burden of my own book on the contemporary significance of the diversity of Greek goddess traditions.

(I don't find Whitmont's rewriting of Toni Wolff's typology of the feminine helpful. To speak of Luna, Lila, Medusa and Pallas instead of Mother, Hetaira, Medium and Amazon removes few of the inadequacies and strikes me as an artificial and still abstract mythology which does little to illumine my experience. However, men may find it relevant to their experience of women and to the varied aspects of their own femininity, and I do applaud the attempt to provide a more differentiated sense of what femininity may mean than is provided by exclusive focus on The Mother Goddess.)

Whitmont wants very badly to speak of a shift in consciousness in which contemporary men and women both participate. He affirms that the return of The Goddess is important to *him*, not an experience exclusive to women. I grant that, yet believe we need to move more slowly than he seems to. I would like to have him first be content to speak of the male experience of the Goddess and to let us women speak of our experience. Together we might then discover how they are alike and how different. In his introduction Whitmont presents some of his own dreams which seem clearly and powerfully to mean what he takes them to mean; the interpretation of his female patient's dreams in Chapter 1 seems more forced (though I recognize the difficulties in any capsule case presentation). This difficulty has been with us ever since Freud created depth psychology by bringing together the results of his self-analysis with his interpretations of his female hysterics' dreams. Whitmont tells us that "modern women: want to be listened to, especially when they feel inarticulate," want a man to "help [them] discover what [they] do not yet understand about [themselves]" (p. 205). He seems still to believe that we women need men as our interpreters.

I am not saying this in anger. The task of sorting through what constitutes "masculinity" and "femininity" and how these relate to actual men and women is enormously difficult—and essential. I want to help, to talk with rather than be talked to. I feel left out when I am told "The new woman will need...; tomorrow's woman must..." (p. 211). Whitmont seems to know this abstractly, for he acknowledges: "The feminine instinct refuses to *have* to give, to be told how it *should* feel" (p. 216, his emphasis). Nevertheless, the implicit message still seems to be that of Jung's "Modern Woman in Europe": "Be our anima."

I see the difficulty as inherent in Whitmont's failure to separate anima and femininity clearly enough from woman. The initial task would seem to be to name as best we can what constitutes "femininity" and "masculinity," acknowledging that the polarity is deeply imbedded in our history, literature and language and in our unconscious. I would agree that the "opposition and complementariness of male and female belong among the most basic representations of the experience of dualism" without agreeing that they "underlie" all such other polarities as solar/lunar, active/passive, spirit/matter (p. 114). I can accede to Whitmont's decision to use "anima" and "animus" to refer to the psychological feminine and masculine respectively rather than "Yin" and "Yang" as he did in *The Symbolic Quest* and applaud his willingness to give up trying to make use of Jung's Eros/Logos formulations. I find value in his recognition that aspects of both femininity and masculinity are unconscious in both women and men; we each have both anima and animus. Nevertheless he then goes on to equate women with the anima, as when he writes, "For women and the anima, the new femininity requires..." (p. 201). He seems to want to insist on the importance of the difference between archetypal masculinity and femininity: "An egalitarianism that disregards [it]...is a remnant of the repressive, monotheistic, and monolithic patriarchal outlook" (p. 163). He proclaims that "self-affirmation for women means, first and foremost, acceptance of their differences from men" (p. 202). Yet he seems unable to see that women's relation to the feminine may be different from men's, unwilling to acknowledge that he is writing of the feminine primarily as men experience it.

For Whitmont The Goddess is seen as necessarily in relation to Dionysos. The focus on archetypal image (rather than on myth) and the amplification method encourage Whitmont to use Dionysos as a name for the son of The Goddess as such. Thus he can both speak of Dionysos, Adonis, Tammuz, for example, as though they were entirely equivalent figures, and apply everything he can learn of Dionysos from Kerenyi or Otto to any dream image he interprets as a Dionysos representation. "She never appears without him." The Goddess of son/lover/victim constitutes one totality (p. 53). For a psychology of the son this is obvious. Whitmont's real fear seems to be that Dionysos may appear without The Goddess:

> The way of the phallus alone, without the personality and integrative attitude of the Feminine, its sense for wholeness and containment, would fail to satisfy our growth needs.... Without the reassimilation of feminine values, [he] would be truly Satan (p. 132).

Whitmont's conviction that the Grail myth represents the key symbol of initiation into the new consciousness represented by The Goddess's return confirms that his vision is focused on the male quest. He himself defines this myth as representing the injury to male creativity engendered by disregard of the great Feminine (p. 183). The myth seems peculiarly appropriate to the emergence of the new consciousness he heralds because of its recognition that the quest is essentially individual not collective. Though the knights set out from Arthur's court together, "each chooses his own individual and separate way for the search."

The Goddess, as Whitmont understands her, represents the recognition of birth and death as one whole, the acceptance of the fullness of existence, of what *is* rather than what should be. She teaches the intrinsic significance of suffering and destruction, the inevitable reality of aggression and death. The Goddess means spontaneity rather than duty, "You may but be careful," rather than "You shall" or "You shall not."

The return of The Goddess is intimately associated with Whitmont's central theme of the containment of aggression. For The Goddess represents a way to release instinctual energy rather than repress it. "The inner meaning of the return of The Goddess is self-assertion in the service of life renewal" (p. 31). The last section of the book is devoted to how we might create rituals that would enable us to express these Goddess-given energies symbolically rather than acting them out literally. Whitmont sees therapy as helping us experiment with both imagination and discipline, helping us find individual expressions that yet acknowledge the transpersonal dimensions of Her reappearance. He is well aware that there are no guarantees that She will come or that the threatening disaster will be averted.

He writes in the same hope and fear, the affirmation and wonder, expressed in the poem by Yeats with which he prefaces the volume:

> Surely some revelation is at hand,
> Surely the Second Coming is at hand...
> And what rough beast, its hour come
>   round at last,
> Slouches toward Bethlehem to be born?

3

The Mother Goddess Among the Greeks

The goddesses of Greece with whom we are most apt to be familiar—Hera and Athene, Aphrodite and Artemis, even Demeter and Persephone—are participants in a polytheistic pantheon dominated by all-father Zeus, whose meeting place is high on Mount Olympus or in the sky. They are complex and vivid personalities, clearly defined, easily distinguished from one another, very humanlike creatures whose connections to aspects of the natural world are no longer directly apparent. Yet implicit in some of the myths and more visible in the cults devoted to them is evidence that each of these goddesses has some original connection to vegetation ritual. They are highly developed and specialized forms of the primordial mother goddess. The Greeks called this goddess of the beginning Gaia (or Ge), which means earth.

> The mother of us all,
> the oldest of all,
> hard,
>> splendid as rock
> whatever there is that is of the land
>> it is she
>> who nourishes it,
>> it is the Earth
>> that I sing.[1]

Gaia is not simply mother, she is earth mother. Indeed she differs from the later goddesses in that she is and remains earth, earth recognized as animate and divine. Gaia is never wholly personal, never entirely humanized—not even in

14

Homer or Hesiod. This is not a deficit; it does not mean she is thereby somehow less than the so completely anthropomorphic Olympians (who may wield the thunderbolt or drive the chariot of the sun but are not themselves the lightning flash or the solar disc; who may take on the shape of a bull in sexual pursuit or of a swan in flight but without forfeit of their humanlike personalities). Gaia reminds us that the divine is transhuman and prehuman—there from the beginning—not simply a human projection. Because of this she is the primordial source as no humanlike mother can be.

Yet she is not earth as an abstraction, not *the* earth but earth, especially that particular expanse of earth that for each of us is earth, from which we know the earthiness of earth. For the Greeks the particular place where Gaia's presence was most evident was Delphi. Most of us probably associate Delphi and its oracle with Apollo, but before Delphi was Apollo's it was Gaia's. The Greeks experienced Delphi as the navel of the earth. The omphalos that marks it as such is its most sacred monument. This is where the world came into being. This is preeminently the place where earth and sky, human and divine, come together. Even in classical times there was still a temple to Gaia near the Castalian spring.

When the oracle was Gaia's it probably took the form of dream incubation, the quest for the kind of knowledge that emerges from hidden depths. Aeschylus suggests that the transition from Gaia to Apollo was a peaceful evolution; Hesiod and the Homeric hymn to Pythian Apollo present a more violent struggle. Python, a female dragon created by Gaia as guardian of the shrine, was slain by Apollo to make possible his usurpation of the oracle. Gaia responded by sending dreams to all those who might otherwise have come to consult Apollo's wisdom, until Zeus was persuaded by Apollo to order her to desist.

Gaia is the living presence of earth; a reminder of the time when matter was still rebellious, long before one could imagine it as terra firma. She reminds her worshipers that matter is still rebellious, alive and eruptive. Gaia is earthquake and volcano, molten lava and shifting rock. She is earth as it is in itself, not earth as subdued by humankind. She is goddess of all that grows but never the goddess of agriculture. (Indeed, in Greece the agriculture rites are so entirely civic, political affairs that a goddess as far removed from being a fertility goddess as Olympian Athene can be their patron.) Gaia signifies all that cannot be brought under control. She is divine; she transcends the human. She is that very transcendence but as an earthly, shaped, present, appearing reality.

To understand Gaia as *only* earth, to reduce her to being a personification of an aspect of the natural world, is to miss the point. Gaia is earth made invisible,

earth become metaphor, earth as the realm of soul. She is never just vegetal fertility nor even the physical globe at its most volatile and destructive.

She is for life but for ever-renewing, ever-changing life, for life as it encom-
passes death. Gaia rituals included animal sacrifice as well as offerings of cereal
and fruit; they may in archaic Greece as in many vegetation cults have included
human sacrifice. The Orphic hymn addresses her thus:

> Divine Earth, mother of men and of the blessed gods,
> You nourish all, you give all, you bring all to
> Fruition, and you destroy all.[2]

There is a within-ness to Gaia; souls live in her body. The Greeks understood
that souls inhabit earth, not sky. The dead live in her depths. There is much evidence that Gaia is a chthonic deity. On the Areopagus her statue stands with
those of Hermes and Hades. At Athens, Mykonos, and probably Delphi, she was
worshiped in association with the dead. Indeed, the omphalos at Delphi was very
likely originally a grave mound, clear evidence of a connection to a chthonic cult.
The Attic *Genesia* (also called a *nekyeia,* a descent into the underworld) was an All
Souls festival when offerings were brought to family graves. The *Anthesteria,*
which in classical times was celebrated in honor of Dionysos, was probably originally a mournful festival consecrated to Gaia and the dead, and even in the classic
period Gaia was still involved. Gaia's rituals, like other chthonic rituals and the
rituals of the mystery cults, suggest the possibility of a different kind of identification between the worshiper and the goddess than we find in the worship of her
Olympian offspring. Gaia's devotees experienced ecstatic and orgiastic possession
(as was also true in the cults devoted to her biforms, Rhea and Cybele).

Gaia is also the giver of dreams and of mantic oracles. Though Hermes is the
divinity most closely associated with the interpretation of dreams, Gaia is their
source. Understanding her prophecies comes not from being able to read the stars
or the entrails of birds or beasts, but from attunement to her deep knowledge of
what is really (and inevitably) going on.

One cannot understand Gaia simply in human or psychological terms. Nevertheless, she is nature moving toward emergence in personal form. The most usual
artistic representation of Gaia expresses this beautifully—she is shown as a
human woman emerging breast-high from the earth itself.

In Homer, though Gaia has a definite shape, though she is more than a vague
and inchoate conception of the whole earth as animate and conscious, she is not
as concrete and personal as her Olympian offspring and not personally active. She

is the presupposition. Because earth is always near at hand and cannot be escaped, she is guarantor of the most serious oaths. Even the gods swear by her.

In Hesiod, though Gaia is still clearly *earth*, she is, nevertheless, conceived in a more personal way. According to his *Theogony*, in the beginning there was Chaos, by which he means simply emptiness, pure potentiality, a yawning abyss. Then, by a process of spontaneous emergence, appear Gaia and Tartarus, along with Eros, Erebos (Darkness), and Light. Tartarus represents the within-ness of earth, its dark unknowable interior; Gaia its giving forth. Tartarus its chthonic aspect, earth's relation to death and soul; Gaia its relationship to vegetation, physical life, fertility. But the two cannot really be separated. Tartarus is Gaia's within-ness; Gaia is Tartarus's self-externalization.

Gaia and Her Offspring

To be creative is Gaia's very essence. To be Gaia is to give birth to something other than herself, to heterogeneity. Her first creations are her parthenogenetic offspring, sea and mountain and sky. Though she then mates with her own dark double, Tartarus, and with sea and sky, she is still their origin. All things begin with the mother, even fathers. Of these primal divine beings only Gaia has a cult. The others belong to mythology, to cosmogonic reflection, but are not experienced by the Greeks as living, active principles, as is she. The others are supplanted, Ouranos by Zeus, Pontus by Poseidon. She is not; indeed, she participates in the supplantation.

According to Hesiod, Ouranos and Gaia co-parented not only the twelve Titans but also a race of one-eyed Cyclops and of hundred-handed monsters. Because Ouranos found these latter creations ugly and terrible, he hid them in Gaia's depths and did not allow them to emerge. But it is Gaia's very nature to give forth. Thus, she is in great distress at having to contain these creatures within her. She solicits the aid of the youngest of the Titans, Cronos, to accomplish their release. When next Ouranos comes to make love to her, Cronos springs forth from his hiding place and, using the sickle his mother had fashioned precisely for this task, cuts off his father's genitals. The falling drops of blood are received by Earth, who conceives and gives birth to the Erinyes, the Giants, and the tree nymphs. From the foam surrounding the sea-tossed member Aphrodite emerges. Ouranos is henceforth relegated to the sky, and there serves as the very figure of distance, un-involvement, abstraction.

Cronos (with his Titan sister Rhea as consort) takes his father's place and gives birth to six children. But Gaia and Ouranos warn that he is fated in his turn to be overcome by one of his children. So, one by one as they are born, he swallows them. Once again it is Gaia who intervenes on behalf of the emergence of life. She deceives Cronos into swallowing a stone instead of his last-born child, Zeus, and she secretly rears her grandson. When Zeus grows up, he tricks Cronos into disgorging the swallowed stone and children and then fights against his father, with his siblings, the Cyclops, the Hundred-handed, and at least one of the female Titans, Themis, as allies. The battles are of truly cosmic proportions—sea and earth and even the wide heavens are shaken by them. Hesiod's descriptions of the clamor, heat, and confusion are magnificent.

But though Gaia sides with Zeus against the Titans, when he next begins to battle them she is on their side. The Titans are Ouranian; they seek to contest the Olympians for heavenly supremacy. The Titans win her support because they are truly earth-born (not at all the huge ogres of fairy tale). It seems to her that Zeus intends to deny his common origin with all her other creations and offspring. This so enrages her that she proceeds to engage in the creation of new monstrous forces to pit against him, most notably the fearsome dragon Typhoeus, from whose shoulders grow a hundred snakeheads. Here as always, Gaia shows herself for life and against any stifling order.

It is in her very nature to create, to bring forth variety, heterogeneity. She is ever fertile; a drop of Ouranos's blood or of Hephaestus's semen impregnates her, but she is as likely to give birth to the monstrous as to the beautiful. She groans and protests, feels essentially thwarted when Ouranos forces her to contain her own children in her body (in contrast to Cronos, who swallows his progeny in order to feel safer, who feels threatened by what he does not contain). Gaia's emanations are projections of her own being, each catching one aspect of her own protoplasmic fullness. To know her fully is to see her in that which emerges from her.

Among her offspring the most important are Themis, the Erinyes, Demeter, and Persephone. Each reflects a different aspect of Earth. *Themis*, daughter of Gaia and Ouranos, shares many of her mother's functions and attributes, including her knowledge of the future. (It is she, for instance, who warns Zeus against the threat posed by any son born to Metis.) Delphi was hers after it was Gaia's and before it became Apollo's. As bride of Zeus Themis is mother, among others, of Dike (Justice) and of the Fates. She comes to be associated particularly with righteousness and communal order in society. But it is important to see the significance of its being an earth goddess that thus represents righteousness—for this suggests that for the Greeks right order in the human realm meant harmony with the natural order.

The *Erinyes*, the Furies, also represent forces that insist on such right ordering and emerge to reestablish it when it is disregarded. They come into appearance especially to extract retribution for the most heinous crimes—matricide and oath breaking. But the Erinyes are all along also the *Eumenides*, the consoling ones. The aboriginal conception associated them with marriage and childbirth, with retribution (though the former, too, are bloody events), and as bringers of a gentle death (as to Oedipus), not only as avengers.

Demeter and Persephone in their essential bond with one another represent the two aspects of Gaia, the vegetative and chthonic. But Demeter is associated more with cultivation than is Gaia; she is the corn mother, not really the earth mother. She is also humanlike, especially in her bereavement and grief, as Gaia never is. Persephone is the goddess of the underworld but never just a goddess of the world of soul; she is always also the beautiful young goddess of spring as it manifests itself in tender leaf and half-opened bud, in the rushing streams and the freshness of bird song. To hold soul and earth together, the hidden and the appearing—that is Gaia's gift.

Gaia is the all-mother, the mother not only of the gods but of human beings as well. There are many different tales of how the primordial human sprang directly from Earth: one speaks of Erichthonius, whom Gaia conceived when Hephaestus's semen fell to earth; another of Cecrops, who was born from the earth with a snake's body. There is a story to the effect that once in anger Zeus determined to destroy the whole human race with a flood. Only Deucalion and Pyrrha were saved; as they longed for human companionship they were told to throw over their shoulders the bones of their mother. They picked up stones and tossed them behind them: Deucalion's stones became men, Pyrrha's women.

All humans have their source in Gaia. But Pandora, the first woman, is Gaia in human form. Her very name, *Pan-dora,* "rich in gifts," "all-giving" (a name also of Earth itself), suggests this. In Hesiod's account, she is fashioned by Hephaestus of earth and water. In vase paintings, where she is often represented as a creation of Prometheus, her iconography is indistinguishable from Gaia's—she is Gaia emerging in human form from the earth, an earth worked upon by Prometheus's (or Epimetheus's) hammer. In Hesiod she is associated with the letting loose of many evils into the human world, including sickness and death. Pandora is indeed Gaia's manifestation: the giver of all gifts, both welcome and unwelcome.

Eclipse of the Goddesses

Probably each of the Olympian goddesses was originally a preHellenic local earth goddess—Hera in Argos, Athene in Attica, Artemis and Aphrodite somewhere in the Near East. In this sense, each is Gaia. Nevertheless, Hesiod's attempt to distinguish the Olympians from the original mother derives from a genuinely mythopoetic sensitivity. It is of the essence of the first mother to give birth to a rich variety of daughters. To remember Gaia's relation to these later goddesses is not to say that they are nothing but Gaia herself under other names, but rather that she is the ground out of which their figures emerge.

Today, the most familiar goddesses are, as we are so often reminded, the goddesses of patriarchy. As they are presented to us by Homer, Hesiod, and the tragedians, the Greek goddesses are not very attractive creatures. These texts all exhibit a deep suspicion of feminine power; they all seem concerned to validate the priority of the social over the natural order, and to record the establishment of a "rationally based" policy in which rulership is no longer to be determined matrilineally. The original ties of the goddesses to the natural world have been rationalized or reduced to metaphor. Athene is no longer the Acropolis rock and Artemis no longer the Arcadian wilderness. Aphrodite is no longer the mist rising from sea to sky, or the rain falling from sky to earth, though she may still envelop a favorite hero in a cloud to hide him from an enemy's fatal attack. Some once-potent goddesses (Ariadne and Helen, for example) are in the classical literature reduced to human status. Artemis, the goddess who within the Olympian pantheon is seen as still bound more to the natural than to the interhuman world, is represented in the *Odyssey* as a clumsy child, out of her climate when she leaves her forest haunts. The goddesses' chthonic aspect, their relation to death and transformation, like their relation to the natural world and to vegetal fertility, is emphatically ignored, except in the case of Demeter, the goddess of the grain, and Persephone, the goddess of the underworld (and Homer manages to avoid paying much attention to them).

The establishment of the Olympian order was a revolution, as is made plain in Hesiod's *Theogony* in the account of Zeus's battle against all the generations of divine begins who had preceded him (including eventually even Gaia, the mother who had at first encouraged him against his father). Within the hierarchy thereafter ruled by Zeus (especially in Homer's accounts) the goddesses clearly become subordinated divinities. Aphrodite, who in Hesiod is recognized to be generations older than Zeus, is in the *Odyssey* represented as the daughter of Zeus and Dione. That Hera was known to be a more ancient divinity than Zeus is symbolized in Hesiod by her being his elder sister; in Homer she becomes not only a needy, dependent spouse but a younger sibling. Even Athene, whose stature is less diminished, is made into a goddess entirely dependent on male power, proud to be motherless, Zeus's parthenogenetic creation.

The goddesses are not only subordinated to the god, they are defined as being in their very essence related to men, each in a very particular way: Hera is wife, Athene is father's daughter, Aphrodite is the responsive beloved, Artemis is she who shuns men. Thus they are represented from the perspective of male psychology, and consequently both sentimentalized and denigrated.

Each goddess, too, has had her dominion and powers much more narrowly delimited within the Olympian world than was true earlier. Aphrodite is now only the goddess of physical beauty and human sexual love; Artemis is primarily the goddess of the hunt; Athene the protector of cities and patron of the arts. Not only is each given a distinct sphere of power but, especially in Homer, the goddesses are represented as implacably hostile to one another. It is the unmitigated rivalry between Athene, Hera, and Aphrodite that gives rise to the Trojan War (a rather backhanded recognition of the continued potency of the goddesses).

Goddesses and Motherhood

It is striking that in the classical presentations the domination of the Olympian goddesses by patriarchal power is symbolized by their being represented as cut off from their mother. Demeter, Hera, and Hestia were swallowed by their father immediately after birth; Aphrodite was born (at least according to Hesiod's account) out of the semen that surrounded her father's severed genitals after Cronos had thrown them into the surging sea; Athene (according to the same source) emerged full-grown from father Zeus's head.

Of the major Olympian goddesses only Artemis had a mother—a mother whom she seems to have mothered from almost the moment of her own birth. The newborn daughter immediately sets about assisting with the delivery of her twin brother Apollo, and on many other occasions rescues Leto from insult or danger. There is much that is instinctively motherly in Artemis, especially her tender solicitude for all that is young and vulnerable, animal or human. Indeed, at Ephesus, she was worshiped as the many-breasted great mother. Yet the classical Artemis is a virgin who never bears a child of her own; she shuns the world of men and lives in the forest on the fringes of the inhabited world. She represents the persistence of the natural, the untamed, even within the Olympian hegemony—but a naturalness that had become infertile.

Nor are any of her sister goddesses more whole in their mothering. Like Artemis, Athene and Hestia are childless. Though Hestia can love generously and impartially—and in Rome, as Vesta, becomes a prototype of the good mother—she seems, perhaps in consequence of the early loss of her own mother, to be deeply suspicious of close personal attachments. Athene is a devoted and dependable friend, she is a protector of the generation of young children on whom the future of the polis depends, but she carefully protects herself from sexual passion and explicitly (in Aeschylus's *Oresteia*) avows an allegiance to father-right and implicitly accepts Apollo's declaration "that the mother is no parent of that which is called her child." Aphrodite's marriage to Hephaestus is sterile; her children are the incidental consequences of the self-indulgence of her passionate attraction to an Ares or an Anchises. She loves Aeneas, the issue of the latter liaison, and tries to protect him as best she can during the Trojan War and his subsequent journey to Italy, but she takes no part in rearing him. In her mothering, she displays the same kind of adventitious dispensation of favors that characterizes her sexual involvements. Though Hera is wife to all-father Zeus, their marriage, too, can hardly be regarded as bounteously fertile; Hera is preeminently wife, not mother. Her daughters (Hebe and Eileithyia) are but pale shadows of herself; her sons, Ares and Hephaestus (who, at least according to some accounts, are her parthenogenetic offspring), serve her primarily as pawns in her incessant battles with her husband. Her stepson and namesake, Herakles, is the prototype of the hero who must take on one impossible task after another in the never satisfied hope of receiving her blessing. Demeter's boundless love for her daughter, Persephone, seems at first glance to represent an idealized version of maternal devotion—yet a closer reading suggests it may be her overinvestment in her child that makes Persephone's abduction by Hades a necessary denouement. In these goddesses the Greeks represented in divine proportions the mother who abandons her children or holds them too tight, the mother who uses her children as agents in her marital struggles or to fulfill her own frustrated ambitions.

Childhoods of the Goddesses

The myths about the childhoods of the goddesses seem to offer us a vision of the sadness and pain, the vulnerabilities and weaknesses, inherent in childhood. To paraphrase Nietzsche: the goddesses justify human life by living it themselves, the only satisfactory theodicy ever invented.

The fantasy element seems evident in the myth of Persephone's childhood. The representation of a primal dyad between mother and daughter, not intruded upon by a father or siblings, could fairly be called "a family romance"—as if the blissful first weeks at the breast could be prolonged forever. Zeus, the most royal and powerful father imaginable, never appears, so the mother never turns away from the child and is never disparaged. This is truly a divine childhood, and though Persephone outwardly becomes a maiden she remains until her abduction a dreamy self-enclosed child.

But Demeter's own childhood is different, spent within her father's body along with the other four children he swallowed as soon as they were born. Robbed of a connection to her birth from birth, she tries to create a fantasy bond with her daughter, over-identifies with her, seeks to give her the childhood she was herself denied. She is childish (not harmoniously childlike) in her raging grief when Persephone is taken from her. Because she had no real childhood of her own, she seems to see childhood sentimentally and to be easily overwhelmed by its negative aspects.

Hera's childhood is essentially the same as Demeter's, but as an adult she lives out her unlived childhood differently. First, she, too, tries living through her children. But whereas Persephone was a more beautiful and vibrant version of Demeter, Hera's daughters, Hebe and Eileithyia, are but pale shadows of their mother. Because they are reduced in her mind to being but pawns in her battles with Zeus, her sons are crippled, Hephaestus physically, Ares psychologically. She had sought to mother Zeus, to make him her well-sheltered son; she had asked him to mother her, wholly enclose her as her father had when she was young. When she discovers the inadequacy of all these modes of asking others to provide her with a childhood, she realizes she must herself go in search of that lost childhood. She returns to her motherland and re-imagines the unlived childhood; only then, knowingly carrying her own childhood within her, is she represented as ready for real relationship.

Artemis's childhood has some of the same elements as Persephone's. Zeus is again the absent father. Experientially, Artemis has only a female parent, one who is inordinately proud of her. But Artemis is robbed of her childhood by having a mother much more obviously childlike, dependent, and vulnerable than is Demeter. The myths suggest that her childhood midwifery may lead Artemis to be insistently self-sufficient in her adult form and unwilling ever to renounce the solitude of the child. She remains tender toward children but easily becomes impatient with the childishly dependent adult. There is something eternally young in her way of being alone and distant; she, too, carries her childhood with her always.

At first glance Athene seems truly to have no childhood. She emerges full-grown out of the head of Zeus, dressed as a warrior, emitting a triumphant battle cry. She seems to begin life as the adolescent, closely identified with her father, with so-called masculine attributes like self-confidence and courage, intelligence and dispassion, and with the male world. She epitomizes the particular kind of strength that can come by denying childhood and the mother bond. The denial is hers: she seems proud of having had no mother. Yet we feel something missing;

we feel that until we can connect her to her maternal origins there is something one-dimensional about her. Without her childhood she is incomplete. So we go in search of it and discover Metis, her wise and intrepid mother whose potential progeny threatened Zeus, and we understand Athene differently.

Aphrodite is motherless and fatherless; she is born of the depersonalized phallus immersed in the impersonal oceanic womb. She represents a self-sufficiency that is nonetheless warm, receptive, and open. Older than Zeus, coeval with the Titans, she symbolizes a more cosmic beginning than just individual human birth and childhood. She reminds us that the archetype of the child, like that of the mother, pertains not only to personal psychology: part of the divinity inherent in the archetype comes from its transpersonal, cosmic aspect.

The mythological representations of the childhoods of the goddesses evoke the archetype of the divine child and the wonder of all beginnings:

> In the image of the Primordial Child the world tells of its own childhood, and of everything that sunrise and the birth of a child mean for, and say about, the world. The childhood and orphan's fate of the child gods have not evolved from the stuff of human life, but from the stuff of cosmic life. What appears to be biographical in mythology is, as it were, an anecdote that the world relates from its own biography.[3]

Which returns us to Gaia, to the beginning of all beginnings, the primordial mother.

Notes

1.   Charles Boer, *The Homeric Hymns* (Chicago: Swallow Press, 1970) 5.

2.   Apostolos N. Athanasakis, *The Orphic Hymns* (Missoula, MT: Scholars Press, 1977) 37.

3.   C. G. Jung and C. Kerenyi, *Essays on a Science of Mythology: The Myths of the Divine Child and the Mysteries of Eleusis* (Princeton: Princeton University Press, 1969) 80.

4

Diotima and Alcibiades

Although I am neither classicist nor philosopher, I ordered Martha Nussbaum's *Fragility of Goodness* when it first came out after reading Bernard Knox's appreciative review in the *New York Review of Books* and read it then with profit and pleasure. I returned to it, especially the chapters on the *Symposium* and the *Phaedrus*, this summer while working on the Plato section of a book on same-sex love.[1]

A few months earlier a dear friend had come to tell me that he had AIDS and that he had always hoped I might write about the Greek mythological representations of male-male love in a way that would explore the relevance of those representations to contemporary experience (as my book on Greek goddesses had explored their present-day relevance). In response I began working on a book that begins by re-examining the dominant images through which both male and female homosexuality have been viewed in this century, the myths about homosexuality attributed to Freud and Jung and those they actually put forward. I then go on to consider how same-sex love was viewed in ancient Greece, in a culture where at least some expressions of it were socially validated. This has entailed some demythologizing of modern popular notions about sexual attitudes and practices in classical Athens to provide a basis for understanding the mythological representations and also seemed to require some consideration of both Sappho and Plato.

My re-readings of the *Symposium* and the *Phaedrus* led me to a somewhat different interpretation of those dialogues from those put forward by Nussbaum, an interpretation which I put forward here more as an alternative reading than as a replacement of hers. I do not imagine that I offer perspectives that will be new to her; indeed, her texts and footnotes show that she has considered and on reflection rejected many of the readings I find persuasive. I reintroduce them because I find myself not wholly convinced by her interpretations and yet find her book too important to ignore. Alternative readings must, I submit, engage in dialogue with hers.

I value Nussbaum's work for several obvious reasons. I appreciate not only the clarity and close reasoning of her writing but also its passion, its personal voice, and its inclusion of the full range of her own response.

I honor her turning to the poetry and philosophy of ancient Greece convinced of their relevance to our own attempts to make sense of our lives, to our struggles to articulate what constitutes a livable life. I agree with her view that Greek polytheism makes available a still helpful way of representing the painful collision between binding obligations. I share her belief that we require a view of human life that honors its messiness and complexity, contradictions and contingencies, and that takes account of our feelings, our bodies, and our vulnerability to circumstance, to loss, conflict and suffering. I am moved by her recognition of how pulled all of us—not just Creon or Antigone or Socrates—are to evade or close off conflict and pain, to be self-sufficient and in control. She sees that there is a kind of beauty in that pull to transcendence, as well as a kind of tragedy (and, I'd add, perhaps a kind of comedy, too.)

I also value her work because she recognizes the significance for her inquiry of the tragic as well as the philosophical texts (and reminds us of the anachronism inherent in imposing our genre distinctions on classical literature). She recognizes how the tragedians' focus on concrete stories makes evident our vulnerability to passion and circumstance as more generalized descriptions often do not and celebrates their appeal to our feeling as well as our intellect. I agree with her that interpreting tragedies is a less determinate and more mysterious matter than interpreting Aristotle—though Nussbaum seems more confident than I about the possibility of finding *the* moral conception communicated in a play as a whole. (This is relevant to my reservations about her interpretation of the *Symposium*, because there too I find her equating the meaning of the dialogue with a position voiced within it.)

Although Nussbaum reads her chosen texts from tragedy with care, she still reads them as a philosopher—looking for a moral thesis, and, indeed, discovering the same thesis in each of the plays she discusses. Though I would agree that in each of these dramas (*Agamemnon, Seven Against Thebes, Antigone,* and *Hecuba*) we see demonstrated the moral cost of yielding to the temptation to avoid the struggles and remorse associated with an honest engagement with ethical conflict, I am less sure that this is the central message of each play. Because Nussbaum is interested in how accidental circumstance brings to light moral deficiencies that might never have been exposed, she minimizes the degree to which both Agamemnon and Eteocles (Agamemnon in his murder of Clytemnestra's first husband and child, Eteocles in holding on to the kingship of Thebes beyond his pre-established term) are already culpable before the scenes which reveal their lack of moral courage. In her interpretation of the *Antigone*, by identifying the "conclusion" of the play[2] (89) with Haemon's example and Tiresias' advice (64, 79, 81), she seems to miss the awe as well as pity that Sophocles' Antigone herself inspires in most viewers of the tragedy. All that Nussbaum says about Antigone's single-mindedness and the abstractness of her conception of familial obligation is, of course, true. Nussbaum also acknowledges that the play's implicit criticism of Antigone leaves her moral superiority to Creon untouched (66). Yet I find her reading of the play with its emphasis on the Chorus, on the messenger and Tiresias, on Ismene and Haemon, strangely off center. She reads the play as telling us that "human beings had better stay with 'established conventions' in spite of the risks these leave in place" (89). But surely the play is also celebrating the fearful beauty (as well as human limitation) of a woman who chose differently.

In Nussbaum's reading of Plato I value her recognition of the importance of the dialogue form (but her insistence that Plato was the main creator of the austere, unambiguous style of philosophical discourse is puzzling) and her awareness of how difficult it can be to ascertain what choice between the alternative responses articulated within a dialogue Plato wants us to make:

> This makes it dangerous to speak of Plato's views unless we simply mean his view of what the open alternatives are and what the choice of either involves giving up—no trivial view in itself. But we do often want to go further than this and to speak of Plato as defending one alternative over another. It would be a mistake to abandon this way of speaking. His students, Aristotle included, had no doubt that he was defending views in works such as the *Republic* and the *Phaedo* (87).

As I recall how one-dimensional, how literal, Fenichel's or Jung's readings of Freud are, I wonder about that invocation of Plato's students. Relatively reductionist readings may, after all, express that same rage for control that Nussbaum elsewhere explicates so well. Indeed, I find puzzling her continued identification of the Platonic with self-sufficiency and pure rationality despite the quite different Plato that emerges from her own close readings.

I am not persuaded that ultimately she takes the dialogue form as seriously as she claims to—for, as in her reading of the tragedies, she seems quite confident of her ability to discover the thesis communicated in the dialogue as a whole. She dismisses the dramatic elements as existing only in order to engage us initially and as thereafter insignificant (131). This leads, I believe, to her imposing cruder polarities on Plato than the texts justify. For example, she believes that in the

Phaedo Socrates' visitors begin to learn only when they put their love for Socrates away and turn to thought (133); 1 would say it is their love that motivates them to turn to thought, that Plato is encouraging a sublimation rather than a rejection of Eros. (That is a theme to which I'll return in my discussion of the *Symposium*.) Yet Nussbaum does admit that in some of the dialogues, including the *Symposium*, it is more difficult to speak with confidence about Plato's view, and she explicitly recognizes that "there are many ways in which a reader who also takes the dialogue form seriously might object to the solutions at which I have arrived" (88).

As one such "objecting" reader I find the *Symposium* a less harsh and alarming book than does Nussbaum and find its Socrates less a coldly self-sufficient Nietzschean Socrates than does her reading. I find less tension between Diotima and Alcibiades, less radical disjunction between the *Symposium* and the *Phaedrus*. But remember, I come to these dialogues by way of a focus on Socrates as a teacher whose one subject was Eros. My reading is in many ways an old-fashioned reading, informed more by the work of Paul Friedlander than of any more recent scholar.

Friedlander speaks of Plato's youthful acquaintance with Socrates as the "fateful encounter" of his life. He believes that if Plato had not been one of the young men like Charmides or Lysis (or Alcibiades) who found in Socrates someone "who turned his soul upside down," he might have become an author of tragedies like Agathon or a political figure of some consequence like his uncles—and Socrates might have been remembered as just one among the mass of Sophist teachers. But Plato met Socrates and saw in him a compelling model of a life devoted to *philosophia*, a passionate Eros directed toward wisdom. "The strength of this love and the transforming power of this unique personality combined to throw the young Plato out of the course for which he seemed to have been destined."[3]

In his writing Plato sought to introduce an understanding of Eros different from the assumptions of his contemporaries about *paiderastia* and also different from what was shown in the inherited mythology. To do this he created a new myth whose central figure was Socrates, represented not only as a teacher of Eros but as an embodiment of Eros, and a new form of mythical representation, the philosophical dialogue. In Plato's representation of him, Socrates' interactions with the young Athenian aristocrats who were his students, his conversations with them, the homoerotic ambience of these encounters, was as important to what made him *the* philosopher as the content of his teaching. Socrates himself was suspicious of writing and believed that only words directly spoken to another have the power to touch the soul. Plato invented a literary form that he hoped might convey his teacher's erotic presence and draw us into the dialogue, thereby awakening *our* eros for wisdom.

It follows that we cannot understand Plato by trying to extract a philosophical doctrine from the dialogues—as I was taught to do when I was in school—or a "dialectical method." The dialogues as a whole communicate the Platonic vision. Because Plato's Socrates taught that it is from the interaction between the lover and the beloved that "the deepest insights spring," we cannot even identify the meaning of the dialogues with Socrates' speeches but must examine closely the complex interplay among the contributions to the discussion of all those participating.

My focus is on Eros, the one subject of which the always ironically modest Socrates was willing to admit any knowledge. In the *Lysis* (204b) Socrates announces: "Ignorant as I am in all other things, God gave me the power to recognize one who loves and is loved." In the *Theages* (128b) he confesses: "I know nothing about these lofty matters—how I wish that I did!—but as I am always saying, I am quite ignorant in general save for one small subject: the nature of love."

My focus is on Eros—and more specifically on Eros among men. Most scholars who have sought to articulate Plato's view of love have focused less than I do on what I take to be more than an historical accident—that when he spoke of love, he spoke of male love directed to men (although they would not dispute that such was the case).

Plato's dialogues are full of allusions to Socrates' love of young men. At the beginning of the *Protagoras* Socrates is teased about his infatuation with Alcibiades; in the *Charmides* he admits that "pretty well all youths of that age seem beautiful to me" and continues, "Then I saw what was inside his garments and I was aflame and beside myself" (155d). Such passages make evident Socrates' susceptibility to physical beauty and convey a taken-for-granted acceptance of his sensual responsiveness. Yet they also suggest that there is another beauty that stirs him even more deeply. Socrates declares that the nobility of Charmides' soul is even more important than the beauty of his face and body: "Before we see his body, should we not ask him to strip and show us his soul?" (154e). As the *Protagoras* unfolds, Socrates reveals that although Alcibiades was present, "I paid no heed to him. Indeed, I forgot him completely"—for there was someone more beautiful present, wise old Protagoras (309d). In the *Gorgias* he calls himself an *erastes* (a lover) of both Alcibiades and philosophy and tells us that philosophy is a less capricious and unstable *eromenos* (beloved) than Alcibiades (481d).

Although these stories about Socrates' infatuations are told in jest, they never-theless communicate the strength of his responsiveness to physical beauty. They suggest that the sensual element, though "a steppingstone to a higher level," is nonetheless "a necessary steppingstone whose absence would make that higher level inaccessible."[4] In the *Symposium* as I read it, Diotima *teaches* that one cannot omit the preliminary stage, the love of one body; in his representations of Socrates' interactions with his students, Plato *shows* how attainment of the higher level does not imply a simple negation of the starting point.

The dialogues also reveal that the relation between Socrates and the youths is not that typical between an *erastes* and a group of *eremenoi*. The *Charmides* ends with the beautiful boy threatening to rape the resistant philosopher (176b); in the *Alcibiades Major*, Alcibiades admits, "We shall in all likelihood reverse the usual pattern, Socrates, I taking your role and you mine" (135d). In the *Lysis* Socrates concludes, "It is necessary then for a genuine and not a pretended *erastes* to be loved by his boy" (222a), and in Xenophon's *Memorabilia* he says, "When I desire someone, I give the whole strength of my being to be loved by him in return for my love, to arouse longing in return for my longing, and to see my desire for companionship reciprocated by his desire" (II 6.28). The roles are reversed, or perhaps erased; there is a novel emphasis on reciprocity. We begin to glimpse that there is a new myth about male-male love being introduced here.

We also begin to see that Eros itself is being understood in a different, more extended way. Philosophers are said to be *erastai* of Being and truth, of under-standing and knowledge. As David Halperin observes, "Plato's language is designed to emphasize the active, restless character of the desire that is common to the passionate pederast and the aspiring philosopher," to show that philosophy begins in desire.[5] Socrates seeks to draw his students to participate in his own love for wisdom, for the soul, for the community. For the Platonic Socrates male love becomes the privileged path that leads to the growth of the soul, to creativity and to the mode of immortality available to us humans.

I have been intrigued for a long while by the role Diotima plays in Plato's *Symposium*. The setting of this dialogue is a banquet given by Agathon on the occasion of his having won the prize for tragedy in that year's competition. The men who are gathered together are old and close friends; several are recognized love pairs. They decide to take turns making speeches in praise of love. It soon becomes clear that for all of them the love most worthy of praise is love between men. Socrates' turn comes last. He begins by confiding that most of what he has to say will be but inadequate recapitulation of what he in turn had been taught by a Mantinean woman called Diotima. What is this unseen feminine presence doing there in the middle of that gathering of homosexual men?

The interweaving of the various speeches constitutes perhaps the most famous composition ever devoted to the inner meaning of love among men. What does Diotima communicate that would otherwise not be expressed? What are the "deepest mysteries" of love that (Socrates tells us) she was not sure even he would be able to attain?

Despite my fascination with this question I do not believe that we can reduce the meaning of this dialogue to Diotima's contribution. The setting within which it is introduced subtly qualifies and interprets her views. All the speeches play a role in helping us to understand what the deepest mysteries might be and why they might be so difficult to apprehend. Each is a necessary part of the way. Each represents a stage in the rite.

Plato's dialogue purports to be a repetition by Apollodorus, a young follower of Socrates, to an unnamed friend of a story he'd been pressed for by another young Athenian a few days earlier. His version is secondhand; he'd originally been told the story by someone who had been present at the banquet itself as one of Socrates' most impassioned young admirers—then. For despite the current interest in the event, it had all happened years ago, "when you and I were in the nursery." And Diotima's conversations with Socrates were even then events of a long gone past.

In the interval the party has clearly already assumed mythic significance. The setting serves to communicate that at the time of the retelling Socrates is still inspiring the love of young men like Apollodorus, and that they are fascinated with the details of their beloved teacher's life. They love him and want to know him. To know him includes knowing such tales; to retell them is to enact their love. Remembering the frame within which the dialogue is set may help us "read" Diotima's teaching about the stages of love with more complexity than we might were we to ignore it.

A symposium is a drinking party; the banquet is in honor of Dionysos as well as of Eros—Dionysos, the god of theater, mysticism, love, and wine. Dionysos is present all along; he does not arrive with Alcibiades. The party is being held to celebrate an event that had taken place in Dionysos' theater the day before. When Socrates arrives and begins his mocking praise of Agathon, the other retorts, "Let Bacchus judge between us," suggesting that another dramatic competition is about to take place.

But though they are initially gathered in honor of Dionysos, Eryximachos soon suggests (he says the idea is really Phaedrus's) that they spend the evening with each one present taking his turn to speak in praise of Eros—to which Socrates readily agrees, for "Love is the one thing in the world I understand" (177c). Eros is from the beginning present among them in many guises. In the *Protagoras* (whose dramatic date is some fifteen years earlier than that of the *Symposium*) Agathon had already been identified as the beloved of Pausanias; in Aristophanes' *Women at the Thesmophoria* (written in 411) Agathon is mocked for never having moved beyond the *eremenos* stage. Here in the *Symposium* their friends' response to this long-term relationship is more complex; it is clearly accepted, perhaps even a little envied, and yet it also provokes teasing. Socrates, for example, pretends to be flirting with Agathon throughout the evening. Another relationship given recognition in several other of Plato's dialogues is that linking Phaedrus to the physician Eryximachos as his younger, respectful companion. At the time of the banquet Socrates is fifty-three, Alcibiades thirty-four; their relationship, too, as we shall see, has a long history.

These are the men who take turns responding to the question "What is love?" The asking is the practice. They search together, beget together, and though the contributions of some may be slight, sentimental and conventional, nevertheless each builds on what the others have said. In other dialogues Socrates is engaged in focused interrogation of one or two youths or in a relatively formal debate with a famous Sophist; here he is meeting informally with a group of his peers, among whom are included two poets—as though this topic could not fully be explored without their participation. The insights grow out of the interactions, these people, this occasion. Even Diotima's discourse, supposedly told to Socrates long ago, is closely connected to what precedes. Each speech is part of the way. Plato's view emerges only through an interaction in which Socrates' contribution is but one part.[6]

I cannot review all the speeches here, but cannot afford not to attend at least to the one attributed to Aristophanes. Into the mouth of the greatest of Athens' comic poets (who, as all his readers would recall, had mocked Socrates in his play *The Clouds* [4231]), Plato puts the myth about the primordial "round people," which may well be the most widely remembered passage in the *Symposium*. Aristophanes tells how these first humans came to challenge the authority of the gods and how Zeus, hoping to undermine their rebellion without destroying them, cut them in two ("just as one might slice an egg")—leaving "each half with a desperate yearning for the other" (191a). Though the images Aristophanes invents are undoubtedly humorous and some of his phrasing consummately flippant, like many readers over the centuries I find this newly created myth deeply moving. I believe it was meant to be moving. What Plato communicates here of the power of our conviction that we can be made whole only through relation to another, a particular other whom we recognize as uniquely akin (whereas Eryximachos had seen love as reconciling opposites), is not simply an understanding of love that Socrates will contest, but like Alcibiades' passionate utterance an important complement to Socrates' own discourse.

The comic tone may mask the radical criticism of the dominant conventions, may lead us to miss that Aristophanes is here acknowledging that the desire and pleasure felt by women and *eremenoi* is in principle no different from that of adult men. As Foucault notes, "His mythical tale upsets the generally accepted principle of dissymmetry of age, feelings, and behavior between the lover and the beloved"—and thus makes irrelevant the traditional moral focus on the issue of consent."[7] Though Aristophanes, like the other speakers, gives most attention to the desire of males for males, his tale makes clear that it is the same desire that animates the yearning of those sliced off from the original hermaphrodites (now heterosexually-oriented men and women) and that also moves the women who are slices of the original female. (This, we might note, is the only reference outside of Sappho in classical literature to what we call lesbian love.) "What I am trying to say is this—that the happiness of the whole human race, women no less than men, is to be found in the consummation of our love, and in the healing of our dissevered nature by finding each his proper mate" (193c).

Aristophanes describes how in pity for the desperate longing of the severed pairs to be rolled back in one, Zeus moved their genitals so that they might at least have the solace of sexual intercourse and its momentary overcoming of the gulf between one human and another. But he also names how sexual desire is but a surrogate for a deeper longing, for "a something else to which they cannot put a name" (192c) but that is actually the return to their original state, a complete merging in an utter oneness not just of bodies but of souls.

His tale, which communicates how our sexual need for another emanates from our sense of incompleteness, of being subject to a primal wound, reminds us of Freud's recognition of our inexpungeable woundedness—as Aristophanes' emphasis on how all longing is really a longing to find again the lost first other reminds us of Freud's conviction that all later loves are but substitutes for our first love, our mother. As Nussbaum observes, Aristophanes gives us an account of love as directed to "entire beings, thoroughly embodied, with all their idiosyncrasies, flaws, and even faults. What makes them fall in love is a sudden swelling up of feelings of kinship and intimacy" directed to another "as a unique and irreplaceable whole" (173). Yet he also communicates how unlikely, how much a matter of chance, it is that we will, indeed, find our other half (and jokingly says that perhaps Pausanias and Agathon are among the lucky ones). So it is likely that most of will us always be driven by our desire—longing for a lost other, longing for an impossible fusion.

As Aristophanes presents love, the discovery of the other is an end in itself, the satisfaction of our deepest yearning, rather than what makes possible a mutually engaged-upon higher pursuit. His tale offers no criteria for our choice of beloved beyond that powerful sense of recognition—neither physical beauty nor beauty of soul. The mysterious compulsive power of sexual attraction is beautifully rendered; but the moral choices involved in our erotic life are obscured and no recognition is given the creative energies that love may release.

The next to speak is Agathon. When he is done and with evident self-satisfaction takes back his seat, Socrates ironically acknowledges his eloquence and observes that he had not realized earlier that the group had agreed to flatter rather than to praise the god of love, something he could not willingly undertake to do. "But I don't mind telling you the truth about Love, if you're interested, only if I do I must tell it in my own way" (199b). Of course, those gathered all assure him that he should go ahead and make whatever kind of speech he likes.

Diotima

Socrates then proceeds to tell his friends about the lessons he'd been given "once upon a time, by a Mantinean woman called Diotima." Like Apollodorus promising to retell Aristodemus' account of the Symposium as best he can, Socrates now promises to repeat Diotima's teaching as well as he can.

Thus when it is time for Socrates to speak about the one topic he claims to know, he presents himself as an initiate and explicitly compares his relationship with the priestess to that of Agathon with him. Long ago, he says, he found himself occupying the position that the youths surrounding him now hold. Playfully he recalls Diotima's "almost professorial authority," the self-confidence with which she asserts, "Of course, I'm right," and his own ignorance, his eagerness for instruction, and his difficulty in keeping up with her arguments.

As Socrates rehearses Diotima's long since passed interrogation, he communicates that whatever he knows about love he learned through interchange. Love can be learned only through love, only through a mutual searching. To speak of Eros, Socrates has to tell us a story—a story of a teaching, an initiation.

For Diotima's language is that of the mystery religions. She is a priestess, not just a skillful dialectician. There are stages of initiation, and there is a final revelation. As she says toward the end of her speech, "Whoever has been initiated so far in the mysteries of love and has viewed all these aspects of the beautiful in due succession is at last drawing near the final revelation." (21 1a)

Diotima, as I have already confessed, fascinates me. There is no evidence that she was an historical personage; she is Plato's invention. Even within the dialogue her evident familiarity with the earlier speeches (her mockery of the suggestion that "lovers are people looking for their own halves," her reinterpretation of Phaedrus's encomium of the self-sacrificing devotion displayed by Alcestis and Achilles) reveals the playfulness of the conceit. And yet it is more than playful. To understand this dialogue and Plato's view of love between men requires that we understand why he brings this female teacher into the midst of this male gathering. Why is Socrates presented here, as in no other dialogue, as a mouthpiece through whom another announces her wisdom?

Perhaps it is in part a device that permits the introduction of the familiar interrogative form within the set speech required by the symposium setting, perhaps in part an acknowledgment that the words Plato is here putting into the mouth of his teacher go beyond anything the historical Socrates had taught.[8] Perhaps by putting the praise of *paiderastia* in a woman's mouth he would make it appear disinterested (as Pausanias's praise so clearly was not).[9]

But I am persuaded that there is more to it than that. Diotima is and isn't Socrates, but there is a reason for his concealing himself behind a female mask. She serves as a kind of anima (to use Jung's term), as that in Socrates which gives him access to an understanding of love that has a distinctively feminine cast.[10]

Eros, Diotima informs Socrates, is not a god but rather a daimon, an intermediary between the divine and the human. As she goes on to describe this unkempt and barefoot Eros, "a lifelong seeker after truth, an adept in sorcery, enchantment, and seduction" (203cl), he (as Friedlander notes) is clearly "nobody but Socrates, even though the picture is ironically exaggerated."[11]

When Diotima defines Eros as really meaning the longing for the good, the longing for the good to be ours forever, the youthful Socrates, as he recalls their conversation, had had but little difficulty in following her. But then Diotima takes a leap that puzzles him—and that, I believe, Plato deliberately attributes to his female psychogogue. For Eros, as she goes on to describe its deepest manifestations, is presented very differently from the conventionally masculine ways of conceptualizing erotic experience reproduced in the earlier speeches. Diotima identifies love with procreative activity, an understanding of love that (as Halperin reminds us) the Greeks took to represent a feminine perspective. Women's nature, they believed, desires to give birth.[12]

The authentic aim of erotic desire, she tells him, is procreation. "To love is to bring forth upon the beautiful, both in body and in soul" (206b). Where in one of the earlier speeches Pausanias had clearly distinguished between procreative heterosexual love and the spiritual love of *paiderastia*, Diotima now proposes that conceiving and giving birth are the true aim of love as such. Love is not a longing for the possession of the beautiful but for its conception and generation.

Diotima, as Halperin suggests, is an almost necessary invention. How else but through a woman could Plato introduce this unprecedented image of male pregnancy? The language of pregnancy—of fecundity, conception, gestation, birth giving, child rearing—this, Diotima asserts, is the privileged language for describing the true nature of Eros, of active male love. Thus she proposes a "feminine" dimension to male love very different from the celebration of "effeminate" passivity suggested in Agathon's speech.

Underlying her emphasis on procreative love is Diotima's conviction that love longs for the good to be its own forever. With all our longing for immortality, we are mortal creatures, and propagation "is the one deathless and eternal element in our mortality." The only way we can perpetuate ourselves is by leaving new life behind (208b). Though in a sense accepting Aristophanes' description of the insatiability of love, Diotima goes on to suggest a way in which infinite longing may be appeased—not through possession, but through creation. Thus the recognition of *death* lies at the heart of Diotima's teaching. Because of death (and our yearning to transcend it), Eros cannot mean simply gratification or self-fulfillment, but must mean new creation.

Such generativity may be expressed not only through literal procreation, by turning to women and conceiving children with them and together raising a family, but also through turning to a young man of beautiful soul and undertaking his education. But as Diotima goes on to describe this homoerotic bond, it becomes clear that she has something quite different in mind from the educative *paiderastia* recommended by Pausanias earlier in the dialogue. For she speaks of the lover, through his association with his beloved, being finally "delivered" of his pregnancy. "And what is more, he and his beloved will help each other rear the issue of their love—and so the bond between them will be more binding, and their communion even more complete, than that which comes of bringing children up, because they have created something lovelier and less mortal than human seed" (209c). Thus it is not the *erastes'* love for an *eromenos* that is focal here—but their mutual co-creative love. As examples of such spiritual progeny she mentions the work of Greece's great poets and her lawgivers.

Diotima is speaking of a mutual and reciprocal eros. Plato's contemporaries would have accepted the notion that the aim of *paiderastia* is to move from an erotic hierarchical relationship to a more equal bond; but for that more mutual relationship between adult males they used a different word, *philia* (friendship), with different connotations. Diotima's use of Eros is radically innovative and actually undercuts the well-defined distinction between *erastes* and *eromenos* that all the other speakers (with the exception of Aristophanes) had taken for granted. The image here is not of pursued and pursuer but of mutual responsiveness.

A loving in which one might be able to both give and receive pleasure at once was a loving that the Greeks thought of as typically feminine. It was deemed acceptable for women to enjoy the receptive role, and heterosexual intercourse was imagined to give pleasure to both partners simultaneously. Thus Plato here transposes the "kind of mutuality in eros familiar to women" into the erotic dynamics of male love.[13] In Diotima's model the lover and the beloved are both educated and transformed by Eros; indeed, the distinction between the two is all but erased.[14] Nor is the love by which the beloved is moved simply "answering love"; both partners love in the same way. She even moves beyond Aristophanes' recognition that the same love may move both partners, in seeing that what they love is not one another but something that lies outside either, that which they have together brought to birth. The apprehension of beauty releases the power to create.

The move to a reciprocal model of love is possible because the love Diotima is describing does not involve physical consummation and therefore need not involve the penetration of one male's body by another which the Greeks saw as so problematic. From Diotima's perspective the avoidance of literal expression is not motivated by the need to honor the integrity of the *eremenos* but by the recognition on the part of both partners that that is not what they really want. Thus the roles are reversed—the beloved must learn to love, the lover teaches the renunciation of physical gratification and by modeling the beauty of his dedication to wisdom himself becomes the object of love.[15] This is thus a model of male love in which the phallus essentially disappears and through its disappearance makes possible an image of male-male love that is not polarizing.

Yet Diotima's insistence on calling the relationship she is describing "erotic" makes clear we should not move to too simplistic an understanding of "Platonic" love. The persistent reference to bodily metaphors suggests that they are not "only metaphors," that she sees real continuity, not radical disjunction, between embodied and spiritual love. Thus her position is very different from that voiced by Pausanias. The soul's love for the good and the beautiful is a passionate love, a knowing of the good that includes desire, that is anything but sterile cognition.

This is the point at which she tells Socrates that she is moving to the "deepest mysteries," which she is not certain he will be able to apprehend. She proceeds now to initiate him into the stages of love. "The candidate for this initiation cannot, if his efforts are to be rewarded," she says, "begin too early to devote himself to the beauties of the body" (210a). Thus, the necessary beginning point is appreciation of physical beauty. Nor is there any suggestion that such appreciation must be given up—only that one is not to stay stuck there, as though no other beauty existed. Instead, she lays out a series of stages, each of which depends on the other, the last being *philosophia*, the love of wisdom itself.

Having reached this stage, the initiate approaches the final revelation, which bursts upon him all at once as a wondrous vision (as in the Eleusinian mysteries in which the culminating revelation was the disclosure of sacred symbols in a sudden blaze of light[16]). The ecstasy of that culminating epiphany lies at the very heart of Diotima's teaching. The real goal of the whole initiation is the seeing (as in the mysteries) of the "very soul of beauty"—not in any of its appearances, not as a face or hand, or even words or knowledge, but in itself—the beauty of which every beautiful thing partakes. Diotima here admits that this "universal beauty" is beyond words, inexpressible. It can only be "seen" by "inward sight," by the imagination, by intuition.

Again she insists that mounting this ladder, which begins with the response to one beautiful body, with "*prescribed* devotion to boyish beauties," is "the way, the only way, to approach, or be led toward the sanctuary of Love" (211c). Diotima expands the meaning of Eros in a way that reminds me of Freud's expansion of the meaning of sexuality. Just as Freud asserted that psychoanalysis stands or falls on the basis of the expansion of sexuality beyond heterosexual intercourse to include the nursing of the newborn child and the creative activity of the artistic genius, so Diotima says that true understanding of Eros means moving beyond its association with paiderastic relationship to the most profound experience of human life, the ecstatic experience of oneness with beauty itself—which is immortal as no particular beauty can be. Diotima intends the connections, the undertones.

She teaches how passion can enter into a relation to the nonpersonal. The sense of self-completion that according to Aristophanes we hope to find in one another, Diotima promises is really available in this mystical union. This vision is what makes human life worth living, and what frees one from the seductive power of "lads just ripening to manhood," of "the beauties that used to take your breath away" (211d).

But Diotima is not inviting us to some abstract realm of Ideas. Her last words, as Socrates recounts her teaching, are: "Remember, that it is only when he discerns beauty itself through what makes it visible that a man will be quickened by the true virtue" (212a).

In Diotima's teaching, beauty and love (not truth and dialectic) are proposed as *the* way; our esthetic sensibility to physical beauty, our emotional responsivity, lead us on. "It is not exclusion of the body that characterizes true love in a fundamental way,"[17] but rather the shared recognition by two lovers that the other is not the aim of their love but rather the partner for the "bringing forth" to which she returns in her last words.

The most serious questions raised by Diotima's teaching are of course those put forward by Gregory Vlastos in his important essay, "The Individual as Object of Love in Plato's Dialogues."[18] Does she, he asks, include in her vision any recognition of love directed to the particular other human person, not as an assemblage of beautiful parts but as a unique whole? Vlastos concludes that her vision of lovers engaged in the joint pursuit of beauty itself, a relation that is not reciprocal, subsumes the particularity of the other person. What Vlastos finds missing in Diotima's account is trust, forgiveness, tenderness, imaginative sympathy.

Nussbaum (who agrees with Vlastos) focuses on the important step in which Diotima recommends relaxing one's passion for a particular body, agreeing to "deem it of little or no importance"—which she believes is being recommended as a *therapy* that would alter our way of looking at the world by "making the related the same, the irreplaceable, replaceable." For "Diotima connects the love of particulars with tension, excess, and servitude; the love of a qualitatively uniform 'sea' with health, freedom, and creativity." For Nussbaum Diotima's teaching removes us from vulnerable attachments and the conflict between them. When beauty itself is the object of our love, it is always available and we are freed from being slaves to passion and luck as we are in Aristophanes' myth (79).

But my reading of Diotima is different; it sees her teaching as warmer, more passionate, more accepting of desire and embodiment—and therefore my reading of the next part of the dialogue differs, too. Where Nussbaum sees radical discontinuity, I see a more subtle continuation and confirmation.

Alcibiades

When Socrates finishes his account of Diotima's teaching, all applaud except Aristophanes. Just as he is about to voice his objections, there is "all at once" a sudden knocking at the door, followed by the notes of a flute and the sound of festive brawling, and Alcibiades enters, clearly drunk, "with a mass of ribbons and an enormous wreath of ivy and violets sprouting on his head," the very image of a Bacchic devotee (212c,e).

As he enters the room and is welcomed, Socrates makes room for him on the couch. Alcibiades exclaims, "Well, I'll be damned! You again, Socrates! So that's what you're up to, is it? The same old game of lying in wait and popping out at me when I least expect it," (213b) and proceeds to tease him for having managed to sit himself next to Agathon, the handsomest man in the room. Socrates laughingly protests, "It's a dreadful thing to be in love with Alcibiades. It's been the same ever since I fell in love with him. I've only got to look at anyone who is the least attractive, or say a single word to him, and he flies into a fit of jealous fury" (213d).

Remember that Socrates has just said that since receiving Diotima's instruction in the long ago past, he has lived by that teaching and sought to bid others do the same. Thus his joking response implies that the love he acknowledges feeling for Alcibiades is part of following the path he has just been describing. The "all at once" of Alcibiades' appearance recalls the "all at once" of what Diotima called the final revelation—suggesting that the scene to follow will constitute a showing-forth of the hidden mysteries. Yet Plato's contemporaries would immediately remember Alcibiades as a profaner of the Eleusinian mysteries. No wonder readers ever since have argued about his role in the dialogue.

After having yet another drink and persuading Socrates to join him, Alcibiades is asked to make a speech, as the others have done, and Eryximachos suggests that he address his eulogies not to Eros but to Socrates. Alcibiades agrees and says, "I'm simply going to tell the truth," (reminding us of Socrates' promise to tell only the truth as he began his speech), and explicitly challenges Socrates, "If I say a word that's not the solemn truth, I want you to stop me right away and tell me I'm a liar" (215a). Socrates' silence, his failure to challenge Alcibiades' account at any point, gives warrant to its claimed truthfulness.

Fully to understand this speech as Plato would have expected his readers to requires that we remember that Alcibiades was, indeed, a favorite of Socrates. This extraordinarily beautiful and brilliant young man had been loved by many who deserted him as it became clear how he would waste his youthful promise through ambition and recklessness. An early dialogue, the *Alcibiades Major*, "begins with the puzzling question of why, out of an entourage of lovers, only Socrates remained loyal, and it concludes with the answer that only Socrates, among all others, has loved the youth himself (i.e., his soul)."[19] The others who had pursued Alcibiades abandoned him as "the flower of his youth began to fade"; it was just then that Socrates, who had long observed him, approached him for the first time. Socrates explains that until now his daimon had kept him away. "The god who has hitherto held me back now sends me to you." (We sense a connection between this daimon and the daimonic Eros of the *Symposium*.) This early dialogue makes clear that though only Socrates had loved his soul, for him too, the attraction of Alcibiades' physical beauty had been a "necessary stepping-stone whose absence would make that higher level inaccessible."[20] The dialogue reveals how initially annoyed Alcibiades was by Socrates' approach and how at its end Socrates' passion had engendered Alcibiades' answering love. Socrates says that his love for the younger man had "hatched the winged fruit of love." Yet the conversation Socrates initiated was not the typical *erastes'* praise of youthful beauty but instead praise of the polis and philosophy. The early dialogue already implies much that Diotima seeks to teach. It also confirms the truth of the story Alcibiades will tell.

Nussbaum speaks of Plato's "loving recreation of the speech of the other side" (187), whereas I read Alcibiades' speech as the necessary complement to Diotima's discourse. Friedlander agrees:

> It is indispensable that after the path to the Forms has been shown, i.e., after clarification in words, there should follow a human-active movement revealing the nature of the goal. The pronouncements of the priestess could not be the end of the work. There had to be a concluding part in which the ascent to the heights would be depicted in the reality of actual life. The *Symposium* reaches its climax in the episode involving Alcibiades.[21]

I take this episode to function much as do the myths introduced at the climactic moment of some of the other dialogues (the *Republic,* for instance, and the *Phaedo*): it presents the truth that cannot be presented in the discursive mode. I'd go further, and suggest that the tragedy of Alcibiades from Plato's viewpoint is that he saw and understood Socrates' beauty more clearly than anyone else (except Plato himself—that he speaks for Plato in his eulogy), but was tragically flawed, so that he couldn't make his own the love devoted to wisdom and beauty that he glimpsed. Friedlander makes much the same point: "As far as Alcibiades' description of Socrates goes, could Plato have written anything like this without having experienced it in his own encounter with Socrates?"[22]

Alcibiades' speech takes a different form from that of any of the others. For one thing, he is drunk or nearly so, under the influence of Dionysos, exhibiting that god-inspired madness that Socrates celebrates in the *Phaedrus*, for which

Diotima's emphasis on the passion inherent in true Eros has already prepared us. For another, he will, of course, be speaking of a particular love, his love for Socrates, not of Eros as such. And he will be telling the *history* of his love, not speaking of it in general terms—but then Socrates had told us the story of his initiation also.

Alcibiades begins his eulogy with an image. He compares Socrates to the little Sileni statues which one opens to find a figure of a god and to Marsyas the satyr. He says he means by the image to communicate Socrates' bewitching power, but clearly we are meant to remember that satyrs were noted for enjoying being anally penetrated, so that the confusion between the roles of *erastes* and *eremenos* that so much of Alcibiades' speech centers on is already introduced in the image.

Alcibiades attributes Socrates' magical power not to his music but to his simple unpoetic words, not to their eloquence but to *what* he says, which has the power, Alcibiades proclaims, to smite him "with a kind of sacred rage." The wild abandon Alcibiades had displayed on entering was due to Dionysos, but he tells us that Socrates has just the same effect on him. Socrates' words have the power to "turn my whole soul upside down," to make Alcibiades feel, as he says, that "I simply couldn't go on living the way I did" (216a).

As Alcibiades talks, he calls upon the others (whom he names "fellow sufferers") to acknowledge the truth of his tale, its correspondence with their own experience of Socrates. He says he's been "bitten in the heart, or the mind, or whatever you like to call it [and surely one of the points of the dialogue is the rightful conjunction of heart and mind] by Socrates' philosophy," as though by a poisonous snake that will not let go. "And looking round me, gentlemen, I see Phaedrus, and Agathon, and Eryximachos, and Pausanias, and Aristodemus, and Aristophanes, and all the rest of them—to say nothing of Socrates himself—and every one of you has had his taste of this philosophical frenzy, this sacred rage." None present denies it, though invited to (218a,b).

In his portrait of his teacher Alcibiades emphasizes precisely all that is unique, particular about him. It is through this particularity that he sees beyond it. He speaks of feeling in response to Socrates "one thing I never felt with anybody else." He says that Socrates is "the only man in the world" who can make him feel shame. Toward the end of his speech he returns to this theme: "Personally I think the most amazing thing about him is the fact that he is absolutely unique; there's no one like him, and I don't believe there ever was" (221c).

He also says that he sees through Socrates, past the superficial admiration for beautiful boys to the deep inward sobriety and temperance. He claims to have at least once had access to that inner truth. "I don't know whether anybody else has ever opened him up"—note the sexual language—"when he's been being serious, and seen the little images inside, but I saw them once, and they looked so godlike, so golden, so beautiful, and so utterly amazing that there was nothing for it but to do exactly what he told me" (217a).

Reminding his "fellow drunks" that he has sworn to tell the truth, he tells how, even when they were alone, Socrates would speak not "the sweet nothings that lovers whisper to their darlings" (217l)) but just go on talking as he always did. More and more intrigued, Alcibiades finally resolved to ask "him to dinner, just as if I were the lover trying to seduce his beloved, instead of the other way round" (217c). Having talked him into staying the night, Alcibiades confides to him that he sees him as "the only lover I've ever had who's been really worthy of me," and that therefore I've decided that "it'd be just as absurd to refuse you this as anything else that belonged to me" (218d). But Socrates responded that if indeed Alcibiades recognized how the beauty of an outwardly ugly philosopher outshone his own youthful beauty, then he should also realize that his offer was no bargain at all. Alcibiades, still hoping, crept under Socrates' mantle and slept through the night with this "godlike and extraordinary man" in his arms; but "when I got up the next morning I had no more slept with Socrates, within the meaning of the act, than if he'd been my father or elder brother" (219d).

When Alcibiades finishes, there is "a good deal of laughter at his frankness—especially as he still seemed to be in love with Socrates" (222c).

In Alcibiades' account of his relation to Socrates we see enacted that reversal of sexual roles described by Diotima. Alcibiades begins as an *eremenos* but finds himself taking on the *erastes* role of pursuer. He has felt himself to be really seen by Socrates, in his soul, his personhood, as by no one else—which is so frightening he runs away—and yet such a gift that he returns. He also wants to really know Socrates, to get inside, and imagines that the path to such intimacy would be intercourse. But indirectly and yet clearly, Alcibiades also shows that precisely what gives Socrates his power, what makes him unique, is that he doesn't yield to the opportunity for physical gratification (though he doesn't seem to object to falling asleep cuddled by the beautiful Alcibiades' body).

Alcibiades offers the tale of the "test" as the most telling revelation (the equivalent of Diotima's "final revelation"?) of who Socrates really is; but he had to experience Socrates' refusal of the proffered physical intimacy to "get" it. As Cornford says, "It is Socrates' 'indifference' which Plato is presenting as an instance—*the* instance—of the 'love' which finally emerges from the dialectic of the *Symposium*. But it is being presented with a delicacy so sure that there is not so much as a hint that the claim of Alcibiades' passion to the name of 'love' is being impugned."[23] (I can't help but see the abstinence that Freud requires of the analyst in responding to a patient's transference love as an expression of a love akin to that manifested here in Socrates.)

Socrates responds, not by contesting a word Alcibiades has spoken, but by acting as though he believes the whole point of his discourse had been to interfere with Socrates' flirtation with Agathon. Just at that point the party is broken off by the entrance of a group of revelers. Everyone gets drunk or leaves or falls asleep except for Agathon and Aristophanes and Socrates. Socrates tries to persuade the other two "that the same man might be capable of writing both tragedy and comedy" (223d). As, in my reading, Plato has shown himself doing here.

Nussbaum believes the dialogue leaves us having to choose between Diotima and Alcibiades; but I read Diotima (and the whole dialogue) differently. I see Diotima offering a more sensual, a more emotional, a more *human* teaching about Eros than does Nussbaum, and consequently I also find less tension between the Socrates of the *Symposium* and the Socrates of the *Phaedrus* than does she. She can recognize Plato's identification with the role assigned Phaedrus in the later dialogue but not his empathy with Alcibiades here.

Yet Nussbaum recognizes that readers who take the dialogue form seriously may come to interpretations different from hers (198, 87). Different readings are no doubt shaped in part by coming to the texts with different questions. Because this time around I come to Plato out of an interest in his understanding of male love, I find in his writing clues to a new myth that goes beyond those he inherited and in significant ways enriches our understanding of the "deeper mysteries" of male love.

Notes

1. Cf. my *Myths and Mysteries of Same-Sex Love* (New York: Continuum, 1989).

2. Martha Nussbaum, *The Fragility of Goodness* (Cambridge: Cambridge University Press, 1986). Page references are given in the text.

3. Paul Friedlander, *Plato: An Introduction* (New York: Harper & Row, 1964) 127-30.

4. Friedlander, 46-9.

5. David M. Halperin, "Plato and Erotic Receptivity," *Classical Antiquity* 3.1 (1986) 71, 73.

6. R. A. Markus, "The Dialectic of Eros in Plato's Symposium," in Gregory Vlastos, ed., *Plato: A Collection of Critical Essays* (Garden City: Doubleday, 1971) 134.

7. Michel Foucault, *The Use of Pleasure* (New York: Random House, 1986) 232.

8. F. M. Cornford, "The Doctrine of Eros in Plato's Symposium," in Vlastos, 125.

9. K. J. Dover, *Greek Homosexuality* (Cambridge, MA: Harvard University Press, 1978) 161.

10. David M. Halperin, "Why is Diotima a Woman," in David M. Halperin et al., eds., *Before Sexuality* (Princeton: Princeton University Press, 1990) 259.

11. Friedlander, 174.

12. Halperin, "Diotima," 276-7. Although in Aeschylus's *Oresteia* Apollo claims that women play no real role in generation, classical period medical texts describe female orgasm as seed-producing and in the *Timaeus* Plato speaks of the womb as a *living* animal so passionately desirous of making children that when fruitless for a long time it wanders all about the body producing all sorts of illness.

13. Halperin, "Diotima," 280.

14. Halperin, "Erotic Receptivity," 68.

15. Foucault, 240.

16. Cornford, 127.

17. Markus, 114.

18. Gregory Vlastos, *Platonic Studies* (Princeton: Princeton University Press, 1981) 1-34.

19. Paul Friedlander, *Plato: The Dialogues, Second and Third Periods* (Princeton: Princeton University Press, 1969) 227.

20. Friedlander, *Introduction,* 148-9.

21. Friedlander, *Dialogues,* 28.

22. Friedlander, *Introduction,* 130.

23. Cornford, 149.

5

Masks of the Goddess

The mother is really a more immediate parent than the father because one is born from the mother, and the first experience of any infant is the mother. I have frequently thought that mythology is a sublimation of the mother image.[1]

While I was a graduate student Joseph Campbell was invited to participate in a colloquium that brought to our campus a series of brilliant and celebrated intellectuals. I remember many of those lectures, some more vividly than others, but Campbell's presentation stands out from all the others because he didn't lecture; he told stories. Actually he didn't so much tell stories as dance them; his whole body, his whole being, was engaged in his telling. (When a few months later I saw his wife, Jean Erdman, perform her dance based on *Finnegans Wake*, "The Coach With Six Insides," I understood how much each had given the other.) Campbell was a gifted storyteller. I remember him; I remember the stories; I still retell many of them. For me there is no higher praise: to tell the old stories in a way that honors them, renews their power, moves others—what a blessing!

But, of course, we never just retell the old stories; we use them to tell our own, and what I want to focus on here is the story Campbell uses the old stories to tell, the story he tells about the stories. For, though Campbell seems to respond more sympathetically to James Joyce's "creative mythologizing" than to Thomas Mann's, his own practice more closely corresponds to Mann's:

[Mann] explains, interprets, and evaluates discursively the symbols of his art, whereas Joyce simply presents, without author's comment. Furthermore, in his approach to symbols Mann comes to them from the secular world, through literature and art [as Campbell came to myth through Joyce's fiction], not by way of the ingraining from childhood of the iconography of a seriously accepted, ritually ordered religion.[2]

Campbell is addressing us, seeking to persuade us to a particular view of the history of mythology and of its function, and ultimately, like Mann, to a "life-way."

Campbell's Natural History of the Goddess

From my feminist perspective it is to his great credit that in his history of mythology Campbell accords an important place to the role played by goddesses, and that he did so already in the first volume of the *Masks of God* series (published in 1959) long before the revival of interest in the goddess among contemporary feminist scholars (which we might date as becoming visible in 1976 with the publication of Merlin Stone's *When God Was a Woman*). In the third volume he explains:

> I am taking pains in this work to place considerable stress upon the world age and symbolic order of the goddess; for the findings both of anthropology and archaeology now attest not only to a contrast between the mythic and social systems of the goddess and the later gods, but also to the fact that in our own European culture that of the gods overlies and occludes that of the goddess which is nevertheless effective as a counterplayer, so to say, in the unconscious of the civilization as a whole.[3]

As Campbell understands the history of human religiosity, the goddesses were there from the beginning. The goddess shows herself as there "at the very dawn of the first day of our own species." She "lures us beyond even our longest archaeological fathom-line." She can truly say, "No one has lifted my veil."[4]

He finds evidence of her presence in Neanderthal burials. The supplies around the skeletons, the evidence of animal sacrifice, the attention to the solar axis in the placement of graves, the arrangement of the dead in sleeping or fetal position—all suggest that burial was understood as a return to mother earth for rebirth.[5] Campbell believes that the earth as both bearing and nurturing mother was prominent in the mythologies of both early hunting and planting societies.

The importance of the goddess among the earliest hunting, fishing, gathering peoples is confirmed by the many nude female figures (often with a highly stylized emphasis on loins, genitals, and breasts) found at early Paleolithic sites. Their placement on shrines makes clear they were cult objects. Indeed, these female figurines were apparently the first objects of human worship. Thus among the Paleolithic hunters as in the later planting societies "the female body was experienced in its own character as a focus of divine force, and a system of rites was dedicated to its mystery."[6] Campbell believes that in these small and relatively settled societies there was neither a strong patriarchal or matriarchal emphasis, but rather an essential equality, indeed, that even puberty rites did not distinguish significantly between male and female initiates. All worshipped the goddess, because from her womb came the game animals upon which their life depended.

> There can be no doubt that in the very earliest ages of human history the magical force and wonder of the female was no less a marvel than the universe itself; and this gave to woman a prodigious power, which it has been one of the chief concerns of the masculine part of the population to break, control, and employ to its own ends. It is, in fact, most remarkable how many primitive hunting races have the legend of a still more primitive age than their own, in which the women were the sole possessors of the magical art.[7]

Later the goddess's importance among hunting peoples declined. A second stage of primitive hunting societies came into existence with larger hunting groups ranging more widely for big game. The change to a warmer, drier climate during the late Paleolithic and the appearance of great grazing herds of bison, antelope, and wild cattle issued in a more continuously ranging nomadism; women's domestic work came to be disvalued and men developed a "fine sense of their own superiority."[8] In these societies men came to dominate in the religious and political sphere; women were excluded from the men's secret initiation rites, which included ordeals and mutilation. In the regions of the Great Hunt an essentially masculine psychology came to prevail, with an emphasis on achievement, and women became ancillaries to male achievement.[9] The paintings in the underground caves where the men performed their rituals focus on animals and male hunters; there are no female figures. The costumed shaman now exercises the magical role previously assigned the naked goddess. Outside these caves one sometimes finds female figurines so violently shattered as to lead to the suspicion that there had been a deliberate attempt to break their power.[10]

In planting societies, on the other hand, women who were responsible for the transition from gathering to cultivating enjoyed the magico-religious and social advantage. By their discovery they had made the earth valuable; thus they were seen as knowing its secrets. Woman did the planting and reaping "and, as the mother of life and nourisher of life, was thought to assist the earth symbolically in its productivity."[11] During the basal Neolithic period between 5500 and 4500, characterized not only by the beginnings of agriculture but also by the domestication of animals, by pottery and weaving, and by settled village life, women probably predominated socially and religiously. Again, many female figurines have been found, attesting to the importance accorded the goddess in whose body are sown the seeds upon the growth of which human life depends.

Campbell comments on how reluctant male scholars have been to admit the significance of these sculptures:

> We have no writing from this pre-literate age and no knowledge, consequently, of its myths or rites. It is therefore not unusual for extremely well-trained archaeologists to pretend that they cannot imagine what services the numerous female figurines might have rendered.... However, we know perfectly well what the services of such images were in the periods immediately following—and what they have remained to the present day. They give magical psychological aid to women in childbirth and conception, stand in house shrines to receive daily prayers and to protect the occupants from physical as well as from spiritual danger, serve to support the mind in its meditations on the mystery of being.... They go forth with the farmer into his fields, protect the crops, protect the cattle.... They are the guardians of children. They watch over the sailor at sea and the merchant on the road.[12]

Campbell recites the many titles by which the goddess was known in the Neolithic world; he lists the many symbols associated with her, and describes her characteristic postures: standing pregnant, giving birth, nursing a child, holding serpents, riding a bull. The goddesses are often accompanied by male gods who are both son and consort, who die (often as a ritual sacrifice) and are reborn. He explains how the rituals dedicated to these goddesses derive from recognition of death as the presupposition of life, not from the perception of harvesting as a killing or as a heroic act on the part of the reaper but as a sacrifice by the grain. He shows how this leads to rituals of sacrifice, including human sacrifice—sacrifices which are not so much gifts to the goddess or god as re-enactments of their gift of themselves. He interprets these often violent rituals as representing a "willed affirmation" of "the ruthless nature of being," a reconciliation to the "monstrosity of the just-so of the world."[13]

> In the Neolithic village...the focal figure of all mythology and worship was the bountiful goddess Earth, as the mother and nourisher of life and receiver of the dead for rebirth. In the earliest period of her cult...[She] may have been thought of only as a local patroness of fertility, as many anthropologists suppose. However in the temples of Sumer (3500-2350)...[she] was certainly much more than that. She was already...a metaphysical symbol: the arch personification of the power of Space, Time, and Matter, within whose bound all beings arise and die.... And everything having form or name—including God...was her child, within her womb.[14]

But then once again the goddess was obscured. In the Neolithic village, men were close to being superfluous. "Small wonder," Campbell says, "if, in reaction, their revengeful imaginations ran amok."[15]

With the beginnings of plow agriculture, the preconditions for the establishment of the hieratic patriarchal city-state appeared. Planting became men's work; the greater productivity led to larger communities, to specialization and stratification. Writing, astrology, the calendar are introduced; there are male priests and male kings. For the first time social order was imposed from above by force. The "stars"—the five visible planets, the sun and the moon—and their hierarchical order were looked to as providing a model for a hierarchical social order. Myth was consciously used, not to foster the growth of the young to maturity, but to render the authority of the king unchallengeable.[16] The lunar bull is suppressed by the solar lion, the goddess by the god. "The progressive devaluation of the mother goddess in favor of the father…everywhere accompanied the maturation of the dynastic state and patriarchy."[17] In these monarchies the focus has shifted from the goddess to her son, with whom the king (by way of what Campbell terms an act of "mythic inflation") identifies himself. The new mythology implies a new psychology, the rational, divisive functions of the mind under the aegis of the male hero overcome the dark mystery of the deeper levels of the soul represented by the goddess.

The move away from the goddess correlated with the appearance of the city-state was then aggravated by invasions of nomadic hunters with their masculine ideology, both into areas where it simply amplified a transition already underway and into areas still dominated by the Neolithic village perspective. Toward the end of the Bronze Age (c. 1250 BCE) the mythology of the mother goddess was radically transformed, reinterpreted, and, in large measure, even suppressed by suddenly intrusive, patriarchal nomadic herder-warriors like the Hebrews who entered Canaan and the Aryans who came to Greece, Persia, and India.

Campbell traces the impact of this patriarchal god-worshipping invasion on both oriental and occidental mythology. But everywhere, he finds, the sense of the power of the mother remains as an ever-present threat. He uncovers the ubiquity of the goddess, even in myths where she is not supposed to be playing any part.

He shows how in India, the old Neolithic Bronze Age goddess reappears when the Upanishadic view triumphs over the Aryan gods. "The enduring power in that land has always been the same old dark goddess of the long red tongue who turns everything into her own everlasting, awesome, yet finally somewhat tedious, self."[18] In her first appearance in Hindu literature the goddess presents herself as guru of the gods; she teaches them to know Brahman. And in Mahayana Buddhism with its viewing of the world as a Buddha Realm, woman returns as prime symbol of the positive way—"a living image of the wonder of the world in which we live."[19]

In the West, on the other hand, the freely willing hero wins—and yet, as Campbell shows, in the myths of Israel and Greece the ultimate life and spiritual depth continue to rest with the dark presences of the earth, which "though defeated and subdued, are with their powers never totally absorbed."[20]

In a detailed reading of the Genesis stories as carriers of symbols borrowed from the deep past, Campbell explores how biblical mythology inverts the meaning of images drawn from the Neolithic organic nonheroic vegetal-lunar goddess complex. "There is consequently an ambivalence inherent in many of the basic symbols of the Bible that no amount of rhetorical stress on the patriarchal interpretation can suppress. They address a pictorial message to the heart that exactly reverses the verbal message addressed to the brain."[21] He also reminds us how the Bible itself testifies to how important goddess worship remained in Israel until the Babylonian Exile.

When he turns to Greece Campbell applauds Jane Ellen Harrison's discovery of how vestiges of the pre-Homeric goddess survive in later epic and tragedy. In the myths of the gods subduing the Titans, of heroes slaying monsters, he discerns an anxious protest against the worship of the Earth.[22] He also acknowledges that in Greece, unlike Israel, the patriarchal gods married the goddesses of the land and so the goddess survived in agricultural cults, in women's ritual life, and in the Orphic and Eleusinian mysteries. And where he criticizes the Hebrew emphasis on obedient submission to transcendent male deity, he communicates how he values the Greeks' emphasis on human reason, on their having learned to live as neither servants of a god nor "of the ever-wheeling, cosmic order."[23] He also appreciates how the Greeks (like the Orientals) recognized that their gods were "masks," human images, how they never confused the Olympians with "the ultimate Being of being," but understood that, "like men, they had been born of the Great Mother."[24]

Campbell does not minimize the role of goddess worship in early history nor settle for a simple linear evolutionary view that would relegate the goddess only to those archaic beginnings. He accords value to both the perspectives of the early hunters and the early planters, of the hero-worshippers and the goddess-worshippers, though he clearly regards the former's focus on life as opposed to death as "childlike" and "superficial" compared to the integration of life and death characteristic of the latter. He recognizes the violence and loss involved in the suppression of the goddess, though he sometimes writes as though it were just a matter of an oscillating alternation of female-and male-oriented mythologies.[25]

Campbell discerns how many male myths and rituals are really reaction formations, attempts to deny the mother's power or to take it from her. He describes male puberty rituals that assert that though a woman gave birth to the boy's temporal body the men will give him spiritual birth as attempts to arrogate women's birth-giving function to men. Many of these rituals involve forced separation from the mothers; many include the infliction of a sub-incision wound that is identified as a vagina. The boy undergoes a painful metamorphosis into a self-sufficient androgynous being.

Campbell is also sensitive to the distortions imposed by our reliance on male sources:

> It is one of the curiosities and difficulties of our subject that its materials come to us for the most part through the agency of the male. The masters of the rites, the sages and prophets, and lastly our contemporary scholars of the subject, have usually been men; whereas, obviously, there has always been a feminine side to the picture also.[26]

But perhaps he has not always been fully aware of the male bias that informs his own view of the goddess—and of mythology in general.

Campbell's Male Perspective

Campbell writes that woman is a "permanent presence" in mythology:

> both in her way of experiencing life and in her character as an imprint—a message from the world—for the male to assimilate…. The mystery of the woman is no less a mystery than death. Childbirth is no less a mystery, nor the flow of the mother's milk; nor the menstrual cycle in its accord with the moon…. Woman, as the magical door from the other world, through which lives enter into this, stands naturally in counterpoise to the door of death, through which they leave.[27]

However, he says this without ever quite acknowledging how much his own account—quite naturally—falls on woman as a mystery to men rather than on woman as *she* experiences life. His accent falls on the goddess as mother, on the mother as sons experience her, not as daughters relate to her nor as mothers know themselves.

Despite his attempt to acknowledge that the goddesses of the Neolithic world were more than fertility goddesses and cannot be understood only in relation to the fertility of the crops, the herds, and human mothers, his accent always falls on their motherly aspect. Little is said of the warrior goddess, the artisan goddess, the celestial goddess, or the vulnerable goddess.

The accent also falls on the mysteriousness of the goddess, rather than on the sense of familiarity and kinship she may have inspired in her female devotees. In his *Primitive Mythology* Campbell observes that prehistory corresponds to a layer of our own experience, so that in archaic mythology we find clues to "our own most inward expectations, spontaneous responses, and obsessive fears."[28] He reflects on how the earliest experience of the relation to the mother is an imprint that functions to shape the imagination of all humans, our remotest ancestors and ourselves. He notes there how this is particularly true for sons. The mythology of our entire species, he says, gives "innumerable instances of the unrelenting efforts of the male to relate himself effectively" to the mystery of motherhood and the fearfulness of woman.[29] Mother images serve as almost inevitable symbols of the mystery of life and the image of the child in the womb provides us with our most powerful image of bliss—a bliss that myth and ritual seek to help us regain.[30]

> For Campbell the mother goddess typically suggests fantasies of bliss and fusion: The image of the mother and the female affects the psyche differently from that of the father and the male. Sentiments of identity are associated most immediately with the mother; those of dissociation, with the father. Hence, where the mother image preponderates, even the dualism of life and death dissolves in the rapture of her solace. [31]

Daughters are more likely to recognize that one can be close to the mother without dissolving in her; sons more typically see only the radical alternatives: autonomy and separation or dissolution and fusion.[32] Rapture and bliss: Campbell often tells us that the most important function of mythology is to lead us to experience the rapture of being alive, the wonder of existence, to elicit and support a sense of awe before the mystery of being. He says it beautifully and yet again I see this as in part a man's perspective. Bliss and rapture are for him so intertwined with images of reunion with the mother. All myth is seen as an expression of the longing for that return (or as an attempt to deny or overcome it). As he acknowledges to Bill Moyers in the comment that serves as the epigraph to this essay, "I have frequently thought that mythology is a sublimation of the mother image." But what if there is a mythmaking that does not proceed from fusion-longing or from fusion-fear, but from a celebration of intimacy and diversity?

Campbell has a deep appreciation for the role of the goddess in ancient mythology and modern psychology, though, not surprisingly, his understanding of her is shaped by his male perspective. It is my sense that this perspective informs not only his view of goddesses but of all mythology. I think, for example, of his emphasis on its homogeneity, on the universality of its central themes. He recognizes diversity, recognizes how landscape and history shape the details of particular mythologies, acknowledges how diffusion always includes "creative absorption," but what matters in mythology is "the one, shapeshifting yet marvellously constant story."[33] Thus to him all the goddesses—the Virgin Mother, Aphrodite, Cybele, Hathor, Ishtar, and the rest—are really one.[34] Zeus's many mistresses and wives are each "a local manifestation of the goddess-mother of the world."[35] He applauds the Greek identification of Isis and Demeter, Shiva and Dionysus.[36] Many feminists would protest that this is to ignore the affirmation of the particular, the concrete, the earthbound in contrast to the universal, the transcendent, the heavenly that is so central to goddess worship. But our celebration of the many rather than the one, of the local deities rather than the universal, is denigrated by Campbell as a religion of the extroverted and the superficial. He distinguishes two types of mythology—one where the stress is placed on the historicity of the episode, the other where the episodes are meant to be read symbolically.[37] The deeper thinkers, the "tenderminded," see the local as merely a vehicle, recognize myth as myth, the gods and goddesses as masks; they see the psychology beneath the history.

For in our time, Campbell believes, mythology is left with only one function: the psychological, initiating the individual into the realities of his own psyche, guiding him toward his own spiritual enrichment and realization. Thus in his myth about myth all the history of human myth-making he reviews in such detail is in a sense but an allegory: the different stages of mythology are equated with different levels of the psyche. To know the history is to know ourselves. Campbell speaks of the "vanishment" of all the earlier masks of god, masks that are now recognized as simply images of developing man himself. I have retained the sexist language here because I believe it may be more appropriate than Campbell intended. The hero of his myth, the autonomous creative individual, is in some sense inevitably a male figure.

And the celebration of the outmoding of mythology's cosmological and social functions may also represent a male vision. For surely we need myths to remind us of our emotional and erotic bonds with the natural world and of our interdependence with all that lives. Science has not superseded this function; indeed, it may have made it more pressing. Much of the energy for feminism's rediscovery of the goddess has come precisely because she may help us recover a more whole relation to the natural world—before we autonomous humans destroy it.

Campbell also devalues mythology's sociological function in his claim that disengagement is a deeper truth than social engagement. Thus in his reflections on the costs of the disappearance of the goddess from modern consciousness, he emphasizes the psychological costs, in a tone reminiscent of Jung's regrets over the loss of an integrated relation to the anima on the part of most modern men. But he rarely reflects on how a patriarchal mythology has served to support the social oppression of modern women. He does recognize how mythologies have been used oppressively, but proposes as an alternative not more generous, more inclusive mythologies but a turning inward, away from the social realm.

In India women rarely chose the Forest Path, perhaps because they were often prohibited, but perhaps in part because they glimpsed a different truth. Perhaps the masks of *god*, the male deity, are but masks of the creative individual—perhaps masks of the *goddess* are masks of women with women (and, I would want to say, with men). And perhaps "masks" is not quite the right word either—since it implies that we would see more truly if we removed them.

For one of the strange things about this wonderful storyteller, Joseph Campbell, is that he sees myths as penultimate, gods as but convenient means.[38] The ultimate function of mythology, he tells us, is SILENCE.[39] Unfortunately, "not all of us are philosophers"; many of us need the stories.[40] Yet, for Campbell, there is always the regret that, too often, taken literally, the symbol, the myth, occludes truth.

He is persuaded that "the known myths cannot endure. The known God cannot endure." The only honest possibility is that each of us become our own "creative center of authority," each of us become our own mythmaker, beginning with our own experience and finding images for it. Having listened to the stories of the past, we are encouraged to "an intelligent making use" of all the mythologies of the past "to activate…the centers of [our] own creative imagination."[41]

I, too, following Monique Wittig, would recommend that we "remember and invent." But not alone. I so much value that my own mythmaking about the goddess has been done in the context of a community of women engaged in the same task.

Notes

1. Joseph Campbell, *The Power of Myth* (with Bill Moyers) (New York: Doubleday, 1988) 165.

2. Joseph Campbell, *Creative Mythology* (New York: Viking, 1968) 366.

3. Joseph Campbell, *Occidental Mythology* (New York: Viking, 1964) 70.

4. Joseph Campbell, *Primitive Mythology* (New York: Viking, 1959) 334.

5. Campbell, *Primitive*, 67.

6. Campbell, *Primitive*, 313.

7. Campbell, *Primitive*, 315.

8. Campbell, *Primitive*, 324.

9. Campbell, *Primitive*, 389.

10. Campbell, *Primitive*, 325.

11. Campbell, *Primitive*, 139.

12. Campbell, *Primitive*, 13.

13. Campbell, *Primitive*, 180-1.

14. Campbell, *Occidental*, 315.

15. Campbell, *Primitive*, 321.

16. Campbell, *Creative*, 388.

17. Joseph Campbell, *Oriental Mythology* (New York: Viking, 1962) 112.

18. Campbell, *Oriental*, 164.

19. Campbell, *Oriental*, 320.

20. Campbell, *Occidental*, 25.

21. Campbell, *Occidental*, 17.

22. Campbell, *Occidental,* 22.

23. Campbell, *Occidental,* 179.

24. Campbell, *Occidental,* 237.

25. Campbell, *Creative,* 58.

26. Campbell, *Primitive,* 352-3.

27. Campbell, *Primitive,* 388-9.

28. Campbell, *Primitive,* 6.

29. Campbell, *Primitive,* 60.

30. Campbell, *Primitive,* 62.

31. Campbell, *Occidental,* 70.

32. Cf. Nancy Chodorov, *The Reproduction of Mothering* (Berkeley: University of California Press, 1978) 92-110.

33. Joseph Campbell, *Hero with a Thousand Faces* (Princeton: Princeton University Press, 1972) 3.

34. Campbell, *Occidental,* 42.

35. Campbell, *Occidental,* 149.

36. Campbell, *Occidental,* 240.

37. Campbell, *Occidental,* 139.

38. Campbell, *Hero,* 256.

39. Campbell, *Creative,* 42.

40. Campbell, *Occidental,* 254.

41. Campbell, *Creative,* 677.

6

The Wounded Healer

That woundedness, illness, suffering are a prerequisite for taking on the role of healer is a truth recognized in the myths and rituals of traditional cultures throughout the world. It underlies the shamanic vision of the healer in Siberia, North America, Africa and Australia. Everywhere we learn that initiation into healing comes through falling radically ill of a disease that often cannot be diagnosed and for which there seems to be no cure. Recovery comes only when the patients recognize the illness as a call, only when they agree to become healers. The woundedness is understood to signify an unusual sensitivity to the spirit world, the realm of visionary experience, which unless used on behalf of others will destroy. The apprentice shamans must then learn how to use their access to that realm, to channel their gifts and bring them into harmony with their culture's traditions. When others fall ill, the shamans re-enter the strange and terrifying otherworld to learn whom their patients have offended and what retribution they must make or how to recover their stolen soul.

The persisting power of this image of the wounded healer and its relevance to our contemporary understanding of soul-healing, of psyche-therapy, was revealed to me by a dream. Reflection on this theme still always conjures up for me remembrance of this particular dream, though it was dreamt long ago and not by me. The dreamer, a woman friend in Jungian training, dreamt that she and her training analyst were together undertaking the exploration of an undersea world, making their way through all of the fantastically beautifully colored coral and other plants that grow deep at the bottom of the sea. All about them were brilliantly tinted fish and other wondrously strange inhabitants of the sea. The passage was a difficult one. They knew it was important to make their way without brushing against the fatally poisonous coral and without disturbing the living creatures whose world they had entered. My friend's hands clasped her analyst's ankles as he led the way through the unfamiliar terrain. She found herself utterly trusting his guidance, confidently following his lead, until suddenly he made a turn that seemed to push her directly against a sharp piece of coral. The wound was deep and began to bleed. Soon after, they emerged from the water. Feeling utterly betrayed, she turned to him and asked, "How could you let that happen to me?" "Only the wounded healer heals," he replied.

Those words reverberate because they are confirmed by my own experience. I know that it is my own fragility and vulnerability, my experiences of overwhelming depression, of what I can only call loss of soul (for one of its most painful dimensions was that for months that in me which dreams seemed to have died)—it is these that underlie whatever power I have as healer or as teacher. I understand how essential it is to know the experience of woundedness from within in order to learn to trust the process. How important it is to have discovered that such experiences have intrinsic meaning though they are not the only reality, to know that one returns from them although not unchanged. I have also learned that healing often involves wounding, that the teacher may often need to reveal ignorance and heighten confusion, that the therapist may often need to uncover hidden pain, to take apart carefully wrought defenses, as part of her work.

Freud and Jung, the two healers of the soul of our time from whom I've learned the most, both clearly knew of this complex interrelationship between wounds and healing. Freud was really initiated into his depth understanding of the psyche by the death of his father, by the painful discovery in the months that followed that death of the murderous resentment and unrelenting rivalry he had felt since childhood toward this parent whom he knew he loved. It was attending to the isolating depression and the disruptive dreams that preoccupied him during the next few years that led him to acknowledge, "I am my most difficult patient." Through the exploration of his own patient-hood Freud came to recognize the woundedness of all of us. It is not only the neurotics or psychotics among us who are ill, for to participate in civilization (as all humans must) is to be deeply discontent, diseased, inevitably restrained from true fulfillment of some of our most powerful longings. As a healer Freud could aid the transition from hysteric misery to common unhappiness; he could offer sympathy, understanding, courage but not cure, not the elimination of our woundedness. In one of his last essays, "Analysis Terminable and Interminable," he acknowledges how even after a long sustained analysis one is changed and yet in another sense the same and suggests that the most important task in analysis is acceptance of our finitude and preparation for our death.

Jung's call came by way of the symbolic death of his symbolic father, by way of his break with Freud. This led him into those years of psychotic-like immersion in the unconscious that he reports so vividly in "The Confrontation with the Unconscious" chapter of *Memories, Dreams, Reflections*. Later, in "The Psychology of the Transference," he reaffirms how important it is that therapists remember the experiences of woundedness that led them to become involved in therapy to begin with—and that they remain open to further wounding. Jung believes in the mutuality of transference. In the therapeutic relationship the therapists, too, get involved in a transformative process that like their patients they may often find difficult, confusing, and painful. Effective therapy depends on the therapists' readiness to risk being hurt in the process and changed by it and their willingness to communicate that readiness. Jung also speaks of the importance of healers remembering that they too are wounded in order to protect themselves from the danger of inflation, the danger of being pulled into identification with their healing role. How much depends on our remembering that we are not only healers but also wounded.

The "Wounded Healer" is thus not only a figure who appears in other traditions but also one who has played an important role in the history of twentieth-century psychotherapy. The frequent re-emergence of the image suggests that it is an archetype—in the everyday sense of a spontaneously reappearing image, not necessarily in the strictly Jungian sense of a universal *a priori* figure—that informs our work as healers whether or not we or our patients are fully aware of its influence. Thus the more aware we are of just what this image represents, the more likely we are to recognize its role in our own work.

Not surprisingly, this figure plays an important role in Greek mythological traditions about healers. It is these traditions that I would like to examine here. For, rich and illuminating as other traditions may be, it remains true that for those of us raised in the dominant culture of the West the images that lie deep in our language and literature (and, I would submit, probably in our psyches, too) derive from Greece (and Israel). What we individually may have first found elsewhere can also be found here.

Indeed, most of our language for healing comes from Greece—and words that we may often use carelessly and one-dimensionally still carry within them echoes of ancient assumptions resonant with ritual significance. "Medicine," for example, may be related to the ancient mythological sorceress, Medea (who claimed to have the power to restore youthfulness), and to the fearful gorgon, Medusa (whose blood was used by Asklepios to restore life to the dead). "Pharmacy" comes from *pharmakos*, the designation for a ritual substitute victim, a scapegoat. "Therapist" comes from the Homeric *therapon*, one who takes on the suffering and death due another (as Patroclus took on the destiny of Achilles) or one who receives his essence from another (as Hesiod received his inspiration from the Muses), and more directly from the word designating an attender upon the sacred, a priest: *therapeute.*

Again and again I have found Greek mythology profoundly illuminative of human experience. The Greek goddesses have taught me much about the multi-dimensionality and complexity of female experience and power; the Greek hero-ines have deeply enriched my understanding of the subtle intricacies of sister-sister bonding. I value especially how the polytheistic assumptions of this tradi-tion reveal how manifold are the ways in which one may be a mother, or a sis-ter—or a wounded healer. There are many different figures and stories, male healers and female healers—yet in each healing and woundedness (and often the inflicting of wounds) seem to be closely intertwined.

In the religious healing tradition of ancient Greece it was assumed that the god who can heal is the one responsible for the wounding in the first place. Thus sufferers must seek to discover which deity has been offended and what ritual acts they must undertake so they might be purified of their pollution. Plato tells us that the Korybantes (the male attendants of the mother-goddess Kybele) diag-nosed illness by attending to the patients' response to music; if they responded to music associated with Hekate then it was she whom they must appease; if the songs associated with Dionysos produced catharsis, then this was the god by whom they had been possessed.[1] Thus, ritual healing was based on homeopathic assumptions: the agent of wounding and healing are one. The Greeks also believed that the deities had themselves suffered whatever they might impose on others.

Until the 4th century BCE rational and religious approaches to healing were assumed to be complementary. After that, influenced by Plato's radical separation of soul from body and Aristotle's radical separation of intuitive and imaginal con-sciousness from reason, his high valuation of objective, abstract, dispassionate, distancing thought, this was no longer true. The rational approach to illness henceforth concerned itself with abstract postulates concerning the variety of dis-eases and their causes (as in Galen's theory of the four humors) rather than with the treatment of patients; the religious approach degenerated into superstitious reliance on magical remedies. Earlier, in the strata of Greek thought represented by ancient myth and preserved in the 8th century epic tradition and in the lyric and tragic poetry of the classical period, reason encompassed imagination, mind and body were inextricably intertwined, the gods were believed to be at work in human affairs.

In the preSocratic world medical practitioners were craftsmen who worked for their livelihood with their hands and thus were of low social status. One was initiated into the craft through an oral apprenticeship. Like singers and builders they were often itinerant (and always welcome) foreigners.

Because the Greek saw the processes of the natural world as themselves divine, there was no disjunction between natural and supernatural cures, between rational and religious approaches to healing. To Hippocrates, a contemporary of Socrates, a physician was still a servant, a *therapeute*, whose concern was properly directed toward the healing of patients rather than the study of disease syndromes. He believed the appropriate source of medical knowledge to be not abstract speculation but clinical practice. Central to his ethos of responsible medicine was recognizing the limits of one's knowledge and refraining from interference when one was ignorant. He saw temple medicine as the appropriate last resort when the physician's knowledge had been exhausted.[2] The physician and priest were regarded as allies. Asklepios was invoked by both. Hippocrates came to be seen as a "son" of Asklepios, as his human agent; he, in turn, passed his wisdom down to his sons; later all physicians came to be seen as adoptive sons of Hippocrates and as "Asklepiads."

The Greek conception of the divine was polytheistic and hierarchical. All aspects of human experience were associated with at least one of the twelve Olympians, though minor deities might be assigned sovereignty over some particular domain. The major Greek deity associated with healing is Apollo. To understand this means letting go of our superficial identification of this god with dispassionate abstraction, with formal perfection and invulnerable self-sufficiency. It means going behind Nietzsche's heuristic contrast between Apollo and Dionysos; it means going behind the Delphic vision of Apollo to older, more complex representations.

I know of no tale in which Apollo is literally wounded, though there are many which portray his distress at the death of young beloveds, like Hyacinthus and Cyparissus. Apollo also received serious wounding to his dignity as a god when—as punishment for killing the Cyclopes who had made the thunderbolts with which Zeus slew Apollo's son Asklepios (a story we'll examine further on)—Zeus sentenced him to a year's stint as servant of a mortal king, Alkestis. Indeed, some say that he served Alkestis not only as a servant but as an *eremenos*, a receptive partner in a homosexual relationship, an even more radical loss of status. The year with Alkestis represented a year of purification; the connection to our theme may be more evident if we remember that the Greeks saw pollution as homologous with a wound.

But the recognition of Apollo as a healer seems to proceed more from his being a wounding than a wounded god. His arrows brought disease and swift death to men, as his sister Artemis' arrows were held responsible for women's deaths not caused by visible violence. Last summer almost by chance as my partner and I were driving through Arcadia we came upon the serenely beautiful, isolated and rarely visited, mountaintop temple at Bassae dedicated to Apollo as the god who sends and banishes illness, the god of plague and healing. The temple, we learned, was built by the far away town of Phigaleia in gratitude for Apollo's finally bringing to an end a plague he himself had visited upon them. One approaches it by way of a long and steep ascent through wild terrain; the temple is invisible until the last moment; constructed of stone quarried on the site, it seems to grow out of the hills themselves. Vincent Scully says the columns of this temple communicate "absolute quiet, calm and unaffected by the natural tumult around about," "an expression of human order against the chaotic hills," a representation of "the god as savior of humanity making his presence felt in the heart of the wild." He finds the interior of the temple deliberately archaic, sees the contorted depiction of struggling Lapiths and Centaurs as evoking a dark inwardness that suggests, the dark, chthonic aspect of the god.[3] The sculpture known as the Apollo Belvedere is a Roman copy of a statue initially made in response to a community seeking to bring a similar devastation to an end. "Erect a statue to Apollo," the oracle commanded.

As Apollo comes to be identified primarily with his temple at Delphi, his work as healer is more and more often accomplished through his oracular activity. According to tradition Apollo had wrested control of the Delphic oracle from the primordial earth mother goddess Gaia by killing the Python she had established as its guardian. Originally the oracle had probably been incubational; petitioners received the directions they sought through Gaia-sent dreams. In Apollo's time female seers, called Pythia, responded to the seekers' questions. Scholars still disagree as to whether the Pythia's utterances were frenzied and maenadic, requiring interpretation by male priests, or, though dramatic and poetic, clear enough to be appropriated without reliance on such intermediaries. They are agreed, however, as to the uniqueness of this Apollonian oracle, which depended on neither dream nor the interpretation of physical signs like animal entrails or stars, and which relied for generations on the inspiration of a single person holding a permanent office at a designated site. To this oracle came those who sought to know how they might purify themselves or their city. Consultation of the oracle represented an attempt at a rational approach to the resolution of suffering; one came to learn the source of one's pollution and its remedy. Yet (at least in the mythological accounts) the answers were cryptic and usually one's first or even second interpretation of what action they directed was wrong. Following the oracle often made things worse before it made them better.[4]

Full understanding of Apollo's role as healer also requires attending to him as the leader of the Muses. The still beautifully preserved theater at Epidauros is dedicated to him. There last summer I watched a performance of Aeschylus's *The Seven Against Thebes*, a simple, powerful retelling of sibling hatred and love. Two brothers, so estranged that neither can bear to have the other live, end by killing one another. Their two sisters are committed to giving each brother the ritual recognition due the dead, though the state has decreed that one is a hero deserving ceremonial burial and the other a traitor whose body should be left to the dogs and vultures. As I watched, I understood again how Asklepios' visionary appearances in the temple close by and the tragedians' re-visionings of how the divine enters our lives to wound and to heal are closely intertwined. I understood again why Freud took over the word *catharsis* (Aristotle's word for that purging of our fear and terror that our vicarious participation in the enacted suffering of others can effect) to describe how the emotional as well as intellectual remembrance of our own most painful memories can issue in release. For the Greeks the theater as well as the temple was associated with the art of healing.

Apollo's power to heal was also associated with the *paean*, the hymn sung in gratitude for healing or for success in battle. Before it referred to the song, the name had been an epithet of Apollo. Before that Paieon was an independent deity, the healer among the gods, the healer of the gods, who heals two immortals, Ares and Hades, of wounds that no mortal could have survived. Ares, the god of war, was wounded at Troy by Diomedes at Athene's urging; crying in pain he fled to Olympos where he received little sympathy from Zeus who let him know the injury was but the just consequence of his own mindlessly destructive blood lust. But since Ares is a god, he must not die and so he is sent to Paieon for healing. Hades, god of the underworld, received his wound from a poisoned arrow shot by Herakles during his attempt to abduct Cerberus. The excruciating, unremitting pain led Hades to leave his dark domain (as he did on only one other occasion, his abduction of Persephone) to have it cured by the physician god. We can understand that Paieon, the god who heals the gods, would be an unwounded healer—but he is available only to the gods. For mortals only healers themselves vulnerable avail.[5]

Remembrance that we are mortal and not divine is a prerequisite to receiving healing from Apollo. In his realm healing depends upon true knowledge of one's situation. We must remember, though, that Apollo's famous dictum, "Know

Thyself" meant not as we might suppose: "Know the truth about your individual personal history," but: "Remember that you are mortal." The god of healing remains the god associated with death. Among the Hyperboreans with whom Apollo spent the three months of winter, life was miraculously prolonged and death when it came was easy, *euthanasia*. For such a death one might invoke Apollo.

Like all the major deities, Apollo is a god associated with many realms, not only healing—though his particular way of being a healer is integrally related to his other functions and attributes. Often it is among members of the next generation, among the children of the Olympians, that we find more specialized divinities. Thus it is Apollo's son, Asklepios, who becomes preeminently *the* god of healing. [The son's power derives from his father; even at Epidauros, the site most identified with Asklepios, his temple is built above the ruins of an ancient Apollo temple and the Asklepian sanctuary in the gentle, peaceful valley was in classical times overlooked by an Apollo temple erected on the hilltop far above. Once long ago as Apollo Maleatus, Apollo himself had healed the sick by visiting them in their dreams, but as Apollo becomes more and more the Apollo of Delphi such visitations come to seem incongruous.[6] Now it is another god, his son, who makes such nocturnal appearances.

As so often, the story of Asklepios' birth encapsulates much of who he is. He was the issue of a love affair between Apollo and a beautiful mortal woman named (in the most widely accepted traditions) Koronis, a grand-daughter of Ares, the god of war, and a sister of Ixion, the first human murderer. The genealogy thus again brings together the motifs of healing and death. According to the most often cited version, when Koronis discovered she was pregnant she decided to find a mortal man who might wed her and give her child legitimacy. (Other later traditions represent the marriage to Ischyus as forced upon her by her father or show her as victim of Ischyus' seduction.) Apollo, affronted that any woman might prefer a human husband to a divine lover (though the mistresses of many other gods, like Theseus' mother, Aethra, and like Leda, had made a similar choice with impunity) sends Artemis to kill Koronis and the bridesmaids assembled for the wedding; he himself kills the groom. Unwilling to have his as yet unborn son die in this holocaust, Apollo, acting as surgeon and midwife, cuts open his dying mistress's womb to rescue the almost full-term child and thus Asklepios is born (the first caesarean, it is sometimes jokingly said)—saved from death so that he might grow up to heal others. As Kerenyi interprets this, Apollo's power to kill is here reborn, transformed into Asklepios' power to heal.[7]

Achilles' beloved Patroklos. Gently and skillfully Achilles applied a medicinal ointment and dressed Patroklos' wound. Attentively watching, Patroklos learned enough so that much later when another Eurypylos, one who fought for the Greeks, was wounded by Paris, Patroklos was able to heal his injury.

The stories are almost too intricately intertwined to follow, but over and over again we see warrior heroes who wound and kill, who heal and themselves suffer wounds and die. The heroic "syndrome" seems to imply that, of course, warriors must know how to bind wounds, warriors must also be healers.

Thus many heroes learned the art of healing from the wounded centaur healer, but none as profoundly as Asklepios. The others gave or received healing in the course of their exploits as warriors or hunters; he dedicated his life to healing. In recognition of his gifts as a physician, Athene shared with him the vials of blood collected when Perseus severed the gorgon Medusa's head from her body. The blood that dripped from the left vein was a magically potent poison; the blood from the right was reputed to have the power to restore the dead to life. On several occasions, so it is told, perhaps in sympathetic remembrance of his mother's unjust death (though Pindar claims it was for monetary gain), Asklepios used the magic potion to bring back to life heroes unjustly punished by the gods, heroes prematurely sent to Hades. The stories vary as to who benefited from this gift; Orion, Hippolytos, Campaneus and Lycurgus are most often named.[8]

There is no dispute, however, about Zeus' anger at Asklepios' presumption in transgressing *the* boundary between humanity and the gods: men are mortal; only the gods are free from death, *athanatos*. (The exemplary sinners in Hades, the only figures subject to punishment there, were those such as Sisyphus, Ixion and Tantalus who had sought to win such immortality for themselves or to wrest it from the gods.) In punishment for his unforgivable crime, Zeus struck Asklepios with his thunderbolts and sent him to Hades, so that he, though a god, might himself experience the fate of mortals. (It was Apollo's anger at this further unjust punishment that led him to kill the thunderbolt-forging Cyclopes—a challenging of Zeus difficult to reconcile with the Delphic Apollo.)

Thus Asklepios becomes the only god in Greek mythology to experience death. For the Greeks then *the* god of healing is the one who knows what it is to die. Though as a god his stay in Hades is only temporary, though as a god he can experience mortality without forfeiting his immortality, it is his own experience of vulnerability to death that makes him seem to the Greeks a god more kindly and more benevolent than any other.

There are other figures in Greek cult who died and were then worshipped as having healing power. But they were mortal heroes whose power derived precisely from their having died and now living in the underworld. Their powers were chthonic and localized; worshippers came to their tombs to consult with the dead or for healing. For instance, Trophonios, the architect son of Apollo, credited with building the temple at Delphi, was associated with an oracle which one consulted by descending to a cave deep within the earth. The tomb of Amphiaraus (a beloved of both Zeus and Apollo who was killed during the attack on Thebes by a thunderbolt of Zeus to preserve him from the shame of being speared in the back) was the site of an important incubation oracle; devotees came to the tomb hoping to be given a healing dream. But, though there may be disagreement among scholars as to whether Asklepios had always been regarded as a god or whether he had initially been a hero, it is clear that his cult from the beginning was no chthonic hero's cult. There are no references whatsoever to Asklepios being worshipped at his tomb nor to his powers being available only at a single site.

As a god who had spent time in the underworld, it is not surprising that Asklepios was seen as a participant in Persephone's mysteries, an initiate of Eleusis. Indeed, when the god came to Athens (that is, when the cult of Asklepios was brought to Athens after the plague of 420 BCE), he was first brought to the temple of the two goddesses at Eleusis—indicating that the god of healing understands his work as subordinate to hers. Though not himself an underworld deity, Asklepios urges those who come to him to offer prayers to Demeter and Persephone. He can save one from death *now*, but not for good. The respite his healing provides gives those who are not yet ready for death an interval to prepare for the death that still inevitably lies ahead. The healing of the body he makes possible gives us time to attend to the health of our souls. And if the god refuses to heal, it means that the time for one's death has come.

And sometimes, of course, death is a release from illness. As the Orphic hymn says, Asklepios grants a good end to life. I recall also Sokrates' last words: "Krito, we owe a cock to Asklepios; pay it and do not neglect it." In Edelstein's reflections on this cryptic saying he suggests that for Sokrates life was a kind of illness or death and death was itself a kind of healing, marking the beginning of real life, the life of the psyche.[9]

Thus there is a shrine to Asklepios at Eleusis. But his own cult center was at Epidauros—and the rituals there were different from those at any other temple site. For this god was available whenever his need was sought; his temple was open every day, not only on designated ritual occasions. Though not a chthonic hero associated with the underworld, Asklepios was also not an Olympian; he was a god who stayed on earth. Those who came to Epidauros were the hopeless cases, patients who had exhausted the medical resources of their own communities, who knew they were threatened with death and felt they were not ready. We should note, however, that the acutely moribund were not allowed within the god's precincts. Literal death was excluded from this realm of healing, as was literal birth—pregnancy needs no cure. (Barren women, however, came to the shrine in the hopes of being impregnated by the god.) The ritually impure, the criminal, were also excluded.

One went through this ritual alone; it was not a communal event as the rites associated with other gods were. There were three days of ritual preparation—fasting, bathing, offering sacrifices to Asklepios and Apollo, to Mnemosyne (Memory, the mother of the muses; perhaps the prayers to her expressed one's hope of being remembered), and to Tyche (Success). Then, dressed in one's ordinary clothes, one was led by a *therapeute* to a small stone chamber, empty except for a simple stone sleeping platform, a *kline* (the origin of our word "clinic")—a space one might often have visited in daylight during the period of preparation. Even the attendant withdrew to leave one alone with one's dreams and with the god. After offering a prayer to Themis (right order) one settled oneself down to sleep (directly on the stone, rather than on animal skins as in the incubation rites associated with the chthonic heroes)—in hope that the god himself would come as one dreamt.

The Greeks believed that when we sleep our *psyche*, that in us that is quiescent during conscious, active waking life becomes active. It is the psyche that dreams and that persists after the death of our bodies and lives on in Hades. "Psyche" represents the core of our individual being, our personal essence, the aspect of the patient that will encounter the god. The psyche sees dreams, it receives them; dreams are god-sent, are theophanies. In the Asklepian ritual the epiphany, the god's appearance in one's dream, was understood as itself the healing event. His coming marked the always hidden transition between illness and the return to health. Every cure was a divine act, a mystery, which could only happen in the dark. At Epidauros unlike Delphi it was the patient who had the healing vision rather than the priest or priestess. At Epidauros unlike Delphi the vision itself accomplished the cure; there was no need for interpretation nor for action based on the dream's prescription. (Though in the Hellenistic period Epidauros, and especially the Asklepian shrine at Kos run by Hippocratic physicians, may have functioned more like other oracles, with the dreams understood as providing prescriptions for treatment rather than effecting the cure directly.)

In the patient's dream the god might appear in his humanlike form or theriomorphically—as snake or as dog. Many of the recorded dreams describe a snake or a dog licking the afflicted part and thus healing it; barren women told of dreams in which a snake appeared and copulated with them. (In waking life, too, the Asklepian snake, a harmless species of tree-snake that might grow to be six feet in length, was viewed as a manifestation of the god. Snakes were everywhere underfoot at Epidauros [and still are!] and when a new Asklepian temple was initiated at Athens and later at Rome a snake brought from Epidauros represented the arrival of the god.) Snakes were, of course, associated also with many of the goddesses and with chthonic religiosity; as in so many other religious traditions the snake was seen as emblematic of the mysterious relation between death and rebirth. Dogs, too, were associated with underworld experience: three-headed Kerberos welcomes the dead to Hades but eats those who try to leave; night-roaming Hekate is accompanied by baying hounds, the restless spirits of those not given ritual burial.

When the god appears in dreams as a humanlike physician he acts on the pattern of rational medicine; his cures are medical cures. He applies salves, makes use of drugs and operates, though his procedures were often contrary to human theories of treatment, his surgeries more radical than those any mortal healer would dare undertake.

Dreaming, the patient was alone with the god. In the morning the *therapeute* returned to the sleeping chamber to record the dream—only that, though the patient's retelling may no doubt have had some salutary effect and in that retelling the dream (through what Freud calls "secondary elaboration") may quite unconsciously have been subtly revised to accord with the culturally expected dream pattern. Afterwards the patient would offer a song of praise (a paean) in gratitude for what he had been given and sacrifice a rooster to the god, as token that daylight has overcome the dark, health has overcome disease. Despite his recognition of the ultimate power of the underworld deities, Asklepios remains a son of Apollo, dedicated to life on the sunlit earth, to the never ultimately victorious struggle against death.

Most of the traditions associated with Asklepios focus on his role as healer. He had a wife, Epione, whose name like the last part of the god's own, derives from a word meaning "mild," but there are no stories about their relationship. Homer names two sons, Machaon and Podaleiros, two warrior physicians who were among the Greek forces at Troy. Machaon, the "slaughterer," is spoken of as the first surgeon. We have already referred to his own fatal wounding and death. He had a hero's tomb that served as a cult site. His brother, Podaleiros, could treat invisible illnesses including those of the soul, psychic wounds, like the madness of Ajax and the paranoid isolation of Philoctetes. On the way to Troy the latter was bitten by a snake (perhaps sent by Hera, angry at him for helping Herakles achieve immortality). Like Cheiron he suffered from a wound that would not heal. Upset by the wound's noxious stench and by Philoctetes' unceasing cries of anguish, his companions abandoned him on Lemnos. There, alone and in continuing torment, he stayed for ten years—until an oracle foretold that Troy would fall only if Philoctetes came to fight with the Greeks. The wounded hero refused to leave his island until the divine Herakles appeared and promised healing if he went. There one or the other of Asklepios' sons (or perhaps the god himself, with the aid of an herb whose secret he had learned from Cheiron) at last released Philoctetes from his suffering.

Asklepios' other children appear more as figures of allegory than of true myth (though Edelstein believes they may have originally been independent healing diamones). They include Iaso (whose name, meaning "healing," might remind us of the Argonaut hero, Jason); Panakeia (panacea), cure; Telesphoros, completion; Hygeia (hygiene), health. The Greeks still toast Iaso as they drink their wine. Telesphoros, represented as a dwarf-like nocturnal figure may, so Kerenyi suggests, have been associated with the completion represented by death. Hygeia was a drink imbibed in gratitude for one's cure; it may have had psychedelic properties.

There are no stories about Hygeia; she exists as little more than a name. Yet she was said to be the one daughter "worth as much as all the others."[10] There is a lovely sculpted head of her in the National Museum at Athens that to my mind beautifully communicates healing power—her face is calm, serene, her gaze direct and gentle. There are reliefs in the Museum at Epidauros (and in other places as well) that depict her accompanying Asklepios. Often these reliefs depict her standing commandingly while he sits; sometimes the goddess is larger than the god; sometimes she appears in the guise of an enormous snake. There are suggestions here that perhaps he gets his power from *her*, that perhaps healing was originally associated with the goddess not the god. Perhaps she was originally seen as a giver and preserver of health and Asklepios as only a healer of the ill. If so, hers would have been seen as the greater gift in a culture where health was viewed as the greatest boon and old age as a burden. We do know that in later periods the emphasis in the Asklepian cult fell on rituals for the healthy not for the sick. The iconographic evidence may preserve ancient traditions about the health-giving goddess, but according to the literary evidence, Hygeia is a minor figure, a daughter without attribute or story. A wounded healer in that prototypically feminine sense of being devalued, almost invisible.

To discover more illuminating Greek mythological representations of female healing power, we must look at the traditions about the major goddesses. Long before there are any extant evidences of a particular divinity called Hygeia, Hygeia was an attribute of Athene. Athene, as the goddess of all artisans and craftspersons, was the goddess of physicians. The divinity most associated with the life of the polis, she was dedicated to serving the health of the community, of individuals as citizens. In this goddess of practical wisdom the Greeks expressed their belief that the capacity for rational thought was itself a sacred and divine gift. Thus Athene helps us understand that for the Greeks there is no conflict between rational and religious healing; to use our minds for the sake of our shared life is a religious act. Athene also represents a view that reflection may serve to protect us from being overwhelmed by our instincts, our fears, our impetuosity, our enthusiasms. Though it is not difficult to discern Athene's relation to healing, it is at first glance not easy to see her relevance to the theme of the wounded healer. Yet we must recall that Athene wears Medusa's severed head on her aegis—that her pharmacopoeia includes the vial of healing blood gathered from Medusa's right artery and the vial of death-bringing poison gathered from the left. In Athene Medusa's fearful petrifying gaze has been reformed into a power to restore order. That which is most fearsome, most threatening about female energy has in her been transformed, sublimated, made healing.

Another important female goddess of healing is Hera in her aspect as midwife, an aspect evident in more concentrated form in her daughter, Eilytheia (as Apollo's healing power is represented more focusedly in Asklepios). Hera is an obviously wounded goddess, wounded in what is at the very center of her existence, her marriage. Hera is wife—wife betrayed over and over again by unfaithful Zeus, wife as possessive, jealous and vengeful. She is sympathetic toward all other suffering wives, but cruel towards the women with whom Zeus makes love, regardless of how violently they may have sought to avert his advances. In the literary representations of Hera, which express a male perspective, she becomes an epitome of the wounded healer whose own woundedness distorts her exercise of her healing gifts. She refuses to allow Eilytheia to go to the aid of Leto as she struggles painfully for nine days to give birth to Apollo. When Herakles' mother's birth-pangs begin, she sends Eilytheia to bind her legs together to delay his birth, thereby assuring that another child will be born as heir to the kingdom that otherwise would have been his. The evidence we have of women's rituals dedicated to Hera present a different picture, emphasize her helpfulness—but perhaps the women wanted to be sure she would be helpful to *them* or perhaps they saw her as an advocate against unfaithful husbands and shared her animus against their mistresses.

Childbirth was a *women's* mystery. As we noted above, the preeminent god of healing, Asklepios, explicitly excluded women about to give birth from his sanctuary. It is not surprising then that there would be more than a single goddess associated with this central aspect of female experience. Thus not only Hera but also Artemis was a midwife goddess, one who did not share Hera's prejudices. Goddess of woods and wilderness, herself a virgin without children of her own, Artemis came to the aid of all females struggling to give birth—as in her own infancy she had immediately after her own delivery turned to help her mother in her difficult struggle to give birth to Artemis' twin, Apollo. Artemis' attention is available to all; she comes to assist legitimate and illegitimate deliveries, the births of human children and the births of animal young. She is a female-identified goddess, especially concerned with the particularities of female bodily existence, with being born and giving birth, with the onset of menstruation at puberty and its cessation at menopause, with the loss of virginity, and with death. Her mysteries are blood mysteries—those female sheddings of blood that are a given part of female functioning, not wounds in any ordinary sense, yet wounds from which we may die. Birth in Artemis' realm is itself a moment when death hovers near; how likely it is that child or mother or both may perish. Artemis, the agent of such death, also stands ready to nurse the orphan, be it a human child or a wolf-cub or a fawn, at her own breast. As goddess of the forest, Artemis is a huntress—but she is also hunted. Her virginity is that of the vulnerable maiden whose very unavailability is seen as enticement. Though she herself has the power to resist her would-be ravishers, she cannot prevent their pursuit. It is easy to see her as a wounding goddess; she is pitiless toward those she considers strong enough to have the capacity to protect themselves. Yet she is fully available to aid those who are not.

Though all the goddesses have some relation to healing, I see the two celebrated in the Eleusinian mysteries, Demeter and Persephone, as most intimately connected to my theme. Demeter was the goddess associated with the blessings and griefs of motherhood. Herself separated from her own mother at birth, when she had a daughter of her own she longed to give her all the motherly love of which she had been deprived. Not surprisingly, she could not imagine that there could be a surfeit of maternal devotion. No more surprisingly, the most important story about Demeter and her daughter Persephone is one that tells of Demeter's loss of that beloved child when she becomes a marriageable maiden. One spring day Persephone goes to play in a flower-filled meadow with several other young women; that night she doesn't come home. Eventually Demeter learns that Persephone had reached to pluck an especially large and beautiful narcissus; the whole plant had come up as she pulled and out of the ever-widening hole made by the torn-up bulb Hades, the god of the underworld, had appeared. He had gathered the maiden in his arms and carried her down to his underworld realm. Demeter is overcome with anger and grief over the loss of her daughter. So all-consuming is her rage that she neglects her responsibilities to assure the growth of those crops on which human lives (and the human capacity to serve the gods) depend—and so eventually Zeus has to intervene to allow Persephone to return to her mother, not permanently, not on the same basis as before her abduction, but for a good part of each year.

The rites associated with "The Two Goddesses" focus on the reunion and on Persephone as bride of Hades—but the Thesmophoria, Demeter's own ritual, focuses on her loss and grief. Once a year married women left their husbands and children to spend three days in Demeter s temple. They prayed for children and easy births, they indulged in obscene language and vulgar behavior, they felt free to share not only their passive grief but their active rage—much as women did in "consciousness raising" groups a decade or so ago. Demeter was the goddess who knew how much of motherhood is pain and loss. To share one's wounds with her (and to know how truly they were shared by the other women participants) was to receive some assuagement of the pain. The goddess could not undo the loss—anymore than she could undo her own—but she could initiate one into its archetypal and sacred dimensions.

Her daughter Persephone, the goddess of the underworld and of death, may, paradoxically, be the most important of all Greek images of the wounded healer. For what Persephone offers is healing of our fear of woundedness and vulnerability, our fear of finitude and death. Herself abducted by Hades, she comes to love him; herself taken to the underworld against her will, she comes to be its queen. The Greeks saw the underworld as the place where psyches *live*; they saw Persephone's mysteries at Eleusis as the rituals whereby one learned that entering Hades might be blessing rather than curse. What they had rituals to help them learn, we may need to learn from our own experiences of being wounded: release from what may be the most serious illness of all—the fantasy of a health without wounds, a life without death.

Notes

1.   E. R. Dodds, *The Greeks and the Irrational* (Boston: Beacon Press, 1957) 78.

2.   Ludwig Edelstein, *Ancient Medicine* (Baltimore: The Johns Hopkins Press, 1967) 205-246.

3.   Vincent Scully, *The Earth, The Temple, and The Gods* (New Haven: Yale University Press, 1979) 124ff.

4.   Joseph Fontenrose, *The Delphic Oracle* (Berkeley: University of California Press, 1981) Ch. 7.

5.   Carl Kerenyi, *Asklepios* (New York: Pantheon, 1959) 80-82.

6.   Emma J. Edelstein and Ludwig Edelstein, *Asclepius* (Baltimore: The Johns Hopkins Press, 1945) Vol. II, 99.

7.   Kerenyi, 46.

8.   Orion was killed by Artemis whom Apollo, jealous of his sister's friendship for the hero, had tricked into an archery contest; Hippolytos died because of Aphrodite's jealousy of his exclusive devotion to Artemis; Campaneus was killed by Zeus for his presumptuous challenge to Zeus during the siege of Thebes that ended in the fratricidal slaughter recounted in that play I saw at Epidauros; Lycurgus was driven mad and sent to his death in punishment for having driven Dionysos from Thrace.

9.   Edelstein and Edelstein, 131.

10. Edelstein and Edelstein, 89.

7

A View from the Parthenon

Guilia Sassa's *Greek Virginity* (Cambridge, MA: Harvard University Press, 1990) seeks to clarify our understanding of Greek images of virginity through careful examination of myths, vase paintings, literary texts, and medical writings. She is convinced that our ignorance of how different the ancient Greek conception of the female body is from ours occludes our understanding of women in the pre-Christian world and may blind us to some of the peculiarities of *our* view.

The first section of her book focuses on the relation of the virginity of the Pythia, Apollo's priestess at Delphi, to her oracular function. Unlike many other recent scholars Sassa gives credence (despite the absence of confirmatory archeological evidence) to ancient texts that testify to the Pythia's delirium and to vase paintings that represent her sitting above a vaporous fissure in the earth. Thus, the divine spirit, the *pneuma*, was believed to enter the priestess from below, whereas usually it descends from above. Early Christian writers interpret this pornographically: they describe the Pythia as a visible body obscenely possessed by a demonic Apollo and imagine the vapors entering her body by way of her genitals and filling her with delirious madness. But to Greek authors such as Plutarch it is "with the soul of a virgin that she approaches the god." Yet Sassa notes that despite the high degree of significance attached to the sexual purity of Pythia, there is no evidence that her virginity was ever tested before her appointment or verified later, and extensive testimony to suggest that the Greeks, too, understood the relationship between her and the god in sexual terms. What then did the Greeks mean by calling her a virgin and how does this relate to their more general understanding of virginity?

Sassa reminds us of how central a role desire plays in myths about Apollo's relations to other prophetesses: the Cumaean Sybil, Cassandra, Daphne. But where these prophetesses seem to represent a rebellious virginity, the Pythia's is a consented offering. The model for her relation to Apollo is that of a bride's obedience to her husband, "the power devoid of brutality that a man exercises over a free but feeble individual whose nature is taken for granted." Apollo uses the soul of the Pythia as his instrument; her psyche is as sensitive to him as is the moon to the sun. The words she speaks are the work of both, the effect of possession in language. The priestess must be a virgin because she must be available exclusively to the god; no other desire may distract her. She is a woman at once faithful and possessed; the language that best describes her is the language of legitimate sexual union. The Pythia's consent is essential and yet it is impossible for her entirely to stifle her own feelings. It is the interference of her emotions, her inability to remain purely passive, that gives rise to her *mania* and to the obscurity or obliqueness of her oracles.

Sassa suggests that the Pythia reminded Greeks of gynecological practices with "obscene and occult" connotations: her posture on the tripod resembled that of a woman seated over a cauldron with her legs open, ready to receive the vapors that would cure her of menstrual or conceptional difficulties, as it also resembled that of a woman giving birth. Indeed, the priestess's oracles are the equivalent of an impregnation by the god. The Pythia carries the god's words within her like an embryo; she supplies her soul to the god as in procreation the women supplies her blood as the raw material for the male's form-giving sperm. What happens between the priestess and the god has about it something of the *obscene*: it belongs "off stage"; it is something not to be seen.

Therefore the classical Greek texts speak of the Pythia as only a voice, invisible to all, as "a female body that was not present when the god who inhabited it borrowed its voice." Outside the temple the priestess resumes the ignorance of the perfect virgin, like a virtuous woman who opens her mouth only to speak to her husband. Her oracular pronouncements were the result of an encounter with the god that had to remain secret. Sassa concludes it is the *clandestine* quality of her relation to the god that serves as the correlate of the Pythia's virginity.

In the second part of her study Sassa continues to probe the interconnection between secrecy, silence, and virginity. She is fascinated by the importance attached to the analogy between mouth and vagina, between the garrulous and the adulterous, the silent and the faithful wife. The focus is now on trying to understand just what the Greeks meant by *parthenos*. Sassa agrees with the scholarly consensus that the Greek word *parthenos* does not denote the intact hymeneal membrane implicit in our word "virgin" but dismisses the view that it denotes simply the interim period between childhood and marriage. She does not believe that the concept is determined simply by age and marital status without any reference to sexual experience. There is a difference between the Greek conception and ours but it is not the difference between a social status and a physical state.

Since *parthenia* means child of a *parthenos*, the Greeks clearly assumed that a "virgin" might bear a child and thus she is obviously not necessarily a woman who shuns all sexual activity. Sassa admits to the many mythical occasions when a woman who has made love outside of marriage (usually to a god to whom she also bears a child—since divine lovemaking seems always to issue in pregnancy) is still called a virgin. One becomes a women (*gyne*) only through marriage. But Sassa, convinced that virgin does not mean simply "not married," insists that the *possibility* of using *parthenos* to refer to a girl who had had sexual relations should not be the *decisive element* in a definition. That the term refers not just to age and social status but to sexuality is evident to her when we take into account how definitively the *discovered* sexuality of a *parthenos* changes her status. Sexuality and virginity may be compatible—but only if the sexual activity remains hidden, only in the absence of suspicion in the minds of others. Discovered sexuality changes a maiden's status even more drastically than does marriage, for she becomes a "nobody." If a father discovers that his daughter is pregnant or has been seduced, he must banish her from his family and may sell her as a slave. Thus it is *possible* for a *parthenos* to have a sexual life, but it is *forbidden*. In tragedy if a maiden is seduced against her will, she is still regarded as a virgin; but in Athenian law the girl's consent is irrelevant. Not her subjective state but what has happened is determinative.

What interests Sassa here is that the Greeks did see the loss of virginity as correlated with discovered sexual experience, as a fact to be found out. To her mind the crucial question then becomes "What was the physical correlate of virginity?" She is fascinated that only a seduction, not virginity itself, could be verified. The event of deflowering *existed* only if *discovered*. Tests of virginity were not within the competence of medicine; the Greeks knew of no anatomical investigation capable of revealing the truth about a girl's sexual life. Greek physicians explicitly denied the "so-called virginal membrane"; indeed, if a girl was born with such a membrane it was surgically removed as an *anomaly*, inimical to women's essential, that is, maternal function. Virginity was an invisible condition detectable only by means of mantic vision or ordeal. The investigation of a maiden's virginity was not directed to a particular part of the body but to her whole being.

The loss of virginity, then, is not correlated with the rupture of an intact hymen, with an irreversible wounding. If a maiden has intercourse, nothing irreparable has taken place. A husband would be unable to find any physical evidence of defloration—unless there were a child or the woman were caught in the act. What Sassa wants to highlight about the Greek understanding of the female body is how it viewed the female genitals as "tending naturally to reseal themselves" (as they were imagined to do in pregnancy). Thus she returns again to the analogy they drew between the oral and the vaginal cavities: both have lips that can open and close. The virgin and the chaste widow are seen as equivalent. "Nothing in the body of a woman…visited by a man's sex is irretrievably lost"!

The last section of the book focuses on the Danaides, who function to represent the negative image of the reversibility of the loss of virginity represented by the Pythia. That the husband-murdering Danaides are punished in Hades by being condemned to try to fill a bottomless jar with water carried in leaky sieves, Sassa interprets to signify that those who refuse the *telos* of marriage remain in a permanent state of incompletion. These women have lost their virginity, but by killing their husbands on their wedding night they have prevented the consummation of their marriage; they have been opened up by their experience of intercourse but because they have not conceived, they are stuck open. They unfillable vessels; neither virgins nor mothers, their lips will never reseal.

Sassa's interpretation of the Greek understanding of virginity is penetrating and well argued and yet not entirely satisfactory. There is an implicit or at least potential feminist agenda in her argument that never becomes fully explicit.

In her introduction and again in her last pages she acknowledges that her interest in a conception of virginity for which the hymen is irrelevant arises from a concern about a fetishizing of the hymen that she takes to be characteristic of present-day views, but which I would suppose most women and many men have long ago discarded. When she speaks of the role assigned to the hymen in Christianity where it is precisely "the physical detail" that makes the immaculate conception a miracle, she writes as though this Christian perspective still has preemptive authority for most of us. Although she quotes Enlightenment physicians who long ago challenged the fantasy of a membrane whose dissection and even observation to readily disproved, she writes as though belief in it were today intact.

When Sassa writes that the assumption that there is an obvious physical correlate of virginity can serve as a camouflage for "the most perverse forms of erotic behavior," I find myself agreeing—and cringing. I remember how very sexually experienced the "technical virgins" of my adolescent years often were and how distorted a sexual encounter obsessed with the importance of refraining from penetration can be. I understand her critique of a view of sexuality that confines purity to a single location and thus "transforms a moral virtue into a physical fact." But I am dismayed at Sassa's describing sexual behaviors that do not culminate in intercourse as "perverse"—and disappointed that she cannot see the value (especially in the era of AIDS) of a celebration and cultivation of the pleasures of noncoital sexuality.

I am also disappointed that Sassa does not deal more explicitly with the hymeneal fantasy as a *male* fantasy. She does ask why the fantasy has been so persuasive for so long, but fails to explore possible answers at any length (though she alludes to an illusory male desire to have sovereign authority over the female body). Nor does she emphasize as much as I would have wished how the Greek view of virginity she explicates for us is also a male view (although she acknowledges that it is "the paternal gaze that determined the strict rules of virgin behavior"). The notion that what the father (or bridegroom) doesn't know doesn't matter is intriguing, for it suggests that there is a sense in which the Greeks recognized that a women's sexuality is her own. But this Sassa never discusses. She never even asks what virginity may have meant from the perspective of Greek women. Granted that the literary evidence gives us direct access only to male views, some speculation would still have been possible. My guess is that consideration of the female perspective would have issued in the same downgrading of the salience of age and marital status but also in less emphasis on physical experience discovered or undiscovered and more on psychology, more on the sense of one's soul and body being one's own, what Esther Harding (in *Woman's Mysteries* [New York: Bantam, 1973]) called "in-one-selfness."

I would doubt that for the Greeks or for us "virginity" is a univocal concept—that it can be defined as a matter of social status *or* physiological state *or* inner attitude. But the view that Sassa brings to us in her valuable book, of virginity as something that can be lost and regained, as something that pertains to our personhood and not to a particular part of our anatomy, seems profoundly consonant with women's own understanding of the female body.

8

Mirrors Of The Self

Archetypal images reveal a rich mirroring of our inner experience and our interactions with the world outside ourselves. As Jung discovered when he went in search of "the myth that was living him," the encounter with a dimension of the unconscious, which is a living, creative, transpersonal source of inexhaustible energy and direction, is life-changing.

Many of us, when we first read Jung, feel we recognize immediately the dimension of experience for which he used the word archetypal. I remember my own first reading of him when I was in my early twenties and imagined myself as fully and fulfillingly defined by the roles of wife and mother. Suddenly my self-understanding was opened up as I began to pay attention to my dreams and was introduced to an unsuspected multitude of unlived potentialities waiting to be acknowledged and nurtured. I discovered also how these roles had archetypal and numinous dimensions (both threatening and life-giving) to which I had been blinded by my involvement with their more trivial aspects. I felt myself in touch with elements of my own experience that were not mine alone. The recognition that I shared my deepest feelings, my most profound hopes and fears, my most valued accomplishments and most regretted failures with others gave me an entirely new sense of being connected to all humanity not just through outward relationships but at the very core of my being.

This experience felt very real. Jung had introduced me to a new word and, more important, to a new vision of myself that I recognized as both liberating and challenging. Although I have many theoretical reservations about the details of his presentation, reflection on Jung's theory of archetypes still renews my gratitude for the way it helps us—both personally and theoretically—to move beyond the limits of a psychology focused only on personal history and pathological issues.

Jung named the images through which the collective unconscious manifests itself "archetypal images." He used the word archetypal to communicate the power some images have to bring us in touch with what feels like the very source of our being. The Greek root, *arche*, refers to beginnings, to origins; *type* derives from a Greek verb meaning "to strike" and from the related noun that refers to an impression or model. Archetype thus signifies the model from which copies are cast, the underlying pattern, the beginning point from which something develops. Though Jung sometimes writes of archetypes as imprinted on our psyches, he also applies this etymology in a more dynamic way when he defines archetypal images as having the power to impress us: "These typical images and associations...impress, influence, and fascinate us."[1]

Jung distinguished between archetypes and archetypal images. He recognized that what comes into individual consciousness are always *archetypal images*—particular, concrete manifestations that are influenced by sociocultural and individual factors. However, the archetypes themselves are formless and unrepresentable, psychoid rather than, properly speaking, psychic: "The archetype as such is a psychoid factor that belongs, as it were, to the invisible, ultraviolet end of the psychic spectrum...One must consistently bear in mind that what we mean by 'archetype' is in itself irrepresentable, but that it has effects which enable us to visualize it, namely, the archetypal images."[2] Archetypes themselves, Jung says, are empty and without form; we can never really see them except as they become conscious, except when filled with individual content.

What it means to posit the reality of archetypes apart from their manifestations is a much-debated issue whose metaphysical dimensions I will mostly sidestep. Because I tend to see archetypes as abstractions from the concrete, diversified images, like many other recent appreciators and critics of Jung I find myself not very interested in them—precisely because I am interested in psyche, soul, and the imagining activity which I take to be the psyche's most characteristic activity.

Jung's interest in archetypal images reflects his emphasis on the *form* of unconscious thought rather than on the content. Our capacity to respond to experience as image-making creatures is inherited, given to us with our humanness. Archetypal images are not remnants of archaic thought, not a dead deposit, but part of a living system of interactions between the human psyche and the outer world. The archetypal images that appear in my dreams spring from the same human capacity that gave rise to ancient mythologies among our remote ancestors. The myths are not causes of the contemporary and individual manifestations, but rather exist on the same plane as analogies.

The focus on the archetypal emphasizes the importance of our images in making us who we are. Our lives are shaped by our thoughts and deeds and, even more powerfully, our fantasies and dreams, and the complex feeling-toned associations with which we respond to the persons and events we encounter everyday. I am not merely what I have thought, as Descartes proposed, nor simply what I have done, as the existentialists claim, but also, as Gaston Bachelard has so powerfully shown, what I have imagined and remembered.

When we speak of archetypal images we are not referring simply to dream images or to mythological or literary images. We are, instead, speaking of a way to respond to our ordinary lives with our imaginations, rather than only pragmatically or logically. We are speaking of a way of being in the world that is open to many dimensions of meaning, open to resonances, echoes, to associative and synchronous connections, not only causal ones. We are speaking of a world discovered to be full of sign-ificance—of signs, symbols, metaphors, images.

Thus, the point of attending to the archetypal is to bring us to appreciate and nurture the natural, spontaneous human capacity to respond to the world not only conceptually but also symbolically. Image-making is as fundamental a human way of responding to the world as are the categories of space, time, and causality described by Kant. Symbolic thinking is associational, analogical, concrete, feeling-toned, animistic, anthropomorphic. It may seem more passive, more simply receptive than organizing conceptual thought, because images, unlike ideas, feel given to us rather than made by us and may, therefore, as Jolande Jacobi suggests, feel like revelations, "convincing by virtue of their immediacy."[3] Or, our involvement with archetypal images may lead us to feel ourselves engaged with an *inner* world, a world of interior objects. But actually, as Jung clearly saw, symbolic or archetypal thinking is a mode of response *to the world*, which may help free us from entrapment by the illusion of the separation between inner and outer and the disjunction of subject from object.

For Jung this capacity for symbol-making, not reason, is the truly human-making function. Attending to these images (which are not translated ideas but the natural speech of the soul, its authentic *logos*) helps get us beyond the tyranny of the verbal and rational modes, which have issued in the suppression of those human faculties we encounter as "unconscious."

When we focus on archetypal as adjective rather than on archetype as noun, the question, according to James Hillman, becomes "What is it about an image that draws the modifier archetypal?"[4] His answer is that so much wealth can be gotten from it, that it is experienced as rich, deep, fecund, generative. *Archetypal* is a word that connotes the value and importance we attach to particular images. It means we endow them with the deepest possible significance. Calling something archetypal is a *valuing* process, not the positing of an ontological fact.

Archetypal refers then to a way of seeing. We don't so much look at archetypes as *through* them. To call an image archetypal is not to say it is some special, different kind of image but a different way of viewing or valuing the image.

Whether an image is archetypal or not depends chiefly on the attitude of the observing consciousness, on our response to the image, rather than any inherent quality. I also believe that there are some common features of human life, such as the birth of a first child or the appearance of a rainbow after a storm, that seem to compel or often evoke this kind of response. There are situations in which it is difficult to respond only rationally or pragmatically; these situations stir us as whole human beings. Though it is often said that archetypal images are formed in response to recurrent typical experiences and to widespread, relatively constant, and consequential aspects of human experience, Hillman reverses this theory: images that merit our repeated attention are archetypal. The repetition pertains not to what instigates the image but to what it engenders.

When we focus on the archetypal *image*, it becomes clear that there is no absolute distinction between the personal and the collective, for the archetypal image marks the juncture where inner and outer, personal and collective meet. It represents the continual dynamic interaction between the conscious and the unconscious, the personal and the collective. Jacobi suggests that archetypal images exist on a continuum from the more particularized to the more general: "The more personal and current a problem is, the more intricate, detailed, and clearly defined is the archetypal figure by which it is expressed; the more impersonal and universal the situation it concretizes, the simpler or more blurred it will be."[5]

Which aspect we emphasize will depend on our purposes, situations, and needs. Yet it is important to recognize that archetypal images will always carry a personal valence and appear in a specific context. Apprehending their meaning for us will always require paying attention to their particularity and not simply their generality.

Then what makes us respond to an image as archetypal? As I recall my discovery of the power of the engagement with the imaginal to transform my very being, I conclude that what is important is not that archetypal images *are* a priori, universal or numinous, but that we *feel* that they are. Archetypal images feel basic, necessary, and generative. They are connected to something original, not in the sense of what they are caused by, but rather in what they help to cause or make possible. They seem to give energy and direction. Archetypal images give rise to associations and lead us to other images; and we therefore experience them as having resonance, complexity, and depth.

They feel universal. Jung claimed, "From the unconscious there emanate determining influences…which, independently of tradition, guarantee in every single individual a similarity and even a sameness of experience, and also of the way it is represented imaginatively."[6] Though I question the accuracy (or even the relevance) of the claim to literal universality, I nonetheless believe that the sense of being in touch with something that feels collective, shared, is indeed part of what archetypal connotes. Perhaps "transpersonal" is a better designation for this than "universal" because it does not imply that the experience or the imaginative representation of it is necessarily apropos of all cultures or all individuals.

But quite apart from the possibility of establishing literal universality, I am troubled by the manner in which claims to universality so often proceed from a view that the socially (or individually) specific aspects of an archetypal image are somehow nonessential. This implies a prioritizing of the abstract over the concrete, the spiritual over the embodied. It also ignores the social oppressions that may seem to be sanctioned by the supposedly sacrosanct universal image, for we are all likely to be unconscious of our involvement in our own culture's assumptions. The relegation of women to subservient roles, for example, may appear sanctioned by traditional notions of archetypal femininity.

Archetypal images feel objective, in some way given, not dependent on prior personal experience, not explicable on the basis of our conscious knowledge. We feel in touch with something hitherto unknown and are often amazed to discover parallels between the images and motifs that appear in our own dreams and those that figure prominently in myths or folktales we know nothing about. The impact of these correspondences is powerful. To experience the unconscious as an objective rather than simply a subjective realm may help free us from the ego's view of the unconscious as "my" unconscious.

These images feel numinous, magic, fascinating, daemonic, or divine. They seem to have a transcendent, autonomous source beyond individual consciousness, beyond ourselves. There is a dangerous aspect to this feeling, the danger of being inflated or possessed, the danger of taking this to mean that these images are sacred and thus inviolable, unchangeable, that they come endowed with a cosmic endorsement.

All archetypal images seem to evoke ambivalence in us. We are both drawn to and repelled by them; they have dark, fearsome, destructive aspects as well as a benign, creative side. We often try to deny this, to emphasize only the creative aspect, or to moralize and divide the archetype into good and bad parts—the positive mother and the negative mother, for example—and thereby lose some of the dynamic energy intrinsic to the images.

They feel transformative. Jung always emphasized that archetypal images are connected to future as well as past: "The self...not only contains the deposit and totality of all past life, but is also a point of departure, the fertile soil from which all future life will spring. This premonition of futurity is as clearly impressed upon our innermost feelings as is the historical aspect."[7] He warns against taking this teleological aspect literally. We are not to think of archetypal images as having a ready-made meaning; rather we should think of them as indicators; otherwise we degrade them to being the mental equivalents of fortunetellers. The images present us with lifelines to be followed provisionally, for "life does not follow lines that are straight, nor lines whose course can be seen far in advance."[8]

It remains important, however, to recall that *we* give archetypal images this value, this significance. We are so easily led to separate the archetype from the psyche, to act as though we could freeze the ever-changing context in which the images appear.

Archetypal images are not absolute or unchanging. Indeed, when we treat them as if they are, we make them into stereotypes. Literally, a stereotype is a metal duplicate of a relief printing, the imprint taken from a mold. Stereotypes are rigid; they have lost the flexibility of the living archetype, the dynamism inherent in the image. Archetypes can become stereotypes when the images are no longer functioning as living images. Paradoxically, it is precisely when the socially or subjectively constructed aspect of the archetypal image is ignored, when the image is ontologized and given normative, universal sanction, that it may function as a stereotype. When this happens, we experience archetypal images as constrictive and confining, shaping us in ways that are not compatible with our ego-ideals or with our soul's deepest longings. For example, the hero archetype can be crippling when it becomes rigidified in this way, and the mother archetype can be oppressive to a modern woman in search of her soul.

Jung's way of working with archetypal images was not interpretation, translation into conceptual language, or reduction to some more abstract, general image, but what he called *amplification*—connecting the image to as many associated images as possible—and so, keeping us imagining. The point is to bring us in touch with their multiplicity, their fecundity, the sense of lively interconnectedness among them, not with their dependence on some common origin. Amplifying helps us get beyond our narrow personal selves and helps us "remember ourselves with a wider imagination."[9]

Archetypal images provide us with a "self-portrait" of the psyche and reveal its protean, many-faceted character. They provide energy and direction for the continual renewal of life. To attend to them is to honor the many parts of ourselves that enrich and deepen our lives but may also add complexity and bring confusion. There are aspects of ourselves that we don't see; if we do see them, we don't like them, or we don't know how to harmonize them with our more familiar aspects. Some of these aspects may appear during particular periods in our lives and then seem to disappear. Some feel familiar and friendly, others alien and frightening.

There is no and can be no definitive list of archetypes or archetypal images. After his break with Freud, Jung spoke of going in search of *the* myth that was living him, but actually, our lives are shaped by a *plurality* of myths, of archetypal images. To be informed by only one is to be in its thrall and to abdicate from the living tension of their interplay, for the different images do not always arrange themselves in a neatly ordered, hierarchical pantheon. Often we will find them to be in conflict with one another. Many women artists, for example, have spoken of themselves as torn between the archetypal images of woman and artist.

Jung said that there are as many archetypes as there are typical situations in life.[10] The book in which this essay first appeared[11] focused on a particular group of archetypal images that serve as mirrors of the self, images that help us see ourselves from many angles. The psyche is composed of various interacting subpersonalities that live within us. It showed how archetypal family figures—mother and father, orphaned child and benevolent grandfather—play active roles in our inner lives. It looked at the archetypal aspects of the various life stages through which we move as we experience childhood, youth, maturity, and old age. It also explored the archetypal dimension of the roles that define our social identities and shape our interactions with others.

Throughout, we examined personified images, how the self appears as a dramatic interaction among various personlike forms—the strutting self-important ego; the socially compliant persona; the elusive, fascinating anima. It looked not at youth but at puers and maidens, not at old age but at senexes and crones. None of these figures exists in isolation; each is in dramatic interaction with one another. As Jung put it, "In the unconscious the individual archetypes are not insulated from one another, but are in a state of contamination, of complete mutual interpenetration and fusion."[12] He sees that it is often "a well-nigh impossible undertaking to tear a single archetype out of the living tissue of the psyche."[13]

We need to learn to look at the images ecologically to see how they interpret and change one another. We probably all have had the experience of seeing how a situation in our lives or a figure in a dream changes its meaning as soon as we look at it through another myth or archetypal image. Often archetypal figures appear as part of a tandem: anima and animus, puer and senex, mother and son.[14] The anima appears differently when we link her with the animus rather than the shadow. Mothers appear differently to sons than to daughters, and being a daughter means something different to daughters than it does to mothers.

Thus there occurs an endless mirroring among the many different archetypal images. As in a funhouse or in Hesse's Magical Theater, these images reflect and shape one another, sometimes in distorted ways.

Sometimes we act as though Jung's description of the psyche provides us with a sacred map that cannot be redrawn. It seems essential to me to break out of the notion that an archetypal description issues in canonically fixed entities. Hillman's essay on the anima and Demaris Wehr's essay on the animus[15] radically challenge the received understanding of these figures; reflecting on figures such as that of the double and the friend, which Jung does not include, may help us recover a sense of psyche as an *activity,* the activity of image-making, and of archetypal images as not static things, but as patterns in motion.

Jung always recognized the importance of conscious, active involvement with the archetypal images, of opening up a dialogue between consciousness and the unconscious. This entails neither repudiating nor identifying with the image or the ego. The point of conscious engagement with archetypal images is not to strengthen the ego, but rather to relativize it, to come to see that ego, too, is an archetype. The archetypal perspective liberates us from viewing the ego's perspective as the only one. An archetypal view is inherently pluralistic, polytheistic, and thus inevitably critical of the dominance of the psyche by ego, hero, king, father. The very notion of archetype challenges the supremacy of the conscious, literal, fixed mind.

The point of archetypal images, like the point of myths, is not problem solving but "imagining, questioning, going deeper."[16] Archetypal images free us from identifying ourselves with our literal failures and successes or from seeing our lives as banal or trivial. The aim in attending to these images is to awaken us to a sense of our yet unrealized latent possibilities, to save us from our sense of isolation and meaninglessness. It is to open up our lives to renewal and reshaping.

Attending to the images creates a new bond between our personal lives and the collective experience of humankind. This accounts for the liberating effect so many people can testify to. As Jung said: "Life is crazy and meaningful at once. And when we do not laugh over the one aspect and speculate about the other, life is exceedingly drab, and everything is reduced to the littlest scale. There is then little sense and little nonsense either."[17]

There are many modes of access to the archetypal images that shape and have the power to help us reshape our lives. Among the situations that serve to constellate or activate such imagining are our own dreams and fantasies, our relationships with others, our moments of failure, and our moments of ecstasy. Sometimes a piece of literature come upon accidentally or a myth assiduously sought will arouse our own imagining, awaken us to analogies between our experience and that recorded in the discovered work. Sometimes reading an account of another's may open us to hitherto unexplored possibilities in our own lives. Sometimes it is just a matter of luck, of grace . .

Notes

1. C. G. Jung, *Memories, Dreams, Reflections* (New York: Random House, 1963) 392.

2. C. G. Jung, *Collected Works* (Princeton: Princeton University Press, 1953-1979) 8:213. (Hereafter Jung's *Collected Works* will be cited as *CW* followed by volume number and page number.)

3. Jolande Jacobi, *Complex, Archetype, Symbol* (Princeton: Princeton University Press, 1971) 50.

4. James Hillman, "An Inquiry into Image," *Spring 1977,* 70.

5. Jolande Jacobi, *The Psychology of C. G. Jung* (New Haven: Yale University Press, 1973) 45.

6. Jung, *CW* 9.1:58.

7. Jung, *CW* 8:190.

8. Jung, *CW* 8:286-289.

9. Hillman, "Image," 65.

10. Jung, *CW* 9.1: 48.

11. Christine Downing, ed., *Mirrors of the Self* (Los Angeles: Jeremy P. Tarcher, 1991).

12. Quoted in Jacobi, *Complex,* 65,6.

13. Jung, *CW* 9.1: 179.

14. James Hillman, *Puer Papers* (Irving, TX: Spring Publications, 1979) 13.

15. James Hillman, *Anima: The Anatomy of a Personified Notion* (Dallas: Spring Publications, 1985). Demaris Wehr, "Religious and Social Dimensions of Jung's Concept of the Anima," in Estella Lauter and Carol Rupprecht, eds., *Feminist Archetypal Theory* (Knoxville: University of Tennessee Press, 1985).

16. James Hillman, *ReVisioning Psychology* (New York: Harper & Row, 1975) 158.

17. Jung, *CW* 9.1:31.

9

Coming Home:
The Late-Life Lesbian

There are many different forms of lesbian love, each with its own etiology, mythology, and archetypal significance, each with its own gifts and dangers. In writing my book *Myths and Mysteries of Same-Sex Love*, I discovered how the Greek mythological traditions about Demeter, Hera, Athene, Artemis, and Aphrodite bring into view the beauty and power inherent in female bonds—and some of the darker, more fearful aspects as well. The stories in which these goddesses figure illumine the multidimensionality and diversity of the erotic relationships that exist between women.

In this essay I want to focus on the late-life lesbian. I choose this focus in part because her story is my story—though, actually, I know and celebrate that each of us who make our pull to women central in our lives only at midlife or later has her own individual story to tell. But there are many of us—and that in itself has implications that compel attentive consideration. For the prevalence of the pattern implies a radical critique of the dominant Jungian view of homosexuality, which sees it only as a phase preliminary to mature heterosexual adulthood. Reflection on this phenomenon may also reveal some of the most salient ways in which the archetypal meaning of women's love of women differs from that of men's love of men.

Looking back, I can say I have always loved women. My mother, of course. She and I drew very close when I was two and three and four. My father had left Germany because of Hitler, and it was several years before we were able to rejoin him in America (though he did pay us two brief visits during those years). My two younger siblings were born while he was gone. During that time we shuttled back and forth between the homes of my two sets of grandparents, both of whom were pressuring my mother to get a divorce, have an abortion, free herself of him. I was her only confidante. And though in surface ways she and I have sometimes been close, sometimes distant, in the intervening decades since those events the intensity and centrality of our bond have never been in question.

My sister, born just before we left Germany, has been my most important life-long same-sex peer, the primary foil for my discovery of who I am and of what it means to honor and love another as *other*. Other females I have loved include the girl friends with whom I was intensely bonded during latency and adolescence, the teachers on whom I had crushes, the young woman with whom I was sexually involved while I was in college, and the women friends of my early adult life, some of whom on rare occasions became lovers as well. I would also include the younger women who were formally my students and have often more truly been my teachers, and, perhaps more important than any of these, my daughter, who is herself a lesbian.

So I have always loved women, but I wasn't always fully conscious of how important a role this love has played in my life. I see that only retrospectively because of how central that love has become since I went through menopause a decade ago.

Odd, how the beginnings of my life as a lesbian and as a crone, a post-menopausal woman, have coincided. I had already begun to imagine that the love of women might become focal when, in my mid-forties after our children were grown, I'd left my husband and begun to live alone. But it hadn't happened then. I hadn't met the right her (or hadn't yet become the right she). But then suddenly, surprisingly, undeniably, she was there. I fell passionately in love. We moved toward one another gradually, gently, but from very early on I knew I hoped to spend the rest of my life with her, to make love with her and to share a home, to tell her my dreams and have her tell me about hers, to read her poetry before anyone else and to let her be my first reader. I was lucky. She had the same hope and longing (or nearly so)—and some of the same fears. We've been together ten years now, though I guess it depends when you start counting. We've known each other for ten; we began our courtship nine years ago, moved in together eight years ago, celebrated our commitment in a ceremony seven years ago, have just this year bought a home together on an island in the Pacific Northwest. In the process of planning how we'll shape our lives when we move there, we are discovering a whole new level of commitment and love.

But although it is true that on looking back I am now more aware of how I have always loved women, I do not mean that the years I spent in a heterosexual marriage or the years I spent ardently involved with male lovers were in some sense a mistake or a misunderstanding—or even a detour. They were as essential a part of my way as what I am living now. And I still love men—though I do not imagine I will ever make love with one again. I still feel drawn to them some-times, when I am with men who have been lovers and whom I still love, or in my dreams—but to respond to that pull might risk hurting the woman I love in a way I could not bear. So (strange for me to acknowledge, given my history) I sus-pect I will be monogamous for the rest of my life.

My turn to women is not a rejection of my heterosexual past nor of men, but a moving beyond, part of my moving consciously into the last third of my life. It feels like a return—to mother, to sister, to self—which may simply be a way of saying that I feel myself in touch with the archetypal dimensions of this turning. I see my turn to this woman as a turn not only to her but to women and in a sense also to "woman," and thus to self as woman. It feels numinous, sacred, necessary, almost fated. It feels like gift and blessing and culmination.

I see myself as now engaged in a continual circling and recircling around the images that have appeared and reappeared in my dreams and fantasies ever since I can remember—images of a numinous She awaiting my presence in a richly fur-nished secret chamber or in a dark underground cave. Honoring these images has become the central task of my life and now shapes not only my inner life but my outer life as well. What has come to matter is entering deeply into that life, not accumulating ever-new experiences. There is a sense in which being with the woman I love is not so much another episode to be added onto a narrative account of my life as it is a discovery of life as poetry, as shaped by the ever-recur-rent image of Her.

It also feels as though this turning to women, this returning, is not simply per-sonal or accidental, but rather that the pull to intense, focused, centralized engagement with women might become conscious and urgent for many women during their later years. In the post-menopausal phase of life, many of us seem to be pulled toward reflection and integration, to introspection and to a more intro-verted kind of intimacy. We long for a relationship with another drawn in the same direction and have learned that such another is much more likely to be female than male. We long for this relationship to involve us with all our being, body and soul, and so we hunger for something more than friendship, for love, for sexual as well as emotional intimacy. I know it was becoming conscious of this longing that prepared me for my present relationship.

I have always experienced sex as having a sacred aspect in its capacity to take one truly out of oneself, into an ecstatic meeting and merging—but in sexual intimacy with a woman the sacred dimension becomes for me almost overwhelm-ingly powerful. The entrance into another woman's body is the entrance into that sacred cave where Her presence is inescapable. As my fingers and tongue explore my beloved's vagina and approach her womb, I know myself to be returning to the place from which life emerges, the place from which I came and which I also carry within myself. This is an experience of *the* sacred, of the very source of life. Perhaps this is why women's turn to women may often happen later in life when it is time to engage life's deepest mysteries. Of course I know that many women experience their pull to women as having always been primary or even as the only form of sexual attraction they have experienced—but I would venture that the pull to women may have a specific soul meaning when it happens later.

That lovemaking among women may signify this reunion with the maternal source marks it as different from what lovemaking among men is likely to mean, and may relate to why most of the gay men I know feel they have always and inescapably been gay (whereas many lesbians I know tell their story with an emphasis on choice) and why most of my gay friends emphasize their sexual pull to men (whereas many lesbians emphasize emotional closeness).

As I reflect on my own experience, I am not at all sure how focal sexual preference is in my conviction that I, my soul, my body, are in a primary way now dedicated to being with women, and in particular with this woman. I imagine that among late-life lesbians there are many different responses to this question. In my own case, urgent, almost irresistible sexual attraction surely played a central part in pulling me into the relationship—in giving me the feeling *this* is the one with whom I want to spend the rest of my life, in giving me the courage to make a commitment to another when living alone had been so comfortable and when I knew so well that being in relationship is always challenging and difficult.

When my partner and I became lovers I was deeply moved by the discovery of how this was indeed a different sexuality—a truth that had somehow been less evident to me in my earlier sexual encounters with women. Now I learned not only how different it is to caress a woman's breasts and vulva and clitoris and to enter another's vagina with my fingers and lips than it is to make love to a man's body, but also how different it is to he caressed and entered by another whose body and desires are also female. The rhythms of touching are different, the place that orgasm plays in lovemaking is different, the taking the time to focus fully on one partner's longings and then the other's was different. When Adrienne Rich speaks of "a whole new poetry beginning here," I know what she means. I was learning a whole new language of love and, for someone who had thought of herself as an adept lover, this was not always easy. It involved unlearning; it seemed also to involve relearning almost forgotten but remembered-in-my-body modes of physical touch.

I also discovered that same-sex sex does not mean making love with another just like oneself. I learned to my initial confusion that what she desires is subtly different from what I desire, that what stirs her most deeply is different, that her rhythms are different. Over the years it has become clear that she (who is more than fifteen years younger than I) feels sexual longing more intensely and more frequently than do I, at least than do I now. This, too, is a surprise; I had always thought of myself as *so* sexual. .

As domestic rhythms have become more central to our relationship during our years of living together, I have come to question how pivotal the sex part is after all. Was it mostly just the path? The choice to be with her no longer seems exactly a sexual choice, at least not in the genital, orgasm sense of sex—though in the more expanded understanding of the polymorphousness of human sexuality, which I learned from Freud, perhaps it *is* a sexual choice. Physical closeness, emotional intimacy, trust in one another, the sense of being fully relaxed in one another's presence—these are so important. Because I recognize much of this as characteristic of what we think of as "infantile sexuality," I could agree that there is a regressive aspect to the sexual dimension of our relationship. Yet by "regressive" I would intend to invoke not pathology but once again the theme of return, recircling, homecoming. It seems evident to me that really we go forward, not back, that we turn to one another as the persons we've become through all our years of living. An inexpungeable nostalgia for our beginnings is not incommensurable with the recognition that we cannot literally return.

Of course, lesbian relationships, almost irrespective of how central sexuality is to any particular couple, are transgressive, socially-tabooed relationships. To enter such a relationship relatively late in life may entail the taking off of yet another persona, yet another mask. We may come, perhaps even more clearly than before, to know ourselves as we are apart from conventional gender roles. Our whole sense of personhood may be transformed as we discover the irrelevance to our self-understanding of conventional notions of masculinity or femininity. We are not simply making a different "object choice," but we experience ourselves differently. We may even discover that neither *heterosexual* nor *homosexual* nor even *bisexual* adequately describes what is now a much more fluid sense of our sexual identity, or that of others. I have come to question not only the masculine-feminine polarity but also the very notion of opposite sex and same sex. The "opposite" sex is not really opposite, but neither is a same-sex other the same.

Perhaps the *joy* of discovering a different, more subtle, perhaps more vitalizing kind of "difference" is especially vivid when it comes as a gift late in life. I certainly know how amazed I have been to discover how new my relationship with my partner still feels after ten years, how unknown and known she still seems, how much about ourselves and one another we keep discovering.

Of course, the turn of woman to woman inevitably reactivates the Mother-Daughter archetype. Women loving women may feel free to acknowledge our unstilled longing to nurture and be nurtured, to be mother and child, to be mothered and be daughtered—and to indulge those longings as best we can. But because of all we have learned elsewhere in our lives, we may be able to do so without being caught in fantasies of giving or being given a fully sufficient mothering, and without falling into a pattern of interaction where one is always the mother, the other always the child.

Nor is the Mother-Daughter archetype the only one that may inform our relationships. Just as salient is the archetype of Sister-Sister bonding, felt primarily in the ways we challenge one another to be all that we are capable of being and seek to engage one another in ways that are truly egalitarian, mutual, reciprocal. I feel the Sister archetype at work in my partner's demand that I be there toward her as all that I am, that I risk sharing my powerfulness and my vulnerability, my desire and my fear, my appreciation and my anger—and that I encourage her to do the same. Almost every lesbian couple I know struggles to find ways to cultivate intimacy and yet respect one another's otherness and need for some distance, some life apart from the relationship. We struggle to find ways to sister one another well, to bless rather than resent the differences, competition, and conflict that inevitably emerge as the "archetypal haze" induced by the initial hegemony of the Mother archetype begins to dissipate.

Our relationship is certainly not all harmony and fusion. I know it would not satisfy my soul needs if it were. Yet I also know that I usually don't like at all the particular ways in which disharmony manifests. I still fear her anger, and my own. I wish she didn't envy me my worldly accomplishments and recognitions, didn't resent my involvements with my children, didn't fear that I might someday after all abandon her. There are times when the demand that I fully and honestly open my soul to her seems to ask for more than I can give. At times I experience her as a "soul-snatcher" and do everything in my power to protect myself from her. But it is precisely through these only half-welcomed challenges that the relationship activates the archetype of the Self. I am brought into touch with so much that is me and yet unfamiliar and almost inaccessible. All truly vital relationships do this, but I believe a relationship with an intimate same-sex other does so in an especially powerful way. For she seems to know my potentialities and my defenses almost as though from within. She can get through to a hitherto impregnable core. I had not consciously wanted that from this relationship, had felt satisfied with the me I knew, had not imagined that so late in life I could be so flooded with renewed life energy.

Indeed, part of what makes this turn to her feel like a homecoming is the heightened sense of energy, the experience of renewal, that has accompanied it. The sense of being in the world in a new way is comparable to what Jung says happens when we integrate the "transcendent function" and move beyond our familiar reliance on feeling or thinking or whatever has been our dominant function and respond instead on the basis of our inferior functions.

Yet, like all relationships, this late-life lesbian attachment has its "shadow" side. One aspect of this is simply the inevitable "coming down" from the elation that characterized its beginnings, the ebbing of the exhilaration that seems almost always to accompany a re-engagement with the archetypal. I call this "learning again about finitude." Certainly I have had to learn again the limits of any relationship to fulfill me, have had to learn again to rebalance the pulls of intimacy and solitude, love and work, or, as we might say, of Aphrodite and Artemis, Aphrodite and Athene. More painfully, I have had to learn anew the limits of my capacity to change, even when I might wish I could be different in the ways my partner wishes I were different. I am stubborn, resistant, fearful, and controlling. I am me, and though still in process and profoundly affected by this woman I love, I am in some ways stuck with being *this* me—and stuck, too, with *this* her (for I could imagine her as different, too!).

In a deeper sense, the shadow side of the homecoming stems from the fact that everything that I consciously attend to during this last third of life becomes part of my preparation for death. My partner and I have known this ever since we first came together. I remember so vividly how, when she first realized that I wasn't already making plans to leave after our first real moment of intimacy, but rather hoped to be with her for the rest of my life, she cried out, "But then you'll die and leave me anyway." We laughed, but it is likely to be true—not for a long while, probably, given the longevity of my parents, but someday nonetheless. That recognition, of course, would very likely enter into any late-life relationship and perhaps especially into a relationship where there is a significant disparity of age. But I believe there is more to it than that. I believe that there is an intrinsic connection between my coming to love this woman and my awareness of death's approach, though I did not see this until I was already deeply in love with her.

For directing my love to a woman feels like a homecoming in the most profound of all ways. My turning to her, this very particular, flawed, beautiful woman whom I love, signifies, among so much else, a return to the womb that gave us birth and which also welcomes us when we die, a return to earth, to Her, and to all those human women who in some way serve Her and represent Her.

10

Bruno Bettelheim: A Wounded Healer

I met Bruno Bettelheim only once, at the 1985 conference in Phoenix celebrating "One Hundred Years of Psychotherapy." My most vivid memory of those few days is of an evening session planned as a dialogue between one of Freud's grand-daughters and a grandson of Jung's. Because Sophie Freud-Lowenstein was kept away by a delayed flight, Margo Adler, Alfred Adler's granddaughter, attending the conference as a journalist, was talked into being part of the panel, as was Bettelheim. When Margo explained that she knew almost nothing about her famous grand-father who had died years before her birth, Bettelheim explained to her that there was really no way her father could have communicated what his father's life had been like, so different was the Vienna of the early decades of this century from contemporary America. I remember how moved I was by the gen-tleness with which Bettelheim tried to explain this to her and by the evident nos-talgia he felt for the world of his own early years. This may have touched me even more than it did others there, for my parents are of the same generation as he and they, too, were forced by Hitler to leave their motherland as young adults. I had so often heard them speak of the incommensurability of their lives there and their lives here. In the midst of all the American optimism about the efficacy of psy-chotherapy, I also deeply appreciated Bettelheim's witnessing of how a commit-ment to healing need not occlude recognition of how much human pain is incurable.

I realize, too, that I was predisposed to respect and like the man. His book, *Freud and Man's Soul,* has been particularly important to me, because it lent authority to my own long-standing attempts to communicate to my American students how important to understanding Freud an appreciation of his deep immersion in classical culture and German literature is and how different the Freud available to his German readers is from Freud as one comes to know him through the English translation. Bettelheim's *The Uses of Enchantment* had moved me in part because it reminded me of how during our first years in America my mother would read to us children from the well-worn copy of Grimms' fairytales that her own mother had once read from to her. I remember how impressed I was on first reading Bettelheim's early theoretical book *Symbolic Wounds: Puberty Rites and the Envious Males* by his then unprecedented recognition of the importance of male womb-envy. Recently as I have begun working on a book about my own relation to the Holocaust, I have found it important to lay Bettelheim's reflections next to all the many other accounts composed by survivors. I own but I think never read any of Bettelheim's books about autism, though I do remember his speaking about his work at the Orthogenic School one morning during the Phoenix conference and being followed on the podium by R. D. Laing. Bettelheim had left a handkerchief on the lectern and when Laing began to pick it up, he shouted, "Don't touch it. You'll catch my germs." To which Laing replied, "I'd be honored."

So when Bettelheim died in 1990, I was as dismayed as any other admirer. Not by the suicide which, coming after his wife's death and his own increasing loneliness and isolation and incapacity, struck me as entirely compatible with his life, but by the sudden appearance of accusations by former co-workers and patients that Bettelheim had abused, both emotionally and physically, the children entrusted to his care. As I sought to understand how much I wanted to resist letting this new information in, I realized that like many others I had invested Bettelheim with the aura of the healer archetype and that it was painful to see him reduced to ordinary mortal size. My own earlier difficulty in reconciling an idealized image of Carl Jung with the facts of his anti-Semitism, his initial blindness to Hitler's evil, his chauvinism, his self-indulgent exploitation of his wife and mistress had taught me how our longing to find someone on to whom we might project the healer archetype leads to idolization—and then inevitably to demonization. I had also learned how easily being seen by others in terms of this archetype can lead to an inflated sense of identification with it and to an uneasy awareness of the falsity of the identification. I had a hunch that understanding the ways in which this archetype had functioned in how others had responded to Bettelheim, both positively and negatively, and how it had entered into his own self-understanding might enable me to put the new information into some kind of meaningful context, but knew I didn't really know enough to do so.

Thus I welcomed the opportunity to read the two very different recent biographies devoted to Bettelheim: Richard Pollak's *The Creation of Dr. B* (Simon &

Schuster, 1987) and Nina Sutton's *Bettelheim: A Life and a Legacy* (Basic Books, 1996).

Pollak's brother, a patient of Bettelheim's in the mid-1940s, died while on vacation from the school by falling through a chute in a barn floor as the two boys were playing hide and seek. The book reads like a personal vendetta, inspired by Pollak's still smoldering anger at Bettelheim's failure to heal his brother and at Bettelheim's laying the responsibility for his brother's illness on their mother's rejection of him as an infant—and perhaps (though this is never acknowledged) by Pollak's own unconscious guilt at his own role in his brother's death. Pollak seems determined to help others see through the façade to the "real" Bettelheim, the charlatan. My own title for Pollak's book (whose every chapter focuses on a deception) is "Secrets and Lies." He has no interest in trying to understand Bettelheim from within. He shows no appreciation of psychoanalysis, no real understanding of the unconscious, little sense of how different the Vienna of Bettelheim's early years is from his own American world. Indeed, at times the book seems as much an attack on Freud, on psychoanalysis *tout court,* on the general tendency in the 1940s and 1950s to see autism as a developmental disorder, as on Bettelheim—though it certainly highlights the accusations directed against Bettelheim as an abusive therapist and as someone whose success depended on false credentials. Pollak seems never to try to see what might lie behind the accusations or behind Bettelheim's irruptions of anger or his exaggeration of his past accomplishments.

Sutton's deep immersion in European culture and sophisticated understanding of psychoanalysis and her recognition that Bettelheim was "a man from another age, another world" enables her to approach his life with the human empathy Pollak lacks. Her prologue expresses her own shock at the revelations about Bettelheim's deceptions and abusiveness that emerged for the first time immediately after his death and her determination to understand how to integrate *this* Bettelheim with the noble healer whose life she had thought she would be exploring. She assumes that neither is the *real* Bettelheim, that her task is to uncover the relation between the two, to apprehend the complexity of "the flesh and blood man with his little lies and major bouts of rage." She comes to believe that the disclosures bring into view not only Bettelheim's weaknesses but also what made him a truly great therapist. My title for her book is "Surviving," for it seems dedicated to helping us understand how Bettelheim's struggles to overcome his lifelong lack of self-love and deep-seated pessimism underlie both his accomplishments and his failings. Yet Sutton's very ability to uncover the unconscious roots of Bettelheim's more troubling behavior, to see the whole story in relation to him, may lead her to forgive Bettelheim too much. She recognizes that the charges, whether or not true, are part of the Bettelheim story, since they arose in response to his relationship to children entrusted to his care, but evinces little interest in the suffering that lay behind the accusations. That is, she sees Bettelheim's woundedness but seems not fully to acknowledge the wounds he inflicted.

Both books speak of Bettelheim's assent to the central theme of Hans Vaihinger's "As If" philosophy: that we must live by fictions to make life meaningful and bearable. For Pollak this was a way of rationalizing a life of dissembling, for Sutton it explains how Bettelheim managed to live a meaningful life despite the depth of the depression that haunted him throughout his life and the deeply pessimistic worldview that he shared with many of his Viennese contemporaries. Both authors describe the lifelong impact of Bettelheim's mother's initial rejection of her ugly infant son: no matter how successful he became, Bettelheim continued to believe he was ugly, small, and Jewish. Both note how Bettelheim's early years were colored by the household secrecy surrounding the syphilis his father contracted when Bruno was four. Both communicate how young Bruno feared he was responsible for the oppressive cloud that hung over his childhood home. Pollak suggests weakness of character kept the adult Bettelheim from leaving these childhood wounds behind. Sutton quotes Bettelheim's own observation that "those who single-mindedly devote themselves to making this a better world for children are usually motivated by their own unhappy childhoods."

His father's death in 1926 forced Bettelheim to drop out of university and take over his father's lumber business. If not for that, he later observed, "I could have had the life I imagined"; the life, we might say, that he *did* imagine when after his arrival in America he presented himself as having impressive university credentials and as an intimate of the circle around Freud. In actuality, although in 1936 he returned to the university to study the philosophy of art and was one of the last Viennese Jews to receive a Ph.D., he never earned the degrees in art history and psychology he later claimed. It is unclear when Bettelheim's unremitting depression led him to enter psychoanalysis and how long his analysis lasted, but in all probability it was for no more than a year or two (though he had been an ardent, careful reader of Freud since early adolescence). In his later years Bettelheim confessed that although this analysis provided him with insight about the sources of his depression, it did not issue in a full working through of his emotional problems. Yet Sutton believes that despite its brevity his analysis taught him the real mystery at the heart of the analytic process: the healing power of transference.

Bettelheim's later embellishment of his Viennese credentials led him to claim that it was he rather than his first wife Gina who took care of the autistic girl that lived in their home in Vienna for the seven years before the *Anschluss*. Not surprisingly, Bettelheim's story about applying for psychoanalytical training and having Freud himself appear to say that his background in art made him an ideal candidate turns out to be pure fabrication. Like so many of his stories, it represents the kind of thing that *could* have happened (Freud did believe that a background in art and literature would more adequately prepare one to be an analyst than medical training) and should have happened had Bettelheim's education not been disrupted.

Gina reports that although even as a young man Bettelheim was always seeking to make an impression, he didn't start lying until after he came to America, until after his time in Dachau and Buchenwald. Bettelheim was imprisoned by the Nazis simply because he was a Jew and had passed up opportunities to leave Vienna because of his responsibility for his sister and widowed mother. Because his family could afford to bribe the Nazis, he had access to extra food rations and relatively light work assignments while in the camps and was eventually released. After his release he obtained an American visa because of the intervention of influential Americans (though, despite his later claims, Eleanor Roosevelt played no role). As Sutton notes, Bettelheim's experience in the camps gave birth to Bettelheim the psychoanalyst, for he there discovered the strength of his will to live. In order to maintain a sense of his own identity and autonomy, to establish a kind of control in a situation where he had no real control, where he was by definition an object not a subject, he deliberately became an observer of his own reactions and of those around him. In the camps he also quickly learned that survival required one to lie. As Sutton puts it, "The closed barbaric world of the camp provided the ideal breeding ground for those larger-than-life stories that can help one stay alive." Bettelheim's co-prisoners later testified to how the stories he told them about his earlier life gave them hope—and how his listening to their stories confirmed them in their own sense of identity.

After his liberation Bettelheim sought to make sense of his experience and to share what he had learned from it. Wanting to inform Americans about the horrors of the concentration camps, he initially found that no one wanted to listen. Pollak seems to hold it against Bettelheim that though he had a relatively easy time and short stay in what were after all only concentration camps (rather than extermination camps like Auschwitz), his 1943 essay "Individual and Mass Behavior in Extreme Situations," the first account of life in the camps by a survivor, immediately led him to be seen as an expert on the Holocaust. Of course

Pollak is right to indicate how angry after the war those who had been at Auschwitz or whose family had died there were at Bettelheim's presumption to speak about *their* experience, so radically different from his, and by his unwillingness to modify his views in response to later reports about the psychology of those who survived in the extermination camps. Sutton is more interested in how Bettelheim's survivor guilt helps explain why, once given the mantle of authority, he couldn't let it go. She believes that when the corpses and gas chambers appeared, Bettelheim's inner feeling that he had in some way cheated to gain the role of expert retriggered a desperate battle against his lifelong feeling of being a fraud.

Sutton sees how when he came to America Bettelheim must have felt forced to create a whole new life for himself and how this inevitably left scars on a man who so much desired to be admirable and could not stand the idea that he was not. Completely broke when he came to this country, he was thrilled by the opportunity to participate in a University of Chicago study of secondary education because (even though an unpaid position) it might lead to the university connection he had always wanted—and did indeed lead to several years of teaching (first art history and eventually philosophy, psychology, and German literature as well) at a small women's college outside Chicago. Later Bettelheim reluctantly agreed to become director of the University of Chicago's Orthogenic School, although what he had really wanted was not to run a home for emotionally disturbed children but to teach at the university. Yet it is easy to see how his camp experience shaped Bettelheim's determination to provide not just custodial care but to make the school an outstanding center for treatment and study. The premise of Bettelheim's "milieu therapy" was that just as the extraordinarily cruel environment of the camps could destroy human autonomy, so an extraordinarily benevolent environment might heal the severely wounded. Bettelheim's survivor guilt led to a longing to help the helpless and to his conviction that this entailed being able to imagine what the children were feeling, understanding what their behavior *meant*, how it expressed their suffering.

Yet Pollak, who sees the school not as a healing but as an abusive environment, vividly describes the school as dominated by a "climate of fear." Although Bettelheim always said that physical punishment of any kind was completely forbidden at the school, Pollak recounts numerous instances not only of Bettelheim's cruel verbal abuse but of his slapping patients, hitting them with a belt, beating their bare bottoms. He reports that one former patient complained that Bettelheim had pulled her naked out of the shower and beaten her in front of dorm-mates, that he fondled her breasts (though Pollak admits he was unable to corroborate her testimony and that most persons he interviewed, even those otherwise highly critical of Bettelheim, doubted its truth). Even so, the other accusations are daunting enough, even after we take account of Sutton's attempts to put them in context. She reminds us that Bettelheim's defenders were not free to say what they knew about the psychological history of the accusers and notes that all of these accusers were from the generation of patients Bettelheim had abandoned by retiring. She notes how the accusations were amplified by those who see all psychoanalysis as a fraudulent endeavor. Admitting that Bettelheim could be cruelly sarcastic, that (especially in the later years) he could fall into rages, she relates this to his conscious assumption of the role of "Big Bad Wolf," his sense of the need for a strong authority figure in the permissive atmosphere of a school where there were no drugs, no physical restraints, no isolation rooms. But I was struck by the power of a former patient's observation: "One of deepest hurts at the school was constant belief that Bettelheim's brutality was therapy." Because Sutton never really discusses the more troubling episodes Pollak mentions (including the problematic aspects of Bettelheim's taking on the dual role of personal therapist and employer with some of his counselors), the disquiet his presentation evokes is not fully assuaged.

The frustrations involved in trying to work with the autistic children Bettelheim began admitting to the school in 1955 seem to have sparked his increasingly uncontrollable rages. He clearly hoped that an unrelievedly beneficent environment could heal even these most seriously disturbed children; a decade later when he had discovered how little he could really do for them he underwent a severe mid-life depression. Sutton concludes that some of the autistic children at the school made real progress while others didn't, but that all were better off than they would have been elsewhere because under Bettelheim's care they were treated as suffering human beings. But she realizes that this was not enough for Bettelheim who needed to believe in his healing powers and therefore exaggerated his successes. In writing about his autistic patients he couldn't resist making a better story out of a good one. By so doing he reached a wide, popular audience and quickly became viewed as the national expert on autism. His catchy titles *(Love is Not Enough, Truants from Life, The Empty Fortress)* helped, as did his richly detailed anecdotal style. He said he wanted to offer hope, but I think Pollak is right in accusing him of offering false hope to the parents of autistic children.

Once Bettelheim began embellishing, exaggerating, lying, he didn't seem able to stop. Pollak and Sutton both ask why those who could have challenged his stories never did so while he was alive, for their silence seems to have encouraged him to continue elaborating his stories. Some of those Holocaust survivors the biographers interviewed explained that one doesn't denounce a fellow exile, especially one who was in the camps, but it seems that no one ever directly confronted Bettelheim himself either. The hesitation on the part of the former patients to speak out earlier is easier to understand; many seem to have felt that there had been no chance of their being believed until after so much negative media attention was given to Bettelheim's suicide (which many of them experienced as a betrayal).

Both authors also suggest that Bettelheim *wanted* to be found out, that, as Sutton puts it, while covering his tracks, he left a trail of white pebbles that made it relatively easy to uncover the actual path (though during his lifetime he seems to have feared that should his "dark secrets," his lies about his past, come out it could destroy the school). It is as if, though he didn't believe it could ever happen, Bettelheim still deeply longed to be loved for who he really was. Sutton relates to Bettelheim's fraudulence as primarily an inner problem. She sees him as so haunted from childhood by a feeling of fraud that the more he appeared great and beautiful to others the more he felt small and ugly inside. That is, she understands Bettelheim's most troublesome behavior as he sought to understand that of his patients—as expressions of his suffering. I find her view of Bettelheim as someone early wounded in his capacity for self-love and obsessed with his ugliness persuasive and moving. She reminds us that Bettelheim recognized that his analysis had helped him master his suffering intellectually but not on a deeper emotional level. She sees how such unresolved feelings shaped his whole life and how powerfully they emerged again at the end of his life. His work had forced him to be optimistic; without it nothing had power to do so. "The old wounds and obsessions had not healed, despite a lifetime spent trying to help others." After his wife's death, when he no longer felt sustained by her love, his depression and his deep-seated pessimism got the upper hand. He came to believe that one never really gets over the experience of having been in the concentration camps, an experience that makes one lose one's belief in humankind.

My own understanding of Bettelheim based on what these biographies reveal is close to Sutton's but subtly different. Without ever directly invoking the healer archetype she communicates how possessed Bettelheim was by it, how painful it was for him to confront the gap between the magician he believed he should be and the actual disappointing results. Her claim that in writing about his camp experience Bettelheim had fulfilled his mission by transforming his sufferings into a useful message suggests the kind of transformation associated with the mythic figure of the *wounded* healer. Often in myth the wounded healer seems really to be a once-wounded but now-healed healer but sometimes he appears as a still-wounded healer. In Greek mythology, for instance, the healer Cheiron suffers from an incurable wound so unremittingly painful that he comes to regret an immortality from which he cannot escape. It is as a still wounded healer that I have come to see Bruno Bettelheim.

I believe that Sutton sees him thus as well. Her whole book seems dedicated to helping us see how Bettelheim's wounds were the source of his gifts and also of his limitations. She understands and she forgives. To her picture I would only want to add that I see Bettelheim's wounds as also the source of real wounds he inflicted on others. To me it is somehow not quite enough to speak of his "limitations." I see him rather as a wounded *and wounding* healer—and as a reminder to all of us of how closely allied are the power to heal and to wound.

11

Hope Lives When People Remember

◆

Simon Wiesenthal's Fight Against Holocaust Amnesia

Most of us know Simon Wiesenthal as a Holocaust survivor who has dedicated his life to identifying, locating, and bringing to justice Nazi war criminals, most prominently Adolf Eichmann. We may have read his books, among them *The Murderers Among Us* and *Justice, Not Vengeance* or visited the Simon Wiesenthal Center in Los Angeles with its powerful depiction of the rise of Nazi terror and the horrors of the Holocaust and its equally compelling representations of contemporary racial injustice in the United States and of present-day genocides in, for example, Cambodia and Bosnia. Wiesenthal has written of how the years of suffering during the Shoah inflicted deep wounds on his faith in the existence of justice, how he came to feel that "God was on leave." Like Elie Wiesel he seems to have emerged from the camps believing that God now depends on us and to have taken on the role of assuring that justice can still prevail, by working to publicly confront and condemn Nazi leaders in hiding.

We may not have realized—certainly I didn't until I read Hella Pick's biography, *Simon Wiesenthal: A Life In Search Of Justice* (Boston: Northeastern University Press, 1996)—the degree to which Wiesenthal is a figure of controversy, the depth of antagonism he is capable of arousing. This overall sympathetic account nevertheless forces us to recognize how Wiesenthal's combative personality, his love of public acclaim, his delight in controversy, his vanity and his aggressiveness, his need to act as the solitary hero, have led him to play a central role in the distasteful battles for ownership of the Holocaust. Although many of the accusations laid against him—that he collaborated with the Nazis during the Second

World War, that he worked for the CIA against Communist regimes in eastern Europe during the Cold War—are clearly groundless, nevertheless his exaggerated version of the role he played in bringing Adolf Eichmann to justice has won him many enemies in Israel and within the World Jewish Congress.

No one doubts his dedication, his sense of mission, but many question the obsessiveness with which he chose a life permanently tethered to the Holocaust, as though only thus could he justify his survival. He wants so desperately to be accepted as an authentic Jewish hero even his wife, reportedly, begged him after he turned 75 to lead a more normal life. Nevertheless, she accepted, I am not married to a man; I am married to thousands or maybe millions of dead.

In 1941 when the Nazis invaded Lvov in the Soviet-controlled part of Poland, Wiesenthal was a young architect living with his mother and the high-school classmate he had recently married. His 63-year-old ailing mother was soon sent to an extermination camp; she and all his other relatives were killed in the Holocaust. He and his wife were moved to a concentration camp outside the city, and separated. Wiesenthal says that his rejection of the notion of collective guilt comes from the decent treatment he received in this camp. He saw his wife almost daily. Although his initial forced labor assignment involved working on the railroad, he was soon reassigned to work as a draftsman. He was obviously a privileged inmate who established a kind of friendship with his boss and thus won access to information which he was able to convey to the non-Communist Polish underground. This also made it possible for him to help his wife get out of the camp with false papers. Although they had no further contact until after the war and Wiesenthal assumed she had died, she actually made her way to Warsaw where, not recognized as Jewish, she was assigned to work in a gun factory with other Polish women. Wiesenthal himself escaped for a time and joined up with a group of partisans but was then recaptured in June 1944 and spent the last year of the war in several different camps. Even after some of the camps had been liberated, the killing continued in those that remained.

The end of the war found him in Mauthausen, the very last camp to be liberated. He says that his life there was saved by a Polish orderly who gave him extra food. Though an SS guard taunted him that no one would ever believe him if he told the truth, Wiesenthal began keeping a list of perpetrators while he was still in the camp, as though he already had a sense of how he would want to dedicate his life after the war—although he also already wanted to record the names of Nazis who had behaved well. Immediately after his release, he attached himself to the U.S. war crimes commission, hoping to help in the capture of Nazis fleeing from Mauthausen before they reached the West. But he soon discovered that the hunt for Nazis was already compromised by the nascent Cold War and that the West's search for intelligence agents and scientists they could enlist on their side, and for rebuilding West Germany against the Soviets, took priority over deNazification. Thus from very early on he was persuaded of the need for private initiative. He established his own information network by going to the displaced persons camps and asking the inmates for names of perpetrators. There he found his wife; their only child, a daughter, was born in September 1945. His wife really wanted to move on but was trapped by Wiesenthal's obsession.

Wiesenthal saw himself not so much as a Nazi-hunter but rather as a fighter for justice against Holocaust amnesia. If you no longer believe in God, he said, then the focus must be on earthly justice. He believed that the most important consequence of the Eichmann trial was that it showed Israelis that the victims of the Holocaust had not been cowards; that they had no chance of escaping the Nazi genocide program. He wanted to help Jews overcome their guilt at having allowed the Holocaust to happen to them. Thus Wiesenthal had no interest in restitution for the victims; all his energy was directed to bringing the perpetrators to justice. Because he believed in the possibility of educating humanity against the perpetration of the worst crimes, he dedicated his life to the project of seeing that no Nazi murderer would get to die in peace—so that the murderers of tomorrow would know that they would have no peace. He believed that punishment had to be individual, not collective. It was equally important to him that the "righteous Gentiles" who had actively opposed the Nazis and helped victims escape extermination be recognized—and also that even Jewish collaborators should be brought to justice. Because he wanted the Nazi criminals to be brought before courts of law, he was vehemently opposed to Israel's underground tactics, as he was also against capital punishment.

It was, however, the hunt for one particular perpetrator, Adolf Eichmann, that is both the source of Wiesenthal's fame and of the controversy surrounding that fame. Wiesenthal was clearly obsessed with Eichmann, with trying to understand how this ordinary man who loved his family had become a mass exterminator. His hunt for Eichmann began in the 1940s when others were not yet involved: the Americans were more interested in assuring political stability in West Germany than in pursuing Nazis, the Israelis more concerned about establishing their new nation. These delays allowed many of the most prominent Nazis to escape from Europe. Wiesenthal studied their escape routes; he was able to prevent Eichmann's family from having him declared dead (and thus protected from later prosecution). When Wiesenthal learned that Eichmann was in Argentina, he didn't have the resources for the pursuit. He continues to believe that if others had been willing then to trust his research, Eichmann could have been captured in Argentina in the 1950s, but admits that he was not that involved with the actual capture a decade later and that he knew nothing about the Mossad's kidnapping plan. It is probably true that he has embellished his participation even in the earlier search, but also true that his archive of survivor testimony was of real help to the prosecution's preparation for the trial. (It seems not at all surprising that Mossad resents Wiesenthal getting so much of the acclaim, especially in the several popular films [starring Ben Kingsley and Laurence Olivier] that distorted and glamorized his role. "He is a great enough man without invading other people's territory.")

The trial did succeed in arousing more public interest in the hunt for Nazi perpetrators, especially for some of the more prominent Nazis like Stangl (the commandant of the extermination camps at Sobibor and Treblinka) and Mengele—though the Israelis turned out to be not all that interested; for them the Eichmann trial had served its purpose. And Wiesenthal's wife, too, felt enough had been accomplished; she thought they might settle in Israel where he could work with Yad Vashem. But Wiesenthal had no interest in being part of a bureaucratic effort; he established his own Documentation Center in Vienna, where he compiled a list of 22,000 perpetrators, only 1,000 of whom were ever brought to trial. He became profoundly disheartened by how many Nazis had succeeded in reentering public life—and by how many of the trials ended in verdicts of "not guilty." From early on Wiesenthal emphasized that Jews had not been the only targets of the Nazis' genocidal ambitions and took particular account of the suffering of the gypsies—a view not at all popular among Jews who often wanted to insist on the uniqueness of Jewish suffering.

The other most common association with the name of Simon Wiesenthal is the "Museum of Tolerance" at the Simon Wiesenthal Center in Los Angeles. This is really an independent institution that uses Wiesenthal's name to promote its fundraising but also contributes some of its revenue to Wiesenthal's own center in Vienna. The Hebrew name for the museum is *Beit Ha'Shoah*, "House of the Holocaust"—but the museum has always aimed at putting forward a universal and future-directed message, and to focus on the contradictions between the American dream and the painful realities exemplified by, for instance, the murder of Martin Luther King and the 1992 riots in Los Angeles. The exhibits are designed to engage the mind and the imagination of visitors, to help them confront their own prejudices and enlist them in the struggle for the eradication of hatred. The museum is dedicated to support Wiesenthal's deepest conviction: *hope lives when people remember.*

But for Wiesenthal himself his most significant contribution may well be his little book, *Sunflower*. The book centers on a memory from his own Holocaust experience—or at least purports to do so. The recalled event was not included in his earliest memoir accounts of his life during the Nazi period; Wiesenthal first mentioned it in his testimony at Yad Vashem when he was in Jerusalem in 1961 for the Eichmann trial. From then on he told it often, as a stunningly effective way of keeping the memory of the Holocaust alive by focusing on an event that raises deeply perplexing questions about guilt and forgiveness. When pushed about the accuracy of the story, Wiesenthal would acknowledge the haziness of the memory, its hallucinatory quality—and that in his telling of it he had been deeply influenced by those Hasidic tales of encounters between a *rebbe* and his followers and their intertwining of the ordinary and the extraordinary.

Teaching Stories, like the parables of Jesus, the mondos of Zen Buddhism, the tales of Sufi and Hasidic masters, play a central role in many religious traditions. They differ from proverbs because they present us not with typically recurring, general moralistic truths but with a distinctive story set in a particular time and place. They thus communicate that it is in the everyday world that ultimate issues arise and that ultimate decisions are demanded. In these stories which often take form of a dialogue between a teacher and a seeker, the teacher's response may be surprising, puzzling, upsetting. We have a feeling that something is missing that pulls us in and we are left to puzzle out what this story might mean to us. The story may begin to make us feel that it's about us in some odd way. The story itself is somehow transformative, a word-EVENT open to many different responses. The point seems to be that there is no set right response but that we—each one of us in our individual being-here—are being addressed, challenged.

Wiesenthal's *The Sunflower: On The Possibilities And Limits Of Forgiveness* (Schocken, 1997), his account of an encounter between a concentration camp prisoner and a dying Nazi soldier, is a powerful contemporary example of this genre. The book, first published in French in 1969, appeared in English in 1976 accompanied by a symposium of responses. It has recently been re-issued, again with a symposium, although many of the original responses have been omitted and thirty-two new ones added. The new edition testifies to the continued power of Wiesenthal's tale to inspire passionate debate.

The Sunflower reports on an experience Wiesenthal had, not with one of the policy makers, but with a member of the Nazi rank and file. One day on an assignment that takes him outside the concentration camp in which he is imprisoned, he passes a military cemetery and sees that on each grave a boldly waving sunflower has been planted. He sees butterflies going from flower to flower, conveying light and messages to the soldiers buried beneath the soil, connecting them to the living world. He has a sense of how different the death that is waiting for him and his comrades, unritualized burial in a mass grave, will be. The prisoners are brought to a military hospital to clean up the defiled refuse from the operating rooms; he recognizes the building as formerly the town's technical high-school, which he had once attended as a student.

Suddenly a nurse calls him out of the group and asks, "Are you a Jew? Follow me." She leads him into what had formerly been the Dean's office that now holds but one hospital bed. On the bed lies a soldier; his head is completely bandaged; his bloodless hands lie lifeless above the coverlet. The whole scene feels like a dream. The sick man whispers that he knows he's close to death. Wiesenthal feels no pity; he has seen too many prisoners just as young left to die untended and knows this one will get a sunflower. The man says he needs to talk about an experience that is torturing him, a crime he committed a year ago, otherwise he cannot die in peace. He needs to talk to "a Jew." In his agitation, he drops a letter from his mother that he's been holding in his hands. Wiesenthal picks it up and returns it to him and thinks about how he will never again hold a letter from his own mother who he knows has already been murdered by the Nazis.

The soldier tells Wiesenthal that his name is Karl; that though he had been raised as a Catholic by parents who distrusted the Nazis, he had voluntarily joined the Hitler Youth and then the SS. "I was not born a murderer," he says, and then, "My mother must never know what I did. She must not lose her image of a good son." Wiesenthal wonders, "Why do I have to listen to this? Why not send for a priest who could help him die in peace?" He wants to get away. Nevertheless, he brushes a buzzing fly away from Karl's face and continues to listen.

Finally Karl is able to relate the scene that troubles him. "I cannot die without coming clean. This is my confession." His group of soldiers had been ordered to force a large group of Jews into a house, to set it on fire and to shoot any who sought to escape. Karl himself had shot a family—a young man and his wife and their child—who had tried to jump out of one of the burning house's windows. Wiesenthal thinks of a young child he remembers from the ghetto, the last Jewish child he had seen alive.

Karl continues, "In the last hours of my life you are with me. I do not know who you are. I only know that you are a Jew and that is enough. I needed to talk about this to a Jew and beg forgiveness from him." Wiesenthal feels that there is true repentance in Karl's confession. "Two men who had never known each other had been brought together for a few hours by fate. One asks the other for help, but the other was himself helpless and able to do nothing for him…I was in no mood to help him. I kept silent…. At last I made up my mind and without a word I left the room."

The next day the nurse tries to give Wiesenthal the dead man's things but he refuses. Several years after the end of the war he visits Karl's mother. She acknowledges knowing some of the terrible things the Nazis had done, but holds on to her faith that her son had not taken part in them. Wiesenthal refuses to confirm her attestations, but doesn't tell her the truth either. He again keeps silent.

Wiesenthal ends his account with a question. "Was my silence right or wrong?…What would you have done?"

The second half of the printed book, the "Symposium," presents us with almost fifty responses, but, of course, the question is also addressed to US. The published responses help amplify the issue, but they don't protect us from having to respond for ourselves.

The episode clearly didn't end for Wiesenthal when he walked out of the door. The evening of his return to the camp, he tries to talk about it with his two closest friends, the skeptical secularist Arthur and the devoutly observant Josik. Arthur celebrates that now there's one less of THEM. He tells Wiesenthal, "If the world comes to its senses again, there will be plenty of time to discuss the question of forgiveness. There will be votes for and against, but no one who wasn't here will be able to understand anyway." Josik says, "In each person's life there are historic moments and today you have experienced one. I would have done the same but more consciously. You would have had no right to forgive him in the name of others who'd not given you that right. You can forgive only what people have done to you yourself. You acted more unconsciously and now don't know if it was right or wrong." Wiesenthal retorts, "You make it sound too simple. He looked to me as a representative of the other Jews he could no longer reach. He showed his repentance of his own accord." Arthur is insistent, "If you had forgiven him, you would never have forgiven yourself all your life. Let it go."

Many of the published responses also say, "Let it go." Many of the responses written by Jews say, "You did right; it's over." A fellow survivor says, "For Wiesenthal to have forgiven would have been a betrayal of the millions of innocent victims. I am certain Wiesenthal's conscience should not be troubled." Harold Kushner says Karl "doesn't deserve the power to live in your head." Cynthia Ozick claims, "The masters say whoever is merciful to the cruel will end up being indifferent to the innocent." (Although Hans Habe believes that one of the Nazis' worst crimes is how they cut survivors off from their capacity to forgive.

We have to regain this, he believes, not for their sake but for ours.) Several note that Judaism says even God can only forgive those who've sinned directly against him and forbids us to forgive those who've sinned not against us but against another.

Most of the Catholic respondents, equally surely, say, "You should have forgiven." Edward Flannery says, "Forgiveness must always be given to the sincerely repentant." Harry James Cargas says he would be afraid not to forgive lest he not be forgiven.

Both groups tell him to let it go—but he couldn't and still can't. He tells us, "I still see him, whenever I visit a hospital, whenever I see a sunflower." As more than one of the respondents recognizes, Karl has become a lifelong presence in Wiesenthal's journey; it seems likely that they will be bound together until his dying day.

I am reminded of a Zen story about two monks on a pilgrimage who come across a woman unable to cross a suddenly engorged stream. One of the monks picks her up and carries her across. The two monks proceed on their way. Miles later the other one says, "How could you do that? You know we've taken vows never to touch a woman." The first responds, "You are still carrying her. I left her behind hours ago."

Sometimes, though, it may be right to keep carrying the woman. This is certainly the view of some of the participants in the symposium. Hurbert Locke affirms, "Some matters should continue to trouble us." Martin Marty agrees, "I prefer Wiesenthal's lifelong uncertainty." He suggests that to believe there is only one right response in such a situation is to deprive us of an element of our humanity. And Primo Levi, speaking out of his own experience as a prisoner at Auschwitz, wants us to understand how in those conditions there was no absolute right and wrong. One was over and over again faced by situations posing inescapable moral conflicts. Of course, he believes, Wiesenthal is still troubled.

These many different responses suggest how Wiesenthal's parable may help deepen our own reflections on atonement and forgiveness.

Many of the symposium participants wonder whether Karl was really repentant. Several suggest that he wanted forgiveness only because he knew he was dying, that he wanted only to cleanse his own soul and seemed to have no concern for the Jews who were still alive, not even for the helpless Jew who stood before him. Matthew Fox notes that Karl asked forgiveness for his one dramatically evil deed, but not for the many other crimes he helped perpetrate. Others note that it seems that any Jew would do for Karl, that he still viewed the Jews as an undifferentiated group and thus had learned nothing.

There is, of course, no way of knowing. Yet Wiesenthal seems to continue to believe in the authenticity of Karl's repentance. He confesses that he has often wondered what would have happened had Karl lived, had Karl been brought to court like the so many other murderers whom he had hunted out. He recalls how unrepentant most of those others have been when brought to justice but says. "It's hard for me to believe my young SS man would have been like that."

But there is no way of knowing. As Deborah Lipstadt notes, sin is not an amorphous act but something done against a particular person. Repentance means not committing that sin again when you find yourself in the same situation. Repentance in Jewish teaching, *tsuvah*, turning, is not a simple momentary act but a process that includes *acts* of restitution, of reparation. The Mishnah tells us that for sins against God Yom Kippur, the Day of Atonement, brings forgiveness, but for sins against one's neighbor the Day of Atonement brings no forgiveness until one has become reconciled with one's neighbor. This reminds me of Martin Buber's essay on "Guilt and Guilt Feeling," in which he writes that coming to terms with guilt is not just wishing I hadn't done something, not just overcoming a feeling of guilt, but actively going out to the other whom I've injured and working to redress the injury. Clearly, this is something Karl did not do and we cannot know if he would have had he lived. But Arthur Waskow who in his response addresses Karl rather than Wiesenthal cries out, "There is no way for you to repair what you have done, no way to repair the rips and tears that have left us Jews still struggling to be able to trust, no way to repair our sense that God is in hiding from the world."

From this perspective for Wiesenthal to have offered Karl words of forgiveness would simply have been cheap, meaningless grace. Not all are agreed, however, that this is what Karl really wanted. They note that to begin with Karl said he only wanted to talk, only wanted to be heard—and Wiesenthal did stay, did listen, did hear. Again I think of Martin Buber, of Buber's asking, "What do we expect when we are in despair and yet go to a man? Surely a presence…" Perhaps Wiesenthal's silent presence, his picking up the letter, his brushing away the fly were enough to give Karl a sense of still being included in the human community. Matthew Fox believes that Wiesenthal gave Karl the only penance he could bestow, the silence that left him alone with his own conscience, and believes that Karl recognized Wiesenthal's silent presence as a gift. "Some kind of mysterious grace happened between these two," he says. And Fox suggests something else that rings true to me, "Indeed, I wonder if Simon did not receive his vocation from this dying SS man." He sees Wiesenthal's commitment to hunting down Nazis in hiding as a commitment "to allow them a deathbed conversion, a deathbed confession." This seems to correspond to what Albert Speer, the only high-ranking Nazi to admit guilt at the Nuremberg Trials, writes in his contribution to the symposium. Thanking Wiesenthal for coming to visit him in prison, he writes, "I can never forgive myself, but you have shown compassion though not forgiveness to me. You showed clemency and humanity when we sat face to face. You helped me and I thank you."

But perhaps even more than wanting us to think deeply about atonement and repentance, Wiesenthal wants to be sure that we don't FORGET, that it doesn't happen again. As Elie Wiesel has devoted his life to remembering the dead, so Simon Wiesenthal has devoted his to remembering the perpetrators—and, as this tale makes clear, to remembering not only the leaders but also the followers like Karl and the passive bystanders like Karl's mother (and like the former acquaintances who turn their backs on him as he and his fellow prisoners are marched through the town in which he grew up.) These, the ordinary ones, are the ones who broke his trust in humanity. Though subtly, Wiesenthal's parable invites us to recognize that if we are honest with ourselves we might find ourselves to be more like them than we would wish.

This simple tale elicits so many responses. Perhaps the most illuminating would be to return to the beginning and read it once more.

12

Her, Herta

I'm a father's daughter, I say, as though that protects me from having to look too closely at my relation to her.

But, of course, I am also a mother's daughter and at least in my dreams I recognize this as the deeper truth. Twenty years ago I had a dream in which I found myself saying "It is time now for me to go in search of Her." In the intervening years I have sought Her in many guises, but now it's time to return to this first Her. Not the archetypal mother, not the goddess, not sister or lover, not my own early self, not even Self, but *her,* my mother, Herta Fischer Rosenblatt.

I don't want to grow up like her, I used to say, *I don't want to grow old like her,* I've been saying for the last ten years. *But you married her,* another voice—it's mine, too—replies. Which is true, I guess. River, in marrying me, may have married her father, but I have definitely married my mother.

And, of course I *am* like her myself as well; and many of the ways I'm not are ways she didn't want to be either.

So, perhaps it's best to begin at the beginning.

I don't remember much of my first two years, the years before Hitler came to power, the years when all my parents' dreams seemed to be coming into reality. When after their six years of waiting, they'd married and a year later had their first child, me. I know I was a joyfully welcomed child. That having waited so long to get married they weren't willing to wait longer to have a family, even though the other young professors thought them foolhardy. They both remember that when my mother first came home from the hospital, my father picked me up and whispered to her, "We're here just to help her become herself, not for her to fulfill our dreams," knowing he was speaking for both of them.

I know that my mother had happily chosen to become a mother, my mother, rather than continue her career as a pharmacist. I know that from the beginning she thought of us as Persephone and Demeter. Born on the first day of spring, I was her Persephone, goddess of the spring, and she was Demeter, my passionately devoted mother. I know that she felt filled beyond fulfillment by my presence in her life. I know she had longed all her life for the close, fusion-like intimacy she experienced as I nursed at her breast. I think she may never have been held tenderly by her own parents, never been told that she was loved just for being. They were old when she was born and expected so much of their only child. To excel at school but also to help those who did less well, to befriend not those to whom she might spontaneously be drawn but the ones others neglected or teased. Always to see what was missing, who was hurting and why, and to try to assuage, comfort. My sister thinks she was abused. I'm less sure this was so in the literal, sexual sense my sister has in mind but I do think she was exposed to what I think of as a specifically German kind of abuse, distance, withdrawal, expectations. Such a good girl, always.

I think she grew up with a deep, unfulfilled hunger for something else, not praise but warmth. Maybe even passion. And, of course, she married a man who didn't offer that. He was bright and ambitious, kind and shy, but self-contained. They met at the university, she was a student, he a graduate lab assistant. They fell in love, they waited, they married. His father was a converted Jew but that seemed irrelevant to him, to her, too. Though never, I think, to her parents. Nor, as it turned out, to Hitler.

So when I was two, when my mother was expecting their second child, when we'd just moved to the suburbs, my father lost his job. As did all professors who by Hitler's definition were Jews. For six months he tried to find another position in Germany. He made a little money writing abstracts for a chemical journal, but mostly my parents were dependent on support from former colleagues, from his parents, from hers. In the fall, my father left for a postdoctoral appointment in England. While there he received offers for jobs in the Soviet Union, in South Africa, in America. (His dissertation had involved the first research showing platinum's value not just for jewelry but as a catalyst.) He accepted the position in the States and came back briefly to Germany before sailing to New York. My mother got pregnant again. My mother, my brother and I moved out of our own home and alternated between the homes of my parents' parents. Her parents and his urged her to get an abortion. Her parents and his urged her not to follow my father. Hers wanted her to abandon the marriage to a Jew they had thought disastrous from the beginning. His wanted their son to have a chance at a new life unencumbered by a wife and three children.

Much of this I didn't know then. Indeed, parts of it I didn't know until I was married with children of my own. I don't remember having any of it explained then. But I do remember my father not being there, and I do remember that though I was only three, only four, my mother turned to me for comfort, for closeness. As though I was the only one she could really trust. And I sense that even then I knew I had to be there for her and yet also protect myself from being swallowed up by her need. I had an inner life that wasn't hers. I had an imaginary friend, sometimes my size, but sometimes as small as a clothespin, whom only I could see or hear or talk with.

And I had a dream which became my most treasured possession and to which I returned often, both in sleep and in waking life. In the dream, after everyone else was asleep, I would make my way from my bed to a small door at the back of the closet that opened on to a steep flight of stone steps. Carefully, I would make my way down this dark passageway to a landing at the far end of which was a massive wooden door to which only I had the key. I would then enter what seemed to me the most beautiful room in the world. It had crimson velvet drapes and a crimson carpet. In the middle of the room there sat a jewel-encrusted golden chest. This was *my* space, a room to which only I had access, a room to which I could retreat whenever I chose. Now I can interpret the room as signifying both self and womb, my mother's womb and my own. Then it simply meant there was a place of beauty and peace and safety that was mine.

I have another memory from that time when my father was gone. It, too, begins with my lying in my bed. I am almost asleep, touching myself in a way that has become comforting, lost in my own thoughts. My mother and my grandmother come into my room, perhaps to kiss me goodnight. My grandmother gently moves my hand away from my genitals and whispers to my mother, "You'll have to watch that one." Nothing was said to me but I understood that this kind of touching would have to be kept secret.

Three months after my sister was born, we came to America. I was overjoyed to see my father again. My brother fled from him in terror, seeing him only as a stranger. He picked up my baby sister and his face filled with love for this child who symbolized the new life our family was beginning.

Most of what I remember about that first year in America before I began school is about *me*. I remember learning English and beginning to make friends with the neighbor children, the white ones who lived in the houses to the left of ours, the black ones who lived to the right. I don't really remember much about my mother then. Except that she played her piano while we napped, and sang *lieder* as she dusted and swept, and read to us from the same copy of Grimm's fairy tales from which her mother had long ago read to her. And that once a month she had terrible headaches and went to bed and left me in charge. And that she developed a painful and disfiguring tic that wouldn't go away. Mostly though I remember her playing with us in wonderfully silly ways and making us feel that everything in this new world was an adventure. Yet when I look now at photographs of her taken then I see only sadness, pain, loneliness.

Sunday evenings the few people we knew who had also come from Germany joined us for supper. Former colleagues or students of my father and their wives. We children would spend the afternoon helping my mother arrange sliced eggs and radishes, pickled herring and various cheeses to make pretty open-faced sandwiches and arrange them on the beautiful Meissen china she'd brought with her from Germany. My mother was happy then; she'd hum as we were getting ready.

And for a while there was a young German, a violinist, who would come by one evening a week and make music with my mother. But something happened. Either he made an advance that she rebuffed or my father feared he might. In any case he stopped coming. And my mother was sad.

A year later I started school and fell in love with words, with books. I taught my mother to speak English, telling her how to shape her lips and teeth and tongue to make the unfamiliar sounds. I'd liked being read to but I loved being able to read on my own. When adults asked me what I wanted to be when I grew up, I answered "a writer." I didn't know then, didn't know until a few years ago when my mother started telling the stories of her own childhood and youth that she now retells over and over, that when she was six she'd written a poem in honor of her mother's birthday and signed it "*Herta Fischer, Dichterin,*" Herta Fischer, poet.

I don't think my mother was writing poems though in those early years in America. I think her soul had died or was left behind in Germany for a long while. Her father never forgave her for having chosen my father over him and her fatherland. And she had been a father's daughter. Also, something had happened between my parents. My mother has never said much about this, except shortly after my own marriage when she started confiding things it felt that she'd been waiting for years to tell someone, but which I didn't really want to know. I gathered then that they had had trouble reconnecting emotionally, sexually. So a source of warmth and comfort was lost. But I didn't know that then. Wouldn't have guessed it. I remember only how much we three children who all shared a bedroom loved rushing into theirs in the morning and leaping onto their bed, onto them. And how warmly we were welcomed.

How warmly, always, we were welcomed. Into their lives, into the world. How much we were encouraged. How attentive both our parents were to the stories we told at the supper table about our adventures during the day. How proud my parents were of my successes at school. How the best part of every week was the whole family walking each Friday evening the mile and a half to the public library and taking out as many books as we could carry home. I remember that my father read Thackery and Fielding, Dickens, Hardy, Conrad and Joyce, as though the way to become an American was to read English literature. And I remember looking down on my mother for reading only fairy tales and myths and detective stories.

I remember that I was often embarrassed by my mother. She was so different from other mothers. In the mornings she would rush out to the street to scoop up the droppings left by the horses that delivered the milk, the ice, the vegetables. My friends teased me about this and I was ashamed; but our garden was the most beautiful on the street. Especially one red rose bush. But mostly my friends adored her. They always wanted to play at my house where my mother might show us how to make music with the pots and pans in the kitchen or to make a dollhouse out of an orange crate, a toy train out of cardboard cheese boxes and emptied spools of thread. They loved it when she became a juggler or a magician or when she'd pin up a sheet between the dining room and the living room and we'd be invited to a shadow puppet performance, Billie Goat Gruff and the three trolls or Cinderella and her prince.

But I hated that she wore her hair in a pinned up braid rather than in a perm; that she wore homemade dresses and low-heeled oxford shoes and never wore make-up. Once a year, for the annual dinner dance at the elegant home of my father's boss, one of the richest men in America, she had her hair waved and wore a touch of pink lipstick and a hint of perfume and when she came to kiss us in bed before she left, I would realize, "She's beautiful." But mostly she acted as if looks weren't important, were in some way "bad."

I hated that my clothes, too, were homemade and ugly. My sister and I made paper dolls and cut up wallpaper samples to make the beautiful clothes for them we'd never have ourselves. And I hated that I, too, had to wear braids, two long skinny ones, and had to submit to her braiding them every morning when I was wild to be off to school, to my own life.

I loved school, until in fourth grade I had a teacher who resented my abilities and perhaps even my enthusiasm. I didn't say much about it at home but my mother could see that something was terribly wrong. So in her mended stockings and well-worn shoes, in her shapeless dress and with her still marked German accent, she went to talk to the headmistress of the fancy girls school in the next town. To this day I have no idea really of exactly what she said or why it was so effective, but I do know that in fifth grade I started going to that school as its first and only scholarship student. And there my love of learning, of reading, of writing was nurtured and blessed. Of course, going to that school was sometimes difficult in ways that felt more important to me than to my parents. We weren't poor, not at all by Depression standards; my father had a professional job. But my fellow students were rich. They lived in mansions and belonged to country clubs; they had chauffeurs and housekeepers, horses and show dogs, summer homes and yachts, elegant clothes. I never did share their out-of-school life, but in school none of that mattered. And outside of school I soon had another group of friends who cared about things most of my classmates didn't: social justice, peace, spirituality.

That, too, I owed to my mother. For at about the same time that I started going to the private school, we got our first car and what my mother most wanted to do with this car was to visit the Quaker meeting she'd heard of in a town about a half hour away from ours. She had never forgotten being fed by American Quakers after the First World War and liked what she knew about a group that took inner life and the transcendent seriously but didn't see a need for ministers or creeds. So we went that first Sunday and continued going. My closest friends all through high school were other young Quakers in the greater New York area who would get together one weekend a month. I had crushes on some of the boys in this group, because that's what we girls did, but much more important was the intense, intimate connection with one of the girls who, like me, had come to America as a very young child with her parents to escape Hitler. We shared a bed on those weekends and stayed up most of the night whispering our otherwise unspoken fantasies and fears. We wrote one another almost every day that we were apart. We read the same books; we had the same heroines.

It was in that Quaker milieu, too, that my mother, luckily for us I think, started having friends, women friends of her own. For, in my high school years, I consciously separated from her. I became a father's daughter. My father and I spent hours together every evening. He read Ovid and Catullus with me to supplement the Caesar and Virgil we read in school, taught me calculus when I got bored with algebra. He introduced me to Zola and Hardy, Mann and Dostoevski. We argued about politics. He was passionately interested in all the things that most interested me and even our disagreements drew us closer. Much later I asked my mother what this had been like for her. "I was a father's daughter, too," she said. "I knew you would return to me."

It was only later that I realized how deeply the dreams I had for myself as a teenager connected me to her. I wanted a radically different life from hers. I didn't want to grow up to be a housewife, a mother. I wanted to become a world-famous journalist or a Nobel prize-winning author, to have passionate love affairs but no commitments to tie me down. It was my mother's unfulfilled longings that helped shape these dreams. She, too, didn't want me to grow up like her. So there was a strange way that in rejecting her I was choosing her, which I only dimly understood.

Meanwhile, she was happier. After the war, my father's mother had come from Germany to live with us. She often made my mother feel like a servant in her own home. Instead of sympathizing, I tended to be angry with her for not resisting. But now she had women friends with whom she could share her distress and she had *writing!* She joined a reading club and then organized a writer's group. She began writing poetry and short stories. She went to writers' conferences and was welcomed as a "find." She was published.

And when I went away to college, writing became the medium of our relationship. My mother wrote me several times a week and I was always glad to find a letter in my mailbox. But I also didn't like the letters. They presumed a closeness I didn't feel. She wrote mostly about what I was feeling and experiencing; that is, about what she imagined I was feeling, and it wasn't at all what I felt I was feeling. I felt both invaded and not seen, and somehow helpless to change it. I couldn't bear to tell her that the letters that revealed her soul were to me sentimental. I couldn't find a way of telling her what I was feeling, partly because I didn't want to, they were *my* feelings and related to something I didn't know how to talk about with her. Sex.

When I left for college I knew very little about sexuality. My mother and I had never talked about it. I'd never been allowed to date—like many immigrant parents, mine were very strict. I'd masturbated but had no language for what I was discovering about my body's longings and pleasures and no clear understanding of how what I did related to the sexual encounters described in the fiction I loved. In college, I met young men who shared my love of poetry and fiction; who liked to talk about the things that most interested me, young men who were bright and ambitious themselves and appreciated bright and ambitious women. I'd thought that enjoying talking with them meant I'd enjoy becoming physically intimate with them, too, but our actually quite preliminary touching aroused a responsive passion in me which terrified me. I felt much safer in my roommate's bed, cuddling, kissing, gently stroking her breasts and having mine gently sucked, and then slowly, silently, almost secretly, moving to more intimate touch and sometimes to orgasm. None of this was the kind of thing I would have written about to my mother.

But then I met George. And felt safe with him, safe enough to risk opening myself to him and to my own passion. My whole sense of myself was turned upside down. I didn't want a career after all, at least not now. I wanted George and the children we would have together. I married him, became the only married student in the very elite college I attended. I graduated and got pregnant. I had five children in five years, four sons and then a daughter. I loved it. I loved getting pregnant and being pregnant. I gave birth easily and had no difficulty breast-feeding my babies. *This* I could share with my mother; we became very close.

And when after I'd weaned my last child I decided I wanted to go to graduate school, she wholeheartedly supported me. She took care of the children the two days each week that I was in class and it seemed to both of us that being a grandmother was what she'd been born to be. My children were never embarrassed by the playfulness and spontaneity that had sometimes made me squirm. She didn't seek with them the fusion she had sought with me and saw them more clearly than I felt she'd ever seen me. Today she still tells stories about them in their earliest years, stories which so clearly reveal what was already most distinctive about each one of them, most lovable, most worrying.

As I went on and became a professor, she was enormously proud of me and pleased that I could have what she had not, both a family life and a successful career—and, of course, she was envious. I felt her disappointment at what life hadn't given her. Some of it was anger at never having had a chance to fully exercise her gifts and to have them recognized. But there was also grief, grief over her still unfulfilled longing for passion. She so longed to be wanted and to have her own wanting be received. That's the pulse that underlies all her poetry.

The same pulse moved through my veins. Wanting it all. The career, the marriage, the children, the lovers. Wanting it all and choosing to have it all. Including the love affairs, some with men and some with women. Somehow able to live these openly without threatening my marriage. Feeling very blessed, very lucky.

And then in my early forties wanting something different. Leaving my marriage, my Ivy League professorship, to live alone for the first time. Fearing my mother would disown me as her father had her—for leaving her, but also for leaving her world, marriage, marriage to a good man. But instead her saying, "Any woman would understand your going."

That first spring in California I woke from a dream, astonished by the words I remembered saying with such clarity and passion within the dream: "It is time now for me to go in search of Her." The dream led me back to the myths my mother had told me back in the very earliest years of my life, and especially to our *myth*, the myth of Demeter and Persephone. The dream returned me to the mother-world. I began to write from my soul, from my heart, from my hurts.

And she began writing poems in response to my essays. Demeter blessing Perse-phone's choices. Her Hera, her Artemis, her Athene singing in counterpoint to mine.

And then I found River and fell in love with her and began to live with her. Another poet, another woman often unsure of her own gifts, her own worth, another woman often overcome by depression. Another woman who wants things deep and intense, who longs for those moments of fusion that I seem to fear. My mother felt validated by my choosing a woman—and yet so often has difficulty with the particular woman I've chosen, perhaps just because of how alike they are.

My mother is an old woman now, in her nineties, nearly blind. She still writes poetry. Just last week an elderly stranger at the post office showed her a many-times-folded clipping he keeps in his wallet, a poem she'd written over a decade ago. I am ashamed that mostly her poetry doesn't move me as it moves him, that I often find it clichéd, sentimental, sing-song. I am sad that I have never known how to tell her that.

My mother is an old woman now. She is often unhappy, disappointed by what life hasn't given her—an advanced degree, a prestigious position, money of her own, public honors. I see my life as shaped by choices that she knowingly and unknowingly led me toward. She sees hers as having been shaped by others, by fate, Hitler, my father. But she still writes poetry. Her passion, her longing, are not yet stilled.

I am the love of her life. Her message to me has always been: "Choose me; don't choose my life."

And she tells me now, whenever we are together, whenever she writes, "Never wonder, you have loved me enough and in just the right ways."

13

Journeys To The Underworld

Because a psychology engaged with the depths of the soul, of the psyche, cannot help but recognize that "under" is a world, concern with underworld experience seems from the beginning to have been intrinsic to *depth* psychology. Freud became a depth psychologist as he struggled with the depression that overtook him after the death of a dearly loved father whom, he was suddenly forced to realize, he had also resented and been ashamed of. He begins The *Interpretation of Dreams* with an epigraph from the *Aeneid*, in which Juno announces her resolve to turn to the underworld for help that the heavens refuse to yield. Throughout the book Freud uses Hades as a privileged metaphor for the unconscious. Jung's vision of the unconscious was shaped by the dream in which he found himself continually descending from one floor of a house to yet another more ancient one until at last he found himself in an archaic underground cave surrounded by bones and pottery shards.

The underworld seems to be an inescapable metaphor, what Jung calls an archetype, an image which reappears spontaneously in our own dreams and fantasies, and in the myths and legends of most peoples. Stories that refer to it seem to insist on being remembered and retold and to stir us beyond our conscious understanding. The underworld is an uncanny realm, unknown, and yet strangely familiar. It stirs up complex, ambivalent, ambiguous, contradictory fears and longings.

To some of us, at least at times, and in some myths, time spent in the underworld is understood primarily as "time out," referring to periods when we feel ourselves abducted from the everyday world of work and relationships and ego-functioning. We see "underworld" as relevant to our experiences of loss and failure, of abandonment or punishment, emptiness or estrangement, of passivity or paralysis, of guilt and remorse, of depression or even psychosis. Underworld is associated with endings, with death.

My own experience of this aspect of underworld came during a period in my late thirties when I found myself so overwhelmed by guilt and loss that I could no longer even imagine that things might ever be different. I was not dreaming. I had lost all touch with that in me which hopes, which could imagine love or joy. It felt as though my soul had died, was lost somewhere deep in the underworld. It seemed evident to me that there was nothing in me that could pull me back up. When my despair was at its greatest I felt that the only possible resolution was for my body to join my soul in death. The winter solstice was approaching. I flew to a faraway seaside city where the ocean waters that I have always loved, always recognized as the source from which life emerges and to which it must return, would be warm. I had planned to dive into those waters and swim until I could swim no further. But during the night of my arrival I had a dream, the first in many, many months. Magically, when I awoke, there in a chair across the room sat a friend who had divined what I was up to and found me simply in order to say, "You cannot go without saying good-bye." The dream, to my mind, was sent by Hermes, god of dreams, and the friend who helped me to understand that the dream (in which I'd bled to death aborting a child) was signifying not that I should go ahead with my plans but that the dream death, the symbolic death, was death enough. The friend who had helped me to see that I *was* dreaming again, that my soul had come back to life was also sent by Hermes or, as it truly felt, was Hermes.

In other myths or dreams or other periods in our lives, or other understandings of the same myth, dream or life situation, underworld is seen as referring to another and somehow "deeper" reality than that of "upper world" commitments and activities. It evokes images of healing, remembrance, integration, transformation, rebirth, completion, of womb rather than tomb.

In retrospect I came to view that difficult time in my thirties as what taught me that the underworld is itself a sacred realm, appropriately ruled over by a goddess, a place of renewal, not simply of death. This understanding of underworld is, actually, the one I began with. In the earliest dream I can remember (and one I had often as a child) I find myself descending a steep narrow stone stairway that leads deep underground. I find in my pocket the key that will unlock the massive oak door that confronts me at the foot of the stairs. I open the door and find myself in the most beautiful room I have ever seen. It is lined with red velvet drapes; a crimson carpet covers the floor; sparkling chandeliers hang from the ceiling; at the center of the room sits a jewel-studded chest. Even as a child I knew this room was always there and that I alone had access to it. I knew it was a place of safety, of shelter. Some forty years later I dreamt of making my way down a narrow passageway that began in a cave cut into some desert cliffs. At the end of my descent I find myself in a small underground cavern. It is dark. I can see nothing, but I know myself to be in the presence of a goddess, of *the* goddess for whom I have been searching.

The underworld may be a place of desolation or of renewal. It may also be the place where the souls of the dead whom we loved (and love still) now dwell. From there they come to us in our dreams with words of consolation or of warning, or simply to be with us again for a fleeting moment.

There are many different images, stories, interpretations. We need the many stories, yet some will seem more "true," more telling, to particular ones of us than will others. My own understanding has been particularly deepened by Greek mythological traditions about journeys to the underworld, by the myths which communicate how the Greeks imagined the underworld, and especially how they imagined our present relation to it, the relation of the living to those who have died before us, and our relation while still alive to our own "end," our death, our *finis*, and to our purpose, our *telos*, to those experiences that give depth to our lives.

These Greek myths are stories that have been retold often, re-imagined by many poets and artists; they are stories that continue to nurture the soul. They illuminate our lives, as our lives help us to interpret them. These myths lead us to the *depths* of experience, to our own fears and longings about death, about failure, about loss and endings, to our own experiences of such journeys *within life*. They are not primarily about death, though of course death always does come into the tale. They are not about the easy entrance into the underworld of the soul released from the body, an essentially irreversible entry, but rather about the temporary, sometimes deliberate, sometimes forced, forays into the underworld of the still embodied. These are journeys that involve return or at least that are undertaken with the hope or assumed possibility of return.

Hades and Its Shades

The Greeks spoke of the underworld as the House of Hades. They imagined it as lying far to the west, beyond the setting sun, or deep underground. According to Homer it lies next to the village of dreams. It is dark, unlit. It is not a place of punishment or reward but of remembering, a place where nothing happens or, more accurately, where nothing *new* ever happens.

There is one region of Hades, Tartarus, which lies as far below the surface of the earth as the sky arises above it, reserved for the hopefully permanent isolation of the still-dreaded most ancient gods, the Titans (whom Freud likened to our most primal, most repressed, most terrifying instinctual energies). The darkness of Tartarus represents a mystery that terrifies even the gods. Tartarus is the deep within-ness of the earth, as old as Gaia herself. They emerged together out of the primordial void. It is inhabited not only by the Titans but also by archetypal sinners—mortals from the long-ago beginning time—figures who sought to deny their own mortality, to achieve parity with the immortal gods. Their punishment expresses the theme of *repetition*.

These sinners include Tantalus who, filled with resentment at being a *mortal* son of Zeus, sought first to steal the god's nectar, a drink reserved for the immortals, and later to trick them into eating human flesh (by offering them a savory stew made from the dismembered body of his son Pelops). In Tartarus Tantalus forever reaches for the succulent apple, the refreshing water. In life, another sinner, Tityus, tried to rape Leto, the mother of Artemis and Apollo, in order to violate her body; in Tartarus his flesh is continually gnawed on by snakes and vultures. Ixion, whose slaying of his father-in-law constituted the first human murder, and who also tried to rape Hera, is in Tartarus stretched on an ever-revolving wheel. Sisyphus, who raped his sister-in-law and drove her mad, so that in her torment she then murdered her own children, is condemned endlessly to roll a rock up a steep incline and then watch it roll down.

There was also a special afterworld called Elysium (or the Elysian Fields or the Isles of the Blessed) reserved for those mortals made immortal through the arbitrary favor of the gods or because of divine parentage—a place where the dead retain their faculties and engage in the same activities that gave them pleasure while they were alive. But Tartarus and Elysium really exist only to help us apprehend what Hades is not: it is not a place of punishment or reward, only an *after*-world. It is an afterworld to which all will eventually come, whether in the world above one was a hero like Achilles or a murderess like Clytemnestra.

Those who come to this afterworld were spoken of as shades, as shadows, or as *psyches*. For the Greeks of the pre-Socratic period the psyche was not related to waking life consciousness; it was active only when the waking ego was not, in dream, in trance, in intoxication, in moments of intense passion, in madness, and in death. The psyche represented the core of the individual, his or her unique personhood, but was not the seat of thought or feeling (for which the Greeks had another word, *nous*). It was that essential aspect of the person that was not dependent on the physical body, and at death left it for good. Except Teiresias, who even after death retained not only psyche but also nous, denizens of the underworld could not think new thoughts. They could only remember—that is, re-member, integrate, apprehend the depth meaning of their earlier embodied life.

The psyche is sometimes represented as a homunculus, and sometimes identified with the breath, which enters to give life and departs at death. It was imagined as being easily able to slip into the underworld, if ritually buried and mourned. Since the funeral rites were understood to serve as rites of passage, entry to Hades is not assured even for psyches. Hecate is accompanied by the angry spirits of those prematurely dead or inadequately mourned who are caught between worlds, between the world of the living and that of the dead. Antigone fears for the fate of her brother's psyche if his corpse remains unburied.

In Homer the dead are represented as mourning their lost bodies and the sunlit world. Yet they are also imagined as *eidola*, as clearly defined images of their former embodied selves, as *seeming* to have bodies still. They are immediately recognizable to others. But when Odysseus on his visit to Hades reaches out to embrace his mother, his hand goes right through her. She is but shade, shadow, smoke, like a figure in a dream.

Although the immaterial souls of the dead could slip into Hades easily, access was difficult for the still-embodied. The entrances were few, remote and hidden, with gates at Taenarum, at the Alcyonian Lake near Lerna, at Argolis, and at Lake Avernus near Naples.

Underworld Gods and Goddesses

The underworld is a sacred realm ruled over by the goddess Persephone and her consort Hades, who, it was generally held, left his underworld realm only once, in order to abduct Persephone. Neither he nor she otherwise conveys people to their realm; their role is to welcome those who come and to define and maintain the order appropriate to this place.

There are no cults in which Hades plays a central role. There is no period in Greek ritual life in which he is important. There are no records to indicate that he was known to the indigenous people before the Indo-Europeans arrived. In Homer, where there is little recognition that the realm of the dead is sacred, he is almost ignored. And later, in both myth and rite, he is little more than Persephone's shadowy consort. The world of the dead is again ruled by a goddess, as it seems to have been long before it came to be viewed as under his rule. Yet he is still *there* and the place bears his name.

Aidoneus, his oldest name, signifies that he is, by definition, the unseen one. This name was rarely used, perhaps because it evoked the terror associated with the dark, unlit realm over which he rules. Mostly the Greeks sought to sublimate their terror of the underworld god by invoking him with other, more euphemistic names, such as Trophonios, the nourisher, Polydegmon, the receiver of many guests, Euboulos, the good counselor, or Ploutos, wealth-giving. Many of these titles are intended to suggest that Hades is not only the grim god of death but also a god of the fruitful harvest. This renaming may signify aversion, denial, but it may also bespeak a deeper truth, a truth not only about Hades' possible origin as an archaic chthonic fertility deity, but also a recognition of an inner fruitfulness which immersion in his world may yield.

Hades enters Greek mythology as one of the sons of Cronos. According to Hesiod, almost immediately after his birth, Hades (like his sisters, Hestia, Demeter, and Hera, and like his brother Poseidon) was swallowed by his father (who feared that some day one of his progeny would seize power from him as he had seized it from his father). He remained in his father's stomach/womb (the words are the same in Greek) until rescued by their last-born sibling, Zeus. A variant version relates that Cronos, rather than swallowing his newborn sons, threw the infant Hades into Tartarus as he threw newborn Poseidon into the sea. According to the most familiar myth, after Cronos' overthrow the three Olympian brothers divided the world among them by lot: Zeus received dominion over the heavens, Poseidon over the sea, and Hades over the underworld. But these most familiar myths are late myths, deriving from a period when patriarchal religion has replaced the more ancient indigenous worship focused on goddesses.

Perhaps there were three major Olympian gods because there had earlier been a triple goddess—the triad of maiden, mother, and crone, represented in the later strands of Greek mythology by Persephone, Demeter, and Hecate, but once simply the three aspects of *the* goddess whatever name she might go by in a particular locality. The triad of Zeus, Poseidon, and Hades may have come into existence simply to assure that patriarchal rule would be recognized as extending over every domain, including even the underworld.

Although the most familiar strand of Greek *mythology* sees Zeus as chief among the gods and as delegating rulership of the seas to his brother Poseidon, and over the underworld to Hades, and thus suggests that Persephone is subordinate to Hades, to the Greek *religious imagination* she is clearly the more important figure. From the perspective of Greek religious life, Persephone was primarily the dread goddess of the underworld, not the innocent maidenly goddess of spring. There are no accounts of anyone arriving in the underworld and finding her absent—or even of her playing a subordinate role to Hades. The rituals through which the Greeks sought to assuage their fear of death were celebrated in her honor not his.

There are other divine beings associated with the underworld, minor deities such as Thanatos, who (contrary to the view of him put forward by interpreters of Freud) is not imagined as a killer, as a bringer of death, but only as a carrier, one who conveys the psyche from the place of death to Hades. There is Charon, who ferries the newly dead across the river that separates the land of the living from the land of the dead. The stagnant, muddy river, Acheron, was a son of Gaia condemned to the underworld because he had sided with the Titans in their ill-fated war with Zeus. Another underworld river, Styx, a daughter of Night, sided with Zeus against the Titans; her waters were used to witness the gods' own most solemn oaths. Styx was among Persephone's companions when she played in the meadow before her abduction; it was in her waters that Thetis dipped Achilles in the hope of making him immortal. Others include Lethe, mother of the Graces, the river whose waters erased memory, and Cerberus, the three-headed dog, who guards the entry, and prevents premature visitation and impermissible escape.

Among the Olympian gods, some besides Hades and Persephone have important underworld roles. The psychopomp, Hermes, often leads the psyches to Hades and accompanies and guides its more temporary visitors both to and from the underworld. The most important death-dealing deities are Apollo and Artemis, his swift arrows bring death to men, hers to women.

Divine Journeys to the Underworld

There are also two Greek gods, Dionysos and Asclepius, who are said to have spent time in Hades, even though from the Greek perspective what primarily distinguishes the gods from us is that we are subject to death and they are not. Both of these gods are sons of mortal women whose divine fathers had them snatched from the womb as their mothers were burning to death. Both, at least in some traditions, were viewed as human heroes who *become* divine.

It is told of Dionysos, the god of death and rebirth, that after his own apotheosis he determined to rescue his mother Semele from the underworld and bring her to Olympus, as befits the mother of a god. Unable to find a way into Hades, he is finally given directions to one of the hidden gates by an old shepherd who exacts a promise that if his mission is successful, the god will return and allow the shepherd to make love to him. When Dionysos returns to fulfill his pledge, the old man has long since died, and so to honor his promise the god whittles a large wooden phallus and lowers himself upon it. The story suggests that Dionysos' venture succeeds because of his willingness to be submissive.

Dionysos is a god of souls, not just of the grain or even the vine. The most important ritual observed in his honor, the *Anestheria*, though on the surface devoted to celebrating the new wine, was at a deeper level an all-souls festival, an occasion for the souls of the dead ("the thirsty ones") to emerge from the under-world and spend a day in our midst. Dionysos represents the sacredness and fear-fulness of all boundary-dissolving experience: intoxication, sexual ecstasy, madness. The god of ecstasy is also a god of death and of the underworld, a god who suffered dismemberment and death, and who exposes us to a kind of dis-memberment and death.

The story about Asclepius, the Greek god of healing, the other god who spent time in the underworld, begins with his restoring to life heroes he believed had been unjustly killed by the gods. In punishment for this transgression of the boundary between mortal humans and the immortal gods, Zeus kills the healer god and sends him to the underworld where he remains until rescued by his father, Apollo. The time spent in Hades teaches Asclepius that he can delay death, but not ultimately protect humans from it. Those who come to the god in hopes of cure learn that whatever extra life his healing art may give them must be used to prepare for the death that surely still awaits them. In the realm of Ascl-epius therapy, healing, becomes preparation for death.

Human Journeys to the Underworld During Life

Greek myths about journeys to the underworld by mortals in the midst of life suggest a significant difference between male and female descents. The Greek myths about male journeys are primarily myths about deliberately undertaken purposive enterprises—not about abductions. The heroes undertake their jour-neys for the sake of life *here*, in order to demonstrate their daring and courage, to rescue someone or regain a lost love, or to obtain some precious knowledge. Female sojourners more often seem to discover intrinsic meaning in underworld experience, a discovery of self, and an inner fulfillment.

Yet I note that, even in the tales of heroic ventures into the underworld, the notion that the point of journeys to the underworld is to emerge with one's val-ues and character intact is often subtly criticized and undermined. For though that may be the hero's intention in setting forth, sometimes something different happens along the way. In the Orpheus myth, for example, Orpheus approaches Hades with an assumption of the superiority of life above ground, but the end of his story suggests a different view.

My sense is that to be caught in what the myths describe as a "masculine" or in a "feminine" attitude is to miss that each may have its truth, its appropriateness, for all of us irrespective of our gender. For underground to function as an arche-type we need to become free of stereotyped responses to it—*always* fighting against or *always yielding*. There may, indeed, be two quite different ways of relating to the underworld, and for all of us, irrespective of our gender, one of these may sometimes be the more appropriate response, while the other may become more appropriate in different circumstances, at a different life stage. I recall with a smile how in my younger years I sought an underworld guide who would rescue me from my times of depression, withdrawal, despair, who would help me *out* of the underworld, at the same time that my closest male friend saw me as someone who might help him find his way *into* the depths. Almost a reversal of what the myths suggest about the difference between male and female engagements with the underworld.

Rainer Maria Rilke's poem, "Orpheus. Eurydice. Hermes" long ago first made me aware of how different the archetypally feminine perspective on underworld experience is from the so-called masculine perspective. The poem describes the scene when Orpheus, having persuaded Hades and Persephone to allow him to bring his too-soon dead young bride back to the upper world, is leading the way by playing his lyre, knowing that if he looks back to assure himself that she is indeed following, he will lose her forever. But Rilke's focus is on Eurydice whom he imagines as "deep within herself, like a woman heavy with child," as "come into a new virginity" as so "filled with her vast death" that when, abruptly,

> the god put out his hand to stop her, saying,
> with sorrow in his voice: He has turned around—,
> she could not understand, and softly answered
> *Who?*[1]

That "*Who?*" with which Eurydice expresses how far she is from sharing Orpheus' longing that all might be again as it was before she was taken to the underworld communicates in one word the distinction between the male and female responses to underworld experience. Orpheus is intent only on rescue from the underworld. Eurydice is so rooted in the underworld that she no longer even recognizes him.

Male Journeys

The tales about mortal male journeyers to the underworld, not only the one about Orpheus, but also those about Theseus, Heracles and Odysseus are, on the surface at least, told from a perspective that celebrates life in the upper world as the only real life available to us humans.

Theseus' journey, for example, is undertaken on a dare, for the sake of glory. He and his boon companion Peirithous resolve to abduct two daughters of Zeus.

First Theseus kidnaps young Helen (long before her marriage to Menelaus or her more famous abduction by Paris), though she is quickly rescued by her twin brothers, the Dioscuri. Then the two together enter Hades, determined to abduct Persephone *from* the underworld (as Hades had abducted her *to* it). Hades greets them and waves them to sit, and once sat they find they cannot get up again, for their chairs are the seats of Lethe. Perhaps they were tied down by chains or serpents, or perhaps their flesh itself grew into the chairs, perhaps it was simply their own forgetfulness that kept them there. Homer and Virgil say the two remain caught there forever, but in another tradition Theseus at least is eventually rescued by Heracles. Theseus went to the underworld expecting that he could just sneak in and bring something beautiful back with him. He found, instead, that he got stuck there and apparently gained nothing; for, while psyches remember, he only forgot. And it seems as though he got out just by chance, or by the reappearance of the heroic ego (which Heracles might be interpreted as signifying).

But Sophocles apparently imagined that Theseus had learned something after all, for in *Oedipus at Colonus* he casts him as a psychopomp. There Theseus guides the aged blind Oedipus into the mist where the "unlit door welcomes in love" the hero who, after his painful discovery of his true identity, had chosen years of wandering exile rather than immediate death. Then, Oedipus had feared in Hades a confrontation for which he was not prepared, a confrontation with the shades of the father he had murdered, the mother he had wed. Now, with Theseus leading the way, he moves to a death, "beautiful if ever mortal's was."

Heracles' rescue of Theseus occurs when he is sent to Hades to bring Cerberus back with him into the upperworld. In preparation for this last and most difficult of all the labors imposed upon him by King Eurystheus, he has first to undergo initiation into the Eleusinian mysteries. Some traditions say that when he arrived in the underworld Hades agreed to let Heracles carry off Cerberus if he could do so without using any weapon. One version reports that Heracles fought with Hades for the dog and wounded the god so seriously that Hades had to leave the underworld and go to Olympus to be healed. But either way, Heracles succeeded—only to be told by Eurystheus to take the three-headed hound back to where he had come from. Heracles seems to be a hero immune to underworld experience, and in a sense successful in his foray into it, though the injunction to return Cerberus also suggests how pointless his whole adventure was.

Odysseus is yet another male hero who ventures the underworld. Years after his homeward departure from Troy Odysseus is told by Circe that if he is ever to find his way back to Ithaca he must go to Hades and there consult Teiresias, the blind seer who alone among mortals still preserves the capacity for creative thought after death. After Odysseus goes through the proper purifications and sacrifices, the blood of the sacrifice draws the shades of the dead to meet him at the entrance to the underworld. He sees his mother and weeps as he finds no body to embrace. He sees Achilles, who tells him it is better to be a peasant in the world above than a king here below, and Agamemnon, who warns him to keep his arrival at home a secret, and many others he recognizes, all of whom are eager for news of the world above. Then suddenly Odysseus is overwhelmed by their importunities and he retreats. But he has learned from Teiresias not only of the dangers that he must still overcome if he is to return home safely but also that his return to Penelope will not, after all, be the end of his wandering, that he will later take off again and die far away from home. Odysseus receives what he came for—and more. He learns that his urge to travel ever onward is a more essential aspect of his character than is his conscious goal. At the moment he heeds only that portion of Teiresias' prophecy that he is ready to hear, but later, much later, he will recall the rest.

To my mind by far the most important of all these male journeyers to the underworld is Orpheus, son of Apollo and the muse Calliope. The story really begins when Orpheus marries the beautiful Eurydice. Soon after their marriage she, while fleeing a would-be rapist, accidentally steps on a poisonous snake; it bites her and she dies. Orpheus is disconsolate; he experiences her loss as unbearable. Virgil says that Orpheus tried without success to console himself with his own music; Ovid that he could not even try. Unreconciled to his separation from Eurydice, Orpheus descends to the underworld. In a sense he is pulled there by his grief; the experience of being overcome by devastating loss is itself an experience of being in the underworld. But he hopes somehow to undo what has happened, to bring Eurydice back to the land of the living. This journey to the underworld represents the first connection of Orpheus to the Dionysian rather the Apollonian world. For, as Dionysos had gone to rescue Semele, so Orpheus goes to rescue Eurydice.

Although in the versions of the myth most familiar to us, those put forward by Virgil and Ovid, Orpheus fails to bring Eurydice back to the upperworld with him, there are older versions of the tale in which he succeeds and thereby becomes one who knows the secrets of Hades and can teach them to others. The figure of Eurydice of the tale is almost beside the point: what matters is that Orpheus has the power to melt the hearts of the infernal powers.

All traditions agree that he goes to the underworld and uses his art, his music, to seek to win back his beloved. Orpheus seems to persuade Persephone and Hades; they tell him to trust his music, play his lyre, and lead his beloved back to the upper world without looking back to check whether she is, indeed, following. But, of course, *we* know that things forbidden in such tales are always done. Orpheus does not quite trust his music after all or, as Virgil understands it, is overcome by the madness of passion that seizes him and turns him around. Eurydice cries out, "What madness!" and she holds out her hands helplessly toward him. In Ovid (as in the Rilke poem) Eurydice makes no complaint, and when Orpheus moves to embrace her for the last time, he finds he holds nothing tangible in his arms.

We have hints in these poems that Orpheus' failure is seen as betraying a misunderstanding of death, of Eurydice, of love. The second loss of Eurydice is in a sense the real loss, the irrevocable loss, though Orpheus is still not yet ready to accept that irreversibility. He tries to reenter Hades but Charon will now not let him return. Orpheus again goes into mourning; again he turns to his lyre to express his inconsolable sadness. Orpheus sings so beautifully that the very trees gather round to listen and is so absorbed in his own singing that he fails to notice the approach of a band of threatening maenads. When he tries to win them over with his magical playing, he for the first time finds his song having no effect; it is drowned out by their cries.

Now we come to what is from many perspectives the most important part of the story: Orpheus' own death, a death that comes to be viewed as a ritual sacrifice. The maenads kill him. As to why, there are many explanations. Perhaps they are punishing him for a dedication to Apollo so intense as to imply a dishonoring of their god, Dionysos. Perhaps they act out of resentment of the misogyny they see evidenced in his violent spurning of all women after Eurydice's loss. Or perhaps the maenads, women in touch with their own instinctual center, not defined by their roles as wives or mothers, represented that aspect of Eurydice which Orpheus who saw her only as *his* beloved had ignored: her in-herself-ness. This is Plato's view: Orpheus had never really loved Eurydice and for this, and the self-indulgence of his self-pity, the women kill him.

The maenads not only kill him; they dismember him. (Here there are parallels to what happens to that other denier of Dionysos, Pentheus, in Euripides' *Bacchae*, and to what happens to Dionysos himself in the Orphic versions of his infancy, when the Titans cut up the child god they have murdered.) The Muses then appear to gather up the scattered pieces of Orpheus' body and spread them out in the fields. Thus Orpheus becomes amalgamated with the ancient rituals in which a vegetation god is sacrificed. Orpheus, the poet who had refused to accept the necessity of nature's patterns of death and renewal, now becomes a participant in a grim celebration of them.

Yet we are also told that at his death, all nature weeps. The severed head and the lyre float down the river, across the sea, to Lesbos, the island famous for its lyric poets (where the head is buried under a temple of Dionysos, forbidden to women). As it floats away, the lyre utters a plaintive melody, and, according to Virgil, the head cries, "Eurydice, Eurydice…"

And, at least in Ovid's version, after his own death, Orpheus is open to Eurydice's perspective as he had not been before. When Orpheus now returns to Hades, he and Eurydice are rejoined; they walk together, each taking the lead in turn, and Orpheus may look back with impunity upon his beloved.

Female Journeys

It is time now to turn to Eurydice, not as Orpheus' anima or muse but as herself—and it is time to try to understand the female perspective on underworld experience as Greek mythology represents it—which is not simply the opposite of the struggle to resist or transcend underworld experience, not a struggle or desire to remain in the underworld rather than get out, but something different, harder to name. This view may truly be one a little more available to women than to men, but *more* truly it is a view relevant to all of us as humans.

For Eurydice, Hades represents a kind of fulfillment. Rilke's Eurydice reminds me of my own period in the underworld and my resentment of would-be rescuers, who were irrelevant, were in the way—who didn't understand that this was *my* experience, this was what I had now to live, that it had its own organic time which could not be foreshortened.

From the perspective of Eurydice, Hades looks, feels, and *is* different. Perhaps we cannot even use the same words for the underworld, cannot use the words that seem right from the outside or even underway, Orpheus' words or Demeter's—the ego's words, the upper world's—cannot speak of depression, loss, failure, boredom, dead-end, but must instead turn to some of the words Freud used when speaking of death-wish, of death-longing: words such as inwardness, cessation, peace. (In the last pages of one of his very last essays, "Analysis Terminable and Interminable," Freud spoke of the most difficult human task, and the most important, as being this coming to terms with what he calls our "femininity": our vulnerability, our passivity, our finitude and death.)

Journeys to the underworld undertaken while we are still alive are not only about handling difficult times well, in a way that nurtures soul rather than ego, but may also truly serve as preparations for Hades, for the later irreversible journey, so that when death, when "the end," comes we can move to it welcomingly. That, after all, was the point of both the Eleusinian and the Orphic mysteries.

That is what we might learn from Persephone or Orpheus, from initiatory experience.

Orpheus had to learn about ends, had to learn that his relationship to Eurydice really was already over, that his effort to reclaim her from the underworld was a doomed attempt to keep the past intact. He had to learn that she is *herself*, not "his love."

And in herself Eurydice is a Persephone figure, one who *belongs* in the underworld. Her name "Eury-Dike" means broad-ruling; it suggests that she was originally an underworld goddess associated with the maintenance of a mode of natural order, of cosmic justice. Orpheus may also have originally been an underworld god, though in the myth as it has come down to us, he was initially a human with an Apollonian perspective, a human whose understanding was transformed when he came under her tutelage. Even in the myth as we have it, his love for her teaches him underworld realities—slowly. The initiation begins with *falling* in love, and then gradually learning what love means. There are echoes in this tale of the old motif of the goddess and her lover-victim.

Eurydice who, like Persephone, was brought to the underworld against her will, but then finds herself at home there, comes to embody its perspective, a perspective for which Orpheus was not yet ready. Again I turn to Rilke:

> Her sleep was everything.
>
> …
>
> She slept the world. Singing god, how was that first
> sleep so perfect that she had no desire
> ever to wake? See: she rose and slept.
>
> Where is her death now? Ah, will you discover
> this theme before your song consumes itself?[2]

The myth is about Orpheus' discovery of his true theme. He learns from Eurydice what I learned from Persephone, as I came to understand that she *loves* Hades, her underworld consort, and comes to know Hades as her home. The story about Persephone is much the same as the one about Eurydice, with Demeter in the Orpheus role, as the one devastated by loss, as the one determined to rescue. Except that Demeter may remind us of more female ways of being caught in an upperworld perspective. It is not only heroes but also mothers who seek to protect and rescue, who cannot bear to allow another his or her underworld journey.

Persephone needed to become herself; she reached for that beautiful dark narcissus; she ate the pomegranate seeds. And yet it is also true that she was abducted, that she was *taken* to the underworld. Strange: to rule in the underworld seems to require having been taken there. Not to have always been there. Not to have gone there deliberately. It is not the place where one begins but where one ends.

There are two other myths of female journeys to the underworld, one about Alcestis and one about Psyche. Alcestis *chooses* to go to the underworld, to death, in her husband's place. He, Admetus, had fallen ill and was about to die, but couldn't bear to. So he called upon Apollo to repay a debt incurred long before, and in gratitude for the love the mortal king had bestowed upon him in his own dark time, the god succeeded in persuading the Fates to agree that when it came time for Admetus to die he might be spared temporarily if someone else would volunteer to die in his place. Admetus expects that his aged mother or his even more aged father would readily agree to do so, but they refuse. Then his still-young wife, Alcestis, volunteers, out of love, to go in her husband's place. (Though, at least in Euripides' version, when she is already dead but not yet arrived in Hades, Heracles appears and wrestles with Thanatos and brings her back to her husband more beautiful than ever.) One can't help but ask, "How could he let her go?" and also: "How could she return to him?" And yet one senses that though she loved life as much as he, she feared death less, and that somehow her love could encompass that difference between them.

There is also Psyche whose last task on her journey to self is her journey to the underworld. I have articulated my reading of that journey in *Psyche's Sisters*[3] where I spell out the parallels between Psyche's story and Persephone's, and reflect on the deep bond between the goddess and the mortal woman, and how it is through her underworld experience that Psyche becomes psyche, becomes soul. The importance of Psyche is that she is human, that her relation to the underworld—like ours—is that of a still-alive mortal, not that of a goddess who *lives* there.

We journey to the underworld, sometimes willingly, sometimes unwillingly. And return, to live *here* with one another. But hopefully not all that we experienced during the time we've spent *there* is washed away by the waters of Lethe. Hopefully we remember what happened there, not for the sake of being stronger, more courageous or more successful, happier or more mature here, but because the underworld is there, an ever-present dimension of the world—and because it awaits our return.

Notes

1. Rainer Maria Rilke, "Orpheus. Eurydice. Hermes," in Stephen Mitchell, ed. and trans., *The Selected Poetry of Rainer Maria Rilke* (New York: Random House, 1982) 51, 53.

2. Rilke, "Sonnets," I.2, in Mitchell, 229.

3. Christine Downing, *Psyche's Sisters: Re-Imagining the Meaning of Sisterhood* (San Francisco: Harper & Row, 1988) 50-52.

14

Tending Soul In The Age Of AIDS

I don't know for how many others in a conscious everyday inescapable way this *is* the Age of AIDS, but for me it is, has been for almost exactly fifteen years, since the day I returned from a five month trip around the world during which I somewhat unexpectedly went through menopause. Reflecting on what this big transition meant to me at a soul level, I discovered how grateful I was to be a woman, to have a woman's body that so insistently finds ways of reminding us of our participation in the natural rhythms of birth, death, and renewal. My body seemed to be telling me that I was entering the last third of life, entering a life-stage one of whose primary tasks would be coming to terms with endings, both welcomed and regretted, including the biggest ending of all, death. When I came home from that trip I found a letter waiting for me from a former graduate student telling me that his lover was dying of Kaposi's sarcoma and that he feared his own immune system was also irreparably compromised, that he, too, would soon be dying.

Of course, then, in 1982, we didn't have the word AIDS—but we did have AIDS. Soon more and more of the men I loved were dying or dead or living with the knowledge of their own infection, and all were living with the loss of beloved others, not just individual others, but sometimes it seemed of our whole community. And every one of us could say just when we were first initiated into the Age of AIDS, first found ourselves on what Paul Monette called Planet AIDS. Once there, we live there. AIDS is part of our everyday consciousness—though, in another sense, we keep getting hit with its horror all over again. We go numb, think we're acclimated, and then…

So, yes. I inhabit this planet. The others who live there are my people, my community. Perhaps partly because I'm a lesbian. Perhaps partly because I spent most of a decade of my life, my 40's, being lovers first with one gay man and then with another—much to my surprise and certainly to theirs! And Philip, one of those men, is now dead. When the plague first appeared, I didn't know if I'd been infected or not and avoided taking the test. Of course, I didn't want to learn I was positive but I also didn't want to know I wasn't, because that would mean that those who were would be "they" and I would be their "other," not part of the community living on Planet AIDS after all. Eventually I realized that of course I live in that world no matter what. I took the test and learned that I was negative.

By then I had come to believe that we *all* live in the Age of AIDS—regardless of whether or not we're sero-positive, and not only because AIDS isn't simply a gay disease even here in America but also attacks hemophiliacs, IV-drug users, African-Americans, women, children, infants—but because we all live in a world transformed by AIDS. Or, more accurately, we have been returned by AIDS to the world as most humans have always experienced it. Part of what underlies the terror and horror that AIDS evokes is that for the last fifty years or more most of us in the West—at least the white and privileged among us—have imagined ourselves immune to disfiguring illness or early death. AIDS has returned us to an age-old world where death is inescapable, fearful, omnipresent.

AIDS has returned us to the world where souls live. I almost hesitate to put it that way, because recently "soul" seems to have become such a popular word, a word to be found all over the best seller list, a word in danger if being leeched of its meaning. Yet the word's current popularity may also be a sign that we live in a time when we again need this word, need a word with different connotations from those evoked by the word "spirit." "Spirit" implies a viewpoint that sees meaning in transcendence, in moving beyond, above, earth and body; whereas a "soul" perspective finds meaning *in* our embodied earth-bound lives with all their messiness.

The Greeks regarded soul (their word was "psyche") as mostly asleep while we were awake but active in dream, trance, in moments of intoxication and sexual ecstasy, and especially in the after-world, the underworld. They recognized that we find ourselves in the underworld not only after death but while still alive, in those times when upper-world concerns are no longer paramount, in times of depression, times when we are "brought down" by grief or rage, fear or guilt, times when typically unconscious, imaginative, modes of thinking not conscious, rational, ones predominate.

I see AIDS as having the power to bring us back in touch with underworld realities and with soul. For AIDS moves us beyond the illusion of innocence, the illusion of being untouched, invulnerable, into a more mature kind of being-here. In *Heaven's Coast*, a book about his lover's death and his own grief, Mark Doty writes:

> I used to think depression wrong—a failure to see, a rejection of the gifts of one's life, an injustice to the world's bright possibilities. But I understand better than I did before....
>
> Could it be that the more I admit the anger and woundedness—the deep, sealed-off hurt long since turned in on itself—the more I'll be able to move freely and flexibly?
>
> Once it was important to me not to become bitter, a kind of survival skill. I didn't want to be burdened, always, by the shadow of a difficult family; there was an energy in me that wanted to move forward, not be locked in contemplation of the past. But I'm forty, and my life's at midpoint (hard to think, now, living in a battlefield, my friends dying at my age or younger, my neighborhood full of men who maybe won't see forty) and I begin to think maybe there is a need for bitterness in adult life. Are we children without it, self-deluded? Is there something in disenchantment which strikes the balance, a darker chord in the self which lends us gravity, depth? A ballast against the spirit's will to rise?[1]

Probably none of us ever journey into the underworld willingly. Going there usually feels like an abduction, as it did for Persephone, the much-loved daughter of the grain goddess Demeter, who one day while gathering flowers in a meadow in the company of a group of other young maidens was forcibly seized by Hades, god of the underworld. Persephone was filled with fear; her mother was consumed by rage and grief; though eventually Persephone came to feel at home in the underworld and her mother came to accept that though her daughter would still spend part of each year with her, her real life was now that of goddess of the realm of souls.

Even when we think we go to the underworld willingly, we seem mostly to imagine we can control, can shape, our journey. We fail to realize that what being in the underworld means is *not* being in control. I think of the Sumerian goddess of love and fertility, Inanna, who sets out for the Land of No Return adorned with all her seven emblems of power, her golden girdle and her lapis beads, and finds as she approaches each of the underworld's seven gates, that one by one she has to give up these protective tokens, so that by the time she arrives she is naked and bowed low.

For many of us it has been AIDS that has forced this soul journey on us. In saying this I do not mean that AIDS necessarily deepens, nor do I mean that AIDS is some kind of blessing in disguise, a wonderfully transformative gift. It isn't—it's shit. And, of course, many different experiences not only confrontation with AIDS can bring us to the underworld. As Shug says in Alice Walker's *Color Purple*, "trouble do it for most folks," and there are lots of other big troubles.

Yet I believe that AIDS because of how it brings together sexuality and death may bring us to soul in an especially powerful way. AIDS reconnects us to the age-old recognition of the interrelation between love and death. As Freud found, in the light of death, sex becomes Eros, becomes not just pleasure but connection. The challenge is somehow to accept death and still love life, for to live is to love. Because to affirm sex is to affirm the body and bodies die, sex makes us aware of our finitude and mortality. I remember the last time close to the end of his life I made love with Philip (long after our relationship had ceased to be sexual in any conventional sense), a lovemaking as tender and ecstatic and bittersweet as any I have known. As we held each other, as I touched ever so gently what remained of his long-loved body, as he ever so frailly touched me, we remembered all the many other times we'd touched each other in love and knew that we would never do so again.

Sexuality in some sense always has this connection to death, but even more inescapably so in the face of AIDS, for although AIDS is not literally a sexual but rather a blood-borne disease, and is not only transmitted through love-making—nevertheless for those I have known well who have had AIDS, it has been transmitted sexually. Which means these men have had to live with the knowledge that their love-making has also been a death-making, have had to live with the knowledge that the body, the penis, the semen, which were once a source of life-affirming pride may now be fatal to others, have had to live with the knowledge that an act of love may have brought death into their body or that through an act of love they may have brought death to another. How does one live with such knowledge?

AIDS forces us to go into these hard places, forces us to go into all kinds of feelings, including many we may be ashamed of: rage, grief, fear of abandonment and rejection, self-pity, self-hatred, guilt, panic, despair. I've come to believe that tending soul means really being open to these feelings, going into the hard places, the underworld. Attending to soul means trying to learn what these unwelcome feelings are saying to us, means learning they are integral parts of a whole life and that they can cohabit us along with hope, peace, love.

The Greeks understood that real healing can only happen through confrontation with underworld realities. Their myths relate that upon reaching maturity, Asklepios, their god of healing, was entrusted with the vials of blood collected from the wound made when Medusa's head was severed from her body. The blood that dripped from the left vein was a magically potent poison; the blood from the right was reputed to have the power to restore the dead to life. On several occasions, so it is told (perhaps in sympathetic remembrance of his mother's unjust death at the hands of her spurned lover Apollo), Asklepios used the healing potion to bring back to life heroes he saw as having been unjustly punished by the gods, heroes prematurely sent to the underworld. The stories vary as to who benefited from this gift; there is no dispute, however, about Zeus' anger at Asklepios' presumption in transgressing *the* boundary between humanity and the gods: men are mortal; only the gods are free from death. In punishment for his unforgivable crime, Zeus struck Asklepios with his thunderbolts and sent him to the underworld, so that he, though a god, might himself experience the fate of mortals. Thus Asklepios becomes the only god in Greek mythology to experience death. The god of healing is the only god who knows what it is to die. Though as a god his stay in the underworld is only temporary, though as a god he can experience mortality without forfeiting his immortality, it is his own experience of vulnerability to death that makes him seem to the Greeks a god more kindly and more benevolent than any other. Asklepios had learned that though his gifts might serve to postpone a premature death, they could not avert death. Those who came to his shrine at Epidauros learned that what he could give was simply the time needed to prepare for a death that *would* inevitably come. With AIDS, where at least at present we live knowing there is no cure, the hope for such a respite might lead us to a new honoring of this ancient god.

The Greeks had such myths to help them access this connection between death and healing. I believe we, too, need images, poems, myths, to help us mourn, help us remember, help us praise. We need such images because they help us access the archetypal dimensions of this plague, help us express how AIDS touches our souls as well as our bodies, how it affects the ways we see and touch and love one another, how it affects our intimacy and our sexuality. Poems and myths help us express our bafflement and our hope, our anger and our love. They give us words that return us from the world of "them" to the world of "us."

I speak as a lover, as someone who has deeply loved men who have died or are dying, or who are living with AIDS. I speak as someone who deeply loves words, language, metaphors, myths, stories, poetry. And who believes that images can heal. Not cure. Heal. To name, to image, the horror may help us come to terms with it—not erase it, but give it its place. I believe that words can help us become intimates of our experience, get close to its actual, particular details. I believe that words can help us share our experience and share in another's.

I see poets and storytellers as our healers, as shamans who move into the world of images on our behalf, for they are more gifted than most of us at finding the right words, at escaping the clichéd and the sentimental, at keeping their words loud and rude and strong and queer. Their fierceness of perception, their urgent, angry, tender acts of witnessing, their passionate optimism, help us see, and unless we really see, we cannot accept, cannot love.

They remind us to continue to celebrate our sexuality, to continue to rejoice in our bodies, in our capacity for ecstasy and for communion, capacities still mediated through bodily touch. They call upon us not to let AIDS rob us of our delight in being desiring, pleasure-seeking and pleasure-giving beings. There is a wonderful passage in *Heaven's Coast* where Mark Doty writes of how his lover, lying on a hospital bed in their living room, watching Provincetown's beautiful young men parade back and forth past their front window, fantasizes having sex with them. Mark at first finds this strange, almost threatening, but comes to bless this sign that a man who always loved the world continued right to the end to do so.

It is so important to continue to celebrate the affirmation of gay sexuality that blossomed in the later 1960's and 1970's, in those all too short years between Stonewall and our becoming aware of the threats posed by AIDS. But it is important also to find ways of honoring some of the changes that have occurred in the gay world since 1981. The heroism that many have shown. The compassionate care for others that many have exercised. The wisdom of a grateful appreciation of the gift of the most ordinary life filled moment that many have come to. The deeper sense of truly constituting a community that many have experienced. The discovery of more permanent and more soul-oriented bonds that many have made. All these may be recognized as blessings, without our applauding the cause or denying the cost. "Does anybody ever get taught these things by anything other than tragedy?" Paul Monette asks.[2]

A mythic figure newly important to me since the advent of AIDS is the wounded healer, who becomes ill and learns that his wound is a calling, a calling to share what he has learned from his suffering for the benefit of others. I have quite a file of obituaries clipped from the *New York Times* of men whom I see as contemporary wounded healers—dancers, choreographers, artists, journalists, playwrights, actors, novelists, poets, including, of course, Mark Doty and Paul Monette.

But I see this archetype as also embodied in less well-known men I've loved. One was a 38-year-old physician who even just before his death was the most zestful life-loving person I have known. Andy had become so sensitive to the beauty of this world that he was about to leave that an apricot sunset or a Botti-celli Madonna would bring him to tears, tears of joy and appreciation. A physi-cian all his adult life, he resigned from his position as an emergency room physician when he first fell ill four years ago and soon became nationally promi-nent as a doctor with AIDS actively involved with Act-Up, the gay rights protest group. In this unique role he worked to encourage other doctors to support its campaigns for accelerated AIDS research and for making the fruits of that research available and affordable. He put all his energy into serving as an interme-diary between the physicians and researchers on the one hand and persons with AIDS on the other. He often told me that he believed that only in these last years was he doing what he felt he was born to do—fully using all his gifts, as a charis-matic speaker and a compassionate physician. His wound and his healing were deeply intertwined.

After his diagnosis, my other friend, an actor, a playwright, and a director put his energies ever more effectively than before into outrageous, in-your-face queer theater. A year or so after his death I dreamt of visiting Martin in New York. He was pleased to see me but said he had little time to talk; he was on his way to a dress rehearsal of a new performance piece. He invited me to come along, which I did, and gave me tickets for the next evening's opening night performance. When I arrived for the opening, I made my way to my second row seat and saw that the first row was filled by all the men I've loved who've died of AIDS—Philip and Andy and the too many others whose names you wouldn't recognize. I knew then that Martin is *there* (wherever "there" is) still helping others laugh at what is beyond tears.

Notes

1. Mark Doty, *Heaven's Coast* (New York: HarperCollins, 1996) 219, 129.

2. Paul Monette, *Borrowed Time* (New York: Harcourt, Brace, Jovanovich, 1988) 43.

15

Turning Again To Athene

Recent discussion about the importance of applying archetypal psychology and mythology to our cultural and political life have made me newly aware that this is not as simple as it sounds, that there is always the danger of forgetting that myths can't tell us how, that "they simply give us the invisible background which starts us imagining, questioning, going deeper."[1]

There is also the danger of what the novelist Thomas Mann and the classicist Karl Kerenyi in the letters they exchanged during the Hitler period called "mythological enthusiasm."[2] As their correspondence makes clear these two viewed themselves as dedicated to an approach to myth which would bring together depth psychology and the scholarly study of mythology as a way of reclaiming myth from the Nazis' misuse of it for political purposes. Deeply disturbed by Hitler's irresponsibly distorted reanimation of myth, they recognized that the study of mythology poses moral issues. The old ideal of a classics-based education had, they believed, revealed its moral insufficiency in not being able to muster the slightest power of resistance against the totalitarian assaults of barbarism and its sham culture. They understood how the long-established German tradition of taking the inner as the real, of giving priority to *Innerlichkeit*, so prominent in Luther and in Kant—had helped make Hitler possible. As had German Romanticism with its celebration of the will, the unconscious, the Dionysian. The Romantics' valorization of the *Volk,* their emphasis on the importance of recovering the unique cultural heritage of one's own people, of creating a kind of national collective consciousness based on emotional rather than political connections was another contributing factor. Mann and Kerenyi saw that the Nazis had reactivated a romantic hankering after a paganism it never fully understood, a longing for liberation from the repressive constraints of biblical morality, a regressive yearning for paradise lost, for infantile freedom.

Both Mann and Kerenyi felt that the contemporary situation required a greater responsibility than had been true in the 19th century world of Bachofen and Nietzsche lest the investigation of antiquity become a part of the violation of the free intellect and the suicide of humanism. Mann suggests that Nietzsche's thinking was given its fatal cast by two primary errors: the first being Nietzsche's total misinterpretation of the relative power of instinct and intellect. To see intellect as dangerously dominant as Nietzsche had only made sense in response to a momentary historical situation, as a corrective to rationalistic smugness. "We," Mann says, "have seen the folly of this." Nietzsche's second error was to see life and morality as antagonists.[3]

Yet Mann sees Nietzsche as leaving us the challenge of reconstituting human reason on a different basis, of creating a humanism of a greater profundity than that associated with the complacently shallow view of the bourgeois age. In the wonderful essay he wrote on the occasion of Freud's 80th birthday in 1936 Mann spoke of the "historical experience of our own day" as representing "a moral devastation which is produced by a worship of the unconscious, the glorification of its dynamic as the only life-promoting force, systematic glorification of the primitive and the irrational." He reminds us that the unconscious "knows no values, no good or evil, no morality" and emphasizes how "antipathetic deep analysis must be to an ego that is intoxicated by worship of the unconscious…an ego deaf to analysis."[4]

Yet the danger of succumbing to "mythological enthusiasm" is real, as Carl Jung's initial response to the rise of National Socialism makes clear. We should not forget that in 1934 Jung published an essay in which he spoke of his belief that "the arousal of unconscious forces in Germany might bring about positive results in the form of genuine psychocultural and spiritual transformation."[5] "The Aryan unconscious," he wrote, "contains tensions and creative seeds of an as yet unfulfilled future":

> The still young Germanic peoples are entirely able to produce new forms of culture and this future still lies in the darkness of the unconscious of each individual, as a seed laden with energy, capable of a mighty blaze. The Jew, as relatively a nomad, never has produced and presumably never will produce a culture of his own, since all his instincts and gifts require a more or less civilized host people for their development….
>
> Where was the unheard-of tension and energy when there was as yet no National Socialism? It lay hidden in the Germanic soul, in that profound depth which is everything else except the garbage bin of unreliable childhood wishes and unresolved family resentments. In my opinion it has been a grave error in medical psychology up till now to apply Jewish categories indiscriminately to Germanic and Slavic Christendom. Because of this the most precious

secret of the Germanic peoples—their creative and intuitive depth of soul—has been explained as a morass of banal infantilism.[6]

It is clear that at first Jung seems to have been in awe of Hitler's charismatic power and to have hoped that his own vision of a renewal from the depths of the unconscious at the hands of an inspired leader was being realized. Though Jung came to see the evil in Nazism and helped many individual Jews, his initial enthusiasm does raise the question: can Jungian psychology be seen as too susceptible to intoxication with the irrational, the transpersonal, the symbolic at the terrible expense of the rational and the social? I raise this as a warning; Jung himself was aware of this danger most of the time, but not always...

One of the things I value about archetypal psychology as contrasted with other interpretations of Jung is that it recognizes this danger and honors the psyche's direction beyond itself into engagement with the world—though I sense, maybe wrongly, that it's still easier for even those of us pulled to this version of Jung to move toward the world of nature than to the world of history, to concern with the Earth and its creatures, with what Rilke called *die Dinge*, with things and images, than with other persons and narrative, with beauty more than with justice.

And even when we become aware of the importance of psyche's engagement with the polis, with history, I'm not sure we really know where to go with that recognition. I see us as somewhat like Hermann Hesse whose plan for *The Glass Bead Game* was dramatically changed under the impact of Nazism. Originally Castalia, the esthetic mountaintop world, had been envisioned as the ideal, but in the book as completed the protagonist Joseph Knecht comes to know he must leave Castalia for the flatland, the world of everyday human life. But Hesse doesn't quite know what to do with his hero once he gets him there and so has him die, apparently accidentally, almost as soon as he arrives.

I believe we need to recognize that the relation between psyche and polis is both inescapable and conflicted, that, as Freud understood, we are both directed toward community and against it. Polis is inside us as well as outside. What Freud called Eros—the drive toward others—is intrinsic to our being-here, as is our pull away. I am reminded of the last lines of W. H. Auden's poem, "In Memory of Sigmund Freud":

> Over his grave
> the household of Impulse mourns one dearly loved

sad is Eros, builder of cities
and weeping, anarchic Aphrodite[7]

In what Adam Phillips calls "his great elegy on human happiness," *Civilization and Its Discontents,* Freud spoke of Eros and Ananke; Love and Necessity, as the parents of human civilization. Freud's Eros is, of course, not the childish Cupid of popular imagination, but rather the Eros of Apuleius and of Plato and Hesiod and the Orphics, the creative principle which is the source of all being, all life.

Freud clearly distinguishes Eros from what he calls "oceanic feeling," from fusion longing, which he viewed as regressive, narcissistic, directed by death longing. His Eros is an active energy directed outward, toward real, particular others. Not to all, that would be fusion longing once again, but to an ever widening, more inclusive circle of others. Freud sees civilization, communal, political existence as based on love and on our fear and hatred of others. We want and resent society; it fulfills and frustrates us; we accept it and rebel against it; part of us adapts to the restrictions it demands, part doesn't.

The twin brother of Eros is Death. Death is something we both long for and fear. Freud associates death wish with all in us that is pulled toward repetition, inertia, regression; all that longs for a tension-free existence, for Nirvana resolution, completion. When denied death-wish becomes destructive, because of our resentful hatred of anything that intrudes between ourselves and that longed for peace, that reminds us of our incompleteness and our unfulfilled longings.

So, although Freud honors Eros, he also hopes to help us learn to honor that in us that continues to want happiness, resolution, fulfillment. He recognizes the pull of narcissism, fusion-longing, of escape from the world of others, the pull back to an imagined inner world, to the illusion that it constitutes a separate reality. Freud uses the term "primary narcissism" to describe the early pre-psychical, pre-verbal stage in which there is no self and no other, a stage which exists only in memory, in fantasy, only for the imagination—only afterwards. For consciousness begins with the experience of separation and loss. Self and other are co-created—which creates the twin possibility of self-love and other-love. Thus consciousness entails a departure from primary narcissism, a transfer of some of the love that might be directed toward ourselves to another. And when we aren't loved or a beloved disappears from our lives, there is always an enormous temptation to entirely withdraw libido from the outer world and thus fall into what Freud calls "secondary narcissism."

This narcissism arises out of the longing to deny the loss, the dependency, the neediness, to claim self-sufficiency. Our initial turn to an other expresses our impossible longing for that other to give us back that lost wholeness. It is really an expression of fusion longing, expresses a desire to *be* not to *have*. Only after the full acknowledgment of the loss of that imagined once-whole world, only after what Freud calls the work of mourning, does there really arise the possibility of turning to others as other, as genuinely separate with their own desires. Only then does the possibility of real loving, of Eros, emerge.

Narcissism is an illusion; we are in a world with others; we are not self-sufficient, we are not the world. And thus narcissism is death. Freud often quotes Heine: "We must learn to love in order not to fall ill." But it is also true, as he recognizes, that the narcissistic longings never die. For we all long to return to that earlier fantasized world where self and other were one, all long to believe that separation is not the ultimate truth.

Neither narcissism nor death wish is "bad"; both are part of the soul's given direction, perhaps the deepest part. Nevertheless it is important that we move beyond narcissism—at least temporarily. Important that we consciously, willingly, embark on that long detour which takes us into the world of others, into the social, the political world. As Freud wrote at the end of *Civilization:* "But now it is to be hoped that the other of the two 'Heavenly Powers,' eternal Eros, will make an effort to assert himself in the struggle with his equally immortal adversary."[8]

Always, however, we will feel the pull of both these immortal energies, though sometimes one, sometimes the other, will seem to predominate. I remember how I'd always felt myself more in touch with the political, social, historical aspect of our human being-here than I felt most of my Jungian friends to be. So that already back when I was in graduate school I knew I needed to listen to Freud as well as to Jung, to Jaspers and not only to Heidegger, to Mann and to Joyce, to Buber more than Bultmann.

Yet when my book *The Goddess* first appeared, almost twenty years ago now, the criticism that most struck home was one that appeared in some classics journal to the effect that I'd ignored how for the Greeks their gods and goddesses had primarily a political function and that my psychological interpretation was anachronistic and narcissistic. I heard that and knew both that it was true and at the same time irrelevant. I knew that I'd been drawn to the goddesses because of a need to understand my woman self in all its complexity and ambiguity, indeed that they had drawn me to them, one by one. I knew that my interpretation was appropriate to where I was then and to where feminism was then. Clearly, a depth psychological understanding of the feminine was needed to balance the narrowly literal political agenda of the dominant group within the second wave of feminism in the early years.

Nevertheless I couldn't just brush this criticism aside. There was a way my critic was right and another in which I was right, and now I find myself wanting to attend to this political function more explicitly, more fully, than I did then—not as an "instead" but as an "and also." I still find goddesses (and gods) good to think with—but want now to think with them, through them, about our responsibility toward the human community.

This means turning to Athene, turning *again* to Athene. (And I can't help but remember Freud showing H.D. the Athene statue that stood atop his writing desk and telling her, "This is my favorite.") For, as Karl Kerenyi reminds us, in Greek religion, in cult, Athene was more important than even Zeus, precisely because of her association with the polis, with civilization, with history.[9] She was the protector, the rescuer from every danger. Indeed, we might say she *was* the community. Through the mediation of her presence, through the wholeness-creating power of her cult, her worshippers knew themselves as fellow-citizens. The rituals performed in her temples were thought to guarantee the continued existence of the city. Thus Athene keeps us in the world of others and helps us to remember the sacred importance of its problems.

But actually what I want to do is to turn not so much to Athene as to Athene and Aphrodite. For what I most centrally want to say emerges out of my associations to a sentence from Nicole Loraux's book, *The Children of Athena*.[10] In her chapter on the *Lysistrata*, the comedy by Aristophanes, Loraux writes that "to use Athena in the service of Aphrodite and Aphrodite in the service of Athena is a feminine way of serving the city." I have no interest here in getting into a discussion of this notion of a "feminine" way of serving the city, but rather want simply to explore how our understanding of serving the city might be deepened by looking at it through the mythic and cultic associations between these two goddesses. (I also don't intend to address the question central to Loraux's own inquiry: how the myths about Athene undergird and make visible the political ideas current in 5th century Athens about women and men.)

But I do want to acknowledge how in recent years I have come to appreciate the structuralist approach to mythology Loraux adopts—not as *the* approach as it is for her, but as a complement to the kind of archetypal approach represented by Kerenyi, which seeks to discover the essence of particular divine figures. Loraux has no interest in psychological interpretations nor in historical approaches that look for the origin of myths or mythic figures. All that interests her is how a myth was used in the city in a particular period. I have come to see this as an important corrective: Athene may be all the stories told about her and all the rituals dedi-cated to her—but at any given moment she is this particular goddess, associated with these particular epithets, worshipped in this particular rite, revealed in this particular story, engaged with these particular other figures. To read, as Loraux does, myths in their civic framework, to explore how they are actively functioning in history, to examine how mythic themes mold and legitimate civic experience and get reworked as social circumstances change—seems particularly helpful when we are trying to understand the relevance of myth to political life.

So, I want to follow up on Loraux's hint and focus on the relation between Athene and Aphrodite as this is communicated in the rituals and dramatic litera-ture of 5th century Athens. I am drawn to this in part because of my conviction that the Greek gods and goddesses can only be understood in the context of their relationships with one another, that they do not exist in isolation, that to know them we must know them in their *polytheistic* context, engaged with other deities who represent incommensurable but undeniable energies and values. We are not called upon to choose between Athene and Aphrodite—but we should not delude ourselves about the ease of compatibility between them. We must rather honor the tension, hold the opposites.

I have always valued Isaiah Berlin's political philosophy version of this per-spective: Berlin set out to free us from the dream of the single principle that would account for everything and to make us aware of the essential incompatibil-ity of some of our most dearly held values—justice and mercy, for instance, or liberty and equality. "It seems to me," he wrote, "that the belief that some single formula can in principle be found whereby all the diverse ends of men can be har-moniously realized is demonstrably false...If as I believe the ends of men are many and not all of them are compatible with each other, then the possibility of conflict—and of tragedy—can never be wholly eliminated from human life, either personal or social."[11] Although Berlin sees us as called upon to do our best to make rational choices, he believes we are doomed to choose and that the very choice may entail an irreparable loss.

It is immediately easy to see how different Athene, the civic divinity, and Aph-rodite whom Auden spoke of as "anarchic Aphrodite" and Loraux as "the goddess of the race of women" are—easy to recognize the tension between the virgin daughter of Zeus and the goddess of desire, of sexuality, beauty and pleasure, and thus to view them as representing incommensurable perspectives.

And yet, we shouldn't make this too easy. We should, for example, remember the myth that relates how Athene rather than Poseidon became the patron divin-ity of Athens, the myth which tells us that it was the women (who in that mythic time were in the majority) who voted for Athene—and that to appease Poseidon the men then promptly deprived them of their power, excluded them from citizenship. So Athene, too, is (or was) a goddess of women.

And we should remember that Aphrodite has a place on the Acropolis. Athene makes room for Aphrodite in her city: on the western slope of the Acropolis there stood a shrine of Aphrodite and Eros, and near the Propylaea was a shrine dedicated to *Aphrodite Pandemos* and Peitho (persuasion). It is probably also important to recall that (contra Plato) Aphrodite Pandemos is Aphrodite as the goddess who embraces the whole people, who makes available the fellow feeling, the empathy, necessary for the existence of a state, who embodies what Freud meant by Eros.

Athene and Aphrodite were also brought together in ritual, in the *Arrephoria*, a major ritual which initiated the month long series of summer festivals which culminate in the *Panathenaea*, the birthday festival of the city. The Panathenaea began with a sacrifice to Eros and Athena at the grove of Akademos outside the city followed by a great procession ending in the presentation to *Athene Polias* of a newly woven robe that depicted the battle between the Zeus-led gods and the Giants, a battle understood to represent victory over the forces that threaten civilization. The earlier ritual, the Arrephoria, involved two young girls, between the ages of seven and eleven, who had spent a whole year in the precincts of Athene on the Acropolis, helping to weave that robe. At the end of that year in the dark of the night these girls are directed to carry a basket whose contents they are forbidden to discover through a hidden underground chamber to the shrine of Aphrodite in the Gardens, the shrine of Aphrodite and Eros. Then before dawn they are to bring something else back, again something secret and sacred. The hidden contents obviously allude to the myth about the infant Erichthonious, entrusted by Athene to the daughters of Kekrops who were forbidden to open the chest in which he was hidden—but we don't know what the basket contained nor exactly what this ritual was understood to mean. Yet it was obviously a female initiation ritual under the tutelage of Athene into those mysteries of female sexual identity associated with Aphrodite—and the well-being of the entire city was understood to depend in some way on the right carrying out of the ritual.

Further testimony to the importance of the connection between Athene and Aphrodite in fifth century Athens is provided by the dramatists. Loraux writes that in the theater of Dionysos a family dispute between the city and its myths is played out. The dramatists make evident the malleability and resilience of the inherited myths. The tragic genre makes myth work on itself.

We are probably all familiar with Athene's role in the *Eumenides* and may remember best the famous lines in which she asserts "There is no mother anywhere who gave me birth and, save for marriage, I am always for the male with all my heart, and strongly on my father's side."[12] But in this play Athene not only validates patrilineal descent, she also welcomes into the city the ancient feminine divinities, the Furies, now to be known as the Eumenides, the healing ones. And according to at least one tradition, these Furies originate through the same violent act of castration which issues also in the birth of Aphrodite: they are born when the blood from Ouranos's severed genitals falls on Earth, on Gaia.

But, of course, the most explicit dramatic representation of the Athene-Aphrodite connection is Aristophanes' comedy, the *Lysistrata*. This play was written in 412 BCE, during the darkest period of Peloponnesian war, a war that set Greek against Greek, a war that originates in protest against Athenian imperialism and oppression. The war had begun in 431; in 404 Athens suffered a decisive loss and the war came to an end. Although Herodotus had spoken of a common Greekness based on common blood, language, religion, customs, there was no political unity among the various Greek city-states. Athens' attempt to impose unity by force failed—and the Greeks didn't find another way.

During this period Athens' poets tried to use myth as a way of going deeper, of moving against both nationalistic fervor and despair. Many of Euripides' plays can only be fully understood if we recognize this as their historical context. Likewise, this play by Aristophanes has been seen as an expression of his desperate hope that some resolution might still be possible. In a comic vein we might say it was his equivalent of Freud's, "But now it is to be hoped that the other of the two heavenly powers, eternal Eros, will make an effort to assert himself in the struggle with his equally immortal adversary."

The play imagines that Lysistrata, a priestess of Athene, talks the women of Greece (not just of Athens) into seizing the Acropolis and going on a sex strike—in the hope that this might persuade their husbands to end the war and make peace. This collection of women give meaning to the word "Greek"—that is, the women identify with Greece rather than with the narrow literal self-interest of any individual city, including Athens. Their identification as women, with other women, takes precedence over their political loyalties—and yet what they do they do for the sake of men and women, and for their own cities.

The women gathered from all over Greece complain about the difficulty of leaving their households, but Lysistrata persuades them that their civic duty is more important than their ordinary domestic duties, that the hope of all the states rests on them. She tells them that their very recognition of how much they will miss their men (and sex) is exactly what shows that this is the only way to get the men to make peace, for the men will miss them just as much.

"We must abstain from the joys of love," she tells them
"Never, let the war go on," they reply at first
"What if our husbands leave us?" they ask
"We'll find some substitute." she responds.[13]

And so the women swear to abstain from love and love's delights, to sleep like vestals alone at night. But they swear by *Aphrodite*, and call upon Aphrodite to make them irresistibly attractive to the men they plan to repulse.

The play is wonderfully ribald, full of *aphrodisioi logoi*—sex talk (which none of the translations I could find do justice to). The women agree to act in accord with their reputation, to inflame men's desires, to use all their seductive wiles—but to do so for the sake of their city and of all Greece. They leave their marriage beds—but in order to return their husbands to them. They occupy the Acropolis precisely because it belongs to Athene *Parthenos*, because it is a place where they cannot succumb to desire without impiety. There, they, too, under Athene's protection, will be *parthenoi,* virgins. Explicit allusions to the *Arrephoria* communicate that the women have in a sense returned—temporarily—to the childhood years when they had participated in civic service to the virgin goddess (who had secretly sent them to Aphrodite!).

They foresee that they may feel desire but they have sworn to Aphrodite to serve her by not yielding to her power. Though they find this difficult in practice...There's a wonderful scene of husband-sick women trying to leave the Acropolis, complaining that Athene's serpent frightens them, that her owl keeps them awake, saying they need to go home to protect their woolens against moths or to spin their unspun flax. One woman who claims to be starting labor, Lysistrata discovers, has hidden the helmet from the statue of Athene under her skirt to feign a belly swollen with child.

Of course, at first the men dismiss "this silly disturbance." "Fools," the Magistrate berates the women, "What on earth can possess you to meddle with matters of war and matters of peace?" The impassioned (and hilarious) exchange between him and Lysistrata begins with her mocking parody "War is the care and business of men" and ends (when the chorus of women has dressed him up as a spinning-woman) with her triumphant affirmation, "War is the care and business of women."

One of the women pretends to be unable to stay away from her husband. She comes to him and says she can't wait to have sex with him, but then says it just won't work unless they have first a pallet, then a mattress, then a pillow, a rug, some special ointment. He gets more and more turned on as she comes to him and then leaves and then returns once more. By the time she leaves for good, he has a permanent erection. "You'll vote for peace," she calls as she scampers back up to the summit of the Acropolis.

And, of course, he does—as do the other men as well. The women triumph and so does Aphrodite, as the joint chorus's song in her praise at the end of the play makes clear—but so does Athens and thus Athene. And, of course, the play shows how strong the pull of Aphrodite remains—for the women and for the men.

So, what do I make of this? Not exactly that I believe that there's a feminine way of serving the city. Nor that I've been given a simple answer to what we should have done or should still do in Kosovo—or in any particular political situation. Which tears me up. I want to know what is right. I would like to believe that the analogies to the Holocaust that many have drawn make it all simple and clear. But I seem always to see the complexities, the dangers, the losses, the pain. As I did ten years ago when the wall between the part of Germany I'd been born in and the part of Germany I'd so often visited as an adult came down and everywhere there was jubilation—but I cried, partly in joy, no doubt, but also in fear, sensing how much suffering and misunderstanding and conflict still lay ahead. .

I guess that's just what I see the myths (including the comic myth) giving us: both hope—and caution. Just as the lines from the end of *Civilization and Its Discontents* suggest. For I need to confess now that I didn't earlier include Freud's very last line, one he added for the second edition when the Nazi threat had become yet more ominous: "But who can foresee with what success and with what results."

Aristophanes' myth is of course only an illusion—mostly, I believe, a cry of pain over what won't happen, can't happen, except on the stage. And yet that we can imagine it, nonetheless, means something, is a gift. It serves as a reminder that as we try to understand our relation to the political we need to honor both Athene and Aphrodite. That, in Berlin's terms, both justice and love are essential components of our life together, though often not easily reconciled. That in Freud's terms, Eros and Ananke are the parents of human civilization.

I see Aristophanes' play as reminding us of the importance of caring about the people involved, all of them—not just the women, not just the Athenians, reminding us, too, of the importance of trying to move beyond our own view and of trying to imagine that of the others with whom we find ourselves in conflict. This, I believe, is at the heart of that "imagining the real" of which Martin Buber spoke. He introduced the phrase in order to honor the central role the imagination plays in that empathic turning to the other that lies at the heart of any genuine communion between one human being and another and thus at the heart of human community.

Together Athene and Aphrodite remind us of the importance of taking seriously the value of values that aren't our own, the importance of remembering that it's never just black and white. They remind us that the political arena is a sacred real—that what happens there matters, really matters. I believe we must also learn to acknowledge that over and over again we must choose—without knowing enough. That there are always inescapable losses—and no clean hands.

I think again of the exchange between Mann and Kerenyi, of Mann's saying that without a gathering based on a sense of community and of piety the prospects for that strange experiment humankind appear distinctly ominous. And of Kerenyi's affirmation: the humanist will possess a fearless knowledge of the dark, demonic, radically natural side of man along with a sense of piety, a recognition of something transcendent, and of human limitation.[14]

Notes

1. James Hillman, *ReVisioning Psychology* (New York: Harper & Row, 1975) 158.

2. Alexander Gelley, trans., *Mythology and Humanism: The Correspondence of Thomas Mann and Karl Kerenyi* (Ithaca: Cornell University Press, 1975).

3. Thomas Mann, "Nietzsche's Philosophy in the Light of Recent History," *Last Essays* (New York: Knopf, 1966) 141-177.

4. Thomas Mann, "Freud and the Future," *Essays of Three Decades* (New York: Knopf, 1971) 416-7.

5. Stephen A. Martin, "Introduction," to Aryeh Maidenbaum and Stephen A. Martin, *Lingering Shadows: Jungians, Freudians, and Anti-Semitism* (Boston: Shambhala, 1991) 8.

6. This translation of excerpts from Jung's 1934 essay "On the Present Situation of Psychotherapy" comes from Ernest Harms' essay, "Carl Gustav Jung: Defender of Freud and the Jews," in Maidenbaum and Martin, *Lingering*

Shadows, 37-38. The phrases about the "garbage bin of unreliable childhood wishes" and the "morass of banal infantilism" refer to Freud's supposedly exclusively "personal" unconscious.

7. W. H. Auden, *Collected Poems* (New York: Random House, 1976) 218.

8. Sigmund Freud, *Civilization and Its Discontents*, in James Strachey, editor, *The Standard Edition of the Complete Psychological Works of Sigmund Freud* (London: Hogarth Press, 1953-1940) XXI, 145 (slightly modified to better communicate the German).

9. Karl Kerenyi, *Athene: Virgin and Mother* (Zurich: Spring Publications, 1978) 5.

10. Nicole Loraux, *The Children of Athena: Athenian Ideas About Citizenship and the Division Between the Sexes* (Princeton: Princeton University Press, 1993) 151.

11. Quoted by Leon Wieseltier, "'When A Sage Dies, All Are His Kin,'" *The New Republic,* December 1, 1997, 28.

12. Aeschylus, *The Eumenides,* trans. Richmond Lattimore, in *The Complete Greek Tragedies,* Vol. 1, *Aeschylus,* ed. David Grene and Richmond Lattimore (Chicago: University of Chicago Press, 1959) 161.

13. Aristophanes, *Lysistrata,* in *Five Comedies of Aristophanes,* trans. Benjamin Bickley Rogers (New York: Doubleday, 1955) 291-2.

14. Gelley, *Mythology and Humanism,* 132, 143.

16

Sad Is Eros Builder of Cities

Though I see it as an issue of great and urgent significance, my sense is that in the past Jungians have failed to honor the integral interconnection of psyche and polis, soul and city, or have understood it too naively—as I believe Jung himself did in the early 1930s when he plainly hoped that his own vision of a renewal from the depths of the unconscious at the hands of an inspired leader was being realized, that the Nazis' arousal of unconscious forces might bring about positive results in the form of a genuine psychocultural and spiritual transformation.

Though Jung came to see the evil in Nazism, that initial enthusiasm suggests the dangers bequeathed by the long-established German tradition of giving priority to *Innerlichkeit*, of taking the inner as the real, so prominent in Luther and in Kant, and by German romanticism's celebration of the irrational, the unconscious, the Dionysian. We can understand how easy it was to move in this direction in response to the dominant overvaluation of what since Nietzsche we've come to call the Apollonian, the 19th century's smug complacent conformist faith in human rationality, bourgeois morality, material success, and progress, its naive assumption that the ego is master of its own house. Of course this issued in an *enantiadroma,* led to a valorization of an inner world as more real than the outer socio-political world, led to a polarization of inner and outer, psyche and polis. It also encouraged the notion that introverts were somehow better, deeper, more whole than extraverts and that one had to choose between political engagement and soul work.

I imagine that many of us may have initially been drawn to Jung because we recognized ourselves as modern men or women "in search of soul," had experienced in our own lives the cost of being over-identified with ego, with persona, with social role. But I sense a growing recognition of the inadequacy of this polarity, introvert *or* extravert, soul-work *or* civic involvement, a readiness to recognize that the relation between psyche and polis is both inescapable and conflicted, that polis is inside us as well as outside. As Freud saw we are both directed toward community and against it. What he called Eros, the drive toward others, is intrinsic to our being-here—as is our pull away. Civilization, communal, political existence, is based both on love and on our fear and hatred of others. We want and resent society; it fulfills and frustrates us; we accept it and rebel against it; part of us adapts to the restrictions it demands, part doesn't.

We want it and need it, but beyond that—and this is what gives our present explorations their urgency—it, the shared world, needs us! And because of that we need to wrestle with those deep narcissistic urges to retreat from world of others, need to recognize the strength of the longing to pull back to an imagined inner world, to the illusion that it constitutes a separate reality. My sense is that the narcissistic longings never die, that we all long to return to a fantasized world of a beginning time when self and other were one; all dream of fusion, all long to believe that separation is not the ultimate truth. But this is an illusion; we are in a world with others; we are not self-sufficient, we are not the world. Only after the full acknowledgment of the loss of that imagined once-whole world does there really arise the possibility of turning to others as other, as genuinely separate, with their own desires. Only then does the possibility of real loving, of real engagement with others as others—in a shared world—emerge. It seems so important to me that we move beyond narcissism, that we consciously, willingly, embark on that long detour that takes is into the world of others, into the social, the political world.

One of the things I value about archetypal psychology as contrasted with other interpretations of Jung is that it recognizes this challenge and honors the psyche's direction beyond itself into engagement with the world. Recently I have been thinking anew of a lecture on the Oedipus myth I heard James Hillman give eight or so years ago, a lecture which didn't really sink in then. Hillman presented it at a conference on family therapy in Santa Barbara. I was scheduled to be one of the respondents. Looking around I could see how completely bewildered by the talk most of the family therapists in the room were and so most of my attention was focused on what I might say when Hillman was done that might speak to them. But in rereading I've been free to attend to what this essay says to me—now.

Hillman's thesis is that the Oedipus myth has been the myth of the century inaugurated by Freud—not so much because we've been so focused in looking *at* that myth, at the Oedipus story, but because we seem to be stuck in looking *through* it, that is, caught in looking at myths as a way toward self-understanding. Hillman communicates his deep respect for Freud's relocation of the human world, including the familial world, in the mythical imagination. Freud, he says, helped us to see that the actual family is mythical. But Hillman wants us to see that Freud's Oedipus is not Sophocles'. For Sophocles the *polis* is central. What sets the play in motion is the desperate need to find a cure for the plague that is devastating the city. Finding the truth about oneself is not enough.

Hillman calls for a more polytheistic view, one not dominated by this one myth, yet he realizes how difficult it is to get out of this myth. Even when we try to focus on a different myth, try to imagine therapy differently, through Eros and Psyche or Dionysos, or Persephone, we seem "still be trying to find ourselves, our true story, our identity." As long as our method remains "search for self," he concludes, we are caught in the Oedipus myth.

I have come to realize how true this is of my *Goddess* book. No matter what myth or mythical figure I was focusing on, I was looking at the myth as a way toward self-understanding. The book emerged out of a dream I had some twenty-five years ago within which I announced to a Martin Buber figure "It's time now for me to go in search of HER"—which on waking I understood to mean it was time to go in search of the goddess (or, as I soon discovered, the goddesses). A few weeks ago a student asked me if the HER in the dream wasn't really myself in the Jungian sense of my Self. My answer—my usual answer to most questions—was "Yes and No—but definitely in a sense Yes." I had turned to the Greek goddesses (and later to the Greek gods) to help me/us see who we are and what we might become out of a deep conviction that psyche needs images to nurture its growth and that reflection on our own lives can deepen our understanding of the myths.

Rereading Hillman's lecture helped me acknowledge the degree to which my book did involve looking at the goddesses through the Oedipus myth. I also realized that Hillman's critique recapitulates Buber's critique of aiming at the self, Buber's conviction that I become I through saying Thou, through turning to the other with whom I'm engaged as truly *other*—something whose truth I thought I had learned long ago. But I seem to need to learn the same lesson over and over: keep having to discover the right balancing for me of what I've learned from Jung and from Buber, keeping having to find a way of honoring both the call of what Jung calls the Self and the call of the actual human others whom I meet in my day to day life.

I am not saying there was anything wrong about what I did then when I wrote the book. I still see it as valid, as almost necessary for me then. And I'm aware of how much it still speaks to others. Nor am I saying that others will necessarily find themselves at the place in which I now find myself. *The Goddess* is still my favorite among the books I've written, though I am very aware I couldn't write this book now. Partly because I just know more now than I did then. Partly because I may be in a more private place. That book grew out of the only time in my life during which I was living essentially alone, unpartnered. It was a time when I may have felt more free to talk about my life without also talking about another's.

But maybe just because I've done *that*.

Maybe because as a Crone my interests are different.

Maybe because it's a different time, the beginning of a new millennium—even though I don't fully know what that might mean.

But I have a hunch that we may be moving from looking through Oedipus to looking through Athene. Perhaps the 20th century was Freud's century, the century of psychoanalysis, of depth psychology, the century of Oedipus (as the 19th century had been the century of Antigone). I'm imagining that perhaps the 21st century will be the century of Athene…(I'll say a little more about this possibility further on.)

I do know my own perspective has begun to shift—not because of Hillman; I didn't really get what he was saying until I'd gotten to a similar place on my own, but along the same lines. As so often before I discover retrospectively that what feels like something I've come to on my own, along a very idiosyncratic path, is actually part of a *Zeitgeist*—like having five children in the 1950s, like turning to the goddesses in the early 70s. Once again I discover that this redirection is not mine alone.

I have just finished reading Bruce Lincoln's *Theorizing Myth* in which he writes of his turn away from the perspectives of a dearly loved teacher, Mircea Eliade, away from Eliade's focus on the polarities of sacred and profane, cosmos and history, his focus on ecstatic experience as being the central themes of myth. Now, he says, he would define myth as "ideology through narrative" and would now see as of primary importance the role myths play in political power struggles.

I find that I, too, am now more interested in the political meaning of myths than in their psychological meaning. Though that's not quite right either: I'm now more interested in their political meaning *as integral to* their psychological meaning, or in their psychological meaning as having a political dimension. I'm persuaded now we have to attend to both dimensions as implicating one another.

I'm still drawn to the illuminating power of myths—and of gods and goddesses—but differently. When I wrote *The Goddess* the classicists I was most drawn to were Carl Kerenyi and Walter Otto. Like them I was trying to capture what Kerenyi speaks of as "the essence of what the Greeks meant by Hermes" or Aphrodite or Hera, the archetypal aspect of these divinities, the psychological aspect. This meant adopting an a-historical a-chronological view, bringing together what I could learn of the preliterate understanding with all the literary evidences from Homer to Ovid and creating a kind of composite view. I was hoping in my own more awkward way to imitate Kerenyi's deceptive, graceful moving back and forth among all the strata as though all existed at once, spatially rather than temporally. It was then not a big step to see how these goddesses still existed, to discover their immediate contemporary psychological relevance.

I can still feel the tug of this essentialist approach.

But now, as I've said, it's a different aspect of the goddesses that I find most compelling.

I am less interested in how they illumine my self-understanding, more interested in the *otherness* of the Greek perspective, how it might provide *disorientation* rather than orientation. I want to find a way of honoring the historical distance, as Buber tried to honor the foreignness of the Biblical perspective in his *Verdeutsch-ing* of the Hebrew Bible.

That is, my sense now is that—precisely in order for the Greek perspective to help us imagine differently, creatively, hopefully—we need to begin by seeing that how they imagined, mythed, the city is different from the ways most familiar to us.

Yet relevant.

As Nicole Loraux says at the end of *Children of Athena*: "There is no statement about Athens that does not nourish very contemporary passions."

I still find that goddesses (and gods) are good to think with—but want to think with them, through them, about our responsibility toward the human community. To begin to do this means turning to other teachers, different interpreters. I am now more drawn to the post-structuralist approach of classicists such as Jean Pierre Vernant, Nicole Loraux, Froma Zeitlin. I want now to learn what I can from them about reading myths in their civic framework, in terms of how they are actively functioning in history, in the city in a particular period. These authors make it so evident that one can't separate myth from the city, can't look at the history of the city apart from its myths. Their focus is on the city's self-image, how it sees itself imaginally. This, of course, includes idealization and wish-fulfillment; it involves recognizing the political efficacy of the imagination and particularly of myth. Myths were used to articulate and express the dominant perspective, to mold and legitimate civic experience; but they were also the locus of ideological struggle. The inherited myths could be revisioned to contest and challenge the dominant view; they were malleable, resilient, alive.

These scholars have persuaded me that for the Greeks—at least those of classical Athens—the gods were more important in relation to polis than to *psyche*—and that this is the aspect that now interests me. Loraux, for one, makes plain that she has no interest in the origins of the myths nor in their psychological relevance, only in what 5th century texts and rituals and art tell us about how myth was functioning then and there. I can't follow her in this; I want it *all*: the pre-history of the myths before their 5th century appropriation and their post-history, the psychological relevance as well as the historical function—but I *do* want to "get" *this* part. To explore how myths were actively functioning in history then, helps us understand the relevance of myth to political life, to *our* political life.

For even when I, when we, become aware of the importance of psyche's engagement with the polis, I'm not sure I or we—who begin from a depth psychological, archetypal perspective—really know where to go with this insight. I see us as somewhat like Hermann Hesse whose plan for *The Glass Bead Game* was dramatically changed under the impact of Nazism: so that whereas originally Castalia, the esthetic mountaintop world, had been the ideal, in the book as written the protagonist Joseph Knecht knows he has to leave Castalia for the flatland, the world of everyday human life. But then Hesse doesn't quite know what to do with him when he gets him there. I know how struck I was by the thin-ness of Hillman's own answer to a student question about what we should *do* to express our commitment to social justice. Vote, he said, talk about who you vote for. He seemed actually to be saying more when he returned to Plato, to the *Republic*, and to Plato's reflections on justice, his sense of the profound analogies between the health of the soul and of the city and how these weren't just analogies. How the health of either nurtures the health of the other, how if one is diseased, the other will inevitably also be.

My hunch is that the point is not immediately to DO something, in a practical action kind of way.

Maybe that is not our task, the task of us depth psychologists and teachers and writers.

Perhaps our task is rather to imagine differently.

To direct our imagining to the world.

To re-myth the city.

To recognize that cities are always mythic, always ordered by mythic assumptions, always in a sense imaginal constructs—and that the life, the health of the city, depends on the vitality, the life-bringing, renewal-bringing, power of the myths, depends on the sense that the myths themselves are alive, that we are imagining the city creatively.

I believe that the imagination is always pluralistic, polytheistic, that it sees in a variety of ways at once. Polytheism means recognizing the many different energies that sustain community and that if ignored destroy it. (The Greeks, remember, knew that the same gods and goddesses who send the plagues that disrupt communal life are the only ones with the power to remove them.) Polytheism also means imagining the validity of the perspectives held by different members of the community, means recognizing that there is not just one valid standpoint.

I believe that our re-mything of the city, our attempts to envision the city polytheisticly, can be helped along by attending to how the Greeks mythed the city. The Greek world is, of course, different from ours; we don't see as they did, don't worship their gods, don't practice their rituals. Just because of that they may help us imagine *our* world differently.

Which means beginning with Athene—with Athena *Polias,* the goddess of the *polis,* of the human community. "Cities are the gift of Athena," we are told. Indeed, in Greek religion, in cult, Athene was more important than even Zeus (and probably historically a much more ancient deity), precisely because of this association with history, with the human community, with civilization. She was viewed as the protector, the rescuer from every danger. The rituals performed in her temples were thought to guarantee the continued existence of a city. Indeed, we might say she *was* the community, for it was through the mediation of her presence, through the wholeness-creating power of her cult that her worshippers knew themselves as fellow-citizens.

Athene keeps us in the world of others, helps us to remember the sacred importance of its problems. Perhaps the epithet associated with Athene that seems most important to me is that she is called the "Ever Near"—that she's here where we find ourselves, that she's here when we need her. This goddess embodies the possibility of holding onto feminine consciousness in the heart of the city, in the heart of the work-world—not just in the house like Hestia, or in marriage like Hera, or in the fields like Demeter, or in the forest like Artemis, or in bed like Aphrodite—but in the apparently, traditionally, male-dominated world.

We need to remember that Athene (*the* deity associated with civic life) is a goddess, a female deity. The Greeks both knew this and were uncomfortable with it, and so they projected this discomfort on her and represented her as sometimes denying her own female origins. In Aeschylus's *Eumenides,* as you may remember, she asserts:

There is no mother anywhere who gave me birth,
and, save for marriage,
I am always for the male with all my heart,
and strongly on my father's side

So as we think about the relevance of these Greek traditions to our own experience of, our own frustrations with, our own hopes for communal life, we need to acknowledge that Athene was used to validate a very patriarchal society—and at the same time used to contest, to question, its primary assumptions.

There is tension, paradox, inherent in this goddess. The myth that relates how Athene rather than Poseidon became the patron divinity of Athens say that it was the women (who in that mythic time were in the majority) who voted for Athene—and that to appease Poseidon the men then promptly deprived them of their citizenship, of their right to vote. Thus, to begin with, Athene was a goddess of women.

Athene was called *Polymetis*; she is a goddess gifted with a many-faceted, practical and compassionate wisdom as opposed to the cool, calm hyper-rationality associated with Apollo, the god "who comes from afar." In Athene's realm one recognizes the need for political action to achieve concrete goals in particular circumstances, action based on really seeing *these* circumstances, not on a priori theoretical principles. This practical wisdom, this *metis*, Athene *owes* to her mother, *Metis*, the goddess Zeus swallowed, the mother she herself may often deny or forget but who is nevertheless the source of this wisdom.

In art Athene is most often represented as either standing, erect and threatening with shield and spear, or seated and tranquil, with shawl and spindle. The shield is of course connected to *Athena Promacus*, Athene as warrior, the determined protector of those in her care. War as she practices it is defensive not aggressive; one of her emblems is the olive tree—whose branches still serve as symbols of peace and reconciliation.

She is *Athena Nike*, Victorious Athene, but she is also Mourning Athene, for her warrior aspect is integrally connected to her own vulnerability. Not even Athene always wins; not even she can always protect those in her care. Indeed, my favorite relief shows Athena with downcast head, sorrowfully leaning on her spear, as she mourns her inability to have protected her city, those she loved, against the Persians.

She is *Athena Hygeia*, Healing Athene, not only a healer of literal wounds as any war deity must be but of all the rifts that separate us from one another.

Athene, according to Aeschylus, is the founder of juries. There's a recognition here that justice involves deciding between rival interests and claims, that communal life will necessarily be a scene of conflict. Athene is given the deciding vote when a jury is tied—and always, the stories tell us, her vote is for acquittal.

Her almost ever-present shield serves not only to protect but also to reflect. Knowing in Athene's realm is reflective knowing; it involves recognizing that something needs to be done, but then standing back to think out how most successfully, most healingly, to bring it about. Athene represents discriminating, focused energy, both the sudden bright idea and its seasoning.

That is, she protects us against the rashness of acting on impulse, helps us remember to think before we act. In illustration I think of the opening scene in the *Iliad*: Achilles, on the point of physically attacking Agamemnon, feels Athene, visible only to him, gently touching him on the shoulder, giving him a moment to recall himself, collect himself.

She teaches us how to harness instinctive energy, as she teaches Bellerophon what he must do to harness the wild untamed winged horse, Pegasus.

She is *Athena Pronoia*, Fore-sighted Athene, who enables us to look ahead to the future, to plan.

The spindle reminds us that Athene was also called *Athena Ergane*, Athene the Worker, goddess of weaver and potter and silversmith, of artist and artisan, of things made for daily use, associated with the daily, ordinary, cooperative, collaborative tasks that make communal living possible.

She is *Athena Kourotrophos*, nurturer of the young, not as a literal mother but as one who helps raise the young to be contributing members of the community. Athene supports them in the fulfillment of their dreams not hers for them, helps Bellerophon realize his youthful dream of harnessing Pegasus, helps Perseus slay Medusa.

One of her favorite guises is as the wise old man, Mentor. As Mentor she comes both to Odysseus in the midst of his too long delayed journey home and to the son who despairs of ever seeing his father again. She is, we might say, the prototypical mentor.

But fully honoring Athene requires acknowledging the polytheistic context, remembering that Athene exists in a pantheon that distinguishes among different aspects of divine energy by including a rich diversity of goddesses and gods. The Greeks never imagined Athene as the only deity relevant to our life together, our life in the city. The Greek gods and goddesses can only be understood in the context of their relationships with one another; they do not exist in isolation. To know them we must know them in their polytheistic context, engaged with other deities who represent incommensurable but undeniable energies and values. In cult one never simply addressed an Olympian god or goddess, but always a particular aspect or localized epiphany. A primary reason to consult an oracle was the need to discover which name or epithet one would need to use.

For the Greeks it was the pantheon, not the gods in isolation from one another, that made visible the ordering pattern through which they imagined the natural world, the psyche, and especially human society. That is, cities may be the gift of Athene—but our life together brings us into relationship to *all* the goddesses and gods, all have a political function, the rituals dedicated to all of them have a central civic aspect. To ignore any of these deities is to invite those plagues, those disruptions, which only honoring them can heal.

Of course in this short essay I can't do justice to how each of the Greek gods and goddesses can illuminate our understanding of how intimately soul and city are intertwined but perhaps I can say enough to communicate what I mean. Let me begin with the gods and with the pre-eminent god, Zeus. For though cities may be the gift of Athene there is a sense in which Athene is especially associated with *her* city, Athens, whereas Zeus is *Zeus Panhellionios*, god of *all* the Greeks, indeed of all Greek speakers, of all those who honor the Olympian gods, so that in the Trojan War he sides with neither Greek or Trojan, whereas the other gods and goddesses align themselves with one side or the other.

He is also *Zeus Xenias,* the god who insists on the sanctity of the guest, the stranger, the alien—again an opening up of the notion of communal involvement beyond a narrow commitment to a particular community. I think of the tale that Ovid tells of Zeus and Hermes coming to earth disguised as beggars, knocking on door after door in search of a bed for the night and being turned away, until at last they found a welcome in the most modest home of all where Baucis and Philemon shared with them the bits of food left in their cupboard and their last flagon of homemade wine and were ready to sacrifice their only goose, a household pet, all unaware of whom they were serving. The neighbors are drowned, the couple richly rewarded.

As Hesiod tells it, Zeus came into power after Ouranos who couldn't bear to have the tidy universe corrupted with such weird creatures as the Cyclopes and the Hundred Handed, and after Cronos who was so fearful of his own children usurping his power that he swallowed them. Now under Zeus things are in place, a permanent order has been established. Zeus is secure in rule, and maintains order without suppressing diversity, vitality, life. He is the god of things as they are. He rules *with*, not alone, as the head of a family of gods.

As the father-god ruling over a patriarchal family, Zeus epitomizes patriarchal rule, patriarchal order—the world as it is. Zeus helps us *see* patriarchy, or at least a particular patriarchy, with its blessings (there *are* blessings) and its limitations and oppressions. Zeus may help us see that we can't go back, that this is where we go on. To me this suggests that we can't really live as postpatriarchal women unless men become postpatriarchal men; otherwise what we'd have would be only counter-patriarchy. And, paradoxically, the traditions about this paradigmatic patriarch reveal more recognition of male-female interdependence and of a usually left unconscious feminine aspect of men than is at first apparent. Nicole Loraux (and others) have written convincingly of how absolutely central to Greek thinking was the tension between the fantasy of an all male world and the recognition that men are born of women, ultimately dependent on them for their very being. How underneath the vaunted male superiority there lurks a fear and envy of female power. At birth Zeus is rescued from his child-swallowing father by his mother and grandmother and then raised by nymphs; without Metis's wise counsel he would never have succeeded in rescuing his older siblings from their father's belly nor would he have succeeded in his battle against the male Titans without the support of their female counterparts. As we've seen, he turns to his daughter Athene rather than to any of his sons as his heir, as the one who to whom he delegates his authority when he leaves Olympus. Yet clearly he does less well relating to females of his own generation, as though relating to women of equal status is too confusing. So Hera is both the older sister/wife to whom he comes for comfort and the younger sister/wife whom he betrays and misuses. He gives birth to both Athene and Dionysos and takes on a feminine disguise well enough to deceive Callisto. This can be understood as male usurpation of female prerogative—or as a kind of fantasized transcendence of the ultimacy of gender difference. Or should I say AND rather than OR? In any case, reflection on Zeus leads us to reflect on the imaginal aspects of patriarchal rule and its inherent fragility. Here, too, it is not too difficult to see how inner and outer, psychological and political, tensions mirror one another.

Apollo, too, a god not associated with any particular city who comes from outside, from afar, may help us imagine our relation to the civic community in a complex way. At Delphi he presided over a panhellenic institution to which one came not so much to worship *him* as to learn what god had been offended, what god needed to be propitiated. He sided with the Trojans and in the *Iliad* seeks to avoid the infighting among the gods and puts an end to Achilles' rampage after Patroclus' death. He is associated with the distancing that makes it possible to look more objectively, more rationally. But we misunderstand Apollo radically if we associate him with a naïve confidence in the rational. He is a god of purification not of unstained purity. Remember, he is himself a murderer. He wins possession of the oracle at Delphi by murdering the Python and later slays the Cyclops—and both times has to undergo humiliating punishment. The Delphic *Stepteria* ritual celebrates the return of Apollo the polluter as Apollo the purified who now has the power to bring purification to the community. In the Attic *Thargelia*, an annual civic renewal ritual, *two* scapegoats, two *pharmakoi*, assigned the role of agents of civic pollution, are banished from the city and stoned (perhaps to death) and thus the city is purified. Apollo is a god of order and moderation, precisely because of his intimate knowledge of his own murderous side. In the *Oresteia*, too, he is associated with the possibility of putting an end to the seemingly endless cycles of blood vengeance in Agamemnon's family's history. He is the god of the fresh start. Apollo is a god of plague and healing, a healer of disasters that affect the whole community (often disasters he has himself inflicted)—war, plague, drought—as his son Asclepius heals the wounds of individuals.

Apollo is the paradigmatic *kouros*, the youth on the edge of manhood, at the height of his beauty and promise, and is particularly associated with the initiation of young males into full adult status, that is into the privileges and responsibilities of citizenship. As such he seems to embody the male need to separate from the feminine, the chthonic, the emotional. To represent the conflict between our longing for order and our knowledge of the underlying never fully eradicable chaos. To signify the commitment to stand for *this* side, in full acknowledgement of the other. I recall how often I have looked at the columns of Apollo's temples at Delphi thrusting up from earth to sky from the perspective of *Athene Pronoia*'s tholos down below—and then at the mountain beyond which dwarfs that proud erection. The earth, the chthonic, is more primal but Apollo reminds us that we nonetheless must (most of the time) side with consciousness. And above all, he is the god who calls to us, Know Yourself—Remember that you are mortal not divine.

And as mortals we need one another, need community, need to be in communication. The god who most clearly brings that into view is Hermes, "the friendliest of gods to men," the messenger god, the god of trade and merchants—who is, of course, also a trickster figure, god of misunderstandings and of surprises, both welcomed and not. Hermes is associated with the shady side of life—with pickpockets, gamblers, thieves, pimps. Many of his rituals are inversion rituals during which (temporarily) slaves take on the role of masters or thievery is permitted. He reminds us that there is a *shadow* aspect not only of the psyche but always also of the public world. His herms stood just beyond the threshold of every house; he presided over that transition between the private world and the public and indeed over all transitions, including those between sleep and waking, upper world and underworld. He is a psychopomp who leads us into the world below, the world where psyches live, but is perhaps associated even more with guidance *back,* back to the world of others.

Let me more briefly remind us of Hephaistos, the only god who works, the smithy, the metal-worker, the maker of beautiful objects. The Greeks in the classical period tended to disparage making, working with one's hands, but because of course they knew how their lives (devoted to civic and ritual affairs) were dependent on the work of others, even they associated this god with the transition to civilized human existence from a former time when we lived in caves in the mountains like animals. To honor Hephaistos as a god was to acknowledge the alchemical magic involved in the smith's transformations of the base into the beautiful. That in cult and myth he was closely associated with Athene implied a recognition that beauty is an essential part of city life: access to the beautiful (sculpture and architecture, the theater, music) is part of what makes a city a city. His brother Ares reminds us that there are deeply troubling drives that really do threaten society, that really must be rejected—the barbaric past, brute rage—and reminds us how easily these can still overwhelm us. But Ares *is* a god, a god the city must take into account, a god the city may often try to invoke on its own behalf but always at great risk.

Though we may not immediately think of Artemis in connection with the city, the Greeks understood that she represents not the natural world *per se*—for that they had Gaia—but the wilderness defined as *outside the city,* and thus in necessary relation to it. She embodies the human need for moments of solitude and for connection to the natural world and to our own embodied natural selves. In her primary association with females at the moment of transition between childhood and married adulthood she also has a polis function. At Brauron she presided over maiden initiations that prepared young girls for their weddings, for their roles as wives and mothers. The goddess primarily associated with that later phase was of course Hera, *Hera Teleia,* Hera fulfilled in marriage. And although the myths about Hera mostly represent her as very unfulfilled in her marriage to Zeus, her cult served to provide women with the social support that private relations so desperately need. This in turn was complemented by the primary ritual associated with Demeter, the *Thesmophoria,* a ritual that provided these same wives and mothers with an opportunity to vent the anger and grief associated with their constricted lives. Like other inversion rituals, this one in which women for three days symbolically ruled the city, served in the end to support the status quo, the ongoing life of the city.

The gods already named were gods whose association with civic life the Greeks readily acknowledged. But the tragedians of 5th century Athens felt it important to remind the city of the danger for *the city* inherent in ignoring other gods, particularly Dionysos (in whose theater these warnings were enacted), Hekate and Persephone, Aphrodite and Eros.

Dionysos, the god associated with indestructible *zoe,* with life, intoxication, dissolution, ecstasy, had to be included in the pantheon, not only because the energies he represents so clearly *are* divine but because these energies need to be brought into relation to those embodied in the other gods and goddesses. This god has deep appeal when the dominant order puts too much emphasis on restraint, responsibility, and autonomy but his power is inescapably and frighteningly present at times when the traditional order is clearly threatened as during the later years of the Peloponnesian War. Never have these two sides been presented in such disturbingly close conjunction as in Euripides' *Bacchae* but there is a sense in which almost all of the plays performed in Dionysus' theater (as part of a six day ritual celebrated in his honor) served to bring the audience, the assembled citizenry of Athens, into touch with all the latent ambivalences and tensions—particularly those between familial and political commitments and between male and female allegiances and between the chthonic and the Olympian deities. From the dramatists' perspective the health of the city depended on the acknowledgment of conflicts whose obscuring threatened the very stability it was intended to uphold. The other major ritual associated with this god, the *Anestheria,* a new wine festival, provided an occasion for the souls of the dead, "the thirsty ones," to emerge from the underworld and to spend a day in the daylit world—a reminder that the dead, the ancestors, are part of the community still.

As death, its inescapability and its fearsomeness, is part of life here, here in the upper world. So that, of course, there is a temple to Asclepius, the god of healing who might help one avoid death for a time at least, in the heart of the city, and Hekate and Persephone, too, must be given due respect. Hekate represents the importance of mourning rites (though in 5th century Athens because the powers that be viewed the extravagance of female grief as threateningly unsettling, its enactments were legally restricted). As Sophocles' *Antigone* shows, it was believed that without proper burial and mourning the souls of the dead would be caught between the upper and lower world and forced to join Hekate's retinue of ghostly angry howling dogs. Guilt toward the dead makes them fearsome, as does the prospect of our own death. To assuage the latter the Greeks had the rituals dedicated to Persephone at Eleusis. It was important to the Athenians that this cult be under the city's supervision, that the Minor Mysteries in the spring would be celebrated in the city's precincts and that the procession of the major celebration in the fall begin in the city. Participation in the Eleusinian ritual was not obligatory, not imposed by virtue of one's public identity as a citizen or a member of a particular age cohort of gender-defined group or professional association. Thus this ritual also serves to confirm that there are private inner pulls whose power or emergence the city cannot control but must respect. So the honoring of Persephone by the city might also be understood as a recognition of the need for the times of deep engagement with an inner world, with soul, to which Persephone calls.

In my essay "Turning Again to Athene" I wrote of how Athene makes room for Aphrodite in her own citadel, how on the western slope of the Acropolis there was a shrine of Aphrodite and Eros, and near the Propylaea a shrine to Aphrodite Pandemos and Peitho (Persuasion). I noted that (contra Plato) Aphrodite Pandemos is Aphrodite as the goddess who embraces the whole people and makes available the fellow feeling, the empathy, necessary for the existence of a community. Indeed, in Corinth she was worshipped as their equivalent of Athens' Athene. I also noted how the two goddesses are brought together in the Arrephoria, a ritual that involves two young girls, between the ages of seven and eleven, who have spent a whole year in the precincts of Athene on the Acropolis. At the end of that year in the dark of the night they carry a basket whose contents they are forbidden to discover to the shrine of Aphrodite in the Gardens and then before dawn they bring something else back, again something secret and sacred. The well-being of the entire city somehow was understood to depend on the right carrying out of this female initiation ritual under the tutelage of Athene into those mysteries of female sexual identity associated with Aphrodite.

In that essay I also wrote about Aristophanes' comedy, the *Lysistrata,* which again brings these two goddesses together. This play, written during the darkest period of the Peloponnesian War, a war that had set Greek against Greek, expresses the playwright's desperate hope that some resolution might still be possible. His imagined resolution was of course only an illusion, mostly, I believe, a cry of pain over what won't happen, can't happen, except on the stage. Yet it suggests that to be able to imagine such a resolution, nonetheless, means something, is itself a gift. His play reminds us of the central role the imagination (Aphrodite's gift) plays in that empathic turning to the other which lies at the heart of any genuine communion between one human being and another and thus at the heart of human community.

I see Aristophanes' play as also reminding us of the importance of remembering that the political arena is a sacred realm—what happens there matters, really matters—and what happens there depends on us, though we may need to invoke the goddesses and gods, all of them, for help. Which brings me back to Eros, to the Eros of Freud (and of Hesiod and the Orphics), the Eros who is not the always still childish son of Aphrodite but the Eros co-eval with Gaia herself, the god of beginnings, of the possibility of new beginnings, the god who doesn't so much create as bring things together, into connection. Thus he is, as Auden understood, "Eros, Builder of Cities." Auden also sensed the sadness of this god, his apprehension of how difficult it is for us to honor all the gods, to turn to one another with empathy and hope—and imagination. To remember the sacredness of our life together.

17

Dionysos and Aphrodite

My primary aim in this paper is to explore how mythology—particularly Greek mythology, the mythology with which I am most familiar—might deepen our understanding of the erotic, of its complexities and many-facetedness, and bring us back in touch with its sacred dimension.

And I'll get there; but to get there I find I need to begin with a few words about Freud and his poetics of sexuality. I want to begin with Freud because I want to begin by reminding us of what probably drew most of us to our study of sex to begin with, although almost inevitably we tend to forget or half-forget this as we get more professionally involved as therapists or researchers. That is, I want to remind you of your own experience of the numinosity of sex, of how sex has the power to stir up our deepest hopes and fears, to give us moments of ecstatic fulfillment, moments when we feel most fully ourselves, most deeply in touch with another—but also to remind you of how our sexuality (and that of those whom we get to know intimately) is always also wounded, connected with our or their most painful disappointments, failures, and losses.

I would also want us to remember that human sexuality is never just physical but always also psychological. This, I believe, is what Freud most wanted to communicate, that our sexuality is always mediated through the psyche, through *die Seele*, the soul. Almost everyone who knew Freud, whether acolyte or critic, spoke of how Freud responded to sex as a numinous reality. His early 1905 book, *The Three Essays on Sexuality,* remained throughout his life one of the two of his books that he valued most highly; indeed, he subjected each new edition to extensive reworking. Its thesis was that we have both defined sexuality too narrowly and asked too much of it.

Freud's understanding of human sexuality was *transliteral*; he viewed sexuality as that through which we express our deepest longings, our longing to give all of ourselves to another and our longing to have another direct all their love to us alone, our longing to *be* ourselves and to *lose* ourselves. For Freud our sexuality includes all sensual and affectional currents, all the ways we experience bodily pleasure and all our intense emotional attachments.

He deliberately speaks of the sexual *drive* not instinct—drive is need become wish, biology become psychology. What Freud puts forward is a study of this drive and its vicissitudes, its transformations—that is a *poetics*. He describes the mechanisms—displacement, condensation, reversal—by which our sexual impulses become expressed in myriad ways and emphasizes the polymorphousness, the malleability, the divertibility of human sexuality.

He sees how the nonperiodic character of human sexuality requires us to choose where and when, with whom or what, we respond to sexual impulse. It entails the necessity of delay and diversion—that is, of substitution, sublimation, symbolization.

Freud believes that our sexuality is inextricably connected to a primary experience of loss, and is permeated throughout our lives with the longing to return to a fantasized once-upon-a-time of fusion, bliss, and one-ness. He is also persuaded that our earliest sexuality (that so-called infantile polymorphous perversity)—which inhabits every cell of our body, not just our genitals, and which reaches out indiscriminately, not just to socially acceptable others—is still part of us, albeit mostly unconsciously. He draws our attention to the latent, hidden, often unwelcome side of our sexuality, sexuality different from the socially-approved "normal" genitally-focused heterosexually-directed sexuality that we find it easy to admit to.

Noting that to begin with, in infancy, our sexual aim is clearly pleasure not reproduction, Freud concludes that that is always the primary aim. He reminds us of how early on all of us are both active and passive in our loving and completely indifferent to the gender of those whom we want to touch or be touched by. Then, as we become aware of sexual difference and of social expectations, this original "bisexuality" is disrupted; we become aware of two possible channels, one of which is usually repressed and we become (in terms of our *conscious* sexuality) heterosexual or homosexual—although the other current remains alive in the unconscious.

He also maintains that we are from the get-go profoundly ambivalent creatures, who hate those we love, long for what we dread, desire where we are repulsed. (This, of course, implies that the absence of affect—disinterest, impotence, frigidity—is also sexual.) He sees the sexuality of all of us as a *wounded* sexuality, characterized by repression and denial, limitation and constriction.

Sexuality is for him not only the meeting-place of body and soul, but also of self and other. Our sexuality takes us out of ourselves, toward others—particular, actual, also-desiring others—which we welcome and yet also dread. For we would like to be self-sufficient or to fuse, to lose ourselves in the other, rather than have to confront those actual others with their own desires and wounds.

We ask too much of sex, and this, Freud believes, explains that sadness after intercourse of which the poets have spoken, for sexuality brings us in touch once again with our impossible longings for complete satisfaction.

I have begun with Freud because I wanted to encourage us to understand (and share) Freud's awe of the unconscious energies that in his *Interpretation of Dreams* he speaks of as "indestructible beings which the ancients recognized as being due their homage." Freud recognizes how the unconscious is connected to the embodiment we long to transcend—and how that denial enhances the mythic power of these indestructible forces, these *gods*.

So now at last, it is time to turn to these gods, to the Greek mythological representations of these indestructible beings, which give us images for facets of our experience that are often ignored or pathologized. For the Greeks of the archaic and classical world sexuality was recognized as having a sacred dimension. Their gods and goddesses are themselves clearly sexual beings; perhaps even more important is that the energies they represent enter into us, into our sexuality, are at work *in* us. As Carl Jung put it, the gods have become our pathologies. Though I would say, not only that. The gods and goddesses illumine our lives; they help us discover the connections between the joyful and the terrifying or confusing or dismaying aspects of our experience.

Greek mythology communicates the polyvalence of sexuality; each of the divinities brings into view a different sexuality. I will be focusing on Aphrodite and Dionysos; but there is also a Jovian sexuality, a Hermetic and an Apollonian sexuality, and Hera and Athene and Artemis each help bring into view yet another aspect of how sexuality may enter our psyches, our souls, our lives.

To view sexuality as god-or goddess-given is to acknowledge its metamorphic, transformative power. The gods bring fantasy, imagination, depth to our sexual experience: there is always more going on than immediately appears. They seduce us with the illusion of fulfillment and seem to punish us with the profound suffering that so often follows the momentary fulfillment. But, as the stories make clear, there is even more suffering when these goddesses or gods, these indestructible energies, are denied. Think of how Aphrodite punishes Hippolytus, who wants to believe that he can devote himself to Artemis alone and ignore the goddess of love. Or how Dionysos punishes Pentheus for his resistance to the god's claim to be recognized as a god.

All the Greek gods and goddesses were worshipped by both men and women (though there were some gender-specific rituals associated with many of them). The blessings that Dionysos and Aphrodite may bring into our lives are available to all of us, male and female—and all of us are in danger if we try to evade the energies these deities represent.

Aphrodite

The poets tell us that because Aphrodite was born from the foam that surrounded her father's cut-off sea-tossed genitals, she was known as Aphrodite *Philomedes*, member-loving Aphrodite, as the goddess of all erotic love, all sensual pleasure, all delight in beauty, as blessing all lovemaking dedicated to mutual enjoyment rather than to domination or procreation—male or female, marital or adulterous, heterosexual or homosexual.

To honor Aphrodite is to honor female sexuality as powerful, beautiful, and sacred. Her sexuality was her own; there are no stories of Aphrodite being initiated into her sexuality or losing her virginity. Yet this goddess is most fully herself in turning to others, in the giving and receiving and returning of love. She wants to be loved, to be desired, not to force another's love by the power of her own. In her realm love generates love, not progeny or permanent bonds.

But hers is not just a genital sexuality; her love has a cosmic dimension, is the source of all life and renewal. Hesiod tells us that soon after she first emerges out of the sea as an already full-grown goddess she steps ashore on the island of Cyprus—and beneath her shapely feet, flowers grow. In the Homeric Hymn to Aphrodite as she makes her way up the mountain to entice Anchises to become her lover, the foxes and snakes and panthers, aware of her divine presence despite her attempts to disguise herself as but a mortal woman, all scurry into the bushes to make love. A story like this leads Kenneth Clark to suggest that "all who saw her felt that the instincts they shared with the beasts, they also shared with the gods."[1] Empedocles called Aphrodite the giver of life. (I cannot help but think here of my own experiences of turning to others in a way that stirred to life in them potentialities, creativities, hitherto hidden and dormant—and how important it was to me to know that this was Aphrodite's doing, not my own.)

Aphrodite works through us by working on our souls, by creating states of mind, by evoking feelings, rather than by directly influencing behavior. She leads us to feel most ourselves when led by our feelings and when intimately and emotionally involved with others. She encourages us to risk exposing our feelings to another and opening ourselves to theirs. Truth in her realm means being true to genuine feeling, to desire, to spontaneity, to the moment. Loving out of habit or out of duty is from this perspective a betrayal.

The Greek gods and goddesses are themselves said to suffer what they inflict on others. Yet although for Aphrodite herself love seems to be more pleasurable longing than terrifying desire, her presence in our lives is likely to be more complex. Sappho attributes to Aphrodite every aspect of her experiences of love: passion, tenderness, infatuation, frustration, jealousy, and loneliness. The intimacy of her connection with the goddess empowers a profoundly confident acknowledgement of her own active desire for others and her longing to be desired in turn by them.

We tend, I suspect, first to see this goddess in her goldenness, as smile-loving, laughter-loving Aphrodite, but most of us soon learn that there is also a dark side to what Aphrodite brings into our lives: the terror of being overwhelmed by passion, by obsessive longing or incestuous desire, the pain of unrequited love, of abandonment or loss, of the ebbing of passion. Euripides speaks of her as a power causing oblivion to all duty and restraint, as a doom-bringing goddess. The very same relationship that may initially have been experienced only in its joy-bringing, life-bringing side may come to be seen as destructive, to ourselves or another or both—and then it becomes hard to trust love, to trust Aphrodite, again. To understand this dark side it may help to remember that the same act of dismemberment that gave rise to her also generated the Furies and that she is sometimes spoken of as one of the Fates. It may help to know that her children include not only Eros, Himeros, and Harmonia, but also Deimos (fear), Phobus (panic), Hermaphroditus, and Priapus.

This dark side of Aphrodite is intimately connected to what love, what sexuality, in her realm mean: love of another, *a passion that only this particular other can satisfy*—even though that other may be forbidden or unavailable or implacably inimical. Most of the myths are about this kind of exposure to Aphrodite. I think, for instance of Pasiphae and her obsessive lust for the bull her husband King Minos had refused to sacrifice to Poseidon. I think of Medea who out of her Aphrodite-inspired infatuation with Jason betrays her father and murders her brother. I think of Ariadne whose love for Theseus likewise issued in a betrayal of her own family and the death of her half-brother, the Minotaur. I think of Phaedra made a tool of Aphrodite's punishment of Hippolytus. I think of Myrrh, whose sisters all become prostitutes because their father had ignored Aphrodite, and who herself (perhaps because her mother had boasted she was as beautiful as the goddess) is overtaken with a sexual longing for her father that she cannot put to rest. She eventually succeeds in tricking him into sleeping with her, only to be even more deeply devastated by his repulsion when he discovers her identity than she had been by her "unnatural" desire.

Not that being a favorite of this goddess is an unmitigated blessing either! Here, of course, I am most immediately reminded of Helen who abandons her husband for love (and who wins Sappho's praise for having the courage to do so) but who herself both welcomes and profoundly resents Aphrodite's intrusion into her life. She discovers how impossibly hard it is to let go of being the enchantress, to escape Aphrodite's clutches.

In reflecting on Aphrodite's relation to love and sexuality, we need also to look at passion's integral connection with death and loss. Because love and passion are by their very nature evanescent, honoring Aphrodite entails acceptance of this transience. It means finding the courage to love despite knowing it will not last forever.

Dionysos

Turning to *Dionysos* means turning to a god associated with a very different aspect of sexuality—though it is interesting to realize that he is actually a great-grandson of Aphrodite. (His mother, Semele, was a daughter of Cadmus whose mother was Harmonia, the daughter of Aphrodite and Ares.)

Dionysos, as Kerenyi says, represents the most naked form of *zoe*, of biological life force.[2] Dionysos is the god of the extreme, wine and ecstasy, madness and confusion. The Greeks honored Dionysos because they knew that being taken over by the god can be a blessing, that the loss of self can be a gift, that to be released from the narrow bonds of ego and convention can be not only terrifying but liberating.

The merging with the god that was part of Dionysian cult, of the religious worship of Dionysos, was otherwise wholly uncharacteristic of Greek religion. Whereas Artemis is associated with the wilderness that lies outside the city, Dionysos's wildness threatens the city, lurks within it and within us. This gods does not represent a steady permanent aspect of the world, but rather an aspect that always suddenly appears and disappears. Although he is experienced as coming from outside, in actuality he is always already here. Though a native son of Thebes he is greeted as a stranger when he returns. Though historically speaking he is one of the most ancient Greek gods, he is accepted into the pantheon late, as a god from elsewhere.

Dionysos's appearance signifies the transgression of boundaries; his festivals are times of license, of inversion. The suggestion that unrestrained sexual passion is in some sense divine arouses opposition everywhere he appears. For passion as

Dionysos exposes us to it, *there is no other*—except the god—and he is no longer other; he and I are one. Dionysos is associated with the kind of love-making, the kind of sexuality, where the identity of the other is, for the moment at least, beside the point. There is no other. This erasure of boundaries brings joy and danger, for it betokens a threatening loss of self. This need not mean an orgy or the leather bar; it can happen in the conjugal bed. We may accuse ourselves of "using" the other—but how different to see such complete investment in our own pleasure as an honoring of this god—and what a gift it would be were we able honestly to share with our partner afterwards that the god had been present.

The blurring of boundaries in Dionysos's world includes a blurring of gender boundaries, of the supposedly clear-cut distinction between men and women, the masculine and the feminine, active and passive sexuality. Dionysos himself was born from Zeus's thigh and reared as a girl and is often spoken of as the womanly god. Yet the male members of his retinue, both in myth and in ritual processions, were the satyrs, aggressively masculine, hyperphallic figures whose enormous penises were associated not with procreativity but with arousal for its own sake. When vase painters depicted satyrs, they indulged in exuberant penile fantasies: there are representations of satyrs with two penises, with enormous erect penises with glans exposed. Satyrs are shown masturbating, engaging in anal intercourse or in sex with multiple partners. Though there is mockery and derision here, there is nonetheless also a sense of the divinity inherent in this extravagant natural untamed male sexuality, as the worship of Pan and Priapus confirms.

Dionysos thus represents an eros among men that may exalt the phallus, but he also represents a male sexuality that may do without it. He is himself often depicted as a god without a phallus. He is the only Greek god of whom it might be said out loud that he permitted himself to be entered, to take on the passive role in adult male homosexual intercourse. Once upon a time, we are told, soon after Dionysos came to maturity he sought to rescue his mother Semele from the underworld. After all, if he is a god, his mother belongs on Mt. Olympus with the other deities. He is helped to find one of the very hidden entrances to Hades by an old shepherd who in recompense asks to be allowed to make love to the god once he has completed his mission. When Dionysos returns to fulfill his pledge, the herdsman is long since dead, so the god carves an enormous phallus out of the trunk of an old fig tree and lowers himself upon it. This story has a ritual corre-late: generally in the classical world being an adult male meant an exclusive com-mitment to an active, penetrating sexuality, but in the Dionysian mysteries celebrated at Lerna male adults were re-initiated into a passive sexuality that they had foresworn after leaving adolescence behind. Dionysos, this suggests, was associated with a vision of a less one-sided masculinity, one that could encompass receptivity and vulnerability, that could acknowledge the pleasure of being entered, of being made love to.

The womanly god was also, not surprisingly, a god of women. The female followers of Dionysos were called maenads; like the satyrs maenads were both mythical figures and actual historical female worshippers of the god (who were called "maenads" only during time spent on the mountaintops engaged in Dionysian ritual). That is, human maenads were women who temporarily left their conjugal households and during the time they spent engaged in ritual were free to release energies ordinarily repressed. Dionysos called women from their identification with their social roles as wives and mothers and invited them to throw off the patriarchal bonds by which they were usually constrained. The ritual gave them an opportunity to discover the beauty and power of their own sexuality, their bonds with one another, and their connection to the natural instinctual world. This male god was thus seen as having the power to open women to their own sexuality, their own capacity to feel desire, experience pleasure, enjoy orgasm. Female sexuality in Dionysos's realm is a sexuality dedicated to one's own pleasure, a sexuality that is not other-directed, a sexuality that has no need for a substitute phallus. Dionysos is associated with truths about women, about our sexuality, that we can experience only apart from men. Alone among the Greek gods Dionysos is never accused of seduction or rape. He does not violate women but rather brings them to themselves. But why, we can't help asking, is it a *male* god who is imagined as having this power? Perhaps this is a way of signifying that when just among themselves women get in touch with their own *active* sexuality, the kind of sexuality the Greeks thought of as quintessentially male.

The maenads went to the mountains to dance for joy, but sometimes this opening up of themselves to their own pent-up sexuality led to more than joy. Euripides suggests that they only became crazed and destructive when their mysteries were profaned, intruded upon, when spied upon as by Pentheus. The frightening stories about the maenads describe what happens when women are cut off from their own power and sexuality, and from one another. These stories describe how the obsessive insistence on the expression of too long denied sexuality may move into a kind of aggressivity, symbolized in myth by accounts of frenzied dismemberments of fawns and kids by the maenads' bare hands and greedy devouring of still quivering raw flesh. I would say that this Dionysian energy is terrifying not only to men but also to ourselves. To be brought in touch with our raw instinct and its compulsive power is frightening and dangerous, but indubitably the work of a god.

What we can learn from Greek mythology is really something we already know but perhaps need to be reminded of: that sexuality is transformative, many-faceted, life-giving—and life-destroying. And, of course, that Dionysos and Aphrodite represent only two of its many aspects.

Notes

1. Kenneth Clark, *The Nude* (New York: Pantheon, 1956) 63.

2. Carl Kerenyi, *Dionysos* (Princeton: Princeton University Press, 1976) 221.

18

Beyond Psychology

So: what might I have to say in response to the theme of "Threshold"? I'm such a skeptic about big turning points, especially about anything really significant being involved in the turn from the 20th to the 21st century.

It helps me to remember that Janus, the Latin god of thresholds is two-faced, looks forward and backward, inside and out, and thus to realize that my way of looking forward seems to require looking back, seems to involve remembering, honoring what Freud called *Nachtraglichkeit*—for which "deferred action" (the Standard Edition's most usual rendition) is a lousy translation—and "belatedness" (the translation Lacanians seem to favor) not much better. A literal rendering of the German would yield something like "the quality of being carried after," phrasing which communicates Freud's recognition of how experiences and memory traces get revised at a later date to fit in with fresh experience or with the attainment of a new stage of development. These revisions then have the power to endow the earlier moment with new meaning and with fresh psychical effectiveness. Freud emphasized that such revisionings are occasioned by new events or situations and happen primarily in relation to unassimilated experience. They involve not simply repetition or delayed discharge, but a real working-over, a transformation. That is, remembering is always redescription, remaking. The echo is different each time. The German word for remembering is *Erinnerung*—interiorization, inwarding—a word that suggests that remembering means taking the recalled event into our own souls. This is what each return to Freud seems to ask of me: to rework not just repeat, knowing that there are richnesses there still waiting to be recovered.

In a recent reading of Wolfgang Giegerich's *The Soul's Logical Life* I was struck by the claim that his project of *Sublating* Psychology goes beyond Hillman's project of *ReVisioning* Psychology in important and necessary ways, for it led me to realize that I see this theme, "Beyond Psychology," as intrinsic to depth psychology, not as a postscript or an afterward. That it's intrinsic seems to mean that it has to be done over and over again. One way of getting at this is to repeat Adam Phillips' suggestion that there is a PostFreudian Freud in Freud himself[1]—a Freud who is always already beyond the Freud we know—but also an Enlightenment Freud, a Freud who calls forth Jung as Jung calls forth Hillman and Hillman calls forth Giegerich.

To which I want to add that in a sense as we've moved through this chain of revisioners we haven't gotten anywhere that we weren't already at! We can't miss the recurring chant—"Your psychology isn't soulful enough, your soul isn't soulful enough, your unconscious isn't UNconscious enough"—a chant which I see as parallel to the chant among the mid20th century theologians I studied in graduate school—"Your god isn't God, isn't sufficiently other." Because it is so difficult for us not to move into reification or positivism, the chant is inevitably a recurring one.

We seem always to be trying to get beyond reification, beyond positivism, and beyond literalism. Giegerich sees this as inescapably true of an imaginal psychology because the imaginal only exists in relation to the literal as its negativity and is therefore tied to it. He believes that a full-fledged overcoming can, however, happen in thought. I question this. I don't believe there is any Notion, any Idea, no matter how rarefied, how Hegelian, how sublated that is not subject to the literalizing impulse. Literalizing is what we do, one of the things we do, because we want to know (even the unknowable), want to feel secure (even as we recognize both the impossibility and the cost of security), because (to introduce a Freudian theme I'll return to later) there is a death drive (which is what this longing for certainty and security ultimately represents). Furthermore just as the death drive isn't bad, neither is the pull to literalism. What's bad is being stuck there, unresponsive to the pull of Eros or of the imaginal.

Poised as we now are at the beginning of the 21st century it may seem convenient to speak of the 20th century as Freud's century, as Paul Robinson did in his review of the book accompanying the Library of Congress's Freud exhibit. Robinson suggests, "We may safely pronounce him the dominant intellectual presence" of the century that opened with the publication of Freud's *Interpretation Of Dreams* in 1900.[2] In the middle of that century in a book published just as I was beginning graduate school, *Freud: The Mind of the Moralist*, Philip Rieff suggested that (in large measure due to Freud's influence) earlier understandings of the human as primarily political man or religious man or economic man had now been superseded by the notion of psychological man. By "psychological man" Rieff meant a vision of the human in which self-concern takes precedence over social concerns, a vision which encourages careful concentration on the self and withdrawal from the painful tension of assent and dissent in our relation to society. Rieff recognized the appeal of this pull to subjectivity in a soul-less, technology dominated world—but also how it inevitably intensifies alienation. He warned, "We may learn every cure must expose us to new illness."[3] It is clear he would not have been surprised that after one hundred years of psychotherapy we haven't gotten any better!

Rieff himself wasn't quite saying that this is what Freud offered, but rather that it is what we've taken from him; it is how Freud has in large measure been understood. It is this understanding of Freud, of psychological man, that leads us to believe we must now instead turn to post-psychological man. It is, however, my belief that Freud himself saw the focus on subjectivity, on the individual inner person, as problematic. The real problem, as Russell Jacoby says in his *Social Amnesia* (published fifteen years after Rieff's book), is not Freud but the forgetting of Freud, the repression of Freud, the assimilation of Freud to positivism. Unlike Rieff Jacoby believes that "Freud *undid* the primal bourgeois distinction between the private and the public, the individual and society."[4] Freud insisted that we are in society and it is in us. But this got forgotten—in large measure because of the distorted translation of Freud, both in the literal sense of the Strachey translation (which, among other equally disastrous distortions, translates Freud's *Seele*, the German word for "soul" as "mental organization" and Freud's *Ich*, the intimate everyday way of referring to oneself, "I", as "ego") and of the physical translation after Hitler came to power of the center of the psychoanalytical world from German-speaking Europe to America. (This latter "translation" led to the dominance of the Anglo-Saxon medical, conformist version of psychoanalysis that Freud had always valiantly though mostly unsuccessfully criticized.) Along with these translations came a focus on therapy rather than theory. Jacoby argues that when we dismiss theory we all too easily move toward assimilationist therapy—toward empiricism, positivism, pragmatism.

Because of how easily this happens, depth psychology keeps returning to the question of the separation of psyche and society, and seems often not to recognize that the point is not to move from a concern with soul to a concern with the world, for aiming at the world is just as problematic as aiming at the self. The problematics persist as long as we see world and self as separate, as opposed, as long as we see psychology and politics as two distinct concerns. Recognizing the inadequacy of this disjunction is, I think, what we have in mind when we say we now find ourselves in a post-psychological world: we seem to understand that we have to go beyond psychology but in a way that recognizes and includes psychology, the kind of going beyond suggested by the Hegelian term, *Aufgehoben*.

But, I want to insist: there's nothing very new about this. In 1939, the year that both Freud and he died, Otto Rank published a book called *Beyond Psychology*, in which he presents psychoanalysis as representing the end of the bourgeois era. Rank is persuaded of the inadequacy of an individual-focused psychology to explain the social turmoil brought about by the rise of Nazism. He views psychoanalysis as part of the human attempt to control the irrational, to explain and thus restrict life, and announces that it is now time to go beyond individual psychology—beyond any rational explanation, beyond any logos. We are called, he says, to live beyond psychology, beyond the expectation of a cure or interpretation that would resolve the pain of living, called to be courageous, to live irrationally, called beyond individual psychology. We need the Thou, the Other, in order to become a self. We need to be loved, yet we fear dependence and otherness and so are caught between our pull to autonomy and our longing to merge. The psychology of the self is to be found in the Other. Our deepest longing is to surrender to something other than and greater than ourselves. Beyond psychology lies relation, and because no human other can actually fulfill this need for us, beyond psychology lies God.[5]

But long before Rank's book appeared, Freud had also, in his own, admittedly quite different way, been going "beyond psychology," had been doing *metapsychology*. Because we tend to use the term in relation to the conceptual models introduced in the central theoretical works of his later years, we often think of metapsychology as something Freud began doing fairly late, after *Totem and Taboo*, indeed, mostly after the First World War. But theory was always more important to Freud than therapy—which is one of the reasons his support of lay analysis was so crucial to him. "Psychoanalysis began as a method of treatment; but I did not want to recommend it to your interest as a method of treatment, but on account of the truths it contains, on account of the information it gives us about what concerns human beings most of all—their own nature—and on account of the connections it discloses between the most different of their activities," he says.[6] Depth psychology's central aim, I would paraphrase, is to contribute to the way we think most honestly and deeply about our human being-here. As Freud said to H.D., "My discoveries are not primarily a heal-all, my discoveries are a basis for a very grave philosophy;"[7] and as he wrote in the *New Introductory Lectures*, "Without metapsychological speculation and theorizing—I had almost said fantasizing—we shall not get another step forward."[8] Freud was engaged in metapsychology all along; he was already using the term "metapsychological" (and clearly had the allusion to metaphysics in mind) in the 1890s, in the letters to Fliess written as he was just beginning work on *Interpretation of Dreams*.

He was moving into metapsychology, he wrote, because he saw himself to be moving toward a psychology that led beyond consciousness.

In this sense his central insight, that the ego is not master of its own house, is obviously meta-psychological. Freud keeps having to resay this in different ways, because each way is so easily co-opted, so easily literalized, reified. The unconscious so quickly becomes a region we can map, a part of ourselves over which we, our ego selves, can gain control. Therefore Freud comes to move away from the language of conscious and unconscious, to speak instead of ego/superego/id, to speak of the forever resurgent *That* in us. Later still he will shift to speaking of Eros and Death in the hope that this more mythic language might prove more resilient to such co-option. But what happened was, of course, that the death drive was simply ignored or rejected. (Going beyond psychology does seem to be something we resist.)

For Freud "real" psychology, depth psychology, is a psychology of the unconscious, the unknown and unknowable in us. This is, to use a term from Giegerich, the Notion out of which all else Freud has to say derives. Understanding Freud means going back to this center and seeing how the details flow from it. I think Freud would agree with Giegerich that real psychology is about those things one can't speak about, but must try to anyway. Real psychology is about the unconscious, which is not something we "have," is nothing positive, is not an empirical given. Freud both wants to know, to bring the unconscious into consciousness, and knows how profoundly there is that in us that we cannot know—and that our longing to know, to control, is part of our malaise. He does not believe we can ever fully bring the unconscious into consciousness; the project of doing so is like Faust's project of draining the Zuider Zee. Every dream interpretation if pursued will come to the "navel" of the dream, the place that marks its connections to an unfathomable source, to the realm of The Mothers in Faust. There is always a place that must be left in the dark, a tangle or knot that resists unraveling. The dream can't be equated with the manifest dream or with the latent (interpreted) dream, for it is the ungraspable, a testimony to our irreducible complexity and depth. Interpretation can be a way of protecting against the dream. To turn to Phillips once again, we are Tantalos to what we dream.[9]

Freud tries to help us to *think* the unconscious and the soul *and* to imagine them. Giegerich says we can only think the soul because it is no-thing. Something so complex and contradictory can't be imagined, only thought. Like Hegel Giegerich sees the imaginal as halfway between sensory intuition and thought. The task, therefore, is to make the latent thought complete by freeing it from its immersion in the medium of emotion or image. Thus Giegerich buys into the

Hegelian assumption that thought is superior to image, though encompassing it. For him soul is thinking; thought is the soul's openness to what is. I see his perspective as in line with the long theological history of the *via negativa*, but want to recall that there is also an *analogical* tradition which holds that the unknown can best be pointed to through metaphor, through image. I am not a Hegelian and don't accept the hierarchical relation between Image and Idea. I see them as of equal value and necessity and so applaud Freud as someone who both thinks and images the soul. He is engaged in psyche-logos both as he actively thinks and speaks about the soul and more receptively as he listens to the soul's speech about itself (which he takes to be a speech of images).

Freud always speaks of the *un*-conscious, never of the *sub*-conscious (unlike Janet and Bernheim who intend the denigrating connotations). He sees that the unconscious can often best be spoken of through negations, by saying what it is not, but he also sees how helpful, indeed necessary, metaphorical descriptions can be. Thus his writings are full of metaphors for the unconscious, though there is clearly a privileged one: Hades, the Greek underworld (the same metaphor privileged by Hillman).

Freud also recognizes how misleading this word "un-conscious" can be; for it assumes the priority of consciousness, the position of ego looking at the unconscious. Therefore in Chapter Seven of *The Interpretation of Dreams* he speaks instead of the psyche's *primary process* and says that this more poetical, mythic, image-filled, emotionally-toned mode of functioning is not a distortion of normal psychic process but the form of the soul's uninhibited activity; indeed, it represents the core of our being.

Freud's most important thesis is that something beyond ego, beyond the self-aware "I," shapes our thoughts, feelings, and actions. This "something" is our own forgotten and denied past but it also includes trans-individual fears, hopes, and memories (as the centrality of his discovery "I am Oedipus" communicates). Thus metapsychology means not simply a psychology beyond consciousness but also a psychology beyond the individual. There is no ego, no "I" present as a given. The "I" comes into being through a sequence of losses and identifications. When we find ourselves, we find ourselves in a world with others—and we find these others in ourselves. The child becomes a self through its erotic identifications with those close to it. The "I" is a precipitate of abandoned loves, identifications and losses, "an archaeological reminder of grief," to borrow once again a phrase from Adam Phillips.[10]

Though Freud was not a theist and most emphatically not a monotheist, he was pulled to what I call "Beyondness" as can be seen even more clearly in the later explicitly metapsychological texts—particularly in *Beyond the Pleasure Principle* and *Civilization and Its Discontents*. Note the first word of the title of the former text: *Beyond*. The German word Freud used, *Jenseits*, is the one used by theologians to refer to the Other World, to heaven. It is in this book that Freud first introduces the death drive and first speaks of the two primary powers, Eros and Death, as not just drives in us but primal energies at work in us, on us, and in the cosmos. Eros for Freud is the energy that pulls us forward—beyond ourselves, beyond the present, the given—to the new, to the other. The twin brother of Eros is Death, a psychical and not simply a biological reality. The goal of all life is death, he tells us, with ever more complicated detours. Death is something we both long for and fear. Freud associates death fear with our fears of the unknown, the uncanny, the unconscious; with our fears of vulnerability and passivity. Death wish is associated with all in us that is pulled toward repetition, inertia, regression; all that longs for a tension-free existence, for Nirvana, resolution, completion.

In *Civilization and Its Discontents* (which Phillips calls his great "elegy for human happiness"[11]) Freud asks why it is so hard to be happy, and suggests that civilization is largely responsible. He points to the irreconcilable conflict between individual and group, a conflict that presupposes non-gratification and the necessity of renunciation. He takes note of our hostility to civilization and of our erotic connection to it. We both want and resent society; it both fulfills and frustrates us—and we are inescapably involved with it. In this text Freud brings in a different aspect of the death drive from the one focused on in the earlier book. Here he writes of how when denied death-fear and death-wish both become destructive, become aggression. Freud reminds us of our resentful hatred of anything that intrudes between us and the peace for which we long, of anything that reminds us of our incompleteness, of our wanting, of our separation from the All. He writes of the violence that is not just out there but also in us, and of how the two are not really separable. He reminds us of energies more frightening and more intractable (I believe) than those usually associated with the Jungian shadow.

But Death (as I've said before) is not the enemy. The death drive is not "bad"; it represents a given direction of the soul. Freud hopes to help us recognize the importance of accepting this as part of who we are, of learning to bear the conflicts within us, of curing our demand for cure or resolution, the importance of coming to view conflict as enduring and enlivening. But, then, that's Eros's view. Death itself might say: we need to honor also that in us that continues to want happiness, resolution, fulfillment.

So, though Freud honors Eros, he also recognizes the pull of narcissism, of fusion-longing, of escape from the world of others, the pull back to an imagined inner world, to the illusion that it constitutes a separate reality. Neither narcissism nor death is "bad." They are part of the soul's given direction, perhaps the deepest part (if we agree with Freud that the ultimate aim/*telos* of life is death). Nevertheless it is important that we move beyond narcissism at least temporarily, that we consciously, willingly, embark on that long detour which takes is into the world of others, into the social, the political world. Always, however, we will feel the pull of both these immortal energies, though sometimes one, sometimes the other, will seem to predominate.

It is this recognition of Freud's, this recognition of the power of these two immortal adversaries, of their unending conflict, that continues to persuade me that Freud speaks to me, more than do Jung or Hillman—though I have learned so much from both—and more than Giegerich does. (I recognize this may be an expression of my Jewish side, an expression of how I resonate with Martin Buber's affirmation that the Jew knows with every cell of her or his body that redemption has not yet happened.)

In *Terrors and Experts* Adam Phillips says: "It's not the future of psychoanalysis that anyone should be concerned about, but rather the finding of language for what matters most to us."[12] He also says, we know somebody speaks to us, if they make us speak.[13] So: Which language does that for us, for you? I don't expect that we'd agree on the answer, but want to say: this is *the* question.

As Freud noted, "People are seldom impartial where ultimate things, the great problems of science and life are concerned. Each of us is governed in such cases by deep-rooted internal prejudices, into whose hands our speculation unwittingly plays."[14] I'm aware that one of the "prejudices" that plays such a role for me is my conviction that the Holocaust is the central defining moment of the 20th century. It is more important to me that we live in a post-Holocaust world than that we live in a post-psychological one, though I see the two as closely connected. I know that any psychology that speaks to me has to be able to take the Shoah into account—which means recognizing those capacities in us which it brought so forcefully into view: not just the suffering we suffer, but the suffering we cause, not just our longing for justice but our capacity to do evil. Any psychology that speaks to me has to recognize as an inescapable given that we live in a world of others and are responsible to it, to them.

Undoubtedly part of my pull to Freud is that I see him as meeting this requirement more fully than Jung or Hillman or Giegerich do. Freud knows at the deepest place within him—in a way that none of his own formulations ever articulated quite well enough even for him—that we are conflicted, that we are not whole, that there is no cure for the unconscious, that the most we can hope for is the substitution of everyday unhappiness for neurotic misery. The goal is not wholeness, but being able to bear our incompleteness, "to live our conflicts more keenly," as Phillips puts it.[15] Whereas for Giegerich the soul is, by definition, whole, undivided. I don' t believe that, as I also don't believe we ever go wholly into the wilderness (I am referring here to Giegerich's interpretation of the Actaeon myth). I don't believe in a whole person in that sense. Paradoxically perhaps, I seem to be saying that Hegelian though he may be, Giegerich's understanding of soul is not dialectical enough! For Giegerich, as I understand him, honoring soul means a total commitment to "wilderness," to risk; it means foregoing stability, foregoing all delight in symbols and myths, for such indulgence is esthetics not psychology. Whereas I would say, the longing for stability is also part of soul, the death drive part.

I also do not believe that we, the soul-us, live only in the abstract virtual world, though I, too, know the growing reality of that world, and see what it has added to our lives as well as what it threatens to take away. I see how technology may lead to the death of our species—and how it grows out of Eros, out of our delight in change and the new, *and* out of the death drive's wish to control. Giegerich seems to think that to do justice to the soul under the conditions of Modernity, we need to turn from image to idea. Because our world is abstract, the soul can now only be satisfied by the abstract; because we inevitably live in this abstract world whether we admit it or not, our soul problems appear on a different level than in the past. The soul today requires abstract thinking. By proclaiming previous levels of life to be obsolete, Giegerich seems to be proposing a developmental model after all, even if the new is not viewed as necessarily an improvement. The time for indulging in myths and images of the gods is past, he tells us. Imaginal psychology's project of interpreting life in terms of the gods assumes that fundamentally we live in same world as did the Greek, but we don't. Thus we miss the particular character of our world, evade the real life of our here and now, by trying to find analogies from another. The specific psychological character of our world cannot be grasped by the imagination. This is what I understand Giegerich to be saying.

I agree that we can't really enter mythic consciousness directly, that for the archaic mythic mind the distinction between the literal and the imaginal doesn't arise, that (as Giegerich puts it) for the archaic mind the imaginal or divine shines forth from within what we'd call the literal. Though I'd add that most of the myths that imaginal psychology concerns itself with (including Ovid's version of the Actaeon myth to which Giegerich devotes so many pages in his book) come from a Greek and Roman literary world in which the literal/imaginal distinction is already well established. I disagree with Giegerich that once one knows this distinction, one can only *think* the gods. Like Vico I believe that outgrown modes of consciousness are still available to us, through empathic *nacherleben*, imaginally, and that the abstract alone is not what the soul requires. The past is still alive in us, not just as archaic vestige but as life-giving. As Freud said, "Humankind never lives entirely in the present. The past lives on in us and yields only slowly to the influences of the present and to new change."[16]

Giegerich's message, though challenging, is in its way upbeat and therefore consoling. I am thinking of his conviction that we can learn to live in this new world happily and wholly. Thus he is comforting in a way Freud never is. Freud ends *Civilization and Its Discontents* by admitting that he can offer no consolation but then goes on to say—remember this is in 1931, as Nazism is clearly on the rise—"But now it is to be hoped [or "awaited," not "expected" as the Standard Edition has it] that the other of the two heavenly powers, eternal Eros, will make an effort to assert himself in the struggle with his equally immortal adversary. But who can foresee with what success and with what results?"[17]

According to Auden, over Freud's grave "the household of Impulse mourns one dearly loved: sad is Eros, builder of cities, and weeping, anarchic Aphrodite."[18] Like Freud, like Auden, I can speak best by speaking mythically, metaphorically, by speaking of the gods, of Eros and Aphrodite.

"Eros, builder of cities"—not sentimental love but the love that sustains us in the difficult projects of our life together, the love that pertains not just to intimate family life but that pulls us ever forward, outward, into larger and larger worlds, into social groupings much, much larger than the Greek polis. The sadness, of course, grows out of our wondering whether that pull is really strong enough—a question that is not just about us in any individual way but about Eros himself.

And Aphrodite, "Anarchic Aphrodite"—goddess of sexuality, sensuous delight and beauty, the goddess who makes manifest the sacredness of the anarchic pull of desire and impulse. We need to stay enthusiastic about her as well. And all along we need to continue to remember how Death, too, holds us in his thrall.

I have no program or vision for how psychology will move in the world that is coming into shape. I have lots of fears and hopes. I share Freud's skepticism and his tentative hope. I see a lot of Death in the more abstract world that I like Giegerich see us as living in already and that I imagine will become even more dominant. I do not believe that either images or ideas will save us. Like Otto Rank, like Freud, like Jung in the closing pages of *Memories, Dreams, Reflections*, I do know that what takes us Beyond Psychology is LOVE.

Notes

1.   Adam Phillips, *The Beast in the Nursery* (New York: Pantheon, 1998) 6.

2.   Paul Robinson, "Symbols at an Exhibition," *New York Times Book Review*, Nov. 12, 1998, 12.

3.   Philip Rieff, *Freud: The Mind of the Moralist* (New York: Anchor Books, 1961) 392.

4.   Russell Jacoby, *Social Amnesia: A Critique of Contemporary Psychology from Adler to Laing* (Boston: Beacon, 1975) 26, my italics.

5.   Otto Rank, *Beyond Psychology* (New York: Dover, 1958) 290.

6.   Sigmund Freud, *The Standard Edition of the Complete Psychological Works of Sigmund Freud.* (London: Hogarth Press, 1953/1974) XXII, 156.7. Henceforward cited by volume number followed by page number.

7.   H.D., *Tribute to Freud* (New York: New Directions, 1950) 25.

8.   Freud, 23:225.

9.   Adam Phillips, *Terrors and Experts* (Cambridge, MA: Harvard University Press, 1995) 67.

10.   Phillips, 1995, 78.

11.   Phillips, 1998, 72.

12.   Phillips, 1995, xvi.

13.   Phillips, 1998, 84.

14.   Freud, 18:59.

15.   Phillips, 1995, 45.

16.   Freud, 22:160.

17. Freud, 21:145.

18. W. H. Auden, "In Memory of Sigmund Freud," in *Collected Poems* (New York: Random House, 1976) 218.

19

After the First Collapse There Is No Other

A few days after what we've all now learned to call "9/11" my partner River Malcolm wrote a poem called "After the First Collapse There Is No Other," which brings together the collapse of the twin towers of her childhood when her parents divorced with the new collapse in New York City. Here's the poem:

> When the twin towers of my childhood
> hurled words against one another
> words huge and heavy with fuel and innocence
> words ominous as jetliners piloted by terrorists
>
> All that I knew of security
> flamed up in that crash
> and slowly collapsed
> and slowly came tumbling down.
>
> Below the hole in the sky
> where loving parents once stood
> my dog and I searched the rubble
> for whatever might have survived.
>
> If I fled into the imaginary world
> of mathematics and science
> where rules and logic and predictability
> so soothed and amused,

I never once mistook it
for the bombed-out city
of lived experience,
where my first postulate was:

"Chaos rules,"
so that, after the first collapse,
there could be no other.

The poem communicates how there is something about us that makes each fresh assault on our taken for granted stable world seem to be the first. Depth psychology, too, helps us appreciate the power of the pull to restored innocence, to upperworld complacencies, and can help us understand how unprepared we always are for the violent intrusion of underworld realities, for the reappearance of violence and chaos and death, for the reappearance of that world behind the world. Yet depth psychology's deeper lesson, I believe, is that that world is deeply familiar, is one in which our souls feel at home.

Freud's essay "The Uncanny" (which he wrote in 1919, on the other side of the First World War, the same year in which he wrote *Beyond the Pleasure Principle*) says this with powerful clarity.

The German word on which this essay focuses is *unheimlich*, whose most literal translation would be "unhomelike" rather than "uncanny." *Heimlich*, which means "homelike" or "homey," refers to the familiar, the intimate, the comfortable; it is used with reference to the members of one's household, one's family, to tame animals who are companionable to humans—though also, by way of an extension that is easy to follow, *heimlich* can refer to the concealed, the private, the secretive. It is one of those words with ambivalent meanings that so fascinated Freud (who was fascinated by ambivalence wherever it appears)—just a few years earlier (in 1910) he had written a very short essay on "The Antithetical Meaning of Primal Words."

Unheimlich, it turns out, is another of those words that means what we first take it to mean *and* its opposite. In its most apparent meaning the *unheimlich* is the unfamiliar; in its most frightening aspect it refers to that which arouses dread and horror. Freud quotes Schelling's affirmation that everything is *unheimlich* that ought to have remained secret but has come to light. Evidently, he suggests, something has to be added to what is novel and unfamiliar to make it *unheimlich,* to make it "uncanny."

Here Freud makes his characteristic move: the uncanny, he says, is that class of the frightening that leads back to what is known of old and long familiar. The uncanny, he goes on to suggest, is associated with feelings of profound helplessness, like the feelings aroused when we find ourselves in one of those nightmares where a frightening event happens over and over again, as though what was happening were somehow fateful and inescapable. Freud's highlighting of the *repetitive* aspect connects this essay to *Beyond the Pleasure Principle* in which he wrote about his grandson's game of *fort und da* and concluded that there must be some kind of mastery achieved through the repetition of even painful experience, some access to a meaning not immediately available. (I cannot help but think here of how some of us felt compelled to watch the planes hit the Twin Towers again and again, to watch the towers crumble again and again.)

Freud writes that in such situations the ordinary distinction between the imaginal and the real seems to have been effaced. (Again I think of how many people spoke of initially assuming that what they saw on their television screens was just a movie, just an illusion.) He believes that a sense of the uncanny is evoked when something actually happens that confirms what we had thought were outgrown modes of thought, long overcome childish fears. What happens may initially seem unfamiliar, but actually it is something deeply familiar that has been forgotten, deeply forgotten, repressed.

What the present uncanny event has stirred up is somehow related to childhood fears—to fear of the father, fear of what Freud often called "castration threat," that is, fear of my annihilation, of death. But, as Freud goes on to say, my present response is even more powerfully connected to fears associated with the mother of our earliest childhood, with our utter dependence on her who is the very source of our being. Thus the newly aroused fear is associated with the mystery of my being here at all.

So, to try to say this most clearly, the *unheimlich* (and I do think the response of many of us to what happened on September 11 partakes of this dimension of experience) evokes the mystery of being and not-being, evokes our fear of death and our even more repressed *longing* for death, for fusion, peace, resolution, completion. I think we felt *awe*—horror, yes—fear, yes—but also wonder, fascination, maybe even some of what German has a word for but English does not, *Schadenfreude*, a strange kind of (almost inadmissible) joy. Experiences of the *unheimlich* connect longings and our earliest memories, to our most primal fears.

You can see, I imagine, how River's poem (written, of course, completely innocent of Freud's essay) follows a similar course. For her the collapse of the Twin Towers in New York was almost immediately associated with the collapse of the twin towers of her childhood. For me, also, there's a sense in which September 11 brought vividly to mind once again what I feel I've always known—what I've known at least since we learned about the Holocaust at the end of World War II, how precarious and illusory our everyday sense of order and stability is. There have been other reminders, too, of course—John Kennedy's assassination, and Martin Luther King's, and Bobby Kennedy's—and Vietnam, Kent State, Oklahoma City, Columbine—the list goes on and on, and probably for each of us there is a different touchstone moment. Some of these are likely to be more private—a rape, a divorce, AIDS—others more public like the ones I've just listed.

But always—each time the world behind the world reveals itself—somehow it seems new, unbelievable, unassimilable, unforgettable. And always we do forget—at least consciously, at least enough to go on. Each assault is new—and old—and soon becomes again unconscious. It *is* important to live in the ordinary world—to be able again to trust, to love, to hope. But, I believe, it is also important to learn to do so with an awareness of the reality of the other world, that world behind the world.

I think of the lines with which Freud ended *Civilization and Its Discontents*, "And now it is to be hoped that almighty Eros might rise again to take his place by his equally immortal adversary, Death"; and I think of the episode at the heart of the "Snow" chapter in Thomas Mann's *Magic Mountain.* The scene opens with Hans Castorp finding himself drawn into a vision of a beautiful Mediterranean landscape. He is entranced by the blue sky, the singing birds, the fragrant blossoms, the beautiful young men conversing as they walk arm in arm, the beautiful young girls dancing together, mothers with their children. But then, almost against his will, he is pulled to enter a Greek-style temple and comes upon two frightful old women dismembering a child and dropping the pieces of its body in a boiling cauldron. Afterwards, after awaking from this visionary experience, he asks himself, "Were they courteous and charming to one another, those sunny folk, out of silent regard for that horror?"

Most humans, I suspect—now and always—have lived with more awareness of that horror, that world behind the world, than we here in America in the late 20th and early 21st centuries. In a way September 11 brought us back—or at least momentarily seemed to have the power to do so—out of an always illusory eternally sunlit world into the world in which others live.

As I noted earlier, probably for each of us there is a particular event that serves for us as *the* event most powerfully associated with the loss of innocence, as the archetypal reminder of the underworld of violence and chaos that lurks beneath the fragile civilized order. For me, as I've said, it is the Holocaust, the Shoah. Indeed, my major writing project these last few years (whose completion keeps being deferred) has been devoted to trying to understand more deeply its place in my life. Though I was born in Germany and had a father whose own father had been Jewish, my family was spared what many others were not; we left early, when I was only four. Nonetheless, what happened in Germany and elsewhere in Europe between 1933 and 1945 is an inextricable, a profoundly shaping, part of my life. The most important lesson of the Holocaust has always seemed to me to be what it revealed about *us,* all of us—about our vulnerability *and* our cruelty.

My sense that Freud knew about this, and about how much we want to evade its being true of us, that is of *me,* is probably part of what keeps drawing me back to him. (And, yes, I know Jung, too, was pulled to confront this, especially in *Answer to Job,* but somehow it is Freud's articulation of it that speaks more directly to me.) I have, however, come to believe that, too often, when we think about the Holocaust we tend to identify only with the victims (or with the liberators), to see ourselves only as the sufferers, as the good—not as the perpetrators. But isn't one of the most important lessons of depth psychology that it pushes us to move beyond such simple dualities?

In those first few days after September 11 I was moved by how shared awareness of that suddenly discovered/rediscovered fragility of our being-here brought people closer to one another—in shared grief, shared fears, a shared determination to stay connected to one another. It seemed also to issue in a wish to understand the suffering that led *to* the attack and not only the suffering it caused, to a wish to try to understand our own complicity, our own guilt. But all too soon I became aware of another aspect of the response to what had happened in New York and Washington: how visibly we could watch grief become *rage*—how wanting it not to be true, not to have happened, wanting to *undo,* came out as anger that spilled out everywhere, as an impulse to a revenge that knows no limits (like that of Demeter in Ovid's version of her response to Persephone's abduction). This, too, is something that Freud understood all too well—it is the central theme of *Civilization and its Discontents* where he describes the process whereby death-fear is transformed into aggression.

A few months after the outbreak of World War I, appalled and surprised at how easily enthusiasm for the war had overtaken his compatriots, Freud wrote Lou Salome, one of the saddest things is that it is exactly the way we should have expected people to behave from our knowledge of psychoanalysis. I, too, given my deeply ingrained skepticism, should have been prepared—but wasn't. It dismays me that the fears associated with the discovery (or rediscovery) of the insecurity of our being-here seem so easily to issue in black and white, good versus evil, thinking, in acts of unrestrained revenge, in what are to me frightening infringements of those civil rights and freedoms, that are so central to my dream of what America should represent. I find myself deeply upset by the relative lack of criticism of the self-righteous posturing and the deeds and plans that it is used to promote—by the *silence.*

Reflecting on this silence has made me aware that coming to terms with the Holocaust entails not only coming to accept more fully how cruelty, violence, aggression—and vulnerability—are an inextricable aspect of our human being here, are part of *me,* but also the present-day pertinence of the fact that most Germans were not perpetrators or victims (in any clearly visible, dramatic way); they were *bystanders.* I understand so much better now how terribly easy it is to be a bystander, to remain silent, to fail to bear witness.

Yet even when we feel an inner call to bear witness, we may so easily feel overwhelmed by not knowing *how,* not knowing what we should do, what we could do. I think of Joseph Knecht, the protagonist of Hermann Hesse's *Magister Ludi,* who felt the call to leave the spiritually focused world of Castalia for the flatland, the world of everyday human life and struggle, but once there couldn't fathom how he might contribute. In writing the book Hesse was himself struggling with the same question, what did he have to contribute? The threat of a Nazi-dominated Europe had forced him to realize he couldn't write yet another book celebrating the inner world, the timeless world of myth, art, and beauty—but also that what he could do, would still be to write a book. Like Knecht he could only enter the world of history with a toy flute in hand.

So we too—I too—must rely on our toy flutes, on the instruments we've devoted our lives to learning how to play. We are called, I believe, to do what we do—in my case, to teach, to write, to tell stories, to speak out—discovering anew how important doing just *this* is—*and* that as always it's not enough—and yet enough.

"What use are poets in a time of need?" Holderlin asked—or depth psychologists?—or teachers?

The answer, I've come to believe, is: a lot! I think of how important Pasternak, Solzhenitsyn, Havel were during the years of Soviet domination. I think, too, of all the poetry circulated on the Internet in the immediate aftermath of September 11. Poetry, fiction, myth have a power to open the imagination—to open souls—in a way that political rhetoric or even philosophical discourse often cannot.

Of course, I've known this, believed this, for a long time. I wouldn't be doing what I do if that weren't true—but I've become newly appreciative of how really true it is this spring while teaching a class on Greek tragedy. In fifth century Athens the performances of tragedy, as part of a major annual obligatory public ritual, made visible to the assembled citizenry the underlying tensions and conflicts, the precariousness of the social order, the limitations of the dominant ideology. The tragedies reflected the anxieties, not the confident verities, of the audience, revealed the underlying violence and irrationality, made possible a radical questioning of both divine and human justice—safely, because presented within the context of a civically-ordained festival. The tragedies were written to illuminate—not resolve—those tensions. The point was to make the citizens aware of the limitations and precariousness of the civic and religious order and to develop an awareness of simultaneously valid contradictory perspectives. The dramatists used stories from the mythic past to subtly suggest analogies to the present, recognizing that such distancing makes possible a more receptive open-minded, open-hearted response. So, for example, Euripides could present the Trojans sympathetically but not contemporary Spartans, the present-day foe.

That we have no comparable public forum in which criticism is validated as integral to our communal self-celebration, does not mean there is no place for our speaking-out. It helps to remember that our story-ing, our witnessing, need not be directly about Afghanistan or Iraq or the Palestinians, just as Hesse's was not directly about the Nazis.

Jean-Pierre Vernant once said that in tragedy myth became a mirror in which the classical polis could look at itself; its purpose was to develop a tragic consciousness in the spectators, an awareness of simultaneously valid contradictory perspectives. I see my challenge as finding ways of retelling these (and other) ancient stories so they can serve as a mirror in which we might view ourselves. Not to resolve, comfort, console—but to help us see.

The image of the mirror returns me to my beginning, to Freud, to the uncanny, to what Freud wrote about our being frightened by a mirror image which we took to be a stranger and turns out to be ourselves!

20

May the Gods Be Present: Therapy as Ritual

Honoring the sacred and numinous dimension of therapy means inviting in the gods and goddesses associated with liminality, with the crossing of the border between the profane and the sacred, between upperworld and lower world. It means attending to how Hades and Persephone, Hekate and Hermes, Asclepius and Dionysos, Athene and Aphrodite make their presence felt in the consulting room.

It is easy to discern in what happens in the consulting room the lineaments typical of the ritual pattern: separation from the profane world, initiation into a radically different, transformative, sacred realm, and return to the profane world in some way changed. The therapy hour is like the central moment in initiation rituals; the rules of the everyday world are suspended and we are encouraged to re-enter wakingly into dream-making, myth-making, consciousness.

The focus on the liminal, on the crossing of the border between the profane and the sacred, between consciousness and the unconscious, between upperworld and underworld is what makes depth psychology *depth-ful,* makes it a *psyche-logos*—or, perhaps better put, a *psyche-poesis*—a psychology dedicated to the soul not the ego, an imaginal not a cognitive psychology. Depth psychology seeks to help us toward the depth dimension of experience, into what mythologies call the "underworld" and thus into a sacred realm and engagement with gods and goddesses.

In therapy we enter that realm willingly, out of a longing for depth, soul, transformation. Nonetheless we often find entering that realm terrifying; we often feel ourselves subjected to an abduction. I think of Inanna naively preparing herself for a visit to her just-widowed sister, Ereshkilgal, goddess of the Sumerian Land of No Return, adorning herself with all her *me,* all her emblems of upperworld power—as though one could go to the underworld like a tourist visiting an exotic land. But gate by gate, her *me* are taken from her; by the time she arrives she has been stripped naked. Greeted by her sister with the eye of death, she is turned into a piece of rotting flesh hanging from a hook on the wall. I think of Persephone, reaching for the beautiful narcissus that seems to promise something new, and finding herself seized by the dark god of Hades and torn from all she has known. I also think of Jung, after his break with Freud deliberately going after the myth that was living him, but then discovering himself in the midst of a psychotic-like process that might well have destroyed him. We know how it all turned out (just as we know that Abraham did not have to sacrifice Isaac after all), but none of them—Innana, Persephone, Abraham, or Jung—knew that at the time.

This becomes painfully obvious if we allow ourselves to read the "Confrontation with the Unconscious" chapter of *Memories, Dreams, Reflection*, particularly the earlier parts, as the account of a journey whose outcome we don't already know. Jung felt so profoundly isolated and alone as he found himself subjected to one frightening dream after another. Think of the dream of the corpses in the crematorium, of the dream of that long row of tombs dating back to the 12th century with the dead, one by one, coming back to life. Think of the dream of the bloody flood covering Germany, the arctic cold wave slowly freezing everything, the boulders that threaten to crush him. Think of Jung finding himself wading trough soft sucking mud and then through icy water, the sun spurting blood, the chariot made of the bones of the dead. Think of how over and over again he feels himself being transported to the land of the dead.

What made it possible for him to sustain his commitment to this exploration was the creation of ritualized ways of working with these images and the emotions they evoked. He honored the power of those images with the meticulous renderings of the paintings in *The Red Book*. He wrote down the dreams in a deliberately chosen inflated style that he felt served to communicate their numinosity. He gave names to the figures that appeared in some of those dreams and then, wakingly, engaged them in conversation as a way of dreaming the dreams onward. Sitting himself down on the beach in front of his lakeside home and playing in the sand, he experienced a recovery of the long-lost spontaneous playful creativity of his childhood. Discovering analogues between these dream images and games and the archaic myths and rituals he had discussed in his 1913 book *The Psychology of the Unconscious* (the book that in a later reworking became *Symbols of Transformation*) helped him realize that what he was undergoing was not just idiosyncratic or pathological or psychotic—but archetypal and meaningful. The ancient stories and rites also suggested that though eventually there would be a re-emergence, it couldn't be hastened.

Slowly he began to hope that what he had undergone could be made meaningful for others by using what he had learned from his own experience to develop his own therapeutic rituals. This, he came to believe, might be the *purpose* of this almost six-year journey: that others might not have to undertake their forays so radically alone. So that, although their journeys would inevitably also be terrifying, dangerous, and sometimes seemingly endless, their fears about what they might encounter and their confusion about how to proceed, may be somewhat alleviated by being guided on the journey by someone who had made a similar one and could testify to the possibility that it might be more transformative than destructive—though, of course, no one can ever *promise* that. (I wonder though if anyone ever really does do this quite alone; there do always seem to be guides—or at least *witnesses.* Even Persephone had Hekate and Helios, Inanna had Ninshubar, Freud had Fliess, and Jung had Toni Wolff.)

When Jung began doing therapy again after the six year hiatus (though we know now from Deirdre Bair's biography that it wasn't quite as radical a hiatus as the somewhat romanticized account in *Memories, Dreams, Reflections* presents it), the therapeutic rituals he crafted were deliberately different in some ways from those he had learned from Freud. There are, of course, important commonalities: in both psychoanalysis and analytic psychology during the therapy hour we find ourselves in a world sharply set off from the world outside. We come at a set time each day or week; we come for fifty minutes or an hour. What happens in the consulting room belongs to an esoteric world; it is not to be spoken of outside, and makes little sense except to other initiates. We have entered a world where there are different rules, a different language, a different mode of temporality where past, present, and future melt into one another.

Admittedly, the rituals of Jungian therapy are in important and interesting ways different from those established by Freud. Nonetheless, they were created in relation to Freud's, so it behooves us to begin by looking at his. H.D.'s account of her analysis with Freud in her *Tribute to Freud* gives us a rich sense of its mythic and ritual aspect. She speaks of Freud as a midwife to the soul, as Asclepius the blameless physician, as an Orpheus who charms the very beasts of the unconscious and enlivens the dead sticks and stones of buried thoughts and memories, as an old Hermit who lives on the edge of the great forest of the unknown, as a trickster-thief nonchalantly unlocking vaults and caves and taking down the barriers that generations had carefully set up, as Faust, as a Prometheus stealing fire from heaven, as the curator in a museum of priceless antiquities.

It is fascinating to see how many of the typical features of initiation rituals are present in Freud's way of practicing analysis. For instance, nakedness: the "fundamental rule" of psychoanalysis is free association, the requirement that we say everything that enters our minds with no censorship, without the protection of cultural taboos or the expectation that what we say should make sense. Or, radical isolation: what happens in the consulting room is to be kept there, not brought outside, not discussed even with our closest others. Or, starvation: the analyst resolutely refuses to gratify the patient's hungers. Most importantly perhaps: silence and word magic.

Psychoanalysis is, after all, the "talking cure." Freud claims that speech itself, the right speech, heals; he invites his patients to free associate and thus to enter a new linguistic realm—an uncanny realm, unfamiliar and yet in some way deeply familiar. Every word calls for a reply and the analyst's silence *is* a reply, a reply that forces the patient toward free association. The analyst's silence keeps the patient's certitudes suspended, helps us discover that our being has never been more than an imaginary construct.

Without the silence there would not be the radical confrontation with ourselves that it forces upon us. But the silence is a silence within a world created by speech. Of course the analyst does speak, but first he listens—with evenly hovering attention, noticing not just what the patient says, but what he or she doesn't, noticing the silences, the gaps, the omissions, the repetitions. When he speaks it is to help us see how our speech conceals and not only reveals, how our longing for coherence, for narrative, for meaning, is evasive, how bent we are on hiding from ourselves.

The aim of therapy, so Freud believed, is to bring me into the world of words, and by way of words into the world of others. We become aware of self and (m)other as we enter language; thus language separates *and* is the medium of any later re-connection between self and other. Narcissism is death; communication, speech, is life.

The language of therapy is attuned to the erotic, the connective, aspect of language. It is talking with the other, Freud claims, that heals. Dialogue not introspection. This, of course, relates to Freud's emphasis on transference, on the ritual replaying of earlier relationships that occurs within the consulting room. Ritual is *repetition*; it is *effective* repetition, transformative repetition. Freud recognized that *all* love is transference love; we bring old patterns, old expectations, old fears to all our new relationships. We keep repeating the same old story but nothing happens. In analysis we are given the possibility of seeing, of experiencing, how the past lives on in the present and thus here repetition may become effective, transformative. Something might happen! These re-enactments, once recognized *as* re-enactments, make transformation possible (as mere intellectual understanding never will), because they give the patient an opportunity to experience the emotional charge still present in supposedly long outgrown childhood attachments.

Although Freud had already in his *Studies on Hysteria* noted the importance of the personal relationship between patient and physician, he had no inkling then that this could be understood as metaphorical incest—which of course is what "transference" is (metaphor and transference are, after all, really the same word). The case of Dora led Freud to recognize that the failure of that analysis could be explained by his not making Dora's projection of her father-longing onto Freud himself (and not only onto Herr K) an explicit theme of their work together. Psychoanalysis, he was beginning to see, somehow stirs up a re-enactment of the emotional patterns of the child's relation to its parents. He had earlier discovered the power of longings to shape our memories of the past; now he was discovering how those same longings operate to shape the present on the basis of that imagined version of the past. He saw how, unconsciously of course, we keep projecting the old patterns and longings onto new beloveds, and so don't really see *them*. There is no real eros connection, no I-you engagement.

Henceforth working with the transference becomes the most important part of therapy. The transference feelings that he had at first looked upon as in the way of therapy become the way itself. Love, as he writes Jung at the time of the Spielrein crisis, is the medium of our work and sometimes we'll get burned. We cannot escape the risk of being scorched by the love with which we operate. The eros summoned up in the consulting room is dangerous; but to try to ignore it would be to conjure up a spirit from underworld and then send it back without questioning it.

Though transference enters into all our relationships, what distinguishes what happens in treatment is simply that there it is provoked by the analytical situation and somehow intensified by the artificial context in which reality considerations seem beside the point, and in which all taboos are lifted. Within analysis it is possible to bring into view the repressed elements of the relation to the parents: the erotic and the hostile aspects, not just the affectionate aspect of which the patient is already aware. The transference of this whole range of affects onto the therapist makes possible a transformation from literalism to an appreciation of the symbolic aspects of the incest complex, makes possible a realization that what was really wanted was transformation not literal gratification.

In analysis as Freud practices it, it is clearly the patient's love (not the therapist's) that is the source of healing; the analyst's compassion is expressed as dispassion. Freud invokes the incest taboo. In order to work the metamorphosis, the love evoked by therapy is to be admitted but not literally enacted. Its energy is needed to oppose all in the patient that resists cure; the longing for change, Freud believes, is in itself never strong enough. (It was in part this recognition that led Freud to his understanding of the role that death-wish plays in our lives.) Freud is deeply aware of how much psychic energy operates *against* therapy. He notes that if someone tries to take a neurotic's illness away from him, he defends it like a lioness with her young. The patient's love is what throws the balance on the side of wanting cure, wanting change.

If the analyst were to respond directly to the patient's demand for his love, she would not have to get well. She would have been given what she thought she wanted but what is really an inadequate substitute for what she originally came to therapy for. Enactment would not free the patient from attachment to literalism: abstinence is intended to further metaphorical realization. Freud's central criticism of "wild" psychoanalysis was that by gratifying their sexual desires it deprives patients of the possibility of a real transformation of their way of being. The more orthodox analyst uses the appearance of love for the sake of recognition rather than encouraging the reproduction of the same old and self-defeating patterns of loving.

Thus it is signally important that the analyst himself not take transference-love personally, literally, which is why he needs to have been through the process himself. (Freud is well aware how humanly difficult such abstinence can be, especially for a young therapist.)

Resolution of the transference can enable us to relate to the other *as* other, not just as a revenant of childhood attachment figures; the aim is to make it possible for us to *love*. The aim is not so much the elimination of the transference as its transformation. The goal is to make us more conscious, and appreciative of how the inevitable presence of our most powerful memories and expectations can lend depth, resonance, dimensionality to our present relationships. That is, we come to recognize the metaphorical dimension of all relationships, the new beloved is herself *and* my mother *and* my sister (and more mysteriously still, perhaps also my father). The point is not to dissolve the imaginal facets, but to recognize—and celebrate—them as such.

Freud sought to free himself and his students and patients from transferring onto psychoanalysis our illusions of salvation. He voices his own skepticism concerning therapy from the very beginning. As almost everyone remembers, Freud once wrote that he saw the aim of therapy to be the transformation of neurotic misery into common unhappiness—a goal that I know sounds dismayingly limited to some, but that I see as expressing the honesty and depth of Freud's understanding of our human being-here. Analysis, he believes, may help us become reconciled to Ananke, necessity—and may teach us to take delight in our capacity for symbolization. It encourages us to acknowledge ambivalence, tolerate ambiguities, take delight in double meanings and in symbolic (that is, sublimated) satisfactions.

Jung, I believe, was more optimistic about what analysis has to offer. Speaking of himself vis-à-vis Freud, he once wrote: I risked a greater shattering and achieved a greater wholeness. I think he believed that his way of practicing analysis might help others toward a greater wholeness as well. One of the most obvious differences between the rituals of Jungian therapy from those of Freud is that in Jungian analysis the patient sits face to face with the therapist, rather than lying on a couch with the analyst out of sight. This yields a sense that analyst and patient are mutually engaged in the process. The analyst is present not as a blank screen but as a fellow human. When it's working, Jung says, something happens to both—and unless the analysts is open to himself being transformed, unless the analyst is fully present with all of his being, nothing important is likely to happen. It is easy to see that much is gained, but perhaps something is also lost: that radical, fearful confrontation with oneself that the free association rule imposes. And I suspect that having the analyst in view is likely to lead to a (mostly subliminal) awareness of his responses to what we say. We notice when he bends forward with heightened interest, when he crosses his legs, when he surreptitiously glances at his watch, when he frowns in puzzlement. We notice and we monitor, not deliberately, not intentionally, but almost inevitably.

Instead of free association, there is conversation. In place of long-withheld interpretation, there is amplification, which may entail a tendency to move away from the details of the patient's images and conflicts to their mythological and archetypal analogues. Even transference is different or responded to differently. What is understood to be projected on the analyst is less likely to be thought of as the literal mother or father of childhood but rather the archetype of Father or Mother, or perhaps of Savior or Healer or Wise Old Man. Again much is gained by this shift away from a focus on the personal, the pathological, the past—to the transpersonal, the creative, the beckoning future. But again there may also be loss. So much more attention is given to the discovery of inner riches than to preparation for less wounded and wounding involvements with others.

Given these differences, it is nonetheless true that for both Freud and Jung analysis is an initiation into underworld experience that may stir up complex, ambivalent, ambiguous, contradictory fears and longings. We enter a mysterious uncanny realm, an unknown and yet strangely familiar world, the unconscious. This going forward seems in some sense to be a return—a return to beginnings, to archaic understandings of the soul that don't valorize the rational conscious ego as the postCartesian West has tended to do, and to our own beginnings, our own earliest memories and initial dreams. I think of Jung's childhood dream of the underground phallus and how powerfully it came back to him during his midlife "confrontation with the unconscious."

Jung's vision of the unconscious was in large measure shaped by a dream in which he found himself continually descending from one floor of a house to yet another more ancient one until at last he found himself in an archaic underground cave surrounded by bones and pottery shards. Freud begins *Interpretation of Dreams* with an epigraph from the *Aeneid* in which Juno announces her resolve to turn to the underworld for help the heavens have refused to grant her; throughout the book, Hades, the Greek underworld, serves as a privileged metaphor for the unconscious. Hades is not hell; it is a sacred realm ruled over by the goddess Persephone and her consort, Hades. Many of the other gods and goddesses are also associated with this realm and with underworld experience. The sacredness of the underworld is something both Freud and Jung honored. Both knew that what happened in analysis—when it happened—is not just the work of analyst or analysand, but of what Buber called the "Between" or the spirit, of daimones or gods.

At the very core of the rituals of depth psychology, of a psychology devoted to the soul, is the prayer: May the Gods be present. Jung said that the gods *will* be present, invited or not—but that inviting them in makes a difference. Hillman has written about how important it is to know *which* altar to approach, to know which god or goddess has brought our suffering upon us and thus which must be called upon for release. As the Greeks knew, only the god who inflicted the wound can effect the healing.

The gods may make their presence evident in many different ways. They may appear in the person of the analyst—in Greek mythology the gods often appear in human disguise, in the guise of a familiar other, a trusted mentor or even an all too familiar suddenly glamorous husband. Of course, it is important for both analyst and patient to know that the analyst *isn't* the god. (Jung warns of the danger of inflationary identification with the Healer in his essay on the transference.) Or the god may appear as a figure in the patient's dream. Or as an energy in the room—Hermes, god of the lucky find, is clearly present in the room when after having arrived at an amazingly happy interpretation, Freud tells H.D., This deserves a cigar! And I would say, Athene herself, not just the small figurine, enters the room when Freud brings the statuette over from his desk to H.D. on the couch.

Any of the gods or goddesses may appear, but those associated with liminality, with the crossing of the border between the upper and lower worlds and those deities associated with the underworld itself seem to be the ones whose presence we might most welcome as we find ourselves participating in the rituals of therapy.

I will do little more than name them here, since I have written so fully about them in my "Journeys to the Underworld." Of course, we would call upon Persephone, goddess of the underworld, whose rituals at Eleusis helped the Greeks assuage their fear of death. We would ask her to help us overcome our fears of the journey to the unconscious that depth psychology invites us to undertake. I think we should also invoke her consort Hades, the Unseen One, who reminds us that the underworld remains an *other* world, that the unconscious never becomes wholly conscious, that we are never wholly seen nor known even by ourselves. We would also pray to Hermes, the psychopomp, for safe passage back and forth between upper world and under world, between our everyday lives in the world of others and work and the intense self-enclosed world of the consulting room. To Hekate we might pray that we not be caught between the worlds, so taken over by our anger at others that we can't really disentangle ourselves enough to fully enter the underworld or to relate to them forgivingly up above. We might ask Asclepius to help us learn how to discover the healing that hides in our dreams. Of Dionysos we might ask that he help make us brave enough to deal with the most frightening, most raw, most instinctual energies that await us on this journey.

To name Dionysos is to also remember how much we need the gods who pull us back to the upperworld: Demeter who reminds us of our ties to children and family. Athene who calls us back to our creative work and community. Aphrodite who calls us back to love.

May the gods be present. We need them all.

21

Instincts And Archetypes

The instincts are not vague and indefinite by nature, but are specifically formed motive forces which, long before there is any consciousness, and in spite of any degree of consciousness later on, pursue their inherent goals. Consequently they form very close analogies to the archetypes, so close, in fact, that there is good reason for supposing that the archetypes are the unconscious images of the instincts themselves, in other words, that they are *patterns of instinctual behaviors.*[1]

An exploration of what Jung is trying to communicate through these terms, "instinct" and "archetype," leads us to questions that lie at the heart of depth psychology: How can we most adequately speak about our human being-here? How can we speak about our being-here as both connected to other forms of life and as distinct? How can we speak about our own being-here as we experience it from within—and about what we therefore feel we know about yours as *you* know it, not as we know it from outside?

This obviously leads us into questions about how we understand consciousness, the specifically human way of being in the world. Depth psychology begins with the affirmation that our conception of consciousness must be expanded to include the unconscious—and with the conviction that this will help us think more deeply about our relation to the natural world and to our own bodies.

I hope to explore these questions in a way that helps us recognize their mystery and importance. They remain questions, questions that people still argue about passionately, and that are important because how we think our lives helps shape how we live them. That is, the questions about the relation between matter and psyche, body and mind, are big questions, not just theoretically, philosophically, scientifically—but existentially, psychologically.

I want to look at how Jung thought about this—and talked about it, as a way of helping us think it. I believe many of us when we first read Jung recognize immediately the dimension of experience for which he used the word "archetypal" and are drawn to him in large measure because of his emphasis on experiences that bring us in transformative contact with a sense of our participation in the universally human.

I remember so well my own introduction to Jung's notion of the archetypal in my early twenties at a time when I felt myself fully and fulfillingly defined by the roles of wife and mother—and yet inchoately hungry for something more. A friend gave me Jung's "Modern Man in Search of a Soul"—and I suddenly found my self-understanding opened up as I began to pay attention to my dreams and found myself introduced to an unsuspected multitude of unlived potentialities waiting to be acknowledged and nurtured. I discovered also how these spousal and maternal roles themselves had archetypal and numinous dimensions (both threatening and life-giving) to which I had been blinded by my involvement with their more everyday aspects. Most important I felt myself in touch with elements of my own experience that were not mine alone. The recognition that I shared my deepest feelings, my most profound hopes and fears, my most valued accomplishments and most regretted failures with others gave me an entirely new sense of being connected to all humanity not just through outward relationships but at the very core of my being.

That said, I want also to acknowledge that I believe there are many Jung's out there, just as there are many Freud's—and that all I can speak of is "my Jung"—and that furthermore I'm not really a Jungian. By which I mean: not only that I'm not a therapist, but more importantly that his is not for me *the* voice about the soul.

Like Wolfgang Giegerich I find that Jung himself doesn't always find language adequate to his most important intuitions. In *Memories, Dreams, Reflections* Jung writes of his life and work being given their shape by a "stream of lava," some liquid incandescent primal stuff which hardened into unshaped stone and then had to be worked in a way designed to expose its inherent meaning. After quoting this passage, Giegerich suggests that we may need to retranslate Jung's texts back into that primal stuff from which Jung had wrought it—that is, to find *our words* for those insights.

Thus, almost inevitably, my focus is going to be in part on *language*. About how it helps—and gets in the way. How it helps us see—and misleads us. I am interested in why Jung chose to use the particular language he did and want to try to understand what he was trying to say that he believed hadn't been said before—and also to ask whether Jung's is still the best language for us.

My way of doing this turns out to be historical—as was Jung's own in his seminal 1947 essay on "The Nature of the Psyche." Thus I will begin with a brief retracing of the history since Descartes of the mind/body problem and will then move on to some reflections on how this problem was conceived in philosophy from the 17th century onwards and then in 19th century psychology. Next—as a necessary prelude to the consideration of Jung's contributions to the discussion—I will spend some time on Freud's radical revisioning of the issue.

It is often said that the only way to teach quantum physics is through its history; only thus, it is claimed, can we understand the necessary path that leads from Newton to Planck and on to Bohr and Heisenberg and beyond. In reviewing this history I've become newly aware of how *hard* it is—still—to find adequate ways of talking about all this from a depth psychological perspective. That is, how hard it is genuinely to adopt a psychological standpoint, to hold on to the conviction that the psychological perspective is *sui generis,* different from both biology and medicine on the one hand and from religion or spirituality on the other. This *difference* was of great importance to both Freud and Jung, as Freud made explicit in *The Question of Lay Analysis* and *Future of an Illusion* and as Jung made most evident in those essays in which he is writing about instincts and archetypes that I will focus on when I finally get to Jung.

But neither Freud nor Jung fully succeeds in communicating this *sui generis* perspective. Freud gets accused of reducing all human culture to biology, as offering a psychology without soul, and Jung is often interpreted in a spiritual way, as putting forward a psychology without body. These misunderstandings have, alas, been encouraged by their translators. Both Freud and Jung wrote about the *Seele,* the German word whose English cognate is "soul." But Freud's translators rendered *Seele* as "mind" or "mental structure" or "organization" and Jung's as "spirit." Can you see already how different words make a difference? And how to stay in *psychology*—not religion or biology—how really to make the *soul* our subject is no easy matter?

The PreHistory of Depth Psychology

We need to begin with Descartes because Depth Psychology represents an attempt to get beyond the Cartesian mind/body and subject/object splits, a project begun in the 19th century by Kant, the German Romantics, and Nietzsche, continued in the 20th by Freud and Jung—and still not fully accomplished. As John Searle says, we have inherited Descartes' language and it is not innocent.[2] We are caught in the Cartesian mind/body split—*and trying to get out*—and never fully do. Partly because our language seems to make it almost impossible: our sentences are constructed of subjects and objects, and of the verbs that describe what the first does to the second.

I want to begin with Descartes but I don't intend to demonize him. The whole philosophical tradition going back to Plato expresses the same longing for certain knowledge, the same disparagement of sense experience and of the knowledge that depends on it. In a sense the name "Descartes" is just a symbol, a place-marker for a view that radically distinguishes between knower and known, between us, *res cogitans,* and the world outside us, *res extensa*, and for an identification of the human self with our minds, with our thinking capacity.

Cogito ergo sum: I think therefore I am; that is, I am (the self is) a thinking being. Our bodies are regarded as part of the external world, a world that exists independently of our thinking it and that is seen as a vast machine set in motion by God, fully determined, with no capacity for spontaneous activity. That is, Descartes reduces all motion, including animal and human activity, to machine-like, measurable action, and banishes teleology and animism from the physical world. This clear-cut distinction between mind and body provided the epistemology necessary to the rise of science. That is, it was a useful heuristic tool in the 17th century, necessary as a method, but dangerous when expanded into an ontology. For the subject-object split issues in our becoming alienated from the natural world and from our own bodies, and even human others become objects to us—rather than fellow subjects. We find ourselves imprisoned in what Buber called the "I-it."

But obviously Descartes wouldn't have had the influence he has had if his way of looking at things had not felt true—or sort of true, partly true. There seems to be something almost irresistible about identifying ourselves with our minds, as having a body rather than being one. This identification provides a way of evading mortality—and also expresses our longing for control and mastery. And there's something intuitively true about Descartes' conviction that the mind—the psyche, the soul, the self—is not a thing, not part of the spatio-temporal world, and that it cannot be made an object in the way that things can.

It is true: there is no Archimedean standpoint, no third person perspective, no stepping outside, from which psyche might look at psyche. Even introspection does not really give us access to what we might call the "feel" of consciousness. Psychology has only its own inside, for subject and object are one. This means that if there is going to be science of psychology, it is going to have to be a different kind of science. So it is not surprising that there wasn't one for a long time.

Clearly Descartes' dualism played a role in delaying the rise of psychology as a science—since *res cogitans* was seen as free not determined, not subject to causal explanations. In his view the self is known through consciousness, self-consciousness, immediately. This also means that what is not conscious is not the real me. Descartes understands thinking, consciousness, much more narrowly than had the Greeks, as including only the capacity for clear and distinct ideas—not imagination, intuition, empathy; these are all regarded as part of our bodies not of our minds or psyches.

In the 18th century the kinds of questions that we think of as falling within the domain of psychology were still being explored within philosophy, in essays on "man" and on "human reason." Cartesian dualism, oddly enough, led to both materialism and idealism: to the view that the only things that are real are bodies and causal relationships—or to the radically different view that the only real things are minds and that the external world exists only in our minds. Then Kant—with his distinction between the noumenal and the phenomenal—showed a way out of this particular dilemma. He affirmed that the outer world is real but that we can know it only *as* our minds apprehend it—that is, through the categories of space, time, and efficient causality, through engaging in what he called "pure reason." But Kant also said that our knowledge of our own human way of being, of ourselves as moral beings, involves a different kind of knowing—a kind of reason that posits free will and intentionality, to which he gives the name "practical reason."

Meanwhile—almost contemporaneously—Rousseau and then the German Romantics maintained, *contra* Descartes, that the core of our human being-here is not our capacity for objective rational thought but our imagination, intuition, passion, not consciousness but the unconscious (they even use the term). They held that animistic, anthropomorphic, mythological ways of speaking give us access to deeper truths about the human soul than the rational objectifying approach associated with natural science.

Nevertheless in the early 19th century when Newtonian science seemed to have made possible a full understanding of the natural world, the natural sciences had usurped the prestige of the traditional humanities-centered curriculum in the universities—and it was in this context that psychology first arose as a distinct field of inquiry, a move led by persons trained in physiology or medicine. As this new discipline emerged it had to face the question: was it to be defined by method or subject matter? The dominant answer at first was "method"—which meant that to begin with "psychology" was essentially neural physiology, since that was what could be studied "scientifically." (Later, American behaviorism proceeds from the same assumptions.)

But as a field of study defined by its subject matter, the *psyche,* psychology arises only a generation later. I wonder if we really realize how *new* psychology is? That it really began in 1874, the year before Jung was born. The word "psychology," though based on Greek roots and first used by Melancthon, only became part of popular usage at the beginning of the 19th century, and then quickly becomes a professional term (and words like *Seele* disappear from academic discourse).

But the word "psychology"—*psyche-logos*—can be understood in two quite different ways: not only to refer to an expert's speech about another's psyche, as third person, objectifying, discourse. It can also be understood to mean the soul's speech about itself—a speech that (as I'll hope to show) Freud and then Jung wanted to hear, to understand, and honor. But such honoring, it will turn out, will require the invention of a very different language from the nomothetic, conceptual, rational and abstract language of science: a more idiographic, animistic, anthropomorphic, metaphorical language.

1874 is important because it is the year in which both Wilhelm Wundt's *Principles of Physiological Psychology* and Franz Brentano's *Psychology from an Empiricist Standpoint* were published. In his book Wundt (raised on Kant and Hegel) asserts that the proper subject of psychology is not neurology but consciousness, subjectivity, and that consciousness can be studied scientifically, not explained as simply an epiphenomenon of the real thing, physiology. Wundt views psychology and physiology as two parallel closed systems of explanation, very much in line with Kant's distinction between pure and practical reason. His project is to replace the third person objective perspective of physiology by an exploration of immediate first person subjectivity. *Consciousness as the proper subject of psychology implies, he believes, introspection as its method—looking at consciousness from inside.* So Wundt opens a psychological laboratory and attempts to develop scientific rules for experimental self-observation of perception and memory. His understanding of the self is Kantian; it emphasizes free will, intentionality, and views the self as the cause of every intelligible event.

So for Wundt consciousness is what psychology is all about. Consciousness but *not* the Unconscious. He dismisses all speculation about the unconscious as a survival of Schelling's "psychological mysticism." The only aspect of the unconscious he would admit into psychology is what after Freud we have learned to call the "preconscious." As Wundt wrote in his *Outlines of Psychology:*

> Any psychical element that has disappeared from consciousness is to be called unconscious in the sense that we assume the possibility of its reappearance in

the actual interconnection of psychical processes. Our knowledge of an element that has become unconscious does not extend beyond this possibility of its renewal.... Assumptions as to the state of the "unconscious" or as to "unconscious processes" of any kind...are ***entirely unproductive for psychology.*** [3]

Wundt, albeit philosophically sophisticated, came to psychology from medicine; Brentano on the other hand was professionally a philosopher. His understanding of psychology was thus not based on the natural science model but rather on a humanities-based approach. For him, as for Wundt, psyche means consciousness, but for him the proper subject matter of psychology was not a specific function like perception but the whole person: our believing, judging, doubting, desiring, fearing, and loving. He was especially interested in intentionality, in final causes, in purposes. Consciousness, he claimed, in contrast to Descartes, is always *consciousness of something*. There is never any just "I think"; I always think something. That is, consciousness implies a relation to the world. To be human is to be projected beyond one self—toward those somethings, purposively.

Brentano is really important to this story because he was one of Freud's most important teachers at the University of Vienna. But before turning to Freud I want to emphasize again how new psychology was at the end of the 19th century. It was just getting free of speculative philosophy *and* of physiology. Still trying to discover *its* subject and *its* method. Still trying to free itself from a method that regarded as scientific only mechanistic objectifying mathematical investigations of an objective (out there) world. And still trying to free itself from a very narrow definition of mind or consciousness as encompassing only the capacity for clear and distinct ideas.

Freud

I see Freud and Jung as representing the most important voices in 20th century depth psychology and deeply value their attempts to honor the soul's own speech about itself—to speak about the psyche from a psychological perspective and to acknowledge how the psychic emerges out of the biological. For both it was evident that consciousness includes what, given the narrow inherited definition of consciousness, was inevitably called the unconscious—and that this unconscious is more closely connected to the body, to the instinctual than is consciousness. For Freud this meant speaking of the drives and of the *Id*, of the *It* in us; for Jung of the collective unconscious, of the archetypes, of the psychoid. I don't believe we need to choose between these two visions, these two theories. Both to my mind help us see aspects of our own being-here we might otherwise miss. Both have the power to help connect us to our bodies, to one another, to other living beings, to our world. For both it was important to keep their science in touch with the natural science of their day: Freud with the new developments in post-Darwinian biology, Jung with the new perspectives opened up by quantum physics.

Depth psychology begins with Freud's claim that psychology must include the Unconscious as well as Consciousness, *as psychical,* not just as biological, that it has to include a recognition that the unconscious is more than just the preconscious (by which he meant what is implicitly conscious but not being immediately attended to).

Freud, of course, doesn't really *discover* the unconscious—obviously the Romantics were already speaking of it—but he brought it into science. And then discovered that his understanding of science had to be radically modified. We need to take seriously that both Freud and Jung thought of themselves as scientists—and not just trivially, not just in order to be seen as doing something respectable. Although both were to some degree into a human science model of *Wissenschaft,* emphasizing interpretation, hermeneutics, rather than causal explanations, both were also determined not to sever psychology's relation to the natural sciences, not to deny the soul's intimate connection to the body. But they were also aiming at a specifically psychological level of explanation. Like Wundt they assumed that psychology's task was the study of consciousness, albeit of consciousness widened to include the unconscious.

Freud brings together Wundt and Brentano, and in doing so creates a *new science,* a 20th century science, a science that emerges almost exactly simultaneously with quantum physics. Freud's *Interpretation of Dreams* and Max Planck's quantum hypothesis were both introduced in 1900 (which is also about the time that Mendel's work first came to public light and the 20th century version of a post-Darwinian evolutionary biology became possible).

Yet although it is true that Freud didn't really discover the unconscious it is also true that he discovered a different unconscious—and discovered it differently. He discovered it first in his *clinical practice,* in the work with his hysterical patients that issued in the 1895 *Studies on Hysteria.* Not by way of philosophical speculation, not via laboratory experiments.

What he discovered was *repression,* the repressed unconscious. To regard their patients' amnesias as deliberate, as intentional, as motivated, as Freud and Breuer do in *Studies,* issues in the conception of a *dynamic* unconscious radically different from the preconscious that Wundt was ready to accept into psychology. Repression and the Freudian unconscious are inextricably related; the unconscious is that which *resists* being brought to consciousness. Freud saw that much that is unconscious in our psychic life is so because it is too painful for us to let it into consciousness; therefore we have repressed it. Indeed, so painful that the repressing is itself repressed.

Freud's discovery of the repressed unconscious came *via the body*. That is, he discovered (in his work with women suffering from hysteria) that the soul speaks through the body; the psyche uses the language of the body to express itself. He learned to hear somatic symptoms as language, not as gibberish but as expressions of an otherwise silenced soul.

In the theoretical chapters of *Studies* and in the 1895 "Project for a Scientific Psychology" (a text that Freud scribbled in the middle of a night, sent to Wilhelm Fliess, and never asked to have returned) Freud tries to reconcile his new insights with contemporary neurological science and its mechanistic assumptions and finds he can't: that the connections he has discovered between adult hysteria and childhood experience work only retrospectively not predictively, that conscious processes, soul activity, don't seem to be amenable to quantifiable measurement and yet do seem to be energetic. So Freud concludes that for the time being at least there seems to be no way of connecting neurology and consciousness. Nevertheless he finds that Darwinian evolutionary theory is relevant to his understanding of how consciousness emerges from an unconscious substratum to enable us to relate more effectively to the external world. He comes to see that repression, too, may have survival value.

Once it is clear to him that consciousness is not a mere appendage of physiological processes, Freud concludes that his focus from now on will be on consciousness in this wider (including the unconscious) sense, on the psyche, the soul—and on looking for *psychological* explanations for *psychological* phenomena. The challenge now is to study consciousness and the unconscious scientifically—but in a way that honors their specificity, that isn't reductive.

To begin with for Freud there is nothing numinous about the unconscious, no sense of it as primary process, not even really that there is an unconscious stratum in the psyches of all of us, not just of the neurotics among us. Freud was brought to his discovery of the unconscious fairly reluctantly, through his work with suffering patients and then through his own analysis. For Freud (unlike Jung) the unconscious is something discovered late and as until then unknown. It was the death of Freud's father in 1896 and the sustained period of depression and introversion that it provoked that led him into his own analysis and into a recognition of the real power of the unconscious in his own life and thus, he concludes, in everyone's. Neurotic suffering only makes more visible what are actually universal psychological dynamics.

The unconscious, he comes to see, not only has different contents from consciousness but also a different way of structuring those contents. Freud's discovery that there are two modes of consciousness, two types of mental functioning, becomes the basis for a richer, more complex formulation of the interaction of rational consciousness with symbolic or mythopoetic consciousness, so that by the time he writes *Interpretation of Dreams* Freud has come to believe that the animistic, associative, emotionally-toned mode of thinking, of apprehending and organizing experience that we glimpse through slips of the tongue and neurotic symptoms and dreams, is the original mode of psychic functioning, the psyche's *primary process*. This more poetical mode is not a distortion of normal psychic process but the form of the psyche's uninhibited activity and represents the core of our being.

Freud both supports our longing to bring the unconscious to consciousness, to recover its contents, to gain access to its mythopoetic faculty—and is intent on reminding us how profoundly there is that in us that we cannot know. We can never fully bring the unconscious into consciousness. The ego is not and will not be master of its own house.

Psychoanalysis, Freud discovers, represents *a new scientific method.* His exploration of the unconscious is not based on speculation but it is also not based on experimentation, on the positing of hypotheses and their validation. Nor is it based on introspection, since his experience is that the repressed unconscious cannot be accessed simply through an act of will. Yet it is based on *experience*—the experience of clinical practice. This base in experience and the attempt to systematize what is learned through such experience and the willingness to modify one's theory on the basis of further experience is what in Freud's view makes psychoanalysis a science.

The unconscious can't be accessed directly, only as it manifests itself in dream or symptom—and in the consulting room. Through the work of free association in the dialogical context of the analysis and through the made-visible re-enactment of unconscious patterns of loving in the transference, the unconscious emerges as word. As word addressed to another. We come to know the psyche—our own and one another's—not as a self-enclosed first-person world, not through introspection—nor through objectifying third-person observation—but only through a second person encounter, an I-You engagement.

So Freud discovers a new scientific method and a *different mode of confirmation*. His discoveries, theoretical and therapeutic, are not amenable to objective scientific proof. They are "true" only to the degree to which these insights accord with our own experience when looked at as honestly, complexly, and courageously as we can get ourselves to do. And only to the degree they help us move from neurotic misery to common unhappiness.

Freud also created *a new scientific language* in his invention of a new genre, the case history. The term itself—*case history*—brings together natural science and human science assumptions. The conjunction of "case" and "history" creates a mixed discourse that brings together the language of energy and desire with the language of intentionality and purpose. Freud often voiced discomfort that his case histories read like fiction, but knew that he needed to use sophisticated literary techniques—synecdoche, flashbacks, hints, the build-up of suspense, a blind and unreliable narrator—because he wanted to communicate the *process* of discovery, not just conclusions. In these case histories he offers historical explanations not "causes." Having studied Aristotle under Brentano and Theodor Gomperz, he was familiar with Aristotle's fourfold understanding of causality. Thus his interpretive emphasis falls not on efficient but formal and final causes, on retrospectively discovered similarities between present and past, and on the shaping power in our lives of "wishes" (purposes, intentions), especially unacknowledged unconscious wishes.

Freud also finds he needs to rely on *metaphorical language* to point to what he means by soul, since he understands so well that the soul isn't a thing, has no substantive existence, and thus can only be described analogically. His metaphors are drawn from an extraordinarily wide range—from physics, electricity, biology, archaeology, geology, and hydraulics—to name just those associated with some scientific field. Because Freud is also aware of how easily these might be taken literally, be reified, he relies on their plurality and diversity to remind us: these are metaphors, not literal descriptions. The unconscious is not really separated from consciousness by a membrane, or by a bureaucratic censor monitoring what is allowed to cross the border. Freud also finds it necessary to use the language of *myth* to speak adequately about the psyche, most obviously of course in his evocation of the Oedipus myth.

Because for Freud to speak of the soul, of its deepest longings and most profound terror, is to speak of the body, he sought a language for the self that takes seriously that we are embodied souls, ensouled bodies—which that body/soul dichotomy we've inherited from Descartes makes incredibly difficult. Freud's insistence on human embodiment means taking seriously our sexuality, our mortality, and our inescapable involvements with other desiring/acting embodied beings, with family and with society.

"The theory of the drives is our mythology," he writes to Einstein. Freud speaks of *drives* (*Trieben*) not "instincts"—a choice of language intended to emphasize the ultimate unity of soma and psyche. Drive is need become wish, energy become meaning, biology become psychology. Human instincts, he tells us, are always mediated through the psyche.

Although the sexual drive is never the only drive for Freud, he does focus on sexuality, because he understood it as the vehicle through which we express our deepest longings—the longing to give all of ourselves and to be fully accepted, our longing to have another direct all their love to us alone, our longings to *be* ourselves and to *lose* ourselves. His conception of sexuality includes all sensual and affectional currents, all the ways we experience bodily pleasure, all our intense emotional attachments. Freud's understanding of our sexuality was always transliteral; by "sexuality" he always meant more than genitality, more than "normal" (that is conventionally defined, socially approved) sexuality. He describes the mechanisms—displacement, condensation, reversal—by which our sexual impulses become expressed in myriad ways, and emphasizes the polymorphousness, malleability, divertibility of human sexuality.

In the years immediately following the First World War as Freud begins to move toward the second typology—the one that describes the psyche not primarily with respect to the distinction between unconscious and conscious but as the scene of conflict between the three agencies, the I, the That, and the Over-I (usually misleadingly translated as ego, id, and super-ego)—he is trying to find new ways of re-emphasizing that the I is not master in its own house, new ways of re-emphasizing the dependence of consciousness on a primal unconscious substratum (which he has now taken to calling *das Es*—the *That* in us), of re-emphasizing the given power of the never fully knowable and uncontrollable energies that work on us and in us.

In *Beyond the Pleasure Principle* he writes of how the same conservative and creative energies that are at work in the physical world as represented by the first and second laws of thermodynamics are at work in the soul. Now, more than at any time since the 1895 "Project," he writes about the relevance of biology to a deep understanding of our human being-here. He compares the emergence of life from the inanimate to the emergence of consciousness within "higher" living beings, and sees this emergence as an expression of a powerful life urge. He also talks about entropy and the inertial biological urge to return to earlier states, and sees this as an urge toward non-being. Everywhere he sees a struggle between the desire to live and the desire to die. And then in the midst of these scientific, bio-logically-oriented, musings, he again begins to speak mythically—about Eros and Death as two primal powers. Eros is the pull to life, to others, to the new, to the future. The pull of Death is the pull to repetition, inertia, regression, the longing for resolution and completion. Both Death and Eros are energies that operate in us consciously and unconsciously, biologically and psychologically, in species-specific ways. But they are cosmic, physical, biological, not just psychological energies—energies that are at work in us, through us, and in the whole outer world.

Jung

Jung has a quite different way of understanding and articulating the connection between body and soul, and of marking the distinctive concerns of psychol-ogy—which he moves toward because he sees Freud's unconscious as too per-sonal, too causal, too pathological, too sexual, too identified with the repressed unconscious. He believes we need an understanding of the unconscious that takes more account of its collective and biological aspects, of a deeper more *a priori* aspect.

And though I'd dispute Jung's understanding of Freud I understand how nec-essary it was for him, how it helped to free him to emphasize what he thought of as his original contributions to depth psychology. Yet it was clear even to Jung himself that his moves beyond Freud start with Freud, with Freud's recognition of the unconscious as intrinsic to psychology. For him, too, the unconscious sur-rounds consciousness on all sides and is that out of which consciousness arises. And like Freud he stresses the autonomy of the unconscious, affirms I am its object not its master.

Of course it takes him a while to work it all out—and, not surprisingly, he begins doing so with a critique of Freud's understanding of sexuality—though he does not intend this as a way of moving to a more spiritual and less biological psychology.

For Jung, too, sexuality is a centrally important aspect of our human being-here, something that facile contrasts between Freud and Jung tend to ignore. My sense is that Jung and Jungians often exaggerate the differences, tend to attribute an overly literal understanding of sexuality to Freud and to overemphasize the spiritual aspects of Jung's psychology (perhaps encouraged by the decision of Jung's translators that I remarked on earlier to very often render *Seele* as "spirit" rather than "soul"). I believe Jung felt free to emphasize those aspects of his thought different from Freud's because he knew the other side was powerfully being given its due by Freud.

In the original 1912 version of what later became *Symbols of Transformation* Jung says there are always two vectors of interpretation: sexual and spiritual, personal and transpersonal, causal and teleological; but he tends later on (including in the 1952 version) to emphasize the vector he sees Freud as ignoring. But in an important passage at the end of his "The Spiritual Problem of Modern Man" he writes:

> The soul is the life of the body seen from within and the body the outward manifestation of the life of the soul—the two being really one—the striving to transcend the present level of consciousness through acceptance of the unconscious must give the body its due.[4]

Even more important is a passage from the end of Jung's chapter on Freud in *Memories, Dreams, Reflections*:

> In retrospect I can say that I alone logically pursued the two problems which most interested Freud: the problem of "archaic vestiges," and that of sexuality. It is a widespread error to imagine that I do not see the value of sexuality. On the contrary, it plays a large part in my psychology as an essential—though not the whole—expression of psychic wholeness. But my main concern has been to investigate, over and above its personal significance and biological function, its spiritual aspect and its numinous meaning, and thus to explain what Freud was so fascinated by, but was unable to grasp…Sexuality is of the greatest importance as the expression of the chthonic spirit. That spirit is the "other face of God," the dark side of the God image. The question of the chthonic spirit has occupied me ever since I began to delve into the world of alchemy. Basically, this interest was awakened by that early conversation with Freud, when, mystified, I felt how deeply stirred he was by the phenomenon of sexuality.[5]

Earlier in the chapter Jung says that for Freud the sexual libido took over the role of a *deus absconditus*, a hidden or concealed god, and that he sensed that Freud wanted to say, but didn't know how, that regarded from within sexuality included spirituality.

It is clear that Jung's understanding of sexuality was shaped in response to Freud, his interest was awakened by Freud, and that he feels he went beyond him. Yet it is also clear that Jung has a narrower, more literal, definition of sexuality than Freud. Reading the Freud/Jung letters shows us that from the very beginning of their relationship Jung was uncomfortable with Freud's expanded understanding of the sexual function. This discomfort was made public in the lectures he gave in New York in 1912, lectures that were supposedly presentations of Freud's psychological theories, though Jung's own spin on those theories becomes quite obvious.

Jung acknowledges that these lectures represents the first public voicing of his differences and criticisms and publicly avows his discomfort with viewing an infant's pleasure in suckling at its mother's breast as a sexual experience. He insists that infants (up to age 3 or 5) are *pre-sexual.* In discussing the activities Freud associates with the polymorphousness of infantile sexuality, Jung speaks of a gradual migration stage by stage from the nutritive toward genital sexuality. His view is clearly more unidirectional and more teleological; for him the earlier stages are fully gone beyond, the past is left behind. Don't project backward, he says; because something leads toward sexuality doesn't make it sexual.

Clearly in part, Jung is just uncomfortable with extending the meaning of the word "sex." To him it *means* genitality and heterosexuality, coitus, fucking, what Freud called "normal" sexuality. But Jung is also struggling to articulate an intuition that there's something Freud doesn't get that's important and that I believe many of us feel we immediately understand. He *knows* that somehow the beauty and the soul meaning of our art, our religion, of human culture, are not fully appreciated when explained in connection to sexuality; that the emphasis on origins, on etiology, is reductive.

So in 1912 Jung announces that he believes it more appropriate to speak of the polyvalence of libido than of polymorphous perversity. He speaks of "the need to give the concept of libido breathing space and remove it from the narrow confines of the sexual definition."[6] He makes clear that by "libido" he means a single energy capable of many applications (as opposed to Freud's model of drives in conflict with one another). For him "libido" refers to a dynamic unity of undifferentiated energy that can be expressed in a multitude of ways. There is one single continuous life urge, not a self-preservation instinct in conflict with a species-preservation one.

> The theory of libido deprives the sexual components of their elementary significance as psychic 'faculties' and gives them a purely phenomenological value.[7]

He claims that we know too little about the instincts and their psychic dynamism to risk giving priority to any one. Thus when speaking of libido we should understand it as an energy able to communicate itself in any field whatsoever, be it power, hunger, hatred, sexuality, or religion.

It is not until 1919 in his essay "Instinct and the Unconscious" that Jung for the first time uses the word "archetype." Where Freud, as we noted, spoke of *drives* (physiology mediated thru the psyche), Jung speaks of instincts and by "instinct" Jung means body in lieu of soul. Instincts are associated with processes that are uniform, regular, automatic, unalterable, blind, compulsive; "archetype" is his word for instinct become meaning. He begins this essay with a definition of the unconscious:

> I define the unconscious as the totality of all psychic phenomena that lack the quality of consciousness—what's too weak to become conscious—and all more or less intentional repressions of painful thoughts and feelings.[8]

This, he says, is the *personal unconscious*. (Note, however, that most of this is what Freud would call the *pre*conscious; even repression is here understood in a more conscious intentional sense than in Freud's more dynamic understanding.) Then he adds: "But the unconscious also includes qualities not individually acquired but inherited"—instincts and archetypes. Instincts are inherited unconscious processes that occur uniformly and regularly and are characterized by an inner necessity. However, he says, "The question of instinct cannot be dealt with psychologically without considering the archetypes because at bottom they determine one another." Archetypes are "*a priori* inborn forms of 'intuition,'" "the necessary *a priori* determinants of all psychic processes"[9]:

> Just as the instincts compel man to a specifically human mode of existence, so the archetypes force his ways of perception and apprehension into specifically human patterns. The instincts and the archetypes together form the "*collective unconscious.*"

> The way in which man inwardly pictures the world is still, despite all differences of detail, as uniform and regular as his instinctive actions.

> The archetype or primordial image might be described as the *instinct's perception of itself,* the self-portrait of the instinct.

> The archetype determines the form and direction of the instinct.

> The collective unconscious consists of the sum of the instincts and their *correlates,* the archetypes [my italics.][10]

I have included all these quotations to indicate how urgently he wants to honor the specifically psychic *and* the tie to the biological—and how difficult he finds it is to do this satisfactorily, to find *language* adequate to the *intuition* (what Giegerich called "the lava flow"), language that isn't dualistic. As he writes in his 1928 essay, "On Psychic Energy":

> Although it seems certain to me that psychic energy is in some way or other closely connected with physical processes yet, in order to speak with any authority about this connection, we would need quite different experiences and insights.[11]

Jung says that he is persuaded that unconscious processes belong to psychology and not merely to the physiology of the brain and assumes that the unconscious functions ultimately go over into substratum processes to which no psychic quality can be assigned. Because we have no means of dividing what is psychic from the biological process as such, we would probably do best, he suggests, to regard the psychic process simply as life-process and psychic energy as a specific part of life-energy, and thus do justice to "the ever-present problem of 'mind and body.'"[12]

But by far the most thoughtful discussion appears in the 1947 essay "The Nature of the Psyche." As I noted earlier, he begins this essay with a review of the history of psychology and talks about how really difficult it still is to look at the psyche scientifically, that is objectively. He quotes Wundt's refusal to include the unconscious in psychology and then says that with Freud's introduction of the unconscious into psychology, "the soul emerges from its chrysalis," no longer as something immediately known but "in strangely double guise, as both known and unknown."[13] He says he believes this move to be as revolutionary as the discovery of radioactivity in quantum physics but goes on to speak of the danger of thinking that if we have a *name* (like the word "unconscious") we have caught the phenomenon, "like a slain creature of the wild that can no longer run away." But "the psyche is the greatest of all cosmic wonders—we have not caught it!"[14]

And then, of course, Jung tries his best to catch it! "The psyche proper," he says, "extends to all functions which can be brought under the influence of the will."[15] Not just the once-conscious, the repressed, but the not yet conscious—though he agrees that psyche includes only what is at least theoretically *capable of becoming conscious.* In this essay Jung for the first time introduces the term "psychoid"—and for the first time distinguishes clearly between archetypes and archetypal ideas or images.

"Psychoid" is a liminal term, referring to the threshold between the physiological and the psychological; its introduction enables Jung to acknowledge that all psychic processes are bound to an organic substrate. The archetypes, as such, are formless and unrepresentable, *psychoid*, rather than properly speaking, *psychic*; they belong to the invisible end of the psychic spectrum, are not capable of becoming conscious; only the archetypal ideas or images ever become conscious. Even names for archetypes like *coniunctio* or *Mother*, are already ideas. What comes into individual consciousness are always *archetypal images*, particular, concrete manifestations that are influenced by sociocultural and individual factors.

Jung's former patient and friend, the noted quantum physicist Wolfgang Pauli, helped Jung to see that the relation between archetype and archetypal image is a-causal—and Jung is obviously comforted by the fact that causality has been dethroned in modern physics as well. He suggests that maybe archetypes are sort of like particles in physics, where we have access only to their effects and the particles are not themselves directly visible and aren't exactly causes. Jung sees the helpfulness of such analogies, but also recognizes (as too many others fail to do!) that they are not more than that, not more than analogies.

As Jung wrestles with these ideas he sees clearly that he has, perhaps inevitably, had to move *beyond science*. "I fancied I was working along the best scientific lines"—but we *can't* adopt the same subject-object standpoint which is core to science—because here the psyche is observing itself. *Psychology is doomed to cancel itself out as a science and therein precisely it reaches its scientific goal*"[16] [my italics].

But the habits of science, its emphasis not only on the subject-object distinction but also on efficient causality, are hard to let go of. So although Jung's recognition of *a-causality* is tremendously important, it was hard for him (or his followers) to avoid making it into just another cause! That is, to speak as though archetypes *cause* archetypal images, in some kind of before and after way, rather than as being present *simultaneously* at different levels of explanation—as gravity doesn't *cause* planetary motions but describes them. The hold of the language of efficient causality is so hard to detect: how easily we fall into speaking as though synchronous events *cause* one another or to represent teleology as meaning that the future somehow *causes* the present.

Once again in this essay he tries to articulate the relation between instincts and archetypes. When simply physiological, instincts are characterized by compulsiveness, whereas when they become psychic they are subject to the will. Jung recognizes that we, of course, fear being swallowed by instinct and by the unconscious—and that the archetypes, too, can work in us compulsively. But there is a way of approaching the archetypes that allows us a creative access to them—through active imagination, conscious symbolizing. The libido has a *natural gradient*—toward the symbolic; symbols are what make possible the transformation or rechanneling of instinctual energy into cultural activity. Ultimately we reach a point at which the energy ceases altogether to be oriented by instinct in the original sense and attains a so-called "spiritual" form:

> In spite or perhaps because of its affinity with instinct, the archetype represents the authentic element of spirit.... Archetype and instinct are the most polar opposites imaginable, as can easily be seen when one compares a man who is ruled by his instinctual drives with a man seized by the spirit. But, just as between all opposites there obtains so close a bond that no position can be established or even thought of without its corresponding negation, so in this case also *'les extremes se touchent.'* They belong together as correspondences, which is not to say that the one is derivable from the other.[17]

Jung writes that psychic processes seem to be balances of energy flowing between spirit and instinct, though the question of whether a process is to be described as spiritual or as instinctual remains shrouded in darkness. It doesn't work, he says, to choose one interpretation *or* the other. It is our consciousness that makes us human, but when we identify only with that, we have lost access to energy and meaning. Jung's primary purpose, I believe, is to bring us into a renewed living connection to the deep unconscious from which consciousness emerges.

His emphasis on the archetypal gives voice to his sense of our having a profound inner connection to the primordially human. Our connection to others is not just external and horizontal, but rather becomes visible at the deepest layer of our souls—in our access to the realm symbolized by the paleolithic cave with its pottery shards, bones and skulls of Jung's dream on the way to America—or by the "rhizome" he invokes in the prologue of *Memories, Dreams, Reflections*.

But I believe it is an enormous mistake to interpret this as a move away from the body or the biological stratum of our being-here. I see it rather as an affirmation that we are connected to one another through our shared human nature, through those biological instincts we have in common and through their correlates the archetypes, which are also part of our shared inheritance.

Notes

1. C. G. Jung, *Collected Works* (Princeton: Princeton University Press, 1953-1979) 9.1, 43.4.

2. John R. Searle, *The Rediscovery of the Mind* (Cambridge, MA: MIT Press, 1992) 14.

3. Quoted by Jung, *C.W.*, 8, 163.

4. Jung, *C.W.*, 10, 94. (Because the German is *Seele* not *Geist*—soul not spirit—I have modified the translation.)

5. C. G. Jung, *Memories, Dreams, Reflections* (New York: Pantheon, 1963) 168.

6. Jung, *C.W.*, 4, 118.

7. Jung, *C.W.*, 4, 112.

8. Jung, *C.W.*, 8, 133.

9. Jung, *C.W.*, 8, 134.

10. Jung, *C.W.*, 8, 133, 136, 137, 138.

11. Jung, *C.W.*, 8, 7.

12. Jung, *C.W.*, 8, 16, 17.

13. Jung, *C.W.*, 8, 167.

14. Jung, *C.W.*, 8, 168,9.

15. Jung, *C.W.*, 8, 183.

16. Jung, *C.W.*, 8, 216, 223.

17. Jung, *C.W.*, 8, 206.

22

Looking Back at Orpheus

And there they walk
Together now; at times they are side by side;
At times she walks ahead with him behind;
At other times it's Orpheus who leads—
But without any need to fear should he
Turn round to see his own Eurydice.[1]

These lines from Ovid's account of Orpheus's reunion with Eurydice in Hades after his own death suggest that there is a kind of looking back that is creative, that comes from a suffering truly endured, and wholly different from the looking back shaped by an unwillingness to admit to the reality of loss and death. The body of Orpheus has just been dismembered, but the shade, the soul, of Orpheus, descending to the underworld, remembers all the places he had visited before. And we remember that Orpheus is a grandson of Mnemosyne, the Titan goddess of Memory and that, as is the case with all deities, her gifts can bring disaster or healing.

I have long been fascinated by Orpheus and by how the poets of ancient Greece and of our own world have kept remembering, reimagining, and recreating him. As I now find myself returning to the myths surrounding Orpheus for the first time after almost fifteen years I find myself amazed, as I always am when I return to a myth I think I already know, by how much more there is to this story than I had earlier recognized.

Fifteen years ago it was Ovid's telling of the myth (and Rilke's amplification of that telling) which moved me most. Looking at the story from a woman's perspective, I saw an Orpheus who just didn't seem able to recognize that "his" Eurydice was precisely that, *his* Eurydice—and that Eurydice herself now really belonged in the underworld. Now I find myself wanting to give equal credit to Virgil's Orpheus, an Orpheus deeply in love with *her* and really not knowing how to live without her. I want to honor that *both* are true—and also want to move beyond an identification with Eurydice so unequivocal that it blinds me to my own relation to Orpheus.

Part of what delights me about myth is precisely this: that the same myth can be understood in so many different ways, depending on to what aspect, what episode, which figure, which version we choose to direct our focus. The more attentively we look the more we come to appreciate how each detail, each variant account, belongs, deepens, complicates.

I have also come to recognize more and more what it means that myths are part of a mythology, how each of the Greek myths leaks into, involves, implies all the others—so that in order to tell any one myth really well, we'd have to tell them all. (This reminds me of Freud's comment that fully to follow the paths of associations suggested by a single dream fragment would issue in the unraveling of a whole life.) Of course, we can't really do this; but I hope you'll appreciate how restrained I am being when I choose not to tell all the stories that lead into and out of the Orpheus myth.

I am also intrigued by how myths get reimagined over the centuries—how it is such reimagining that kept them alive in the ancient world—and that keeps them alive in ours. Although we, of course, don't have direct access to a purely oral stratum in the history of any of the Greek myths, we can sense an oral bardic tradition lying just behind Homer and can access some understanding of how that tradition is transformed in the literary epics composed by Homer and Hesiod in the late eighth century BCE, and can then actually see how the epic take on myth is reframed first by the lyric poets of the late archaic age and then by the dramatists of fifth century Athens and still again by the poets of Augustan Rome some four hundred years later.

Indeed, one of the distinctive features of the history of Greek mythology is that in Greece, as contrasted for instance with Egypt or Israel, the stories belonged to the poets not the priests. The dominance of Zeus, the articulation of the Olympian pantheon, the clear differentiation between the various gods and goddesses, was really more the work of Homer and the bards who preceded him than of cult. As Herodotus observed, Hesiod and Homer are the ones who provided the Greeks with a theogony, who gave the gods their names, distinguished their attributes and functions, and described their shapes.[2]

It was the poets who cast the gods and goddesses as all members of a patriarchal family ruled by Zeus. It was the poets who viewed them almost exclusively in anthropomorphic terms and who gave each so highly individualized a personality that there is no possibility of confusing any goddess or god with any other. (I have only to get a few sentences into a myth about any Greek deity before a listener familiar with Greek mythology will recognize immediately just which goddess or god is involved.)

Given that the myths belong to the poets, it is not at all surprising that there will be a myth about a poet: the myth of Orpheus. There is, of course, more to Orpheus than his being a poet but that is where this myth begins. That is the kernel out of which everything grows and around which everything else accretes. To understand the history of Orpheus thus requires dis-membering, and then re-membering, the myth.

The myth keeps being added to, but not, of course, in some rationally motivated, conscious, deliberate way but imaginally—much as a psychological complex opens up and also pulls things to it through a complex process of association and of the annexation of later experiences (perhaps particularly experiences of suffering) that add dimensionality and depth.

In early Greece poets were regarded as having shamanic powers, as inspired by the gods, as magicians. Their chants, songs accompanied by the lyre, were incantation, enchantment. In this still predominantly oral culture the primary way to transmit traditional knowledge was through poetic speech. The poet's voice was honored as divinely inspired, as absolutely reliable and authoritative.

Orpheus seems to have been an especially intriguing figure to the poets since through their revisioning of him they could clarify their own experience of being poets. Almost inevitably Orpheus becomes associated with the primary themes to which they as poets are perennially drawn, love and death.

Because Orpheus is such an important mythical figure, there are many allusions to the myth in Greek literature but no full accounts. We don't really know how old this myth is, though the Orphics of the fifth century BCE claimed it went far back—but Orpheus is absent from the epic literature, perhaps because the epic poets viewed themselves as muse-inspired bards. What we might ascribe to the imagination, Homer traces to an actual experience shared with him by the Muses who are everywhere and so know everything.

There is no Orpheus in Homer. But in the *Iliad* Achilles is shown playing the lyre and in the *Odyssey* both Nestor and Odysseus are represented as gifted storytellers and a professional bard appears in both epics. In the *Iliad* we are told of Thamyris, who boasted he could sing more beautifully than the Muses; in punishment they took away his sight, his voice, and his memory. Homer's depiction in the *Odyssey* of Demodocus, the blind bard at the court of the Phaeacians, has often been viewed as a kind of self-portrait.

The other major epic poet, Hesiod, also speaks of the muses teaching him beautiful singing, breathing their divine voice into him and warning him, "We know how to tell many falsehoods that seem real, but we also know how to speak truth when we wish to."[3]

Even the sixth century archaic lyric poets make no mention of Orpheus. For Sappho it is Aphrodite not the Muses who inspire her song. Sappho's poetry makes manifest what it is like to experience the goddess of love at work in one's own soul. Her topic is love—"But I say the most beautiful thing on this dark earth is whomever one loves"—and in many of her poems love is seen as becoming visible through the pain to which it exposes us. Love is marked by its transience; the themes of loss and parting (so central to the Orpheus myth) continually reappear. Poetry is remembrance, a dialectic of absence and presence, whereby an absent beloved can be made present through the poet's evocative recollection, whereby two lovers separated by a great distance can be joined together through their shared memories.

Perhaps it is only in a slightly later period when, with the spread of literacy, the poets' claim of a supernatural origin for their words is liable to be viewed with suspicion that an Orpheus becomes necessary. The earliest references (which appear toward the end of the sixth century BCE) present Orpheus as coming from Thrace, where Greeks probably first came into contact with shamanic beliefs about birds and beasts summoned by a magician's song and about journeys to the underworld to recover stolen souls.[4] Thrace was also the traditional locus of the beginnings of Dionysian worship.

Thus from the outset there is an at least implicit connection between Orpheus and Dionysos. But Orpheus is also said to be a son of Apollo.[5] Indeed, it seems impossible to know whether Orpheus was initially an underworld daimon (who emerges when summoned), a chthonic deity like Dionysos, or a follower of Apollo.[6] Thus taking the connection to both seriously is somehow central to an understanding of Orpheus. The myth seems likely to be at least in part about the tension between the form-giving power of art associated with Apollo and the disruptive death-dealing power of passion associated with Dionysos. We will see that the myth can be—indeed, has been, read—in both ways: with art as triumphant or with death.

A close reading of the myth may also force us to abandon the too simple antithetical understanding of the relationship between Apollo and Dionysos fostered by a misreading of Nietzsche. The Delphic Apollo is quite Dionysian; the Orphic Dionysos quite Apollonian! Both Apollo and Dionysos are associated with music: Apollo with the lyre, whose sweet melody is ideally suited to accompany song;

Dionysos with the aulos, the double pipes whose emotionally stirring sounds tend to drown out the human voice.

Apollo, it is said, gave Orpheus the lyre that Hermes had long ago given him. According to the "Homeric Hymn to Hermes," the infant god, born in the morning, played the lyre by afternoon. Sneaking out of his cradle, the god spied a turtle and immediately had the idea of using its shell to make himself a musical instrument. A few minutes later he cleverly arranges to steal Apollo's cattle and then manages to soothe his older brother's justified anger over the theft by playing the lyre. "Cow-killer," Apollo says to him, "I think our differences can be settled peaceably. My heart has never been so struck by anything as it has by this." "So I'll give it you," Hermes responds, "but remember: give the glory to me."[7] Perhaps we should remember this association of the lyre with trickery, with lying words, from the outset.

Athene is reputed to have invented the aulos but then to have quickly thrown it away when she discovered how ugly her face became while playing it. Marsyas (a satyr and thus a figure clearly related to Dionysos) found the discarded instrument and taught himself to play it. Indeed, he learned so well that he challenged Apollo to a contest to be judged by the Muses, a contest which the god—by cheating—won.

Orpheus's mother was one of these muses—not just any muse but Calliope, the one whose name means "beautiful voice" and whom Hesiod named as the most exalted of them all. It was Calliope who thwarted Aphrodite by awarding Adonis to Persephone for a third of each year and the one who (in Ovid) gets to tell the Demeter-Persephone story and to tell it in a way that lays all the blame on Aphrodite.[8] (So perhaps we should not be surprised to find a second century CE author, Hyginus, blaming Orpheus's death on Aphrodite who made the Thracian women fall so passionately in love with the widowed Orpheus that they tore him apart in their eagerness to possess him.)

But that's to get far ahead. To begin with Orpheus came from Thrace and he played the lyre. The earliest literary accounts mention his being a member of the Argonaut expedition. Thus in their myths the Greeks imagined Orpheus as a contemporary of Herakles and of the other heroes of an age preceding the Trojan War, although a somewhat skeptical Herodotus noted that none of the poems attributed to him could be dated from earlier than the sixth century. Orpheus was said to have been brought aboard the Argo at the suggestion of Cheiron (the wise old centaur who was teacher to Jason, Asclepius, Actaeon and Achilles). His primary assignment was to serve as the chanter who would keep the rowers in harmony with one another, but his beautiful singing was of much more help than that. First it coaxed the reluctant ship into the water and then at the very outset of the journey helped quell a brawl among the sailors. Later the ship was able safely to pass the Sirens as Orpheus's song drowned out theirs. It also charmed the Clashing Rocks, and even put the dragon in Colchis to sleep so that Jason could safely steal the golden fleece the fearsome beast was supposed to guard. Some of this is, of course, later elaboration, but already in the late archaic lyric poetry of Simonides we hear how Orpheus's singing had the power to charm wild beasts: "Above his head flutter innumerable birds and from the dark-blue sea fishes leap straight up in harmony with his lovely song."⁹

There is a hint, too, even in the early period of the eventual superiority of poet to hero—it is poets' songs that give heroes their glory, their immortality. And already the intimate connection of musician and magician, of poet and dissembler, means Orpheus will be looked upon with respect—and with suspicion.

This is the Orpheus of the earliest visual art as well—Orpheus with his lyre, and the enchanted beasts. No underworld journey, no Eurydice, no dismemberment.

Then in the fifth century BCE we begin to hear of a *katabasis*, an underworld journey—as though the only challenge remaining to a poet who could charm the beasts would be to charm the powers that rule the underworld. Orpheus is now said to have gone to Hades to rescue a soul—although the object of that rescue is at this point undefined, unnamed. This journey recalls Dionysos's journey to the underworld to rescue his mother Semele and bring her to Olympus, where as mother of a god, she to his mind rightfully belongs. Dionysos succeeds in his project and so, we surmise, did Orpheus in the earliest accounts. By virtue of his success Orpheus becomes someone believed to know the secrets of death and rebirth and to be able to teach them to others.

This version of Orpheus's descent is clearly influenced by the Orphic tradition in which Orpheus figures as a prophet, perhaps even as a founder, of a Dionysos-centered eschatological mysticism. (Apollodorus claimed that Orpheus invented the mysteries of Dionysos; Diodorus added that he had made many modifications in the orgiastic rites earlier associated with the god of ecstasy.) It was probably also the Orphics who first introduced the theme of dismemberment into the Orpheus myth, a theme that so obviously echoes their myth about the dismemberment of Dionysos at the hands of the Titans. In the Orphic context the dismemberment of Orpheus, like that of Dionysos, is understood as a ritual act connected to renewal and rebirth, associated both with vegetal fertility and with initiation. In this context the death of Orpheus does not represent failure or punishment; it is the act whereby Orpheus fulfills his destiny and is assimilated to the god.

A lost play by Aeschylus may have attributed the slaying of Orpheus to a band of Dionysian maenads angered at his rejection of their god for Apollo and it evidently mentioned that he went to Hades "because of his wife" (the first known mention of this figure, though nothing more is said of her). Jane Harrison suggests that Aeschlyus may have sympathized with the maenads' murder of a too Orphic Orpheus, an Orpheus who had betrayed the "real" Dionysos, "the maddened, maddening wine-god," by transforming him into an ascetic.[10]

But these are speculations about a vanished text; the first definite literary reference to an underworld descent undertaken as a rescue mission appears in Euripides' early play, *Alcestis*. In this early play after his wife's voluntary death, Admetus cries:

> Had I the lips of Orpheus and his melody
> to charm the maiden daughter of Demeter and
> her lord, and by singing win you back from death,
> I would have gone beneath the earth, and not the hound
> Of Pluto could have stayed me, nor the ferryman
> Of ghosts, Charon, at his oar, I would have brought you back
> To life.[11]

The allusion to Persephone who did return to the upperworld and the entire tone of this complaint suggest an Orpheus who succeeded in his mission. But in their final song the chorus says that it has nowhere found evidence of any power stronger than fate, neither Orpheus's songs nor Asclepius's healing potions. Both these sons of Apollo had sought to overcome death—Asclepius at the beginning of his career as the healer god when he tried to use the powerful healing potion given him by Athene to bring back to life heroes he believed unjustly brought to an early death by vengeful gods—and both had failed. Thus the chorus sings of the hopelessness of victory over death—just before Herakles, through brute force, succeeds in bringing Alcestis back to the upperworld. So Euripides keeps the myth ambivalent: might Orpheus have succeeded or must he have failed? In his last or next to last play, *Iphigenia at Aulis,* his heroine comes close to echoing Admetus' words: "If I had Orpheus' speech, my father..." Iphigenia cries to Agamemnon. But she knows she lives in a harsh real world where even a daughter's tears will have no power. So much for myths, she seems to say.

Initially the myth of Orpheus appears to celebrate art's power to triumph over death, an understanding that seems to be little more than an elaboration of the notion of poetry as power. But for there to be a real *story* about Orpheus he may need to suffer a genuine defeat, just as for there to be a *story* about Demeter and Persephone they need to suffer a separation. Unending success, unchallenged love, do not a story make. It may well be in Plato's *Symposium* that Orpheus is for the first time imagined as failing in his attempt. Failing because, so Phaedrus tells us, he didn't love enough, didn't love enough to die with the woman he had lost:

> Orpheus, son of Oeagros, they sent back unfulfilled from Hades, showing him a phantom of the woman for whom he came, but not giving the woman herself because he seemed to them to have acted the part of a coward since he was a singer with a lyre and didn't venture to die for the sake of love, as did Alcestis, but rather devised a means of entering Hades while still alive. Therefore they laid a just penalty upon him and caused his death to be at the hands of women.[12]

In some of the earlier dialogues, Plato seems to speak appreciatively of Orpheus. For example in the *Apology* he has Socrates talk of looking forward to meeting Orpheus, Musaeus, Hesiod and Homer in the other world. But more often he criticizes Orpheus's art for relying on emotion and on hypnotic persuasion. In the Myth of Er at the end of the *Republic* in which Socrates imagines the souls of the dead choosing their next life he tells us that Orpheus selected the life of a swan "because from hatred of the tribe of women, owing to his death at their hands, he was unwilling to be conceived and born of a woman."[13] Thus the criticism voiced by Phaedrus in the *Symposium* is not inconsistent with some of these earlier references. But somehow more damning. For earlier Orpheus is criticized essentially for being a successful poet by a philosopher suspicious of poetry. But here he is criticized for failure as a lover, for not loving enough, for being satisfied with a phantom, an image of his beloved, and not even recognizing that it is not really *her*. (Obviously there is a reference here to the conceit of Stesichorus—picked up in Euripides' *Helen in Egypt*—that the real Helen never went to Troy, that both Greeks and Trojans were deceived by a phantom Helen.) Thus for Plato Orpheus failed in his mission—not because of a violated taboo, not because he'd been forbidden to look back upon his bride while returning her to the upperworld as in Virgil's or Ovid's versions—but because of a failure of character.

It is also in Plato's *Symposium* that for the first time Orpheus is imagined as going to rescue a particular beloved woman, though in Plato she still remains unnamed. Later in the fourth century the beloved maiden gets a name: Ariope, which means "wild-voiced," a suitable name for a Thracian nymph or naiad. The name "Eurydice" does not become part of the myth until the first century BCE.[14]

In the Hellenistic period Orpheus comes to be associated with male homosexuality, a motif probably introduced to help explain his death at the hands of women. There is also an early Hellenistic account which says the muses gathered together the dismembered parts of Orpheus's body and gave them burial. Harrison suggests that these muses are the maenads recovered from their madness and compares the relation of the maddened maenads to the gentle muses with the relation of the Dionysos of the *Bacchae* to the Dionysos of the Orphics, and also with the relation of the *Erinyes* to the *Eumenides* in Aeschylus's *Oresteia*.[15]

So now the pieces of the myth are all there—for Virgil and Ovid to assemble, to re-member. It's what they do with the story that I want to focus on, which means noting context, allusions, emphases, omissions, innovations—the subtleties and ambiguities. It's their Orpheus that has lived on.

It is still amazing to me that Virgil's masterfully condensed 75 lines in the *Georgics* (written around 29 BCE) should actually be the first narrative account of the myth—that before that we have only allusions, references, fragments. The *Georgics* mostly consists of descriptive celebrations (clearly inspired by both Hesiod's *Works and Days* and Lucretius) of the ordered routines of country life, which Virgil hopes will be restored now that the devastating civil wars, which had followed Julius Caesar's death, have been brought to an end. The stories in Book 4 are so different that many scholars have wondered whether they were part of the original conception, although certainly what a modern audience is most likely to respond to and remember. The Orpheus myth appears in Book 4 as an *epyllion*, a tale within a tale, a miniature epic. *Epyllia* were expected to be presented in a more emotional vein than that characteristic of true epic and to recount an unfamiliar episode in the life of an important mythic figure. Because the frame and inset tales are expected to be thematically related, to understand Virgil's take on Orpheus we have to take account of the Aristaeus myth within which he sets it.

In Greek mythology Aristaeus is a son of Apollo (like Orpheus) and the sea nymph Cyrene, raised by Cheiron and tutored by the muses who taught him the arts of healing, prophecy, hunting and agriculture. He was also known as the father of Actaeon, cousin to Dionysos. Virgil invokes this familiar Aristaeus as a deity in the prologue to his poem, but in Book 4 he presents a new facet: here Aristaeus is a devoted beekeeper suddenly exposed to the inexplicable death of all his bees. Bewildered and dismayed, Aristaeus turns for help to his divine mother whom he comes upon surrounded by nymphs and muses (one of whom is entertaining the others by telling the story borrowed from the *Odyssey* of Hephaistos's jealousy of Aphrodite's dalliance with Ares). Cyrene advises her son to consult Proteus, the ancient shapeshifting soothsaying seagod (who, Segal suggests, may represent "the ungraspable mystery of life"[16]). Once held fast, Proteus tells Aristaeus, "The anger that pursues you is divine" and can be traced to Orpheus's anguish at being separated from his wife. He then proceeds to tell Aristaeus the full story: how Orpheus's wife, while fleeing from Aristaeus' unwanted embrace, had been bit by a death-bringing venomous serpent—and how this unnoticed, unremembered moment in Aristaeus' life had been pivotal in that of Orpheus.

Thus for Virgil the story of Orpheus begins with the death of his as yet unnamed wife, a wife who assumes an importance in this retelling she has never had before. (When Persephone was abducted in the underworld, none of the maidens with whom she'd been gathering flowers even noticed her absence; whereas here the young wife's peers, the Dryads, are said to have filled the world with their wailing grief.) Never before in the tales told about Orpheus had we had an account of his wife's death—only of Orpheus's attempt to undo it. Never before had we had an account of Orpheus's grief, of his experience of her loss as unbearable. Virgil says that Orpheus tried without success to console himself with his own music:

> And you, sweet wife,
> You on the desolate shore alone he sang,
> You at return, you at decline of day.[17]

Unreconciled to his separation from Eurydice, Orpheus descends to the underworld, hoping to use his music to soften the hard hearts of Hades and Persephone. In a sense he is pulled into the underworld by his grief; the experience of loss *is* being there. But he hopes somehow to undo what has happened, to bring Eurydice back to the land of the living. Virgil does not attempt to describe the poet's song, only how it drew all the too-early dead, the young mothers, the unwed virgins, the youths in fugitive bloom toward him, only how it struck with awe even the Furies and Cerberus and Ixion. Nor does Virgil make any direct reference to the gods' response. He only tells us that "having evaded every hazard," Orpheus was returning with Eurydice following close behind. Then suddenly "on the very brink of light" Orpheus forgets and "yielding in his will, looked back at his own Eurydice." Now, at this painful moment, just when she isn't "his," Eurydice is named for the first time. And only now are we, still indirectly, told of the taboo against looking back that has been violated. This, the prohibition against looking back and the consequent second loss, the very center of the myth as Virgil presents it, is almost surely his invention. And, of course, we know that things forbidden in such tales are always done (and suspect that maybe Hades and Persephone did as well). Orpheus is overcome by a *furor*, a madness of passion (similar to that described as taking hold of both wild and domestic beasts in Book 3), which seizes him and turns him around.

Eurydice, now not only named, but given *voice*, subjectivity, is overwhelmed:

> 'Orpheus,' she cries, 'we are ruined, you and I!
> What utter madness is this? See, once again
> The cruel Fates are calling me back and darkness
> Falls on my swimming eyes. Goodbye for ever.
> I am borne away wrapped in an endless night,
> Stretching to you, no longer yours, these hands,

These helpless hands.' In Mary Zimmermann's beautiful enactment of this scene in her theatrical production "Metamorphoses" we watch Eurydice blindly following Orpheus until he turns and then we see the two lovers piteously, hopelessly, stretching out their hands, never quite touching, to one another. This happens once and it is almost unbearable. But then the whole scene is played out once again, and then a third time—as though maybe, maybe, the story might turn out differently. But, of course, it cannot—and we *feel* how this goodbye is, indeed, forever.

In Virgil's account it is Eurydice who speaks so plaintively; Orpheus is given no words except for one final plaintive, "Eurydice." As Eurydice finishes speaking, she vanishes like smoke, unable anymore to see Orpheus as he vainly grasps at shadows. Then back in the upperworld and powerless to return, Orpheus, wandering ever further north through a cold and barren landscape, weeps for seven months, singing his tale of woe so movingly that tigers are entranced and oak trees draw close to listen. "No thought of love could touch his heart, no thought of marriage-rites," Virgil writes—perhaps an indirect allusion to the tradition of Orpheus turning to homosexuality and its barrenness—but perhaps only an indication of how obsessed he still is with his Eurydice and how consumed by his loss. For in a sense Virgil's Orpheus never does really leave the underworld. Though forever separated from Eurydice, he is completely lost in his grief, can sing of nothing else, think of nothing else, feel nothing else. Yet for him, unlike Sappho, his singing cannot do enough to make the absent present. He is so deep *in* mourning—that his own death when it comes can only be release.

Virgil tell us of this death thus:

> Thracian women,
> Deeming themselves despised by such devotion.
> Amid their Bacchic orgies in the night
> Tore him apart, this youth, and strewed his limbs
> over the countryside.

This account (which reminds us of ancient rites in which a vegetation god is sacrificed) gives the death and the dismemberment a ritual context and significance. Orpheus who had at first refused to accept the necessity of nature's patterns of death and renewal now becomes a participant in a grim celebration of them. At the end of the framing tale Aristaeus (who is never shown feeling any remorse for his attempted rape) offers a sacrifice and is rewarded with the rebirth of his bees, an almost miraculous renewal of life. What Orpheus's sacrificial death accomplishes is more ambiguous. The river carries his severed head, still crying "Eurydice," down toward the sea; the riverbanks echo back, "Eurydice." What survives is this cry, this song, this name. And though Orpheus had once attempted to challenge nature's laws about the irrevocable character of human death, the oak-trees' sympathy, the river banks' echoing, suggest an ultimate harmony with the natural world (which connects the story to the *Georgics'* overarching theme).

Nevertheless, Virgil's account is profoundly sad. There is no reunion, no release from suffering, separation or death. And yet the poet in Virgil is also saying: But SONG is beautiful and it endures. Orpheus has given Eurydice a kind of immortality—her name still sounds—the kind that poets can confer (and Virgil has done the same for him). Art can't overcome death—but neither can death overcome art.

When Ovid comes to retell this story in Book 10 of his *Metamorphoses* Virgil's beautiful account serves as an inescapable model, one he can count on his audience knowing, and one against which he will explicitly be setting his own. Ovid's retelling will also inevitably carry echoes of Virgil's more elaborated description of an underworld descent in Book Six of the *Aeneid*, which includes hints of a quite different version of the Orpheus myth, a version in which Orpheus succeeded in bringing Eurydice back to the upperworld. Aeneas, hoping to persuade the Sibyl to allow him to enter Hades to consult there with Anchises, implores her, "If Orpheus could recall the spirit of his wife, relying upon his Thracian lyre's enchanted strings," so I, "another son of a god," should be allowed at least a visit with the spirit of my much-loved father. Unlike Orpheus, Aeneas came to Hades not to rescue but to learn and yet the discovery that his beloved father really is now but a shade is painful:

> He tried three times
> To throw his arms around his father's neck.
> Three times the shade untouched slipped through his hands,
> Weightless as wind and fugitive as dream.[18]

While in the underworld Aeneas actually meets Orpheus, dressed as a priest or prophet, playing his lyre in the Groves of Blessedness.

Ovid's telling of the Orpheus myth echoes many of Virgil's phrases, but (like Echo's echoing of Narcissus's words) they will have a different meaning in their new setting. He adds many details to Virgil's compact telling and in so doing changes the story—not its basic plot line but its meaning. Ovid's version is more than ten times as long as Virgil's and there are losses as well as gains associated with the elaboration. Ovid is a very different artist, with different gifts and a different understanding of art.

Ovid's theme in the *Metamorphoses* is transformation. He deliberately transforms the received myths: his version of the Demeter-Persephone myth is vastly different from that of the *Homeric Hymn*; his Orpheus is similarly different from Virgil's. By reminding us of the inherited masterpieces he honors them—and demands that we take note of his attempts to go beyond.

Ovid's telling of the Orpheus myth can be read as a deeply self-critical reflection on what it means to be a poet, and especially as a profound examination of what he takes to be the artist's inescapable narcissism. His own hubris is acknowledged in the very last word of his long poem, *Vivam* ("I shall live on"):

> And now my work is done, no wrath of Jove
> Nor fire nor sword nor time, which would erode
> all things, has power to blot out this poem.

....

> … With the better part of me, I'll gain
> A place that's higher than the stars, my name,
> Indelible, eternal, will remain. My lines
> Will be on people's lips, and through all time—
> If poets' prophecies are ever right—
> My name and fame are sure, I shall have life.(XV 871-9)

We cannot help but smile at this narcissistic assurance—*and,* gratefully, acknowledge its truth.

It is through Ovid's consummately skillful complex design, through the way he uses juxtapositions, repetitions, subtle variations, the framing of tales within tales, subnarrators whom we have reason to regard with suspicion, that he suggests his interpretations. Orpheus is one of the most prominent of these subnarrators and it is in large measure through the stories he has Orpheus tell that he conveys his understanding of Orpheus. And yet, even knowing that, we may find it difficult to be sure we know just what that understanding is.

For Ovid's use of wit, irony, parody makes him difficult to read, to interpret. There is an amazing degree of disagreement among good, careful scholars as to when Ovid is being serious, when playful; when judgmental, when sympathetic. Ovid insists that we notice his perspective and leaves us unsure if we've understood it rightly.

Ovid's telling of the myth begins with Hymen, the god of marriage, hastening to Thrace from Crete where he has just blessed the wedding of Iphis (who though born a girl had through the generosity of the gods been transformed into a boy so that he might wed Ianthe, the girl s/he has always loved). But Hymen brings no blessing to Orpheus's wedding, an ominous beginning. (We are meant, I believe, to recall another wedding similarly unblessed, that of Tereus to Procne, and to think of the many parallels between that story and this.) "The start was sad—and sadder still the end." Almost immediately the bride, "just wed" (in Virgil Eurydice seems to be a long-loved wife), while in a meadow accompanied by nymphs (the obvious allusion to Persephone suggests an almost virginal state) steps on a snake, is bit, and dies. The death is accidental, there is no Aristaeus, no attempted rape, no one to blame.

Unreconciled to his separation from Eurydice, Orpheus descends to the underworld (some say more out of fascination with the role of bereaved lover than out of true deep grief) and pleads with Persephone and Hades to restore Eurydice to life. (Only now does Ovid introduce the name, as though only now when lost does Eurydice begin to have an identity of her own rather than just that of "bride," "my bride.") Ovid dares to give us the song that Orpheus sings in hope of winning the dread gods' favor—though many readers believe that he has deliberately put into Orpheus's mouth an artificial, highly rhetorical speech devoid of true emotion (just as in Book V he had deliberately made Calliope's telling of the Persephone story sentimental and awkward). Perhaps Orpheus had never before sung so self-consciously, with so desperate a hope that his song might once again have the magical power he had until now taken for granted.[19]

As I suggested above, it is hard, truly hard, to be sure we're reading Ovid aright. Perhaps it's best to say Ovid invites the questions, demands that we wonder: Is Orpheus sincere or not? Does he love Eurydice or his own singing? Maybe more important than arriving at an answer is getting that these are important questions, that in a way both answers are true. For some of us, on some days, one version may seem more compelling than the other—and that may tell us more about ourselves than about Ovid or Orpheus. Ovid may help us realize that the myth HOLDS these ambiguities—that that is what myths and archetypes do. Ovid, I've come to believe, is deeply in touch with the tragedy *and the comedy* of life—which reminds me of Socrates' claim in the *Symposium* that the truly gifted artist would be able to write in both genres.

On some days I find myself deeply moved by Orpheus reminding Persephone and Hades of the love which had long ago brought them together. On such days, like Charles Segal I see Orpheus as assuming that even this is a world sensitive to love, projecting his own sensibility on the gods, imaging them as his fellow sufferers in love.[20] I am ready to trust Orpheus when he tells the underworld deities that he knows Eurydice must eventually come under their rule, and assures them that if they won't agree to his plea, he does not want to return to the upper world either. On other days I suspect that Ovid sees Orpheus as doing his best to flatter the gods, as putting forward his offer to stay in the underworld if necessary only as a persuasive rhetorical motif. I do know that my own reading of the *Metamorphoses* as a whole finds in Ovid a celebration of truly reciprocal conjugal love (like that of Deucalion and Pyrrha, Cadmus and Harmonia, Cephalus and Procris, Baucis and Philemon, Ceyx and Alcyone) quite unique in the classical world—not that such love in any way prevents suffering or disaster. But Orpheus and Eurydice hardly seem to have had enough time together to achieve that kind of bond.

Ovid's description of the response to Orpheus's plea echoes the *Aeneid's* richly detailed description of the inhabitants of Tartarus (all sent there because they, too, had sought to challenge the primary distinction between humans and gods:

that we die and they don't) more than his sparse few lines in the *Georgics*. Ovid writes that as Orpheus continues his song even the Furies find their cheeks wet with tears, Tantalus stops to listen to the poet's lament, the vultures desist from gnawing at Tityus's liver, and Sisyphus sits down on his rock. Segal sees this as Ovid's representation of a more human, more sensitive underworld, others have found it comic.

In any case Persephone and Hades yield; they call Eurydice and she appears, still limping from her wound. (Again, is this a touching detail or is it humorous?) In Ovid's version we learn of the gods' command before Orpheus disobeys it. Here, too, he turns, as of course in this myth he must, but not because possessed by a *furor*, but simply to make sure Eurydice is there and because he longs to see her. It is not some overwhelming outside force but simply Orpheus's own character that leads him to turn. This Eurydice makes no complaint, but simply utters a faint "Farewell." Here his hands not hers reach out, and reach only "unresisting air." Here there is not quite the finality so inescapable in Virgil's telling; the bond between the two seems to remain unbroken, perhaps preparing us for the different ending Ovid will give his tale.

The second loss of Eurydice is in a sense the real loss, the irrevocable loss, though Orpheus is still not yet ready to accept that irreversibility. He tries to reenter Hades but Charon will not let him return. For Virgil seven painful months intervene between this second loss and Orpheus's own death. In Ovid Orpheus stays immobilized just outside Hades for seven days and then heads north and during the next three years, full of despair and anger over the loss of the woman he loved, repulses all the other women who desire him, and turns instead to the love of boys. For this Orpheus, despite his grief, life, it seems, goes on.

Like Virgil's Orpheus, Ovid's turns to his lyre to console himself. But where Virgil's can sing only his own tale of woe Ovid's, calling upon Calliope ("O Muse, my mother") says that he "will now sing of boys whom the gods have loved and girls incited by unlawful lust." This sounds as if Orpheus is somehow angry at *her*, at Eurydice, and then by extension at all women. He speaks as though he sees himself as the one who has been betrayed, as though his loss is somehow Eurydice's fault, and as though this makes all women's love untrustworthy. (Orpheus's apparent anger at Eurydice for being mortal is reminiscent of a typical theme in Hellenistic love elegy: the male poet's disillusioned anger when he discovers that the woman he thought he loved turns out to be human and that he had really been in love with a dream of his own creation.)

Only Orpheus' first song, the one about Zeus and Ganymede, really fits his announced theme. As we look carefully at the stories he goes on to tell, we may sense that Orpheus himself does not fully understand how self-revealing they are: the love of gods and boys brings little joy to either; the females win our sympathy not our scorn. The stories suggest that loss and love seem to belong together, that the grief Orpheus has been exposed to is one that even the gods must suffer. There may also be hints of a not quite conscious sense of guilt; no, Orpheus was not responsible for Eurydice's first death, but it was his looking back that prevented her return, that kept her among the dead.

As Orpheus sings his many songs, a whole grove of trees gathers close to give him shade and to listen. Not just the poplar tree of Virgil's account but linden, oak, laurel, beech, and pine—on and on the catalogue continues—and each tree has its story of suffering, some we've heard already in earlier books, some Ovid tells us now. (Again the question: is including so many trees parody? or does it deepen the impact, give us a richer sense of the power of Orpheus's music over the natural world, an enlarged appreciation of the universality of suffering?)

The second myth Orpheus retells focuses on the infatuation of "my father Apollo" with the beautiful young huntsman Hyacinthus. While engaged in a discus-throwing competition, Apollo accidentally throws the discus so that rebounding it hits the youth full in the face and kills him. Even the healing god can do nothing. Overtaken by guilt and grief, he cries that he wishes that he might die for or with his beloved, but knows that as a god he can't but rather is doomed to grieve forever. "Your name shall always be upon my lips. The lyre my fingers pluck, the songs I chant, shall celebrate you." Obviously despite Orpheus's introduction, this is not a happy story: the god is exposed to the same kind of loss as Orpheus himself, and furthermore seems more aware of his own culpability. Does Orpheus see that?—or only that father and son both turn to the lyre to give expression to their grief?

Another of the longer songs Orpheus sings focuses on the sculptor Pygmalion who is so "disgusted by the many sins to which the female mind had been inclined by nature," that he, like Orpheus, has completely turned away from women. Until, that is, he carves a stunningly beautiful and lifelike marble female figure with which he falls in love. He kisses it, caresses it, speaks to it, adorns it with jewels and beautiful clothes, gives it gifts, and imagines it coming to life. Eventually he prays to Aphrodite that this might really happen and she grants his prayer. Orpheus seems unaware of any connection between this artist who can only love the object he has himself created and his own love for the woman of his songs. Is this a beautiful story about art and love and their power? or about narcissism? or about both?

Orpheus also sings of Aphrodite being accidentally grazed by one of Cupid's arrows and falling in love with Adonis, a youth whose beauty is so akin to that of her son that her passion seems almost incestuous. Overcome with fear that Adonis might be wounded by one of the fearsome beasts he likes to hunt, she tries to warn him by telling him a long meandering tale about how Atalanta and Hippomenes were turned into terror-striking beasts of the kind she wants him to avoid. "But daring is not keen to heed such warnings"; inevitably the day comes when Adonis is fatally wounded by a boar he'd been pursuing. Aphrodite is devastated; she too has to learn how integrally love and loss are conjoined. She tries to console Adonis, "I'll mourn you forever, my day of grief will be eternally commemorated." Yet we wonder, is it Adonis's death or her own anguish that is central?

These are but a few of the songs that Orpheus sings. He sings also of Myrrh and her incestuous love for her father. He sings also (or imagines Aphrodite doing so) of Atalanta who had been warned by an oracle that if she were ever to yield to love she would lose herself. Both stories are told in a way that allows us to enter into the inner struggles of these women—and that seems to communicate Orpheus's (or only Ovid's?) empathy with those overtaken by a passion, which overwhelms their conscious resolution. Myrrh yields and then is filled with guilt; some god takes pity on her and transforms her into a tree, her still-falling tears become myrrh, and she and the precious resin, the song affirms, will be honored forever. Atalanta and Hippomenes are punished by an Aphrodite angry that she received no thanks for her role in bringing them together.

Orpheus sings so beautifully that not only the trees but also savage beasts and even stones gather round to listen. He is so absorbed in his own singing that he fails to notice the approach of a band of threatening maenads.

Virgil speaks of these women as angered by Orpheus' unswerving devotion to Eurydice. In Ovid their describing him as "the man who dares to scorn us" is open to several alternative interpretations. Perhaps they act out of resentment of the misogyny they see evidenced in Orpheus's violent spurning of all women after Eurydice's loss. Or resentment of his having taught Thracian men the same same-sex preference? Or perhaps they are punishing him for a dedication to Apollo so intense as to imply a dishonoring of their god, Dionysos. They call him Apollo's poet; they drown out his lyre with their flutes, Dionysos' instrument. Or perhaps the maenads, women in touch with their own instinctual center, not defined by their roles as wives or mothers, represented that aspect of Eurydice which Orpheus who saw her only as *his* beloved had ignored: her in-herself-ness. This is close to Plato's view: Orpheus had never really loved Eurydice and for this, and the self-indulgence of his self-pity, the women kill him.

For when Orpheus tries to win these maenads over with his magical playing, he for the first time finds his song having no effect; it is drowned out by their cries and music. In Virgil the death has a ritual aspect; it happens as part of the women's "Bacchic rites"; there is even a sense of self-sacrifice implicit, as though Orpheus welcomes this death and as though it becomes part of a ritual renewal of life. In Ovid the maenads' killing seems more a rageful orgy of violence (with as usual some possibly comic overtones). In this account we hear clear echoes of maddened Agave's terrifying murder of her son, and of Actaeon's being killed by his own hounds after Artemis has turned him into a stag. These maenads first direct their violence against all the birds and beasts that had allowed themselves to fall under Orpheus's spell, but this only serves to intensify their bloodthirstiness. Finding their stones inadequate they use their thrysi as spears, they start hurling clods of mud and ripped-off branches, they pick up shovels and hoes and use them as weapons. They murder Orpheus "in desecration" and engage in no ritual scattering of body parts.

But at the poet's death, all nature—the birds, the beasts, the very trees, even the streams and rivers—weeps. The severed head (and here the lyre as well) float down the river, murmuring mournfully. Though just here, where Virgil gives us that plaintive cry "Eurydice," for Ovid there are no words. Yet here, as in Virgil, the river's banks echo back the mournful sounds. When the head comes to rest on the shores of Lesbos, it is attacked by a snake (as Eurydice had been so long ago) but Apollo intervenes to protect it and Dionysos, whose grief over the death of "Orpheus, the poet who had sung of Bacchus' sacred mysteries" was "great," intervenes to punish the maenads by turning them into trees.

The two gods whose protégé he is insure that after his death Orpheus will live on—as poet and as founder and prophet of the Orphic mysteries. As other tradition attest, his lyre is enshrined in a temple of Apollo—and thus Lesbos becomes the birthplace of lyric poetry. The head, buried under a temple of Dionysos, becomes the focus of an oracular hero-cult. This Orpheus, the Orpheus of the Orphics, is the singer of a theogony, which focuses on Dionysos as the man-god whose transcendence of death prefigures our own. Embodied life is seen as a burden from which after several lifetimes of ascetic discipline we might be freed. The afterlife is now seen as the real reality. Thus in this tradition Orpheus becomes one who leads us *into* the afterworld, rather than one who overcomes its claims or one destroyed by his refusal to accept them.

Ovid's version moves beyond the finality of Virgil's tragic ending; it is part of a *carmen perpetuum*—of a seamless song and a fluid world:

> The Shade of Orpheus
> Descends beneath the earth. The poet knows
> Each place that he had visited before;
> And searching through the fields of pious souls,
> He finds Eurydice.

Thus Orpheus, or rather his shade, now returns to the underworld, knowing it as he had not before, and is reunited with his Eurydice. They greet each other with desirous arms, the "tender boys" evidently easily forgotten and forgiven. (Once again there may be a Virgilian echo: During his sojourn in the underworld Aeneas catches a glimpse of Dido wandering among the shades and tries to ask forgiveness—but she turns away unmoved and flees to her former husband who gives her love for love—as Eurydice now seems to give Orpheus love for love.)

> And there they walk
> Together now; at times they are side by side;
> At times she walks ahead with him behind;
> At other times it's Orpheus who leads—
> But without any need to fear should he
> Turn round to see his own Eurydice. (XI 61-66)

After his own death Orpheus is open to Eurydice's perspective as he had not been before. When he returns to Hades, Orpheus and Eurydice are rejoined; now they walk together, each taking the lead in turn, and Orpheus may look back without risk upon his beloved.

The reunion brings together the shades, the souls, of Orpheus and Eurydice, and takes place in the underworld, the world of shades, phantoms, images. To put it another way: the reunion takes place, can only take place, in the imagination, in an *other* world.

It's as though Orpheus learned something from that earlier journey to the underworld after all, that it served as a kind of preparation for the later irreversible journey—and maybe his own songs served the same purpose. For our stories do often know more than we do. Orpheus may have begun his singing to divert himself from his grief and to express the anger aspect of his grief—but by telling stories that were not directly about himself, stories which enabled him to project his own experience onto others, he could begin to *see* his own (as his story may in turn help us see *ours*.)

Thus, when death came, Orpheus could move to it welcomingly. That, after all, was the point of the Eleusinian and Orphic mysteries, of what, they tell us, we might learn from Persephone or Orpheus, from initiatory experience.

Orpheus had to learn about ends, had to learn that his relationship to Eurydice really was already over, that looking back was looking *back*, was a doomed attempt to keep the past intact. He had to learn that she is *herself*, not "his love."

For Eurydice, when regarded not as Orpheus's anima or muse but as herself, Hades may represent a kind of fulfillment. There is a poem of Rilke's called "Orpheus. Eurydice. Hermes." which long ago first made me aware of how different Eurydice's perspective on underworld experience may be from that of Orpheus.

The poem was inspired by a Roman copy of a fifth century relief in the Athenian Agora, which shows the three figures side by side. Rilke (and most others familiar with Virgil's and Ovid's tellings of the myth) sees the relief as depicting the moment when Orpheus (having persuaded Hades and Persephone to allow him to bring his too-soon dead young bride back to the upper world) is leading the way by playing his lyre and is about to look back to assure himself that she is indeed following, and thus to lose her forever. But in the ancient world this relief (given what we have said about the version of the myth current in fifth century Greece) may have been understood to represent Orpheus' successful leading of his bride back to the upperworld.

Rilke wrote this poem during the period he was in Paris learning from Rodin how sculpture though so seemingly inert is alive with latent movement. The poem is too long to quote in its entirety, but here are the lines which have impacted me most forcefully:

> But now she walked beside the graceful god,
> her steps constricted by the trailing graveclothes,
> uncertain, gentle, and without impatience.
> She was deep within herself, like a woman heavy
> with child, and did not see the man in front
> on the path ascending steeply into life.
> Deep within herself. Being dead
> filled her beyond fulfillment. Like a fruit

suffused with its own mystery and sweetness,
she was filled with her vast death, which was so new,
she could not understand that it had happened.

She had come into a new virginity
and was untouchable; her sex had closed
like a young flower at nightfall, and her hands
had grown so unused to marriage that the god's
infinitely gentle touch of guidance
hurt her, like an undesired kiss.

She was no longer that woman with blue eyes
who once had echoed through the poet's songs,
no longer the wide couch's scent and island,
and that man's property no longer.

She was already loosened like long hair,
poured out like fallen rain,
shared like a limitless supply.

She was already root.

And when, abruptly,
the god put out his hand to stop her, saying,
with sorrow in his voice: He has turned around—,
she could not understand, and softly answered

   Who?[21]

From the perspective of Eurydice Hades looks, feels, *is* different. Perhaps we cannot even use the same words for underworld, cannot use the words that seem right from outside or even underway—but must instead turn to words such as inwardness, cessation, peace. Rilke's Eurydice reminds me of my own period in the underworld and my resentment of would-be rescuers, who were irrelevant, were in the way—who didn't understand that this was *my* experience, that this was what I had now to live, that it had its own organic time which could not be foreshortened.

In herself Eurydice is a Persephone figure, one who belongs in the underworld as her name, *Eury-Dike*, makes clear. It means broad ruling; it suggests that she was originally an underworld goddess associated with the maintenance of a mode of natural order, of cosmic justice. Thus there are echoes in this tale of the old motif of the goddess and her lover-victim. Even in the myth as we have it, his love for her teaches him underworld realities—slowly. The initiation begins with *falling* in love, and then gradually learning what love means.

Eurydice like Persephone was brought to the underworld against her will, but then finds herself at home there, comes to embody its perspective, a perspective for which Orpheus was not yet ready. Again I turn to Rilke, to a much later poem, one of the *Sonnets to Orpheus*:

> Her sleep was everything.
>
> She slept the world. Singing god, how was that first
> sleep so perfect that she had no desire
> ever to wake?
>
> Where is her death now? Ah, will you discover
> this theme before your song consumes itself? [22]

For Rilke the myth is about Orpheus's discovery of his true theme. Though the song Orpheus sang to Persephone and Hades may still have been desire-driven, Orpheus ultimately means something else, something beyond desire which it took the first descent and its failure—once absorbed and understood—and his own death, to teach him:

> Song, as you have taught it, is not desire,
>
> ....
>
> True singing is a different breath, about nothing. (I.3)

Rilke believed that a true poet's sole function was to bring the *Dinge*, the "things" of the world to word—not just to express his own feelings. Art is *transformation* not imitation of the natural world. This is what life is for: for poetry. *SINGING IS BEING*. And for him it is always Orpheus where there is song:

We do not need to look
for other names. Where there is poetry,
it is Orpheus singing. (I.5)

The myth of Orpheus has also inspired many contemporary women poets, including H.D. Her "Eurydice," was written to express her angry disillusion over the discovery that for D. H. Lawrence (as earlier for Ezra Pound and for her husband Richard Aldington) she is more muse and desirable woman (though she wants to be that, too) than fellow poet (which she wants more than anything else). What most angers her is that Lawrence had aroused the hope that this time it might be different:

So you have swept me back,
I, who could have walked with the live souls
Above the earth,
I who could have slept among the live flowers
At last;

So for your arrogance
And your ruthlessness
I am swept back
Where dead lichens drip
Dead cinders upon moss of ash;

So for your arrogance
I am broken at last,
I who had lived unconscious,
Who was almost forgot;

If you had let me wait
I had grown from listlessness
Into peace,
If you had let me rest with the dead
I had forgot you
And the past.

Yet in the last lines of the poem H.D. reclaims her own passion and her own identity as a poet:

> At least I have the flowers of myself
> And my thoughts, no god
> Can take that;
> I have the fervour of myself for a presence
> And my own spirit for light.23

Like H.D. my own way into the myth was through an identification with Eurydice that led me to see in Orpheus primarily his inability to see her, to see her as herself and not as his muse or anima (and to lay all the blame for this on him, as though forgetting how tempting the role of anima-woman can be). But as I have stayed engaged with the myth I've come to see it and him differently—as Steve Kowit imagines Eurydice coming to see Orpheus differently during her many solitary years in the underworld:

> Truth to tell he was in many ways a child:
> Impetuous, unthinking, willful in the way
> A child is, who in his single-mindedness
> & the immensity of his desire
> cares nothing that the matter is impossible,
> Am I to blame him for that one mistake?
> ....
> .... Oh, who could
> be so cruel that she would blame that boy.24

Eurydice need not stay where she was when she flung those last words at Orpheus in Virgil's poem ("What utter madness")—remembering Orpheus need not mean seeing him still as she saw him then. For remembering, as Freud wrote in "Remembering, Repeating and Working-Through" is different from repeating; it is working-through, it is looking back with imagination so that something new can be discovered. Orpheus's "looking back" when he hopes to return Eurydice to the upperworld is repetition; his "looking back" when he has rejoined her in Hades, when he looks with what we might call "underworld eyes," with the eyes of the soul, is re-membering.25

My own "looking-back" now also seems different from the "looking-back" of fifteen years ago. For I now see that another way of understanding the story is to see the death of Eurydice as representing the death of a projection, that is, as representing Orpheus's discovery that (to use Jungian terms) Eurydice was really an anima figure and that it was now time to turn from her to a direct engagement with the anima itself, with his own soul. So he went to the underworld, the world where the soul lives. But because he went there to rescue the anima, to bring her back to the upperworld, he still hadn't really yet understood that the anima wasn't his; that the ego doesn't *have* an anima, that (as Hillman puts it) the point is not to develop my anima but to realize that anima-consciousness represents a way of being in the world.[26] It is only afterward, when he returns to the underworld to stay, that Orpheus comes to understand that he and Eurydice have to relate IN the underworld—that he has to look *from* the anima perspective not *at* it.

Once I saw this Orpheus, I of course saw that there are ways in which I am Orpheus and not just Eurydice; that the *myth* and not just this figure or that within it lives in me—and that looking at the story from a gendered perspective opens up some meanings and blinded me to others—as does adopting a Jungian perspective which might make Eurydice an anima figure for men and Orpheus an animus figure for women like me. I—not just "my animus"—AM Orpheus: his longing for depth, for connection, for love. But also his painful desperate wish that things might stay as they were—and his difficulty in recognizing that a beloved other truly is *other* and learning not only to accept that but bless it. Orpheus's guilt, his failures, his narcissistic delight in his own singing—all these are mine. As is the slow, slow learning that all his (and my) storying represents.

I think H.D. also came to see that she needed to recognize she was both Orpheus *and* Eurydice, poet and woman—or, perhaps more accurately stated, needed to learn how to get them *reconnected.* That need eventually brought her to Freud whom she experienced as midwife to the soul, as Asclepius the blameless physician, as the curator in a museum of priceless antiquities, as a trickster-thief nonchalantly unlocking vaults and caves, taking down the barriers that generations had carefully set up—and as an Orpheus who charms the very beasts of the unconscious and enlivens the dead sticks and stones of buried thoughts and memories[27]—a very different Orpheus from the one imagined in her early poem.

But Freud also helped her to discover that she—and not only he—was Orpheus.

He was very beautiful,
the old man,
and I knew wisdom,
I found measureless truth
in his words.

. . . .

he did not say
"stay,
be my disciple"—

. . . . . .

no,
he was rather casual,
"we won't argue about that"
(he said)
"you are a poet"[28]

She learned from him: You are a poet. You are Orpheus. You are Orpheus *and* Eurydice (as in the work we did on your big dream you were Moses *and* Miriam).

And we, too—we, too—are Orpheus and Eurydice—and still, perhaps, not fully understanding all that that might mean.

Notes

1. Allen Mandelbaum, *The Metamorphoses of Ovid* (San Diego: Harcourt Brace, 1993) 361. Book XI, 64-66. All further quotations from Ovid will be from this translation indicated only by Book and line numbers.

2. David Grene, trans., *Herodotus: The History* (Chicago: University of Chicago Press, 1987) 155, Book II, 53.

3. Norman O. Brown, trans., *Hesiod: Theogony* (Indianapolis: Bobbs-Merrill, 1963) 53.

4. E. R. Dodds, *The Greeks and the Irrational* (Boston: Beacon, 1957) 147.

5. (or, in some versions of a rivergod, Oeagros, who then turns out to be himself a descendent of Apollo).

6. W. K. C. Guthrie, *Orpheus and Greek Religion* (New York: Norton, 1966) passim.

7. Charles Boer, trans., "To Hermes," *The Homeric Hymns* (Chicago: Swallow Press, 1967) 22-61.

8. For the sake of consistency I have chosen to use the Greek names for the gods and goddesses even when Roman authors have used the Latin ones, except, of course, in direct quotation.

9. Quoted in Charles Segal, *Orpheus: The Myth of the Poet* (Baltimore: Johns Hopkins University Press, 1989) 13.

10. Jane Harrison, *Prolegomena to the Study of Greek Religion* (New York: Meridian, 1957) 455, 461.

11. Richmond Lattimore, trans., "Alcestis," in David Grene and Richmond Lattimore, eds., *The Complete Greek Tragedies, Vol. III: Euripides* (Chicago: The University of Chicago Press, 1959) 20.

12. Michael Joyce, trans., in Edith Hamilton and Huntington Cairns, eds., *The Collected Dialogues of Plato* (Princeton: Princeton University Press, 1961) 533-534, 179d.

13. Paul Shorey, trans., "Republic," in Hamilton and Cairns, 843. X. 620a.

14. Guthrie, 30.

15. Harrison, 461-4.

16. Segal, 21.

17. L. P. Wilkinson, *Virgil: The Georgics* (New York: Penguin, 1982) 140, Book 4, 466-468. Further briefer quotes from the *Georgics* are from this same translation.

18. Robert Fitzgerald, trans., *The Aeneid of Virgil* (New York: Random House, 1983) 184, Book 6, 696-700. Further references to the *Aeneid* will be from this translation and given in the text by Book and line number.

19. Paul Bresson, "Vicissitudes of Orpheus," *American Poetry Review,* May/June 1996, 19.

20. Segal, 64.

21. Mitchell, 51-53. I can't resist including part of a prose poem that Stephen Mitchell, Rilke's translator here, wrote imagining Persephone's response to Orpheus's plea:

> But this poor boy, this exquisite singer, will have a hard time ahead of him; she can tell by looking at his eyes. It is one thing to charm animals, trees, and rocks, and quite another to be in harmony with a woman. She recognizes his attitude, she has seen it before: fear protected by longing. Hence the bridal image, forever unattainable, forever ideal. No wonder Eurydice took the serpent's way out. Girls who are seen that way grow up to be maenads. If only, she thinks: If only there were some way to tell him. But, of course, he will have to learn for himself. To lose his love again and again, precipitously, as if by chance. To be torn in pieces, again and again.

> She turns to the king, "Yes, darling," she says, "Let him go."

(Stephen Mitchell, "Orpheus," *Parables and Portraits* (New York: Harper-Collins, 1994).

22. Stephen Mitchell, trans., "The Sonnets to Orpheus," *The Selected Poetry of Rainer Maria Rilke* (New York: Random House, 1982) 225, I, 2.

23. H.D. "Eurydice," *Collected Poems 1912-1944* (New York: New Directions, 1983) 51-55.

24. Steve Kowit, "Eurydice," in Deborah Denicola, ed., *Orpheus and Company* (Hanover, NH: University Press of New England, 1999) 23-24.

25. Sigmund Freud, "Remembering, Repeating and Working-Through," *Standard Edition of the Complete Psychological Works of Sigmund Freud,* translated under the general editorship of James Strachey (London: Hogarth Press, 1953-1974) Vol. XII, 147-156.

26. James Hillman, "'Anima'," *Spring 1973,* 97-132.

27. H.D., *Tribute to Freud* (New York: McGraw-Hill, 1974) *passim.*

28. H.D., "The Master," *Collected Poems*, 451-452.

23

Remembering, Repeating, and Working Through

◆

"Mid-Life and Beyond"

As I reflect on the theme, Mid-Life and Beyond, I become aware of how long it has occupied me and how my understanding of it, especially of the "beyond" part, has changed. Indeed, I am struck by how being in mid-life—not just physically or socially but as *souls,* that is, imaginally—seems almost necessarily to lead us into concern with "the Beyond," with Beyondness, with *Jenseits.*

Looking back, it seems to me that my entry into midlife occurred in 1974 when I was just past 40. My five children newly launched, I left a good marriage of twenty-five years and a promising career at an Ivy League university back east and moved by myself to California. A big shift.

But I didn't really think of this as a midlife crisis. It was just what I did, what I had to do—to discover who I was apart from the roles of wife and mother. I didn't consciously look at the disappointments and new hopes that motivated this move nor at the ways it had been encouraged by the nascent feminism of those years, I didn't look at the old wounds that might have shaped my decision and definitely didn't look at the wounds I was inflicting on my parents, spouse, or children.

That is, I lived this at the level of *enactment* not *reflection.*

That spring, my first in California, I had the dream in which I affirmed "It's time now to go in search of Her"—a dream whose meaning has continued to unfold in all the almost thirty years since I first dreamt it.

Ever since I have been the woman who made that move—and who had and listened to that dream.

Now I can see the costs—can wonder: if (for instance) I had been in analysis, would I have had to do that—to literalize the changes I needed to make, to live them in a so dramatic and outward a way.

Almost a decade later, just after my 50th birthday, I had another dream—a dream of finding myself pregnant. Somehow I knew that this was a dream about the conception of my postmenopausal self and I felt called to live this new transition more consciously. I knew I wanted to be really aware of the costs and losses and not only the gains and new possibilities involved in entering into the last third of life. I took a trip around the world, came home to the woman with whom I've shared my life ever since, wrote most of the books as I think of as "my books."

I was, of course, still a very virginal crone—very much in touch with liminality and profoundly curious about what lay ahead, intrigued by the Beyond—by all that would be new and different, by the regrets about what was over, and by a sense that the real challenge of the years ahead would be coming to terms with finitude and mortality.

Now at almost 73 all that seems pretty romantic: I look back at that Chris as, indeed, a very virginal crone.

And yet I also know that I'm not really a crone Crone yet.

I have just returned from helping celebrate my mother's 101st birthday. *She* is the crone—and I suspect that as long as she is alive, Old Age, Old Old Age, will seem to be a Beyond, a kind of mystery.

I see how she is living being old, really old—and wonder in what ways I'll live it differently. As I look at her I appreciate the truth of Helen Luke's claim that the three gifts of Old Age (all, of course, ambivalent gifts) are the bodily changes, helpless rage, and memory. I see my mother coming to terms (or often not) with blindness and limited mobility. I (and others) am often exposed to her rage. And I see how important her memories are to her—how in many ways she *is* the stories she tells. The stories she tells, over and over again. *Repetitively.* There are a few less each year—and even now sometimes there is still a new one. I have come to understand that what she remembers are the *stories*—that there is no longer any possibility of reframing them, contextualizing them, opening them up. She is her memories—and there is a kind of remembering she (in the waning years of the last third of life) can no longer do, a more creative kind of remembering.

But *I* am now in the *middle* of this last third of life—not primarily engaged in looking forward, nor mostly living in the past, but simply *here*—in the middle. Wondering a little—not much—about what might initiate me into that third phase. Might it be the death of my mother, retirement, some physical disability, or something not yet even imaginable.

But, for now, this is where I am.

In the Middle of that Beyond.

Occasionally looking back and forward, but not really much engaged in trying to construct a coherent narrative version of my life—rather simply aware of the co-presence of all that I have been, will be, and am. I seem to be engaged in a different kind of remembering—in wanting to include it all (as honestly as I can), including, that is, all that *had* to be left out earlier—so that I could go on.

I remember that for the Greeks what psyches, souls, did—in Hades, in the underworld, in the afterworld—was remember. There would be no new experience, no new creative thought, just remembering, going over and over the already lived—putting the pieces together and discovering the whole they comprised.

I've always thought of their remembering as a "re-member-ing," a putting together of the dismembered, isolated, fragmented pieces. So I was surprised—and initially disappointed—when I looked up the etymology of "remember" to discover that its root is entirely different from the root of "member" (which refers to a part of the body as I had thought). "Remember," it turns out, comes from a root connected to "mourning"—a connection that I am just beginning to understand.

I have been helped toward that understanding by an essay of Freud's called "Remembering, Repeating, and Working-Through,"[1] whose title struck a chord. I liked its implication that there are different kinds of remembering, its suggestion that in some way real remembering, deep remembering, is different from just reproduction or repetition—and that this more creative remembering is *work,* soul work. So I knew I wanted to reread this short (nine page) essay of Freud's, wanted to really read it, that is, read it in German.

The title suggested to me that it might be time for me to "remember" Freud—not just repeat what Jungians (or even Freudians) tell us he said—or even what I have said about him before. I keep returning to Freud because I keep finding he has new things to say to me and suggests new things for me to say. Adam Phillips once said that we know somebody speaks to us, if they make us speak.[2] Freud does that for me—helps me speak, helps me with this speaking about midlife and about remembering.

We are accustomed to thinking of Jung's as a second half of life psychology, and tend to forget that this is true of Freud as well. Freud was forty when his father died, forty-four when *Interpretation of Dreams* appeared. The death of Freud's father seems to have functioned like a "shamanic wound"; Ellenberger refers to it as instigating Freud's "first creative illness." Coming to terms with this death led Freud into a period marked by depression and sustained introversion, a period in which Freud found himself flooded by troubling dreams and new insights. Until then the unconscious seems to have been for Freud an important force in the life of his hysterical patients, but it was only his grief, his own suffering, his discovery of how ambivalently he had really felt toward a father he had thought he loved unreservedly that brought him into touch with his own unconscious.

The starting point was suffering; the starting-point for Freud's understanding of the human soul remains suffering, *pathos-logos*—the speech of that in us which suffers. Indeed, one might say that psychoanalysis really begins as *mourning*, as a response to loss. Not only was Freud's self-analysis undertaken in response to the loss of his father—but he comes to believe that psychic life, consciousness, begins as mourning. Our first glimmerings of being subjects, selves, emerges in response to the loss of a world where mother and self were one, where the mother was just *there.* When she suddenly *isn't*, self and mother, self and other, self and world, are co-created. Freud sees the loss of this once-upon-a-time fantasized oneness of self and the all as an irreversible loss, so enormous, so painful, that it cannot be fully acknowledged or grieved. It has to be forgotten—or not exactly *forgotten;* it has to be repressed, has to be unconscious. In this view, as soon as there is a conscious self, there is also an unconscious—an unconscious that holds our unappeasable longing, our unavowable grief and rage, our unmitigated terror. Having lost our first love, we always feel threatened by loss. The *Ich,* the self-aware I, arises as a precipitate of loss.

Can you see already how forgetting and remembering and mourning are all tangled up with each other—and are core to what it means to be a person, a soul?

Of course not all of this was clear to Freud immediately. His own mourning, his own "creative illness" (to again use Ellenberger's term) issued not only in *Interpretation of Dreams* but also *Dora, The Psychopathology of Everyday Life, Jokes,* and *The Three Essays on Sexuality*—all in just a few years of one another, all in Freud's early mid-life. After which he thought he was done. And began looking for an heir. And found Jung (whose very name meant youth!) And then, of course, such a few years later, he lost him. I believe it is important to recognize that this break was a shattering event, a big loss, for Freud and not only for Jung. Indeed, Ellenberger claims that the break from Jung precipitated what he calls Freud's "second creative illness."

The essay on "Remembering, Repeating, and Working-Through" stems from this period. It was written in 1914 as Freud was coming to terms with the break between himself and Jung and with the outbreak of World War One. For the impact of the break with Jung was inevitably deepened by Sarajevo and what followed. A few months after the war began Freud wrote Lou Salome: "I do not doubt that humankind will survive even this war, but I know for certain that for me and my contemporaries the world will never again be a happy place, it is too hideous. And the saddest thing about it is that it is exactly the way we should have expected people to behave from our knowledge of psychoanalysis."

The *anger* that the break with Jung provoked in Freud is painfully evident in *The History of the Psychoanalytic Movement*, the disappointment and hurt in the "Moses of Michelangelo," the creativity primarily in the shorter but important essays like the one we'll be looking at, and the two papers on transference, the one on narcissism, and the preliminary sketch of what eventually becomes "Mourning and Melancholia." All of these were written in 1914, all are clearly preparatory to the full working out of the perspectives first explored in these seminal essays in the big books Freud published in the early 1920s, *Beyond The Pleasure Principle* and *The Ego And The Id*—after which Freud again thought he was done!

In 1914 Freud was almost sixty. I believe that these papers make visible the concerns that most deeply engaged Freud as he was approaching his seventh decade, midlife concerns: concerns about the significance of his life work, about repetition and creativity, betrayal and guilt, about loss and mourning, about the narcissistic longings to be whole in oneself and one with the world, about death wish and fear. It was a time when Freud was deeply engaged in *looking back*—in looking back not just at his own history (or that of individual patients) but also at the whole history of human consciousness as he had first sought to do in *Totem and Taboo*. He was no longer thinking of his insights as primarily relevant in a clinical setting; he now saw the whole world as his patient. In all of these forays—in the discussion of the "primal parricide" in *Totem and* Taboo and how the "memory" of this imagined once-upon-a-time lives on in us—in the reflections on how likely we are to "transfer" the patterns of our early childhood relationships onto all our subsequent relations—in the exploration of how tempting it is when relationships fail to withdraw from the world of others and attempt to recreate that fantasized "before" when we were whole in ourselves and at one with the world—Freud is rediscovering how the past is never just past, how it lives on in the present (in ways we mostly fail to recognize).

The most explicit reflecting on memory occurs, of course, in the essay on "Remembering." Actually this essay isn't exactly about remembering, it is about *Erinnerung*. About *Er-Innerung*. That is, about *inwarding, interiorizing*—about taking into our souls, about the soul work of digesting our experience. To use Hillman's language, it is about turning event into experience. So that we may really live our life. Not just *Leben*, but *Erleben*.

Think of Jung's *Memories, Dreams, Reflections—Erinnerung, Traeume, Gedanken*—and how it focuses on what he is to his "inward vision," his *Erinnerungen*:

> In the end the only events in my life worth telling are those when the imperishable world irrupted into this transitory one. That is why I speak chiefly of inner experiences, amongst which I include my dreams and visions....
>
> I can understand myself only in the light of inner happenings. It is these that make up the singularity of my life, and with these my autobiography deals.[3]

Freud's essay is about remembering and how important it is to a life lived deeply, psychologically, soulfully. It is also about how his clinical experience has changed his understanding of what remembering is all about. The essay is one of his papers on technique and is specifically about remembering as it occurs within the analytic context, but its implications are much wider. For from the time of the so-called abandonment of the seduction theory and Freud's discovery of how the imagination reworks experience—his discovery of the poetics of memory, its *poesis*, its creativity—he began to shift his attention from explaining the etiology of hysteria to trying to understand the suffering of all of us. The discovery of the Oedipus complex (which follows so shortly after this redirection) marks this move to a psychology that focuses on the deep longings and fears that inhabit the souls of all of us.

Freud opens the present essay by looking back, by recalling how he and Breuer had understood memory back in the days of hypnosis and catharsis. Back then, he says, the aim had been to use hypnosis to enable the patient to re-enter the moment in the past at which the troubling symptom was formed. The reproduction of the psychical processes (not the *mental* processes as the translation suggests—it does make a difference to read the German!) involved in that earlier situation would, they believed, serve to discharge them of their power. The assumptions were that there was *a* moment; that it was the *cause* of the suffering or of a particular expression of it, a particular symptom; that this moment was in the *past;* and that past and present were clearly distinct—and that bringing the past moment into present consciousness would eliminate the suffering, the symptom.

With this "chimney sweeping" technique remembering seemed idyllically simple; the notion of resistance never even entered the picture. Memory seemed so simple in those days, Freud writes, but now it all looks quite different. The different, more complex, understanding of memory was forced upon Freud by way of the changes in technique, first by the move from hypnosis to free association, and then the consequent focus on the transference. These changes led to quite a different understanding, for now it appeared that we suffer not so much from discrete symptoms but from being who we are.

With the new technique one immediately discovers resistance, which is likely to first reveal itself as silence. Maryse Choisy describes the impact of the analyst's silence and the injunction to "say everything":

> Fifteen hundred kilometers, I had traveled—fifteen hundred kilometers to reach the Berggasse, lie down and say nothing! He waits. It's the custom. Our first relation is a total silence. It is not true in practice that analysis is an action in words. It is silence, which bears the weight of all memories without evoking any particular one; silence which measures all possibilities without broaching any of them, silence which binds analyst and analysand like two accomplices, silence which fills the room with weird voices. Silence is Freud's greatest invention on the threshold of the unknown world.[4]

So the resistance appears from the beginning, but Freud soon learned that just pointing it out accomplished nothing; just giving resistance a name had no real effect either. So the aim was changed: the goal was no longer to access a presumed back-then, literal, objectively verifiable past moment—but rather to *experience* how the past lives in the psyche, in the soul, in the imagination, not as an intellectual realization but as something that is *happening—now—to me*. A memory, Freud is now rediscovering and helping his patients to discover, is never a literal transcription; it is always infused with imagination. The psyche, the soul, *works* events; it exaggerates, condenses, minimizes, concretizes, it makes use of puns, analogies, associations; it is transformative. Remembering is always redescription, remaking; the echo is different each time. The only place the past *is,* is in the soul, in the present.

Freud is here, of course, rediscovering what Augustine had written of in his *Confessions* as he wondered, Where is my past? What is my relation to my past self? and concluded that he could not distinguish memory from the self. To say, I remember, is to say, *this* is me. "Without my memory I should not be able to call myself myself." Augustine calls memory "the stomach of the mind," "the innermost bowels of my soul." Remembering is like swallowing and ruminating and rechewing. He speaks of memory as a subterranean treasure house with many levels and layers, as a weaving which sews together moments from here and there to create an utterly new pattern—and, most pertinently:

> It is now however perfectly clear that neither the future nor the past are in existence, and that it is incorrect to say there are three times—past, present, and future. Though one might perhaps say, 'there are three times—a present of things past, a present of things present, and a present of things future.' For these three do exist in the mind, and I do not see them anywhere else. The present time of things past is memory; the present time of things present is sight; the present time of things future is expectation.

It is this present, this presence, of things past that now seems important to Freud—that and how our failing to recognize this presence causes suffering precisely because we haven not ever really fully forgotten. Indeed, Freud notes how rarely a truly forgotten memory emerges in analysis—rather, a hitherto apparently insignificant memory, an isolated memory unconnected to our preferred narrative of our lives, may suddenly appear as surprisingly potent.

Earlier, we had remembered the fragments but not the connections; thus, our memories are simultaneously both conscious and unconscious. Freud speaks of how often we consciously recall an apparently trivial event which serves as a kind of symbolic condensation of another still earlier more impactful but more distressing one; he calls these more available moments "screen memories." Focusing on such "screen memories" may help us to "remember" moments that have not been forgotten because they were never conscious. They happened so early in our childhood, at a time when we had no way of making sense of them, of assimilating them. (This, of course, relates to that primal grief and rage and longing and fear I mentioned earlier.) But later such very faint unconscious memory traces get revised to fit in with fresh experiences and with the attainment of a new stage of development, and these revisions serve to endow the earlier moment with new meaning and fresh psychical effectiveness. Freud called this revisioning process *Nachtraglichkei*—"carried afterwardness" (or, more conventionally translated, "belatedness," "deferred action"). "A thing which has not been understood, inevitably reappears; it is like an unlaid ghost, it cannot rest until the mystery has been solved and the spell broken."[5]

Past and present are no longer clearly distinct—what interests Freud is the *energy* of the present resistance to acknowledging that past, to acknowledging its still living power (and although the translation speaks of a "failing" to remember, the German speaks of a *"refusal"*). As Freud says over and over again in this short essay: we would rather repeat than remember. So much of this essay is about *rep-*

etition—Wiederholen—the German word has even more of the flavor of "again and again," "over and over" than the English. *Wiederholen* represents a kind of "remembering" that is not soul-ful, psychical. It is closely connected to our suffering, to what goes wrong in our lives, over and over again. We are often tempted to blame this going-wrong on others, on circumstances, on the "outer" world and thus not to admit to our own contribution to it. Because we don't have a psychical relation to these memories, we act them out, we repeat rather than remember. In this essay Freud first introduces the notion of a "compulsion to repeat," a notion which will become central to the discussion in *Beyond the Pleasure Principle* and will there explicitly be seen as an expression of Death wish, of the wish that things would not change or could be again or still as they were once upon a time.

These acted-out memories, these repetitions, are not recognized as such, because they are not identical replications. They are transpositions, translations, into another key, another language. The relation of past to present is metaphorical. Freud's first inkling of this came through his retrospective reflections on his work with Dora, which taught him that much of what went wrong in that analysis was connected to his failure to recognize the "transference," the *Uebertragung*. When he introduced this word into his written account of this case, it was not yet jargon. It was fresh. It was just the everyday word for "translation," a word whose most literal meaning is simply "carry over" from one language to another, from one time-period to another, from one relationship to another. (Note that transference and metaphor are essentially the same word.) The patient doesn't remember but reproduces, without recognizing the repetitive aspect. The patients act toward the analyst as they had toward their parents—or they expect/hope/fear the analyst might act toward them as the parents had.

So: what is it that gets repeated? Often really painful stuff; the enactments are mnemonic symbols. We repeat our pathology, our suffering, our symptoms, our defenses, our habitual unconscious ways of responding, *our character*. We don't do so only in the analysis, but everywhere in our lives—though perhaps in analysis we will come to learn that this is what we do, what we keep doing. The hope, of course, is that this time around the patient can see this, can feel it, can recognize how often it has happened before. The possibility of transformation is based on *erleben,* on a *lived experience* of the resistance, a *lived recognition* of the repetitive aspect of the transference love. This new relation to the past involves something different from either rejection or intellectual acceptance.

The possibility is that now the patient can begin to *remember,* that is to move from acting-out to keeping it inside, in the psychical realm, can begin to *er-*

innern it. This entails being really willing to look at, attend to, what hurts, to my suffering, to what has brought me to analysis, to where I'm stuck. "One can't overcome an absent enemy," Freud writes. We must believe we are wrestling with a worthy enemy and move from acquaintance to conversation, to real sustained engagement. This will require *vertiefen*, a sinking deeper into, a steeping. (Where the English translation speaks of "unearthing one's memories," the German speaks of sinking deeper into them—the translation misses many *tief*, "deep" words.)

There is a real danger that to begin with the suffering may get worse as one conjures up these rejected ghosts (who may represent things of value for our future life). And we don't want to remember, we *resist*—from the arsenal of the past we pull the weapons with which to defend against the treatment. The aim is to keep the emergent memory (and the longings and fears connected to it) in psychical sphere and give it the right to exist *there*.

So: Remembering is work! It is "working-through," *Durcharbeiten*. It is *Verarbeiten*—the hard work of assimilating, digesting inwardly, returning the memory to its rich associative context. It is *Erinnerungsarbeit*, which *is* analogous to mourning-work and much like it: we never stop mourning *and* we find we can live on. Similarly here: for Freud the working-through entails a kind of *reconciliation* with our suffering (that old "common unhappiness" theme), a certain tolerance for being ill, for being ourselves.

It is not a question of getting rid of our memories. Freud speaks of liberating, unfolding, untwisting them, not as in the English "extracting" them. We honor the memories' right to exist—in the soul, imaginally.

It is a *Gemeinsamener Arbeit*—*a together-work*. Freud, of course, focuses on the work of the patient, but also insists that the presence of the other, the analyst, makes that work possible. Paradoxically, one can use the patient's wanting to repeat *for* the therapeutic work. The very eros that one directs toward the analyst makes it possible to do the work that otherwise one couldn't. Transference makes possible turning the compulsion to repeat into a motive for remembering; by admitting the compulsion into a different field, one render it harmless. Often there are periods of stagnation, when a proposed interpretation is not accepted but is working within. There is a perpetual struggle with the patient to keep it in psychical realm, to *er-innern*. It's a deeply mutual process.

Freud speaks of the imaginal realm one enters into in the consulting room as a playground, a *tunnelplatz*, a riding school—and of course I think of Plato (as I assume Freud also did) and his image of the charioteer and his horses. Freud speaks of the transference as a *Zwischenreich*, a between-realm, not quite the ordinary interpersonal world but also not only an inner world; it is a liminal world, an imaginal world.

On the surface Freud's essay is only about the role that remembering plays in the "working-through" of an analysis—but clearly it is about more than that. I see it as articulating not only insights he has gained from his work with his patients but also the musings of an almost sixty year old man reflecting on his own past and present and future. I see it as providing us with ways of imagining our relation to our own pasts and present and futures. What myth, what ritual, what analysis can offer as guides can also, I believe, be accessed without literally believing in the myth, participating in the ritual, or making our way to the Berggasse. I think of how Sophocles, himself a deeply appreciative initiate of the Eleusinian mysteries, in his *Oedipus at Colonus* lent Oedipus the same freedom from the fear of death the ritual promised—as though he had accessed that freedom simply by having lived his long years of exile *deeply*.

What I take away from Freud's essay is this:

Just as we have to love in order not to fall ill, so we have to remember in order not to repeat. I see Freud as inviting us to celebrate the creative dimension of remembering, to become fascinated by how the past that lives in the present is to a large degree an imagined past and how the past that will enter the future will be a reimagined past. We are invited to celebrate how memory is both diachronic and synchronic, how the past is part of a narrative and also part of a simultaneity. (As Jung acknowledged when in his autobiography he speaks of looking back at his life and seeing it not as a linear progression but as a continual circumambulation of the same recurring themes and images.) We are invited to accept that we can never fully know ourselves, never fill in all the gaps—that the dream of doing so is but a narcissistic fantasy. That is, we are invited to admit to our longing for narrative coherence (for coming to know *the* story of our lives) and at the same time to accept that the possibility of the fulfillment of that longing is illusory. We are invited to return to the past, knowing we won't be free of it, but that accepting it as an imaginal dimension of the present transforms it. Even after the working-through, it will not be the case that our past won't still shape whom and how we love, how we mess up, what we fear.

We will keep returning to the same old themes—*and* see something new. (Analysis terminable and interminable.)

As Orpheus kept looking back at Eurydice.

As Sophocles kept returning to Oedipus.

As Goethe kept returning to Faust.

As Freud keeps returning to Oedipus.

As Jung says it was all contained in his childhood dream of the underground phallus—and of course it wasn't *and* in a sense it was.

As I keep returning to my childhood dream and to the dream in which I announced, "It's time now to go in search of Her."

Notes

1. English translation: "Remembering, Repeating and Working-Through," *The Standard Edition of the Complete Psychological Works of Sigmund Freud* (London: Hogarth Press, 1953-1974) Vol. XII, 147-156; German edition: "Erinnern, Wiederholen und Durcharbeiten," *Gesammelte Werke* (Frankfurt am Main: S. Fischer Verlag, 1960-68) Vol. 10, 126-36.

2. Adam Phillips, *The Beast in the Nursery* (New York: Pantheon, 1998) 84.

3. C. G. Jung, *Memories, Dreams, Reflections* (New York: Random House, 1963) 4, 5.

4. Maryse Choisy, *Sigmund Freud: A New Appraisal* (New York: Citadel, 1963) 2-3.

5. Freud, *S. E.*, Vol. X, 10.122.

24

Another Oedipus

As anyone who has ever heard me talk about mythology knows, I am persuaded that what makes a myth a myth is its power to continue to activate fresh myth-making and thus am fascinated by what Joseph Campbell calls "creative mythology," the retelling of inherited myths in ways that make them freshly pertinent to our own world. Accordingly, to honor Portuguese playwright Armando Nascimento Rosa's new version of the Oedipus story, *Another Oedipus,* to discover what *this* Oedipus has to say to us, means trying to set it in the context of its predecessors, both in the ancient world and in ours—for as Karl Kerenyi reminds us there were many Oedipuses in the classical world, both before and after Sophocles, and many modern Oedipuses, both before and after Freud.[1]

The Classical Tradition

Kerenyi and other classicists, Charles Segal, for example, and Timothy Gantz, give us a rich sense of the complexity of the classical tradition.[2] These scholars remind us that Sophocles composed his version with explicit awareness of earlier literary versions by Homer, Pindar, and Aeschylus, and that there were at least six other tragedies based on the Oedipus myth composed during the fifth century BCE (including one by Euripides), each of which differs from the others in significant ways. And the retelling goes on: Apollodorus, Hyginus, Seneca, all add to the tradition.

Carl Roberts once suggested that it all began with a cult centered around a tomb in Colonus dedicated to an archaic hero named Oedipus, "swollen-foot," and that the myth arose to invent a story that would explain the name. An intriguing theory but one that has been pretty well demolished: though there was such a tomb in Colonus there is no evidence for its existence prior to the fifth century and until Sophocles none of the literary references or vases do much to connect the story about the hero to the literal meaning of his name.

So we have to begin elsewhere, not with ritual nor with speculations about a lost oral story but with the earliest literary evidence. That is we have to *begin* with a *re*-telling, as seems always to be true of myths. In the case of Oedipus this means beginning with Homer. There's a brief allusion in the *Iliad* to a funeral celebration in honor of a Theban king called Oedipus who seems to have been killed in battle, but what we think of as *our* Oedipus and *his* story first appears in Book 11 of the *Odyssey* as part of Odysseus' account of his encounters in the underworld:

> And I saw the beautiful Epicaste, Oidipodes' mother
> who in the ignorance of her mind had done a monstrous
> thing and married her own son. He killed his father
> and married her, but the gods soon made it known to all mortals.
> But he, for all his sorrows, in beloved Thebes continued
> to be lord over the Kadmeians, all through the bitter designing
> of the gods; while she went down to Hades of the gates, the strong one,
> knotting a noose and hanging sheer from the high ceiling,
> in the constraint of her sorrow, but left to him who survived her
> all the sorrows that are brought to pass by a mother's furies.[3]

Note how much we tend to think *belongs* to the story is missing here: no oracles, no Sphinx, no self-blinding, no children born to Oedipus and Jocasta, no *self*-discovery, no exile (here Oedipus continues to rule after the revelation of his deeds and after his wife's suicide).

It is difficult to sort through just what gets added to the tradition when, but by the early fifth century, well before Aeschylus puts together his version, Oedipus's relation to Theban mythological history has been spelled out: he is the son of Labdacus, son of Polydoros, son of Cadmus—whereas Jocasta and Creon are the last pure-line descendents of the Sparti, the "sown men," thus inheriting what might be an older claim to power in Thebes. For when Cadmus first came to Thebes he killed a dragon sacred to Ares and was then instructed to bury its teeth in the ground. Where the teeth had been sown armed men (who immediately started fighting one another) sprang forth. The five who survived made some kind of peace with Cadmeian rule (one married Agave and thus fathered Pentheus) but the accommodation was fragile. When Labdacus died soon after his accession to the throne, a Sparti descendent took power, and the still very young Laius (like Orestes in another tale) was sent away for protection to Pelops' house in Pisa. There, so the story already went, he violated hospitality by abducting the king's beautiful young son, Chrysippus and taking the youth back with him to Thebes.

By now the sphinx had also been brought into the tale, perhaps initially by vase painters. This creature is depicted in art as a hybrid creature with the body of a lion (and sometimes wings) and the face of a human female (a face whose artistic representations get more and more beautiful as time passes). In Hesiod's *Theogony* she already appears as a threat to Thebes (particularly to its beautiful young men whom she abducts and kills), sent by Hera as punishment for Semele's liaison with Zeus. There is no literary evidence of her being brought into the Oedipus story before Aeschylus (according to whom she is sent by Hera in retribution for Laius' unrepented forceful taking of Chrysippus). In the older tellings she can only be overcome by force, but Oedipus succeeds in freeing Thebes of her presence by answering her riddle. (There is even a tradition, though it is probably later, that Oedipus initially comes to Thebes in response to a widely broadcast promise by Creon that anyone who can rid Thebes of the Sphinx may have the widowed Jocasta's hand and the Theban throne—though of course any who fail will lose their lives.)

As the excerpt from Homer suggests, in early tradition the parricide and incest are discovered much too quickly for Oedipus and Jocasta to have children together, so Oedipus is often given another wife who bears him progeny, at first only sons. But in Aeschylus (and maybe somewhat earlier) the children are Jocasta's and they bear the names we're familiar with: Eteocles, Polyneices, Ismene, and Antigone. We know nothing of any preSophoclean tradition in which Oedipus is exiled from Thebes after the discovery of his crimes: sometimes he continues to rule as in Homer, sometimes he is imprisoned in the palace and Creon or his sons take over the throne.

We know that Aeschylus wrote a trilogy consisting of a *Laius,* an *Oedipus,* and *The Seven Against Thebes,* of which only the last survives. But allusions in it to the earlier plays and references by others give us a fairly good sense of the whole. The *Laius* seems to have focused on Laius and Chrysippus and on Pelops' curse on his criminal houseguest (thus setting in motion a curse that moves through a family generation after generation, much like the curse that plagues Agamemnon's family in Aeschylus's *Oresteia*). But the horrors that are to come are overdetermined, for Laius also receives an oracle warning him that were he ever to have a son, that child would kill him. Thus it is not surprising that in the second play the motif of the infant Oedipus's exposure appears for the first time: the infant Oedipus is put in a chest that is dumped into the sea but somehow makes its way safely to land. There is no adoption; Oedipus knows that he is a foundling and when grown sets out in search of his parents. He and Laius fail to recognize one another when they meet on the road to Potnia (not Delphi) and the murder ensues. After the discovery of Oedipus's guilt he blinds himself (a new addition to the story) and fiercely curses his children, thus preparing for the last play in the trilogy, which opens with his sons' mutual fratricide.

So that, in brief, is a summary of the preSophoclean tradition.

Sophocles by writing a single play[4] is able to focus his retelling on one moment within the whole long tale: Oedipus's discovery of the truth about his own life. This intense focus on self-discovery is completely new and transforms the meaning of the whole story—an emphasis that is reinforced by all the insistent references within the play to blindness and vision. Sophocles omits the family curse laid on Laius that is central to Aeschylus; here Oedipus suffers for what he himself has done, not for some inherited affliction. He includes the oracle given Laius, but *adds* (that is, *invents*) the oracle to Oedipus and thus the whole motif of Oedipus trying to escape his fate (and *thereby* fulfilling it). The encounter of Laius and Oedipus is for the first time set on the road between Delphi and Thebes. Sophocles adds the foot-piercing—and thus the puns on Oedipus's name. (Though the punning is more extensive still: Sophocles also plays with *oida*'s association with knowledge in this play that centers on a hero so confident of his intellectual powers who doesn't know what he most needs to know.) The exposure on Mt. Kitharon that makes possible the whole scenario of the two herdsmen and the adoption by the Corinthian king and queen is also new. There is more emphasis on Thebes as the city of Dionysos, hinting at parallels between Dionysos and Oedipus; both are Theban-born *and* strangers. The plague, which casts a miasma over everything, is utterly new; it creates an atmosphere suffused with horror and pollution, suggests that even nature responds to the horrendous crimes with sterility and disease. In this telling Oedipus sets out to learn the truth and has himself issued the edict of exile on whoever might be discovered as Laius' murderer. He is son and husband, king and scapegoat, pursued and pursuer. The exile is itself a fresh addition (and, of course, prepares the way for the *Oedipus at Colonus* in which Oedipus at the end of many years of blind wandering comes to the outskirts of Athens to die and thereby to bring protective blessing to the city for which Sophocles' play was written). At the end of the *Oedipus Tyrannos*, at the point where Aeschylus has his Oedipus pronouncing a curse upon his sons, this Oedipus expresses tender concern for the future of his children—and his city. As he prepares to leave, we do not know whether his acknowledgement of all he has been and done will actually bring about the lifting of the plague (though we do know that this city's troubles are far from over).

As we also know there are many other versions of the myth still to come. We know Euripides wrote an *Oedipus*, though we know little about it, primarily only that there was no prophecy to Oedipus and that it is Creon rather than Oedipus himself who ferrets out the truth. We know of many other later variations on the story: for instance, that despite all their efforts to avoid having a child, Oedipus is conceived on a night when a drunken Laius rapes Jocasta. In some tellings Oedipus is said to have been raised by shepherds or Merope is said to have found the infant Oedipus washed up on the Corinthian shore and to have convinced Polybius that is her own child. Or Jocasta is said to have known the truth all along, having discovered Oedipus's identity by the telltale scars on his feet. Sometimes, too, Jocasta does not kill herself until much later than in Sophocles' play, until after she has had to witness her two sons killing each other.

Nonetheless, the version of the myth that had almost canonical status even in the classical world (think of Aristotle's praise) was Sophocles' version. Fully to appreciate its innovations and influence it helps to see it in its original context, to recognize the sense in which it is set as much in fifth century Athens as in ancient Thebes, to see how this particular version of the myth (with its emphasis on Oedipus's self-inquiry and self-punishment) was shaped by the questions a particular society found most pressing.

The play was first performed shortly after the great plague of 430 BCE in which one-quarter of the Athenian population, including Pericles, died—a plague so devastating that it was viewed even in skeptical, sophisticated Athens as a supernatural disaster. The plague's undermining of Athenian self-confidence and trust in a rational world was undoubtedly part of the background, and many see a connection between Sophocles' Oedipus and Pericles, a great man and good ruler whose ambitious plans issued in the Peloponnesian War that eventually brought disaster to his city. Pericles (like Oedipus) was a *"tyrannos"* not a king, someone who had achieved political rulership by virtue of his own deeds and charisma, not heredity.[5]

We need to remember that the *Oedipus Tyrannos* is a drama, a tragedy—and that drama is *agon*, struggle, and involves the representation of multiple perspectives. It still amazes me that tragedy was a vital genre in Athens for only the approximately seventy year period spanned by its extant examples (484-406 BCE), a period of transition, turmoil, and war. This was a time when the divergence between the heroic values of the archaic world and those of the relatively newly established and still fragile law-centered democracy was still painful and troubling, and when the long drawn out Peloponnesian War brought a heightened awareness of the limitations and precariousness of the civic order. It was a time of conflict between the values of the family-based past and those of the new polis-centered world, that is, a time when the priority of political over familial commitments was still recent and tenuous.

The tragedies were written to illuminate—not resolve—these tensions. The dramatists used the inherited myths to reflect on perennial but newly pressing issues and to call for a deeper and more resilient relation to the community and to the gods, to fate, suffering, and death. In their plays the myths, as Jean-Pierre Vernant puts it, became a mirror in which the city could look at itself, could become aware of the limitations and precariousness of the civic and religious order. Tragedy reflected the anxieties not the confident verities of its audience, voiced the hope (not the assurance) of the triumph of order over chaos. The aim was to develop a tragic consciousness in the spectators, an awareness of simultaneously valid contradictory perspectives. (Though like Oedipus, like us as readers of the play, the audience might have longed for clarity, for certainty, for a more univocal truth.)

Ambiguity, double meanings, paradox and contradiction are central to tragedy. In Sophocles' *Oedipus Tyrannos* the central paradox is that Oedipus is both agent and acted-upon, innocent and guilty.[6] He is morally innocent, he acted in ignorance, but his crime is objectively horrifying—and he accepts responsibility for it. It is not an either/or—Oedipus is not just a victim of fate nor simply a free agent; he is *both*. In this play Sophocles explores the terrible mysterious intersection of fate and free will. The hero is the one who can affirm his fate and say "*this is me*" in a way that includes an acceptance of the inescapable contingencies of his life. Oedipus's life was fate-bound, but there was no oracle ordaining that he had to pursue the truth. That he does out of love for his people. What causes his ruin is his strength and courage, his loyalty to Thebes and to the truth (as contrasted with Jocasta who prefers evasion). What happens *in* the play is what Oedipus does because of his commitment to the truth: the rest, the fated parts, the crimes, lie in the past.

The gods (including *Tyche*, chance, necessity), though largely ignored by Aristotle in his fourth century reflections on tragedy (perhaps because for him tragedy was more a *literary* genre than a performative one), are essential to Sophocles' conception. Otherwise, as Bernard Knox observes, it is all just an awful series of coincidences. The discovery of the unspeakable pollution is bearable only because it is somehow connected with the gods, with some sacred transpersonal force. We live in a world of powers greater than ourselves, forces who are not in any human sense just, but for Sophocles nevertheless *are*.[7]

Freud and Oedipus

Sigmund Freud's discovery of the living reality of myth, the living reality of *this* myth, marks the beginning of *depth* psychology. This discovery grew out of his own experience, out of the self-analysis provoked by the death of father and his consequent discovery of his ambivalent feelings (resentment and disappointment, not only respect and affection) about a father whom he had consciously thought he had loved unreservedly. Freud's father died in October 1896; almost exactly a year later, Freud had a series of dreams that led him to memories of a close early-childhood connection to a nanny, of the "*libido* toward *matrem*" he remembered feeling in relation to his beautiful young mother, and of his intense jealousy of a one-year younger brother who died in infancy. Reflection on these dreams led him on waking one morning to a sudden realization, "I am Oedipus."

As he wrote Wilhelm Fliess, his confidant during this transformative period in his life:

> Being totally honest with oneself is a good exercise. I have found in my own case, too, the phenomenon of being in love with my mother and jealous of my father, and I now consider it a universal event in early childhood…If this is so, we can understand the gripping power of *Oedipus Rex*…The Greek legend seizes upon a compulsion which everyone recognizes because he senses its existence within himself. Everyone in the audience was once a budding Oedipus in fantasy and each recoils in horror from the dream fulfillment here transplanted into reality, with the full quantity of repression which separates his infantile state from his present one.[8]

Later, in *Interpretation of Dreams*[9] Freud included a more reflective, extended, public version of the same primary insight. There he notes that he sees neurotics as making visible what is true of all of us: "They are only distinguished by exhibiting on a magnified scale feelings of love and hatred to their parents which occur less obviously and less intensely in the minds of most children." He offers his own summary of the myth and emphasizes the particular shape and focus Sophocles gave it: "The action of the play consists in nothing other than the process of revealing, with cunning delays and ever-mounting excitement—a process that can be likened to the work of a psychoanalysis." Freud sees how Oedipus's cleverness at solving the Sphinx's riddle masks his greater ignorance—and leads him to think he can solve the new puzzle in the same way.

He insists that the point of the play is not human helplessness before fate, but rather something that "a voice within us recognizes":

His destiny moves us only because it might have been ours—because the oracle laid the same curse upon us before our birth…While the poet, as he unrav-
els the past, brings to light the guilt of Oedipus, he is at the same time
compelling us to recognize our own inner minds, in which those same
impulses, though suppressed, are still to be found…Like Oedipus we live in
ignorance of these wishes, and after their revelation we may all of us seek to
close our eyes to the scenes of our childhood.

Our dreams, he claims, reveal the persistence of these impulses in us and Freud
believes that the Oedipus myth must have sprung from some primeval dream-
material as well. He quotes Jocasta's lines:

> Best to live lightly, as one can, unthinkingly.
>
> As to your mother's marriage bed—don't fear it.
>
> Before this, in dreams, too, as well as oracles,
>
> Many a man has lain with his own mother,
>
> But he to whom such things are nothing bears
>
> His life more easily.

Depth psychology, I believe, really begins with Freud's waking recognition: "I
am Oedipus"—*Not* (of course) with his saying to himself "I have an Oedipus
complex."[10] For Freud "Oedipus" was not an illustration or clever designation
but the medium of discovery. Through his years of reflection on this myth he
came to mean by "Oedipus" almost everything associated with the hero of
Sophocles' *Oedipus Tyrannos* (and later also by much of the Oedipus of *Oedipus
at Colonus*).

He especially wanted to suggest that he had discovered as still alive in himself—and he believed in all of us—a profound inextinguishable longing for the
unconditional love we knew at the breast, or perhaps even further back, in the
womb. Pointing to the persistence in us of incestuous wish and parricidal longing
was his way of calling our attention to a voice still alive in us that cries "I want
her, all of her, all to myself"—and therefore to our deep murderous resentment
of anyone who intrudes between ourselves and her, between ourselves and the
fullness of love, of being fully known and fully embraced, we imagine we once
had and still long for.

Freud knew that this experience of being whole in ourselves and at one with
the world was imaginal, was only discovered retrospectively as we experienced its
absence, its loss. He was fascinated by that mysterious moment at which the self

appears, the beginnings of our *psychological* life, of consciousness. He understood that self and mother, self and other, self and world are co-created—in response to her *not* being there, to her *not* existing only for ourselves. Thus, the human soul comes into existence in a reflexive movement when desire is frustrated. And simultaneously with the birth of consciousness comes the birth of the unconscious. For the self-aware self is produced at a cost. The grief and rage associated with that primal irreversible loss are too enormous to bear; they cannot be fully acknowledged—they have to be unconscious.

Clearly, Freud does not understand incest or patricide literally; nevertheless, he does view them as connected to actual experience, bodily experience and childhood experience, as not "only metaphor." He also reminds us that these are *unconscious* longings, as in the *Oedipus Tyrannos* they are acted on *unknowingly.*

Initially when Freud found himself engaged by this myth, he not too surprisingly looked at it from the perspective of the son, the son's attachment to the mother and his rivalrous resentment of the father. Later as Freud came to recognize that since for female children, too, the first attachment is to the mother, he understood that *this* story (rather than the Electra myth) was relevant to them as well. And as he came to acknowledge the full implications of the bisexuality he had in his *Three Essays on Sexuality* attributed to all of us "in the beginning," he further saw that in actuality all of us, male and female alike, both love and hate *both* parents, desire and identify with each. The ambivalence, he comes to see, is there from the outset: we are passionately attached to those on whom we are dependent *and* passionately resentful of that dependence. Thus we need partly to deny the dependency in order to *be*; need to feel we have let go of what we've lost, need to claim autonomy.

As Freud continued in the years that followed to live *vis-à-vis* this myth, he also saw how it shows how it doesn't begin with us: psychologically we enter into a world already there, a world of others and their desires, their terrors—as Oedipus's life was shaped by the curse laid on his father and by his parents' fear, and in turn shaped that of his children.

Freud also meant by "Oedipus" the commitment to self-knowledge (even when painful) exemplified by Oedipus's persistence in his search to discover the true identity of the one whose murderous deed had brought death to his city. Indeed, this aspect was actually the one most emphasized in *Interpretation of Dreams.*

And in his later years of suffering from the unremitting pain of cancer Freud came to identify with the blind exiled Oedipus utterly dependent on being led by his daughter Antigone, as Freud had become dependent on his daughter Anna.

"My Anna, my Antigone," he called her. In those years, he identified with the Oedipus who had come to terms with his life, his limitations, his finitude, the Oedipus who was ready to die.

"I am Oedipus," he said. Fully to know myself is to acknowledge this identification.

In saying this he was rediscovering what myth-oriented cultures have always affirmed: we find our identity through discovering a mythic model. Thomas Mann believed that Freud's most important contribution lay in his helping us move to a mode of being here in which the mythical point of view becomes subjective, enters into the active ego and becomes conscious there, "proudly and darkly yet joyously, of its recurrence and its typicality, celebrates its role…in the knowledge that it was a fresh incarnation of the traditional upon the earth."[11]

Classicists are, of course, very aware of Freud's influence on modern readings of the *Oedipus Tyrannos*. Jean Pierre Vernant's "Oedipus Without the Complex" is radically critical, insisting that the play is to be read in terms of its meaning in fifth century Athens (which signifies for him that it is primarily about political tensions within that community) not in terms of some universal atemporal meaning. He reminds us that in the play the patricide precedes the incest and that it does not occur because Oedipus hates his father, that it is rather a defensive killing of a stranger. The incest does not arise out of Oedipus being overcome by an erotic desire for his mother but out of his agreeing to enter upon a political marriage.[12]

Yet although it is true that in the play the murder of Laius precedes the marriage to Jocasta and that Apollo seems more concerned about the patricide than the incest, and attributes the plague to *it*—nonetheless, when Sophocles' Oedipus speaks of the oracle he had received he always mentions the incest first and the emphasis in the play falls on Jocasta's role in the abandonment of her infant child. "Her own child! How could she! Only three days after giving birth." And it's the thought of the *marriage*, not the long ago scene at the crossroads, that appalls Oedipus.

Other classicists have been more appreciative. For instance Charles Segal[13] values Freud's recognition of how Sophocles transformed the ancient story into a profound meditation on the large areas of darkness we all have about who we "really" are and about the mystery of being alive in a world that does not correspond to a pattern of order or justice satisfactory to the human mind. He sees how Freud helped us recognize that the play is about *our* deepest and most hidden sexual and aggressive impulses and encouraged us to acknowledge that we respond with horror and delight at seeing the hidden reality begin to emerge.

And, as Nicole Loraux insists, even the spectators watching the original performance were moved beyond their identification as Athenian citizens. The tragedies' emphasis on loss, grief, mortality, the haunting presence of death, suggest to her that the spectators discovered that more fundamental than their role as citizen was their participation in the race of mortals.[14]

Jung on the Play and the Complex

Clearly that there are two different issues: the truth of the Oedipus complex for us and the truth of its being the meaning of the Sophocles play. As we turn to Jung we will discover that he challenged Freud on both accounts.

I noted earlier that I see Freud's discovery of the living reality of myth as marking the beginning of depth psychology. It was, in turn, Freud's account of that discovery that first drew Jung to Freud and that first suggested to him the importance of mythology for psychology—as he testifies in the first pages of *Symbols of Transformation*:

> Any one who can read Freud's *Interpretation of Dreams*...(and) can let this extraordinary book work upon his imagination calmly and without prejudice, will not fail to be deeply impressed at that point where Freud reminds us that an individual conflict, which he calls the incest fantasy, lies at the root of the monumental drama of the ancient world, the Oedipus legend. The impression made by this simple remark may be likened to the uncanny feeling which would steal over us if, amid the noise and bustle of a modern city street, we were suddenly to come upon an ancient relic.... A moment ago, and we were completely absorbed in the hectic, ephemeral life of the present; then, the next moment, something very remote and strange flashes upon us, which directs our gaze to a different order of things.... Suddenly we remember that on this spot where we now hasten to and fro about our business a similar scene of life and activity prevailed two thousand years ago in slightly different forms; similar passions moved mankind, and people were just as convinced as we are of the uniqueness of their lives. This is the impression that may very easily be left behind by a first acquaintance with the monuments of antiquity, and it seems to me that Freud's reference to the Oedipus legend is in every way comparable. While still struggling with the confusing impressions of the infinite variability of the individual psyche, we suddenly catch a glimpse of the simplicity and grandeur of the Oedipus tragedy, that perennial highlight of the Greek theater. This broadening of our vision has about it something of a revelation. For our psychology, the ancient world has long since been sunk in the shadows of the past; in the schoolroom one could scarcely repress a skeptical smile when one indiscreetly calculated the matronly age of Penelope or pictured to oneself the comfortable middle-aged appearance of Jocasta, and comically

compared the result with the tragic tempests of eroticism that agitate the legend and drama. We did not know then—and who knows even today?—that a
man can have an unconscious, all-consuming passion for his mother which
may undermine and tragically complicate his whole life, so that the monstrous
fate of Oedipus seems not one whit overdrawn.... the gulf that separates our
age from antiquity is bridged over, and we realize with astonishment that
Oedipus is still alive for us. The importance of this realization should not be
underestimated, for it teaches us that there is an identity of fundamental
human conflicts which is independent of time and place.... That at least is the
hope we draw from the rediscovery of the immortality of the Oedipus problem.[15]

So, in a sense, it was reading Freud on Oedipus that gave Jung his first hint of
what he would later call the collective or archetypal unconscious; he learned from
Freud that these ancient mythic patterns are still alive in us, often unconsciously.

Indeed, it is not difficult to see aspects of this myth, the Oedipus myth, at
work (partly unconsciously) in the Freud-Jung relationship itself—not difficult
to see how Freud saw in Jung the heir he (already 50 at the time they became
close and sensing his creativity might be at an end after the remarkable productivity of the preceding few years) was looking for; not difficult to see how Jung
found in Freud the "father" powerful enough to be worthy of rebelling against, as
his own father seems not to have been.

Thus it is not surprising that in 1912, while lecturing far across the ocean in
New York, Jung feels free for the first time to challenge Freud, to rebel against
Freud, to give public voice to a critique of Freud. In these lectures he challenges
the expanded understanding of sexuality that for Freud was the "shibboleth" of
psychoanalysis and puts forward his own understanding of the "Oedipus complex." By now (not as earlier, when he had been closer to Freud) he interprets
Freud as having understood incest and patricide very literally—and goes on to say
that he sees the Oedipus complex as relevant only to neurotics, not normal persons. He speaks of "the infantilism of neurotic sexuality," of an "anachronistic
clinging to an infantile attitude rather than real incestuous wishes." He questions
Freud's emphasis on the sexual aspect of the child's pull to the mother and
acknowledges how uncomfortable he is with calling an infant's pleasure in suckling at its mother's breast a sexual experience. Taking it for granted that female
psychology would mirror male psychology, that the female child would direct her
desire to father rather than mother, he introduces the notion of an "Electra complex." He also speaks of the normal child's natural move away from a focus of
libido on the parents, as though this means the earlier attachments have been
fully superseded.[16]

In the same year, in the book that in its 1952 reworking becomes *Symbols of Transformation,* Jung puts forward his own interpretation of the Oedipus myth. In the 1912 version he writes:

> In the Oedipus legend the Sphinx was sent by Hera, who hated Thebes on account of the birth of Bacchus. Oedipus, thinking he had overcome the Sphinx sent by the mother-goddess merely because he had solved her childishly simple riddle fell a victim to matriarchal incest and had to marry Jocasta, his mother, for the throne and the hand of the widowed queen belonged to him who had freed the land from the plague of the Sphinx.

In 1952 he adds:

> This had all the tragic consequences which could easily have been avoided if only Oedipus had been sufficiently intimidated by the frightening appearance of the "terrible" or "devouring" Mother whom the Sphinx personified. He was far indeed from the philosophical wonderment of Faust: "The Mothers, the Mothers, it has a wondrous sound!" Little did he know that the riddle of the Sphinx can never be solved simply by the wit of man...It is evident that a factor of such magnitude cannot be disposed of by solving a childish riddle. The riddle was, in fact, the trap which the Sphinx laid for the unwary wanderer. Overestimating his intellect in a typically masculine way, Oedipus walked right into it, and all unknowingly committed the crime of incest. The riddle of the Sphinx was *herself*—the terrible mother-imago, which Oedipus would not take as a warning.[17]

Thus, Jung emphasizes the repetitions—how Oedipus's response to the Sphinx prefigures what happens later—and on how Oedipus (like us moderns) relies on his intellect and misses the deeper aspects of the situation: does not recognize the devouring, scary, aspect of the Mother that the Sphinx represents. As many others have put it, for Jung Oedipus really *failed* the test: "Man" was an inadequate, too abstract, answer; the better answer would have been "Me, Oedipus" who began as the foot-pierced child, was then the successful hero, and ends up the blind exiled old man leaning on his stick. (The emphasis on the riddle is interesting: it is, of course, not included in Sophocles' play and thus was not considered by Freud.) Note, too, how easily both Sphinx and Jocasta become images of "The Mother," how quickly Jung being Jung moves from the particular to the archetypal.

Which brings us to the central theme of *Symbols of Transformation:* Jung's archetypal re-interpretation of incest. Sexual images, he says, are not to be taken literally, but as symbols. He reinterprets incestuous longing, the longing to return to the mother, as *really* meaning our longing for a return to the psychological source of our being, for a renewed living connection to the deep unconscious from which consciousness emerges, a reconnection to symbolic and not just literal consciousness. The basis of incestuous desire, he says, is not cohabitation but a longing to be a child again, to be reborn. The incest taboo, acting as an obstacle, makes the creative fantasy inventive: that is, because of the prohibition we are moved beyond the literal. The "return" is not exactly a return—not a return to undifferentiated consciousness but a turn to symbolic consciousness as consciously symbolic. The effect of the incest taboo is to stimulate the creative imagination. This brings Jung to his central point, his real purpose: to encourage people to recover the lost atrophied capacity for symbolic, spiritual thinking.

Jungian analyst, Robert Stein,[18] agrees that the incest taboo redirects libido from literal incest to symbolic incest, but, like Freud, says we really have to accept, not run away from, the incestuous longings—otherwise they will trip us up. Stein believes that by running—by cutting himself off, out of fear, from his natural connection to his (substitute) parents—Oedipus became an easy victim to unconscious feelings, to living them out concretely, literally. His crime was his *resistance* to incest, his denial of incestuous longings. Stein also writes about the patricide—which was after all, what upset Apollo, what led to the plague. Oedipus, he says, should have been the son who brought renewal, but he messed up because he killed the father instead of receiving mentoring from him. The anger that sons direct at fathers, he suggests, is not about competition for mother, but about not getting from them what they most need: male initiation.

Along similar lines, another Jungian-inspired theorist, Jean-Joseph Goux,[19] views the *Oedipus Tyrannos* as almost a parody of the male initiatory pattern. He writes of how the initiatory trial, usually set by the father, is here replaced by the murder of the father—and of how Oedipus's triumph over the sphinx, by being accomplished by word rather by sword, signifies that Oedipus has substituted intellectual development for the attainment of authentic male maturity. Because Oedipus doesn't kill the Sphinx, he is destined to marry his mother, is caught in the incestuous relation.

Although James Hillman's "revisiting" of the Oedipus story[20] begins with an appreciation of Freud's relocation of the family in the mythical imagination, Hillman quickly proceeds to qualify Freud's interpretation of the myth. He reminds us that the story begins not with patricide but with (attempted) infanticide and thus with a recognition that the murderous father is an essential part of the father archetype. Hillman interprets the abandonment of the newborn child as an attempt to kill what "child" represents, the imagination. The doom, he says, lay not in the oracles but in actions taken by both Laius and Oedipus when they interpreted the oracles literally and blindly searched for a way out. But the repressed returns: Laius's son reappears; the plague comes back.

Like Freud in *Interpretation of Dreams,* Hillman says that actually the aspect of Sophocles' version of the myth that impresses him most is the focus on Oedipus's search for self-knowledge. *This,* he says, is what has caught depth psychology: our looking *through* Oedipus, more than our looking *at* him. Psychoanalysis (by which he intends Jungian and not only Freudian perspectives), with its focus on self-discovery through recollection of our early lives, seems to be almost inescapably Oedipal in method. Its encouragement of our longing to discover the truth about our lives leads us to look at myths, at their gods and goddesses, their heroes and heroines, and see only ourselves—and to forget that the unconscious is unconscious, that we will never fully know ourselves.

Hillman emphasizes the importance of moving beyond an intrapsychic psychology—and reminds us that for Sophocles the *polis* was central: finding the truth about oneself is not enough; the point is to cure the city. Fortunately, he says, the Oedipus myth itself offers a way forward, in the continuation of the story in the *Oedipus at Colonos.* "Freud stops in Thebes. Sophocles dreams the myth along, as Jung advised us all to do." Here Oedipus has moved beyond a concern with his own guilt: he gives his blessing to another man's son, Theseus, and to another city: "To you and this your land and all your people."

Rosa's *Another Oedipus*[21]

Like Sophocles, like Hillman, Armando Rosa in his new play does not stop at Thebes—yet, though his Oedipus is almost as old as the Oedipus of Sophocles' last play, he does not get us to Colonus.

What happens in the interval between the departure from Thebes and the arrival many years later at the sacred grove at Colonus has always been a mystery: how did *that* Oedipus become *this* one? I remember how disappointed I was by Henry Bauchau's novel, *Oedipus on the Road,*[22] which seemed to me to offer only a very stereotyped filling-out of the pattern of the typical heroic journey (as outlined by Campbell in *Hero with a Thousand Faces*) with all the requisite *femmes fatales* and helpful maidens, frightening ogres and benevolent wizards. I concluded from that attempt: better to leave it *as* a mystery.

Rosa, however, manages to escape the danger of trying to provide a narrative version of the interval—instead he constructs a clearly imaginal scene of an engagement between Oedipus and the ghosts—the souls—of the long-since-dead other participants in the drama. His Oedipus is engaged in a search for a deeper truth about his story than the one he had managed to extract from the messenger and herdsman in Sophocles' play. His confrontation in the play with these ghosts is like a dream or a ritual—an initiation into a deeper, more transpersonal, more archetypal understanding. Oedipus is being given an opportunity to move beyond an egoic perspective, beyond seeing himself as at the center of the story, an opportunity to learn how his story is the outcome of forces set in motion long before his birth.

Through this dramatization Rosa hopes to recover the sacred ritual aspects of the myth that he (in agreement with Kerenyi) believes has mostly been lost from modern revisionings or reinterpretations of it—not just Freud's but also those of Gide, Cocteau and Hofmansthal. In the ancient world, the dramatic retellings were closely associated with ritual: tragedy, in all likelihood, emerged out of dithyrambic performances dedicated to Dionysos, and in classical Athens the plays were performed as part of a major six day Dionysian festival in March or April at the theater of Dionysos with priests of Dionysos in attendance. Many have noted the persistence of ritual themes, such as the transition from dark to light, sorrow to joy, in Greek tragedy, and of the ritual pattern of suffering-sacrifice-renewal. Gilbert Murray suggests that the plots of tragedy recapitulate the death and rebirth of Dionysos (a god whom he, following Frazer, sees primarily as a vegetation god, a Year Spirit).[23] Francis Fergusson finds references not only to agrarian rituals but also to rituals of male initiation and rituals associated with the concerns about communal order in the *Oedipus Tyrannos*.[24] There are clear echoes of at least two important fifth century Athenian rituals in the play: the *Thargelia*, a ritual dedicated to Apollo celebrated in May at the time of the wheat harvest, which focused on the stoning (and symbolic killing) of a *pharmakos*; the expulsion of this scapegoat from the city was undertaken to effect a *katharsis*, a purification of the whole community. The *Anthesteria* was a February new wine ritual dedicated to Dionysos, the phallic wine-god; the celebration included ritualized sexual intercourse between the wife of the *archon* with the god (perhaps represented by a priest of Dionysos). In the play the perverted marriage of Oedipus and Jocasta brings about the reverse of the intended consequence of this *hieros gamos* ritual: barren fields and stillborn births.

Of course, Rosa's play is not a Greek tragedy; he calls it "gnostic theatre" or "a ghostly melodrama." *Another Oedipus* offers us the representation of an inner engagement with the sacred, intended to bring us to enter into our own inner worlds, to provide a kind of psychotherapy. Although not explicitly a Freudian revisioning, the focus on Oedipus's inner world to the exclusion of concerns about fertility (familial or vegetal) or politics carries forward a reading first suggested by Freud. Rosa's own sympathies are more Jungian: he wants to connect the story to collective archetypal experience and to move both the characters in the play and the audience of the play to a more imaginal, less literal understanding of desire and violence—for example, he presents Oedipus's self-blinding as too literalized an expression of his longing for inward rather than outward vision.

Bringing ghosts into the tale is not new. In Seneca's *Oedipus* the ghost of Laius is summoned back up from the underworld and is persuaded to reveal the horrifying truth to Oedipus and the world that his own son had murdered him—and a daughter of Teiresias, Manto, reveals the rest.[25] Thus Seneca completely omits what is central to Sophocles' version, Oedipus's own discovery of the truth. Clearly Rosa's ghosts serve a different function: his Oedipus is almost desperate to discover a deeper truth than the one he had accessed while still in Thebes. In his opening monologue, he tells us that he has learned what he believes are the relevant facts but not what they mean; he is aware of not having reached "soul's knowledge." Still searching, still at war with himself, he hopes Tiresias can help him kill "the wild sphinx" that still lives but now within. The confession of responsibility, the self-blinding, the self-imposed exile—none of these have served to bring him the peace he had hoped for. So now he is on another journey—a more inward one. ("I must open my inner eyes.")

Oedipus tells Tiresias that, though still living, he feels dead. So he is between worlds—between the world of the living and the dead—in the in-between world that Corbin and Hillman associate with the imagination. The Greeks viewed this in-between world as Hekate's realm—inhabited by the souls of the no longer living who have not yet made their way to Hades (because not yet ritually buried or mourned) and so haunt the living. In this play Manto may be the only fully "living" character, for Tiresias is imagined as being so close to death as to be halfway between being alive and being ghost and the other characters—Jocasta, Laius, Chrysippus, and in an even more shadowy sense Pelops—are ghosts.

The first of the ghosts to appear is Jocasta. "Teach me how to live my death in full," she implores Tiresias. Unlike Rilke's Eurydice who was "deep within herself," for whom "being dead filled her beyond fulfillment,"[26] this Jocasta is not even fully ready to admit to her death. Tiresias challenges her evasion of the truth of her death but is also reluctant to help her unravel the tangled knots of her family's tragedy: there is knowledge too painful to be borne, he says. But Jocasta wonders if he believes that because there is part of his own story he doesn't want to look at; she challenges him to confront the full story behind his acquisition of shamanic foretelling powers, to remember the "real" story of how he came alone among mortals to have lived as both man and woman. This "real story," wholly Rosa's invention, is for me one of the least successful parts of the new play, but it serves the important function of *preparing* us for the play's later focus on the Laius-Chrysippus relationship. According to Jocasta, Tiresias was to begin with a beautiful young man who (like Hippolytus) scorned Aphrodite, who in punishment sent Zeus to make love to him. Tiresias awakes to find the god groping him; fleeing from an embrace he finds repulsive, he picks up a dagger and tries to castrate the god. Zeus then emasculates Tiresias and transforms him into a woman with whom he has a long affair. Thus the theme of homosexual rape and homosexual panic is introduced into Rosa's play early on.

And soon it will move to center stage. But first it is important for Rosa to move incest from that place. Rosa accomplishes this by making Jocasta deeply regret her participation in the attempted infanticide but not her incestuous marriage. And even her participation in the attempted infanticide is mitigated: Jocasta tells Tiresias how determined she was to get pregnant and how happy when Oedipus was born, how it was only afterwards that she became fearful about the curse and agreed to the exposure. Here is an Oedipus who to begin with was desired and loved! And was truly loved and desired when he reappeared in Thebes. Jocasta says that after the incest was uncovered she would happily have fled with Oedipus to some far-off land where no one would ever have learned the truth. After her death, she says, she realized she no longer felt any guilt or anxiety about the incest because she had come to understand that she and her son had but enacted a universal fantasy. "Man loves woman because he wants to dive once more into the sea of delight which brought him into the world...Love is a universal incest. There was no need to hang myself for such an ordinary cause." Very Freudian: although it is almost as though by realizing the universal and symbolic aspect, she excuses the literalization. As though by providing us with this powerful representation of the archetype she has done us all a favor! Rosa seems to view his Jocasta as "redeemed" when she moves to this kind of symbolic thinking, when she recognizes how all lovemaking, at least all male heterosexual desire, is symbolic mother-son incest.

Later Tiresias (and Rosa?) seems to forgive Jocasta's participation in the incest because it was part of Pelops' curse—in line with a general tendency (very unGreek) to take away personal responsibility for actions that are fulfillments of prophecy. Tiresias wants Jocasta to acknowledge the real reason for the curse that dooms her family. Oh, Laius' crime, she suggests. Of course, he replies.

Now we come to the heart of this version of the Oedipus story: Laius' abduction of Chrysippus as *the* crime from which all else follows. Rosa claims this emphasis is new which *may* be true, for although we know that Aeschylus wrote a lost play called *Laius* and surmise that central to it was the origin of the familial curse that leads to infanticide, patricide, incest, and fratricide, Gantz doubts that Aeschylus, because of his tendency always to focus on contrasexual conflict, put much emphasis on the Chrysippus episode.[27] Euripides wrote a *Chrysippus,* but it, too, is lost and we know very little about it.

To get a sense of the rich and complex tradition about Chrysippus that would have been familiar to Euripides means beginning with Chrysippus's father, Pelops, and actually with *his* father, Tantalus. Tantalus, albeit a son of Zeus, was mortal and deeply resentful of that status, despite being often invited to dine with the gods. So one day at one of these banquets he tried to serve the gods a stew containing the cut up body of his son Pelops. Demeter, so it is said, began to take a bite of the boy's shoulder, but the gods quickly saw through the trick and restored Pelops to life. Poseidon fell in love with the re-member-ed youth and they began a brief affair at the end of which Pelops was sent back to earth. When the young man was old enough to grow a beard he set out to win a bride and successfully implored Poseidon: If you had any joy of me, help me. All of this precisely fits the idealized *paiderasteia* pattern of fifth century Athens: a consummated sexual relation between a beardless adolescent and an ephebe, an only slightly older still unmarried male citizen who takes on a socially validated mentoring role, and later (after the younger partner has himself reached adulthood) becomes a lifelong friend.[28]

However, the story does not proceed so smoothly. The bride Pelops coveted had been promised by her father, the king of Pisa, to whomever could beat him in a chariot race; the loser (as is usual in such tales) would forfeit his life. Being determined to win, Pelops decided he had to cheat. So he bribed Myrtilus, the king's charioteer, to loosen the linchpin on one of the wheels of the royal chariot. The race won, the king killed, Pelops forgets to pay off the charioteer who in revenge rapes Hippodemia, the newly won bride. In turn Pelops murders Myrtilus by throwing him into the sea—but before drowning, the charioteer pronounces a curse on all Pelops' progeny, thus setting the stage for the fratricidal quarrels between Pelops' sons, Atreus and Thyestes, and providing the background for all the events dramatized in Aeschylus' *Oresteia.*

However, long before his marriage to Hippodemia, Pelops had had another son, Chrysippus. According to some sources, Hippodemia was so jealous of Pelops' apparent preference for this oldest son that she persuaded her sons to murder him. In response Pelops sent both into exile with a curse predicting that they would die at one another's hands. But the tradition about Chrysippus that inspires Rosa is the one according to which Laius, because too young to take over the throne of Thebes after his father's murder by rival claimants to the throne, is spirited away for safety to the court of Pisa. There he falls in love with the beautiful young Chrysippus and abducts him. The term that is used is *harpage*, the same term used for Zeus's (welcomed) abduction of Ganymede; it does not mean rape. Upon discovering what has happened, Pelops, the enraged father, pronounces a curse on Laius: if you ever have a son, he'll kill you. For the Greeks what evoked the curse was not that Laius and Chrysippus had entered upon a homosexual relation but that Laius had violated Pelops' hospitality (a serious crime in the ancient world—think of the story of Baucis and Philemon). There are various versions as to why and how Chrysippus comes to be killed: in some Chrysippus kills himself out of shame at having participated in this dishonoring of his family; in others Atreus and Thyestes kill him for this (rather than because of their mother's jealousy on their behalf). There is even a version in which Hippodemia herself kills Chrysippus when she finds him in bed with Laius and then tries to shift the blame onto Laius. There is another, later and even more fanciful version, in which Oedipus has been sent to Pisa to be raised by Pelops and Hippodemia, Laius comes to visit his son and falls in love with his son's beloved companion, Chrysippus, and tries to run off with him. Oedipus intervenes and in so doing, kills his father. Here father and son were rivals for the Pisan youth![29]

Despite the many variants, by far the most familiar version was that Laius had abducted Chrysippus and that Pelops had then uttered a curse. In most versions the curse included only the patricide not the incest. It focused on the father-son relation, since it was the father-son bond that Laius had dishonored.

Rosa adopts this story and *significantly* reworks it. The new account comes into his play as Tiresias begins to remind Jocasta of the story behind the story as she prefers to remember it. But soon the other participants, Chrysippus, Laius, even Pelops, appear to contribute their versions. In Rosa's play the Laius who comes to Pisa is older than in the Greek account; he is already king of Thebes, already married to Jocasta, temporarily ousted from the throne and so in Pisa for political asylum. When he espies the beautiful youth walking around naked, accompanied by his faithful dogs (like another Actaeon), he feels himself "pierced by Eros' arrow."

At this point, in the new play, the ghost of Chrysippus appears and insists on telling us what happened next. According to his account, Laius invited him to climb on his horse and join him for a ride. The youth accepted, they rode for hours, it grew dark, and Laius announced they would have to spend the night out in the wild. After settling into a sheltered cave, Laius began to accost him. "I liked to enjoy Argena the slave and Laius wanted to enjoy me as I enjoyed her. I began to shout and punch, and running out I fled from him." This is a Chrysippus with heterosexual experience, who responds to Laius' advances with homosexual panic (much as Tiresias had responded to Zeus). Note: the attempted rape is *not consummated.* Chrysippus goes on to tell us that in his panicked flight he tripped and plunged to his death in "Cerberus' ravine." Note that there is no suicide and no murder; the death is *accidental.* Nevertheless Pelops, enraged by his son's death, curses Laius as a kidnapper. The curse is that Laius should be sterile—"and should this fail one day, may the son who is born become his father's murderer, just as you murdered mine." (And here, as not usually in the Greek versions, the curse also includes the incest.)

So what Laius did in Rosa's play to evoke the curse was to inspire a homosexual panic that led to death. For this crime, Tiresias says, Laius should have atoned by "wandering like a beggar on the road." This seems to imply that Oedipus's wandering represents his taking on his father's guilt (as he had earlier taken his father's throne and wife)—as though even his exile is not really his own. In Rosa's own comments about the play he suggests that instead of responding literally to his desire for Chrysippus, Laius should have used it as the first step on the ladder toward the philosophical love of beauty and the possibility of mutual reciprocal love as outlined in Plato's *Symposium.*

Tiresias also accuses Jocasta (who in this version knows what Laius has done) of having welcomed Laius back to her bed despite his having engaged in "the type of treachery that humiliates women." That is, she should have viewed Laius' susceptibility to homosexual desire as a betrayal of her; it was because she forgave him that she earned Hera's unceasing punishment. Jocasta defends herself: I still wanted to be queen and from then on Laius was my slave. But then he got killed—in a duel (!) with Oedipus.

At this point in the play Oedipus wanders in and gives his own account of the patricide, acknowledging that he had actually enjoyed the killing and associating his felt pleasure at the other's death with memories of delighted-in childish exploits of sadism. Violence, he says, is inevitably triggered when two males meet on a lonely road.

Chrysippus again intervenes to say, You're lying; let me remind you of what really happened. Now Chrysippus tells his story somewhat differently: he brags that Laius had desired him (and even that Jocasta now does, that she's still into younger men). He tells Oedipus a strange story: on the day you murdered Laius I was on the chariot with him, a ghost yet somehow visible. I'd been rethinking the whole episode and now found myself wondering why I hadn't returned Laius' caresses with pleasure. How foolish I'd been to forgo the pleasure and the fame of being Laius' beloved.

Turning to the ghost of Laius, which is also now present, Chrysippus says, I wanted to tell you how everything could be different for us. Jocasta says, You grieve for him like a widowed bride. On stage the two ghosts embrace, as though there could be love, mutual love, between two men, rather than only rape or seduction.

Prodded by this embrace, Oedipus remembers what he saw when he came upon the chariot stopped in the middle of the road: "Two men entwined like serpents on the crossroads. One older, the other young, young enough to be his son. I felt totally disgusted." He acknowledges that such male-male love may be a Greek custom but it is one that disgusts him. Thus, in this version it is Oedipus's homophobia that inspires the patricide.

As Laius listens to Chrysippus and to Oedipus he turns to his own memories, in which the two, the desired youth and the feared son, almost merge. He finds himself moving toward an understanding of how, because fathers fear that their sons will grow up to destroy them, they, acting pre-emptively, kill them. Acknowledging that the infanticidal longing precedes the patricidal, he seems really to be asking Oedipus to forgive him. Like Jocasta, he has come to see that what happened between him and his son was archetypal, was a response to a universal pattern. (The question that remains, it seems to me, is: how can we get to where we know this and therefore don't have to live it out literally?) Chrysippus adds a further mitigation of Oedipus' guilt as he notes that he believes Laius was ready for his death when it came. But all Oedipus can hear in Laius' words is a confused admixture of killing and affection, desire and violence. So now it is Chrysippus' turn to try to explain it, to try to help Oedipus move beyond his too literal understanding: you want everything clear and simple, but "life is not as one, it is multifaceted, ambiguous." Maybe if you'd understood this, if you'd seen how all this was inside you, you wouldn't have had to kill your father.

So the crime for Rosa isn't after all really homosexual rape—or homophobic panic—it is literalism, monocular vision. Jocasta and Laius and Chrysippus have each—as ghosts, as inner voices—moved toward a more archetypal and more multifaceted understanding of the drama in which they had participated. Whether Oedipus has been able to absorb, to integrate, this perspective seems to me to be left open—though perhaps in performance this is less ambiguous. Yet the message Chrysippus has come to deliver is that simply recognizing that one has been moved by archetypal forces is not enough; one must discover how to transmute patricide and incest, desire and violence, into less destructive, more creative forms.

Yet although in Rosa's play Laius's "crime" is not really the issue, the *repression* of it—the tendency in our reflections on male psychology to focus on mother-son love, on incest, rather than on the relationships between men—is. It seems to me that Rosa's revisioning of the myth shows how phobic *we* are about male-male relationships—as though we can only envisage them in explicitly literalized sexual terms, as though the only alternatives were genital embrace or murder. I hear echoes of Hillman's conviction that we need to shift our understanding of male psychology from a mother-focused view—which entraps men in the roles of being her son, her hero, or a puer[30]—to one that focuses instead on the relationship between *senex* and *puer,* between an older and a younger male figure. (Just as Hillman deliberately does not envisage this as a father-son dyad, so in the play the Laius-Chrysippus and the Laius-Oedipus relationships almost merge but don't quite.) Moving beyond a literalized understanding of this emphasis on homosexual bonds, that is, moving toward an archetypal understanding, issues in a recognition of the importance for male individuation of an inner reconciliation of senex and puer—like that suggested in the play by the embrace between the ghosts of Chrysippus and Laius.[31]

Recalling Chrysippus's valorization of multiple perspectives helps us remember also that in his play Rosa is introducing us to *an* Oedipus, to *another* Oedipus, not to *the* Oedipus, not to the "real" story—but to an Oedipus who has an important message for us, one that the Greeks (less wary of male-male love than we) may not have needed as much as we do!

Notes

1.   Karl Kerenyi, "Oedipus: Two Essays," in Karl Kerenyi and James Hillman, *Oedipus Variations* (Woodstock, CT: Spring Publications, 1995) 1-86.

2.   Charles Segal, "The Oedipus Myth and Its Interpretation," *Oedipus Tyrannus* (Oxford: Oxford University Press, 2001); Timothy Gantz, *Early Greek Myth* (Baltimore: Johns Hopkins University Press, 1993).

3.   Richmond Lattimore, trans., *The Odyssey of Homer* (New York: Harper and Row, 1977) 173.

4.   The *Oedipus Tyrannos* is *not* part of a trilogy. Sophocles' *Antigone* was written in 441 when he was 54; his *Oedipus Tyrannos* between 429 and 425, and *Oedipus at Colonos* in 405, the year of his death.

5. The term *tyrannos* is never *quite* neutral, though not quite the same as "tyrant" in the modern sense: in Sophocles' *Antigone* Creon is the *tyrannos* and the meaning of the term shifts as the play unfolds—initially Creon is honored as a guarantor of the political stability Thebes so desperately seeks, but later condemned for his unyielding intransigence.

6. E. R. Dodds, "On Misunderstanding the *Oedipus Rex*," in Erich Segal, ed., *Greek Tragedy: Modern Essays in Criticism* (New York: Harper & Row, 1983) 177-188.

7. Bernard Knox, *Oedipus At Thebes: Sophocles' Tragic Hero And His Time* (New Haven: Yale, 1998).

8. Jeffrey Moussaieff Masson, *The Complete Letters of Sigmund Freud to Wilhelm Fliess, 1887-1904* (Cambridge, MA: Harvard University Press, 1985) 272. It is probably relevant to note that this insight came to Freud just as in his theoretical musings he was moving from his claim that all neuroses were the consequence of parental seduction (that is, from focus on pathology and a view of children as essentially passive) to an emphasis on the role played in the ongoing life of all of us of our own earliest active desires and fears.

9. Sigmund Freud, "Typical Dreams," *The Standard Edition of the Complete Psychological Works of Sigmund Freud*, ed. James Strachey (London: Hogarth Press, 1953/1974) IV, 260-266.

10. It was actually Jung who first introduced the term "complex" in 1906 *before* any personal contact with Freud to refer to an unconscious cluster of emotionally-laden associations surrounding a nucleus; Freud didn't use the phrase until 1910 in his "A Special Type of Object Choice Made by Men."

11. Thomas Mann, "Freud and the Future," *Essays of Three Decades* (New York: Knopf, 1947) 411-428.

12. Jean Pierre Vernant, "Oedipus Without the Complex," in Jean Pierre Vernant and Pierre Vidal-Naquet, *Myth and Tragedy in Ancient Greece* (New York: Zone Books, 1988) 85-111.

13. Charles Segal, "Freud, Language, and the Unconscious," *Sophocles' Tragic World* (Cambridge, MA: Harvard, 1995).

14. Nicole Loraux, *The Mourning Voice: An Essay On Greek Tragedy* (Ithaca: Cornell, 2002) 14-25.

15. C. G. Jung, *Collected Works* (Princeton: Princeton, 1953-1979) Vol. 5, 3-5.

16. Jung, *CW*, Vol. 4, 102-128.

17. Jung, *CW*, Vol. 5, 181 ff.

18. Robert Stein, *Incest and Human Love* (Baltimore: Penguin, 1974) 65-78.

19. Jean-Joseph Goux, *Oedipus, Philosopher* (Palo Alto: Stanford, 1993) 5-39.

20. James Hillman, "Oedipus Revisited," in Karl Kerenyi and James Hillman, *Oedipus Variations* (Woodstock, CT: 1990) 89-160.

21. This essay was originally written as a critical response to Armando Nascimento Rosa's *Another Oedipus: The Untold Story* (New Orleans: Spring Journal Publications, 2006).

22. Henry Bauchau, *Oedipus on the Road* (New York: Arcade, 1994).

23. Gilbert Murray, "Excursus on the Ritual Forms Preserved in Greek Tragedy," in Robert Segal, ed., *The Myth and Ritual Theory* (Oxford: Blackwell, 1998) 95-117.

24. Francis Fergusson, "The Idea of a Theater," in Segal, *Myth and Ritual,* 245-266.

25. This daughter of Teiresias was not brought into connection with the Oedipus tradition before Seneca, but she does figure in early Greek mythology as a priestess of Apollo who is sent to live at his shrine in Delphi after the final destruction of Thebes (just before her father's death) where she becomes either a famous poet or the first Pythia. Rosa's play reimagines her as wanting to be an actress not a prophet like her father for she sees theater as the true inheritor of the shamanic tradition.

26. Rainer Maria Rilke, "Orpheus. Eurydice. Hermes," in Stephen Mitchell, trans., *The Selected Poetry of Rainer Maria Rilke* (New York: Random House, 1982) 51-53.

27. For example, in the *Oresteia* a story that for Homer was primarily about male-male struggles over royal power—Aegisthus' murder of Agamemnon, Orestes' murder of Aegisthus—becomes a dramatization of female-male antagonism: Clytemnestra and Agamemnon, Clytemnestra and Orestes, the Furies and Apollo.

28. Cf. K. J. Dover, *Greek Homosexuality* (Cambridge, MA: Harvard, 1978).

29. Gantz, 488-92, 544-45.

30. James Hillman, "The Great Mother, Her Son, Her Hero and the Puer," in Pat Berry, ed., *Mothers and Fathers* (New York: Spring, 1981).

31. This implies a move beyond Jung's view of male homosexuality as representing either immaturity or a disturbance in the relation to women. Cf. Ch. 7 of my *Myths and Mysteries of Same-Sex Love* (New York: Continuum, 1989).

25

Narcissus Reflections

> The way of the soul.... leads to the water, to
> the dark mirror that reposes at its bottom.
> C. G. Jung, *C.W.* 9.1,17

The story ends with a flower, the narcissus with its white petals surrounding the yellow center.

But perhaps it *began* there. Not with the boy staring transfixed by his reflection in the still pond but with the flower.

Nor with the other story.

The one about Persephone, captivated by the flower planted by Gaia, that marvelous radiant flower that smelled so sweet that heaven and earth and sea laughed with joy, that awe-inspiring flower from whose root a hundred blooms grew.

Years ago I wrote of Persephone reaching for that particular flower as a reaching (if only half-consciously) for her own in-her-selfness and for that engagement with death that gives depth to life.

But then I thought the other story, the story of the boy and his image, was already there.

Now I know it came later, much later.

For scholars whom I trust tell me there was no story about the boy until Ovid came to tell it.

So perhaps Ovid moved the flower from one story to another (for it does not appear in his telling of the Persephone story).

But before there were any stories, there was the flower—and its name. A name derived from association with the word, *narke,* and thus with sleep, unconsciousness, death.

And the flower gets its name because its sweet smell can make the heavens laugh but may overpower us mortals, put us to sleep, remind us of death.

But of course there would come to be stories and of course the stories would be about longing and beauty and being overpowered and death.

And of course eventually there would be ideas, ideas like narcissism and narcolepsy.

But let's begin with the story, the one about the boy and the image. Not as we tend to remember it, as though what it really meant was narcissism all along (even a fine Latinist like William Anderson makes that mistake[1]) but as it was told the first time around in Ovid's *Metamorphoses.* [2]

And let's begin by looking at it *in* the *Metamorphoses,* remembering how important contexts, juxtapositions, repetitions, prefigurings, variations, contrasts, interruptions, flashbacks are to shaping the meanings of any tale that Ovid tells.

Let's begin by remembering how shortly before turning to our tale Ovid writes of Actaeon stumbling upon a pool and being undone by what he sees.

And how just a little later he tells us of another lovely virginal youth, Hermaphroditus, who comes upon another crystal clear pool and there is set upon by a nymph who wraps herself so tightly around the resistant youth that their two bodies become one.

Let's recall that our tale is framed by two about Dionysos.

And that, as Anderson notes, the story about Narcissus is the first account in Ovid's book, following so many of divine seductions and rapes, of a human lover.

Though even this story begins with the rape of a struggling nymph, begins with a rivergod imprisoning a waterlily by curving tightly around her.

So the water and the flower are there from the beginning.

A child is born and the mother asks the yet untested prophet Teiresias if her beautiful son will have a long life. "Not if he comes to know himself," she is told.

We've all heard enough stories to recognize this as a warning.

We remember (even though Ovid has not yet come to the story) that Orpheus is told can have Eurydice back, if he doesn't look back—and we remember that he does.

So we know: this boy will not have a long life. This boy will in some sense come to know himself. And the story will be about how this comes to happen. And if it's a good story, it will look for a while as though it might all turn out differently.

(And of course many read the story as though it *did* turn out differently, as though Narcissus never did come to know himself except in an empty, superficial way.)

But I think we should stay with the story. Narcissus does come to know himself, to know himself as one in love with an image, as still in love with that image even in death. Isn't that more accurate than to say he's in love with himself? Stay with the story.

But we are getting ahead of ourselves.

Let's return to the story,

Narcissus is sixteen, at that age of fugitive bloom that is the equivalent for a youth of Persephone having just reached maidenhood when her story begins.

Ovid makes much of Narcissus' soft tender androgynous body, of how he's desired by both youths and young girls. But his heart is hard; he is impervious to their longing, perhaps more unaware than hostilely rejecting. (It is not in Ovid that Narcissus sends a sword to one of the more importunate suitors who uses it to kill himself.) He seems self-enclosed (as Persephone was enclosed in her mother's arms), perhaps imbued with the kind of self-sufficiency Freud (in his essay on narcissism) ascribed to women like Lou Salome.

One day a nymph, catching sight of him as he is driving frightened deer into his net, is inflamed with love. But this nymph cannot speak her love, she can only reflect the words of others, she can only echo. Ovid has fun with this—but it's also sad. "I'd sooner die than say I'm yours," says he. "I'm yours," echoes Echo. Narcissus flees. (Ovid uses the same word as that describing Actaeon's vain flight.) Spurned she wastes away, becomes only voice.

But, as we've said, many others fall in love with Narcissus, including one rejected male lover who prays, "May Narcissus, too, fall in love and be denied the one he loves." The goddess Nemesis heeds the prayer.

So on another "one day," wearied from a hot day's chase, Narcissus comes upon a sylvan pool, so virginal that its surface has never been disturbed by shepherd or by bird or beast or even fallen branch—not the stream or spring of many translations or pictorial representations. (In Ovid, we might note, the scene of Persephone's abduction is a lakeside grove not a meadow and many water nymphs enter the tale.)

Narcissus lies down and while he tries to quench one thirst, he feels another: desire for the image in the pool. He believes that what is but a shade must be a body. He cannot turn away, lies there still as any statue.

As Ovid describes his Dionysian locks, his ivory neck, his blushing cheeks, my sense is that we, too, become viewers—as taken with Ovid's image of Narcissus as he is with the image in the water. (And if what Narcissus sees is but his own reflection, is that not true of us as well? I'm getting ahead of myself again, thinking of how Freud will take this image out of pathology—will help us see that in looking at Narcissus we are looking at ourselves, at an image of ourselves.)

Narcissus knows not what he sees but what he sees invites him; unwittingly he wants himself; he is the seeker and the sought, the longed-for and the one who longs, fixated on the lying shape. "I smile and you smile too…. bend to kiss and you move to meet me."

Then the narrator's voice intrudes, reminding us that Narcissus himself is an *imago*, a poetic image:

> But why,
> o foolish boy—do you persist? Why try
> to grip an image? He does not exist—
> the one you love and long for. If you turn
> away, he'll fade—the face that you discern
> is but a shadow, your reflected form.
> That shape has nothing of its own: it comes
> with you, with you it stays, it will retreat
> when you have gone—if you can ever leave!

As Narcissus half knows. He knows that though he and the youth in the water are separated only by a thin film, they can never touch. He cries out to the trees that shade the pool as though his situation were the cruelest ever.

> Yes, yes, I'm he. I've seen through that deceit.
> My image cannot trick me anymore.
> I burn with love for my own self; it's I
> who light the flames—the flames that scorch me then.
> What shall I do? Shall I be sought or seek?

As he cries, his tears temporarily erase the image, as his plunging arms will later do once again. The surface of this once-virginal pool has now been disturbed. But this is no mirror whose shattering would destroy the image forever. The turbulence settles, the image reappears. Watery reflections, as Bachelard tells us, are like flowers growing in the water; they are not simply replications, they shift, they move, they disappear and reappear.[3]

Narcissus understands—and doesn't. He turns away, but leaving is as impossible as touching—either would expunge the image. Death seems the only way out of the impossible situation. But then he realizes, "With death my pain will end, and yet I'd have my love live past my death. Instead we two will die together in one breath."

Strangely, it is through seeing his own reflection that Narcissus is for the first time made aware of real otherness. Until now he had been self-enclosed, self-absorbed, impervious to others. But now he cannot bear that his departure would mean the other's, the image's, death. Reflecting on the reflection takes him out of his self-absorption, not more deeply into it.

Narcissus imagines the other reaching toward him with love, as keen to be embraced. He longs for the other's longing, he dreams of mutuality. As Pygmalion will later dream of mutuality when he gazes upon the statue he has made. Desire, is seems, may always be inspired by an image.

The longing for mutuality enters here as a new theme in Ovid's epic—though not in his poetry, for his early love elegies celebrated the importance of shared pleasure in love as they also revealed how the beloved is always in a sense a fiction, created by the lover's imagination.[4]

Narcissus sees that both moving too eagerly toward and leaving destroy the image.

So he returns, back to the image. And stays, wasting away with love. Almost gone, he cries "Farewell" to the image—and Echo, reappearing, answers back, "Farewell" to him. And when his water nymph sisters come to bury him they find in place of his body, a flower, the white petalled narcissus with which we began.

But Narcissus, we are told, is still gazing at his image in the pool of Styx, in the underworld. All along Ovid has spoken of the image as *imago* and as *umbra,* words used to describe the soul. Now Narcissus is a soul himself, *imago* and *umbra.* Soul gazing upon soul, image reflected by image.

Hillman is right.[5] Narcissus experiences the image as *real* and is in a sense fulfilled by the image, has come to realize that gazing upon it is enough. It's no longer illusion but *image.* Kristeva says that the object of Narcissus's love is an image,[6] a fantasy and that if he *knew* that he would be Holderlin or Freud. But perhaps he does.

◆   ◆   ◆

So there was the word and the flower and the story about the boy and his image.

And then there was the idea.

And then the story of the idea.

One which we tend to read backwards—as though the idea was always the one purveyed by the *DSM*: that narcissism is a pathology, a personality disorder characterized by arrogance, exploitation, grandiosity and entitlement, by an excessive need for admiration, by a lack of empathy.

But that's not an IDEA in a depth psychological sense, in Giegerich's sense. For that we have to go to Freud. We go to Freud to recover the possibilities opened up by his reflections on the idea, not to read him in the light of what we believe he must have been saying.

When the term narcissism was introduced into psychology by Havelock Ellis, he used it as a synonym for auto-eroticism in its most literal sense: masturbation. (It does seem strange that this first use was about achieving sexual satisfaction through looking and touching one's own body—when in the myth it's such a big issue that Narcissus couldn't touch what he desired and saw only the face.)

Freud's use of the word brought some of the full richness of Ovid's telling of the myth into psychology, particularly the close association between narcissism and death, though it is important to note that he nowhere explicitly refers to the myth.

As so often LaPlanche and Pontalis's *The Language of Psychoanalysis* helps us trace the story. Freud's first uses the term "narcissism" in 1910 to account for homosexuals taking themselves as their love object: "They look for a young man who resembles themselves and whom they may love as their mother loved them." Without ever directly evoking the myth Freud reminds us of the homoerotic aspect of Narcissus' desiring gaze.

Freud uses the word again in 1911 (in the Schreber case history) for a *stage* in sexual development between auto-eroticism (a stage where there's not yet a sense of having a unified body-ego) and object-love—an intermediate stage where one takes oneself as love-object. Here he also suggests that psychotics may be immured in this stage, may have withdrawn libido from the external world so wholly that they are unable to develop transference in the analytic context.

But in his 1914 paper "On Narcissism"[7] he moves toward a more complex and richer understanding, one that sees narcissism in structural not just developmental terms and takes it out of a pathological context so that it becomes a descriptive, clearly not a deprecating, term. (Though as always with Freud the more exaggerated manifestations open him to the universal normal ones.)

As we read his essay carefully, we begin to see that narcissism is not "bad," is not a pathology, does not apply only to "them" (or at most to a disavowed shadow aspect of ourselves), but is rather a name for a current that flows deeply through the souls of all of us.

Freud begins by talking about what he calls *secondary narcissism*—the withdrawal of libido from object back to self, a withdrawal of libido from others, even imaginal ones—as a way of introducing us to *primary narcissism*—by which he means that early pre-psychical, pre-verbal stage in which there is no self and no other.

This stage, he suggests, exists only in memory, in fantasy, only for the imagination—only afterwards—for consciousness begins with the experience of separation and loss. Then, as self and other are co-created there arise the twin possibilities of self-love and other-love. Originally, Freud says, we humans have two love objects—our mothers and our selves. The Oedipus myth expresses the soul meaning of one, Narcissus of the other.

Thus primary narcissism represents an earlier, more original stage than Oedipal love; it arises in response to the separation between what is not yet an ego and not yet an object. It arises out of a longing to deny the loss, the dependency, the neediness, out of a longing to claim a self-sufficiency. It represents the fantasy that separation is not the ultimate truth, that to begin with we were whole in ourselves and at one with the world. There is always nostalgia for that imaginal "before."

Primary narcissism is poised at that liminal moment between before and after and so for Freud always remains a "border concept," since the domain explored by psychoanalysis is psychical experience. Anything earlier is outside.

Our initial turn to an other expresses our impossible longing for this other to give us back that lost wholeness. It is really an expression of fusion longing, expresses a desire to *be*, not to *have*.

Only after the full acknowledgment of the loss, only after what Freud calls the work of mourning, does there really arise the possibility of turning to other as other, as a genuinely separate other with his or her own desires which are not just for me. Only, we might say, when we acknowledge the existence of a rival, admit that the mother does not exist only in relation to us, only as we enter the Oedipal world, does the possibility of real loving, of Eros, emerge.

For from the outset consciousness entails a departure from primary narcissism, a transfer of some of the love that might be directed toward ourselves to another. Some of the originally undifferentiated libido is directed to the self, some to others. Often we may try somehow to have it both ways, to love someone who reminds us of ourselves, or of our earlier selves, or of our ideal selves. We are also likely to over-estimate the beloved in order to make up for the forfeited self-love—and of course we also demand to be loved back to recover that lost self-love. And when we aren't loved, there is always an enormous temptation to entirely withdraw libido from the outer world and thus fall into "secondary narcissism."

But this, Freud reminds us, is too simple. Secondary narcissism as self-love can't be understood as independent of relationships with others, but rather as an internalization of them. For elsewhere (more than in this essay) Freud speaks of our becoming selves only gradually, by way of a series of identifications through which we acquire an *image* of ourselves. In his 1917 essay, "Mourning and Melancholia," Freud sees loss as central to the formation of the identifications that form the ego. Lost beloved others are incorporated and imaginally preserved in and as the ego: "The ego is a precipitate of abandoned object-cathexes and contains the history of those object-choices."[8] We are our losses, including the loss of an autonomy we never had. We are but the images of those we've loved—and they? Images, too, of lost beloveds. Image reflecting image. On and on…

At first in the early pages of the essay on narcissism Freud seems to be trying to clarify a distinction between object-libido and ego-libido, between love of the anaclitic/attachment (Oedipal) type and narcissistic love. But by the end of the essay we see it's more ambiguous: all object-love has a narcissistic aspect. "No matter how it looks even in adults not all ego-libido is turned to others," he says, and a bit further on, "In a real happy love one can't distinguish object libido and ego libido."

Something similar happens in the 1917 essay. By its end the initial distinction between mourning and melancholia has been deeply problematized. For Freud has come to realize that "melancholia" (unfinished grieving over a never fully nameable loss) is an inescapable part of human life. Since—although in "mourning" the loss is supposedly conscious—the most recent grief always stirs up memories of the never fully grieved losses that precede it, and especially the ungrievable primal loss, of the mother, of one's own wholeness.

Similarly Freud has here in the narcissism essay radically problematized the distinction between object love and narcissism. It is not accidental that Freud's two essays on "transference" were written in the same year as the one on narcissism, for just as it is true that all the dreams of a single night revolve around the same central themes and wishes, so it is also true that all the writings of a single year are likely to bear witness to the same central concerns. In the essays on transference Freud seeks to make us aware of the metaphorical, the imaginal, aspect of all our relationships. *Metaphor* is after all the same word as *transference*, one is Greek, the other Latin, both refer to a "carrying over." Thus "transference" refers to our propensity to carry over into all our new relationships, mostly unconsciously, echoes of the hopes and fears, the fulfillments and frustrations, associated with our earliest experience. Once we recognize the role imagination plays, how it both distorts and enriches all our relationships to others, it becomes possible to move from unconsciousness, literalism, to delight in this imaginal aspect. We can see the other as other and celebrate the added resonance of personal and archetypal associations. Again without invoking the myth, Freud here evokes Ovid's image of Narcissus returning to the image as image not illusion. That all object-love, all love of others, will have an imaginal (and a narcissistic) tinge should neither surprise nor dismay.

Freud's dip into the theme of narcissism sets in motion ripples that will engage him for the next decade. These early reflections on narcissism lead him to the first hints of what will eventually become the *UeberIch* (superego) in the fully developed structural theory of the 1923 *Ego and the Id.* For here he already notes how narcissistic libido is directed toward an "ego ideal," a kind of substitute for the early megalomania which saw oneself as perfect and whole. Obviously this "ideal" is an *image:* we love our image of ourselves or of our past or hoped-for selves.

And although Freud has also not yet introduced the notion of the *Es* (id), the primary narcissism of this essay is a clear prelude to his later understanding of the primitive psychic stage that precedes the ego's differentiation from the id. He is already writing of a primary undifferentiated energy that "fundamentally persists and is related to the object-cathexes as the body of an amoeba is related to the pseudopodia which it puts out."

Freud's explicit naming of the death drive is also some years away, but he already senses how the self-love of narcissism is death wish. For Freud narcissism is in a sense an illusion; we are in a world with others; we are not self-sufficient, we are not the world. And thus narcissism is death. But it is also true that the narcissistic longings never die. For we all long to return to that earlier fantasized world where self and other were one, all long to believe that separation is not the ultimate truth. Eros, Freud suggests, is the long way round back to narcissism, to death; Eros is an *aufhebung* of narcissism, its overcoming *and* its continuation by other means. Incest love (love of the mother with whom we were once one) is already a substitute for the lost wholeness, but it is life, and then *its* renunciation leads us toward other substitutes. But they are substitutes. The deeper longing is not erotic but narcissistic—to be free of object love, complete in ourselves, at one with the world.

Narcissism is thus for Freud a persistent melancholic undercurrent, associated with a *lost* wholeness and with impossible longing—but also associated with the *imagination*, with the power of that once-upon-a-time that exists only in the imagination to propel us forward toward the world, toward others.

◆   ◆   ◆

Somewhat paradoxically Freud's reflections on narcissism emerged out of what we might call an erotic context, out of his deep friendship with Lou Andreas-Salome. He wrote his paper on narcissism in response to her urging that he put together reflections that had come up again and again in their discussions during the year she spent in Vienna. When he sends a copy of it to her she writes him that this essay and its recognition that there is a "good" narcissism" has confirmed her commitment to psychoanalysis—and that her own understanding of narcissism, though connected to his, is also significantly different in its emphases.

The journal she kept of her 1912-13[9] stay in Vienna makes evident that her interest in narcissism, in the role of self-love in love, long antedates her involvement with Freud. Lou came to narcissism independently by way of her reflections on women, love and God—whereas Freud came to it in initially by way of reflections on the difference between neurotics and psychotics. (The year Lou spent in Vienna was the year Freud was working on the Schreber case.)

In her earlier writings Lou says that for women the aim of love is to expand the self, not to reach toward a distant separate other as a romantic man does in his pursuit of the ever-desirable because unattainable woman. Because she begins with a conviction that self and world first exist in a kind of primal union, she is from the outset unwilling to agree to Freud's attempt to clearly distinguish between narcissism and eros, between self-love and object-love. She believes the separation never fully occurs and understands all object-love as the rediscovery of a lost part of oneself (as Aristophanes had suggested in Plato's *Symposium.)*

Her journal reports on the discussions about narcissism in the 1913 meetings of the Wednesday Evening Group and Lou's reservations even then. She writes that she would want to insist that the narcissist doesn't want to swallow the other; rather, his defect is that "his own love's outburst nearly suffices for him." The other is almost incidental to his enjoying his own loving; he feels gratitude to the other for being the occasion of this experience. She writes of a first narcissism (a universal developmental stage to be transcended) and a second (a later neurotic self-infatuation) and says that finally, a third and beautiful narcissism appears:

No longer just a stage to be transcended; it is rather the persistent accompaniment of all our deeper experience, always present, yet still far beyond any possibility of hewing its way from the unconscious into consciousness. In narcissism the Ucs. still exists only *en bloc,* the primordial form not simply of a foundation but of the all-inclusive.

When (back home in Gottingen) Lou receives Freud's "On Narcissism," she writes him a long four-page letter.[10] She says again that what she most values about this aspect of Freud's thinking—and what she sees makes him, unlike Adler, a *depth* psychologist—is the recognition that the ego is not a given, but emerges from a pre-egoic libido.

Lou tells Freud that she'd like to call what he calls "primary" narcissism *true* narcissism; she wants to emphasize that this pre-differentiated state (*not* taking oneself as a love-object) is "real" narcissism. She writes of the naïve full-immersion of an artist in his work as a kind of *self-less* creative narcissism. She also understands those (rare) moments—which she believes most often occur in a sexual context—when we feel ourselves to be wholly *at one* with our body, those moments when we *are* body rather than *having* one, as being experiences of this true narcissism.

She insists: narcissism is liminal; one is still affiliated at the roots even when already on the way to self/other discrimination. So Narcissus lingers; he doesn't flee, even when he understands.

Responding to her response, it is now Freud's turn to urge Lou to elaborate her comments into a publishable essay. Which, in 1921 after a long incubation, she does. In her essay, "The Dual Orientation of Narcissism"[11] she writes: "We remain embedded in our original narcissism for all our development, as the plants remain in the earth despite their contrary growth toward the light." Note the difference in emphasis: for Freud this original narcissism persists primarily as longing, for Lou as subliminal presence.

She identifies narcissism with a primary undifferentiation; it is too simple to reduce narcissism to self-love. "I want to bring out its other aspect—the persistent feeling of identity with the totality." Narcissism is the connecting link between the desire for fusion and for individuality. You love another as though he were the world, as you loved yourself—and she relates this love of the whole to the love of God (here, I believe, revealing her continued closeness to Rilke).

Our over-valuation of those we love represents an attempt to make them a substitute for that All. For Lou all love objects are transferences from that original All. She sees our over-valuing of those we love as a blessing, a gift. We enrich the other with our fantasies, if we know that is what we're doing. She speaks of transference when consciously engaged in by lovers or artists as "festive adornment." There is a joyous aspect to this: "We live with ourselves and with the world more fully."

Unlike Freud, Lou Salome in her essay returns directly to the myth and reminds us that Narcissus was not looking into a manmade pool, but into a pool in a natural setting. "The Narcissus of legend gazed not at a manmade mirror but at the mirror of nature." Not just his own face and body but also the trees were reflected in that pool. For her the scene represents a delighted-in experience of total union with the natural world—or, rather, the vision of it. Narcissus "saw himself as if he were all—otherwise he would have fled."

"There is a kind of narcissism that is an experience of being wholly at one with the world, not just absorbed in oneself.... Narcissism is in its creative form no longer just a stage to be transcended; it is rather the persistent accompaniment of all our deeper experience."

"What Narcissus sees is not the trees themselves but their *images,* the world as image."

We've come a long way from that flower, that pool, that boy—but wasn't all of this always already there?

Notes

1.   William S. Anderson, *Ovid's Metamorphoses*: Books 1-5 (Norman: University of Oklahoma Press, 1997) 373-388.

2.   Most of my quotes and close paraphrases from Ovid are from the translation by Allen Mandelbaum. *The Metamorphoses of Ovid* (New York: Harcourt Brace, 1993). But I have also consulted the Latin text and prose translation in the Loeb Classical Library's edition (Cambridge: Harvard University Press, 1984).

3.   Gaston Bachelard, *Water and Dreams* (Dallas: The Dallas Institute, 1893) 24.

4.   Later in the poem, when Ovid comes to write of Cephalus and Procris, Baucis and Philemon, Ceyx and Alcyone, he will provide images of genuinely passionate sustained reciprocal love, though these loves, too, will mostly end in suffering.

5.   James Hillman, *The Dream and the Underworld* (New York: HarperCollins, 1979) 119.

6.   Julia Kristeva, "Freud and Love," in Kelly Oliver, ed., *The Portable Kristeva* (New York: Columbia University Press, 1997) 147.

7. Sigmund Freud, "On Narcissism: An Introduction," in James Strachey, ed., *The Standard Edition of the Complete Psychological Works of Sigmund Freud* (London: Hogarth Press, 1953-1974) Vol. XIV, 73-102.

8. Sigmund Freud, "Mourning and Melancholia," in James Strachey, ed., *The Standard Edition of the Complete Psychological Works of Sigmund Freud* (London: Hogarth Press, 1953-1974) Vol. XIV, 248-259.

9. Lou Andreas-Salome, *The Freud Journal* (New York: Basic Books, 1964) especially 109, 110.

10. Ernst Pfeifer, *Sigmund Freud and Lou Andreas-Salome: Letters* (New York: Harcourt, Brace, Jovanovich, 1972) 22-26.

11. Lou Andreas-Salome, "The Dual Orientation of Narcissism" (originally in *Imago* 1921), *Psychoanalytic Quarterly* XXXI 1962, 1-30.

Acknowledgments

"The Eros of Teaching," a paper read at a seminar on "The Academic Novel" at the annual meeting of the Society for Values in Higher Education, Vassar College, August 1981.

"Whitmont's Return to the Goddess," *Quadrant,* 16.1, Spring 1983, 109-113.

"The Mother Goddess Among the Greeks," in Carl Olsen, ed., *The Book of the Goddess: Past and Present,* New York: Crossroad, 1983, 45-59.

"Diotima and Alcibiades," *Soundings,* LXXII.4, Spring 1989, 631-656.

"Masks of the Goddess," in Dan Noel, ed., *Paths to the Power of Myth,* New York: Crossroad, 1990, 97-107.

"The Wounded Healer," *Soundings,* LXXIII.4, Winter 1990, 551-573.

"A View from the Parthenon," *Continuum,* I, 1, 1990, 182-86.

"Mirrors of the Self," prologue to my *Mirrors of the Self,* Los Angeles: Tarcher, 1991, xi-xx.

"Coming Home: The Late-Life Lesbian," in Robert Hopcke et al., eds., *Love and the Path to Wholeness: Jungian Perspectives on Same-Sex Love,* Boston: Shambhala, 1993, 28-37.

"Bruno Bettelheim: A Wounded Healer," *The Salt Journal,* Nov/Dec 1997, 30-33.

"Hope Lives When People Remember," solicited by *The Salt Journal,* 1997, but never published.

"Her, HERTA," in Catherine Reid and Holly Iglesias, eds., *Every Woman I've Ever Loved: Lesbian Writers on Their Mothers,* New York: Cleis, 1997, 202-211.

"Journeys to the Underworld," *MythoSphere,* I.2, 1998, 175-194.

"Tending Soul in the Age of AIDS," *White Crane,* Winter 1998/99, 4-7.

"Turning Again to Athene," *The Salt Journal,* Jan/Feb 2000, 22-28.

"Sad is Eros Builder of Cities," a paper presented as part of a symposium on "City and Psyche," sponsored by The Salt Institute, Santa Fe, May 2000.

"Dionysos and Aphrodite," Keynote address, annual meeting of the Society for the Scientific Study of Sexuality, San Diego, April 2000.

"Beyond Psychology," in Dennis Slattery and Lionel Corbett, eds., *Psychology at the Threshold,* Carpinteria, CA: Pacifica Graduate Institute Publications, 2002, 99-111.

"After the First Collapse There is No Other," paper presented at the "World Behind the World" conference, sponsored by Pacifica Graduate Institute, Santa Barbara, April 2002.

"May the Gods Be Present," a paper presented at a seminar on "Psyche, Spirit and the Power of Ritual," sponsored by The New York Center for Jungian Studies, Rhinebeck, NY, July 2002.

"Looking Back at Orpheus," *Spring 71,* Fall 2004, 1-36—a shorter version of this paper appeared in my *Luxury of Afterwards.*

"Remembering, Repeating, and Working Through," a paper presented at a conference on "Mid-Life and Beyond," sponsored by The New York Center for Jungian Studies, Dingle, Ireland, March 2004.

"Another Oedipus," scheduled to appear in *An Oedipus—The Untold Story: A Ghostly Mythodrama in One Act by Armando Nascimento Rosa,* New Orleans: Spring Journal Publications—due out late spring 2006. "Narcissus Reflections," in *Disturbances in the Field,* New Orleans: Spring Journal Publications, 2006, 192-205.

978-0-595-40036
0-595-40036-1

CPSIA information can be obtained
at www.ICGtesting.com
Printed in the USA
FSHW01n1256280818
51822FS